STRATEGIES FOR BUSINESS AND TECHNICAL WRITING

Seventh Edition

KEVIN J. HARTY

La Salle University

Longman

Boston Columbus Indianapolis New York San Francisco Upper Saddle River
Amsterdam Cape Town Dubai London Madrid Milan Munich Paris Montreal Toronto
Delhi Mexico City São Paulo Sydney Hong Kong Seoul Singapore Taipei Tokyo

Acquisitions Editor: Lauren A. Finn
Editorial Assistant: Sandra Manzanares
Senior Marketing Manager: Sandra McGuire
Production Manager: Ellen MacElree
Project Coordination, Text Design, and Electronic Page Makeup: Pre-Press PMG
Cover Design Manager: John Callahan
Cover Designer: Maria Ilardi
Cover Photo: Top image: iStockphoto and bottom left image: Getty Images
Senior Manufacturing Buyer: Dennis J. Para
Printer and Binder: R. R. Donnelley & Sons, Harrisonburg
Cover Printer: R. R. Donnelley & Sons, Harrisonburg

For permission to use copyrighted material, grateful acknowledgment is made to the copyright holders on pp. 327–329, which are hereby made part of this copyright page.

Library of Congress Cataloging-in-Publication Data
Harty, Kevin J.
  Strategies for business and technical writing / Kevin J. Harty.—7th ed.
    p. cm.
  Includes bibliographical references and index.
  ISBN 0-205-74191-6 (alk. paper)
 1. Commercial correspondence. 2. Business report writing. 3. Technical writing. I. Title.

  HF5721.H37 2011
  808'.066651—dc22

                 2009041838

1 2 4 5 6 7 8 9 10—DOH—13 12 11 10 09

Longman
is an imprint of

www.pearsonhighered.com

ISBN-10:   0-205-74191-6
ISBN-13: 978-0-205-74191-5

Why Do You Need this New Edition?

If you're wondering why you should buy this new edition of *Strategies for Business and Technical Writing*, here are a few great reasons!

❶ One third of the readings are new, better preparing you for today's workplace with up-to-date information about how to apply for a job; how to decide when to use different forms of business correspondence; how to meet ethical demands of the workplace; and how to integrate visuals into your writing.

❷ This edition offers an analysis of the approach an engineer uses to solve writing challenges that he faces on the job and shows you problem-solving methods in the context of real world situations (Part 1).

❸ New essays on style and tone and their role in effective communication help you communicate just the right message in the right way to your audience (Part 2).

❹ An expanded emphasis on the importance of clear, effective and appropriate business correspondence now includes discussions of electronic messages in several forms, reflecting the increasing pace of today's workplace (Part 3).

❺ A new discussion of when to use which visuals—table, charts, and illustrations—to accompany a text further ensures the effectiveness of letters, memos, reports, and electronic messages (Part 5).

❻ A new essay stresses the advantages of collaborative writing in the production of longer, more detailed reports and proposals and helps to prepare you for working in teams (Part 4).

❼ Guidance on conducting a job search now balances advice from university placement officers with that from corporate headhunters (Part 5).

PEARSON

For
Kathleen and Maureen,
Matthew and Charlie,
Richard and Peter—
amici e vino devono essere vecchi.

Contents

Preface

WHAT'S NEW IN THE SEVENTH EDITION?

This seventh edition of *Strategies for Business and Technical Writing* represents a thorough reworking of the previous edition. The new edition retains 18 of the 32 selections from the sixth edition and adds eight new selections. In revising *Strategies*, I have been guided by the same principle that informed the selection of materials for inclusion in previous editions: *Strategies* should present the best advice from the best sources about important issues in business, technical, and other kinds of professional writing.

The changes I have made in preparing this seventh edition broaden the coverage in *Strategies* of key issues in business and technical writing, and increase the usefulness of *Strategies* as both a textbook and a reference. The eight new selections in this edition of *Strategies* reflect the ever-changing demands writers in the world of work face to meet the needs of their many audiences, and the entire edition emphasizes throughout the necessity for the highest ethical standards to inform all business and technical writing.

In particular, this seventh edition of *Strategies*

- offers further specifics about how a process approach can inform business and technical writing;
- discusses the advantages of using collaborative writing techniques, especially for writing and assembling longer documents;
- contains an expanded discussion of e-mail and other forms of electronic communication;
- includes simple, no nonsense suggestions for integrating visuals and text;
- provides an expanded section on the job search, which now offers job candidates advice from corporate recruiters and headhunters as well as from university placement officers.

DISTINCTIVE APPROACH TO THE TEXT

Strategies can be used in three ways. *Strategies* can serve as a supplement to a business or technical writing textbook. *Strategies* can also be used as a supplement to a composition textbook or a writing handbook. And *Strategies* can be used on its own as a textbook or as a reference source.

I have designed *Strategies* to appeal to practical-minded instructors, students, and women and men already working in business and technical occupations and the professions. The contributors to this volume write with the kind of purpose and understanding that come only from a career dedicated to improving the effectiveness of business and technical communication. As a result, the selections in *Strategies* not only teach professional writing but are also fine examples of the genre.

In selecting essays for this seventh edition of *Strategies*, I have been guided by the belief that all courses in business and technical writing should firmly implant one idea in the minds of students (and of those in the world of work). *All* successful writing consists of clear and effective prose, no matter in which medium it is composed or sent. However, students should recognize that business and technical writing differs in important ways from the expository prose usually taught in first-year or advanced composition courses. Because business and technical writers communicate with multiple audiences and with a variety of intentions, learning to write well for the world of work may require multiple adjustments in technique. Therefore, in addition to touching on such broad problems as style, jargon, and diction, *Strategies* includes comprehensive discussions of specific forms of writing—for example, different kinds of resumes, letters of application, business letters, memos, e-mail, reports, and proposals. Students learn the specific techniques used by successful men and women in business, industry, and technical professions who communicate information as part of their jobs.

ACKNOWLEDGMENTS

The essays in this seventh edition of *Strategies* have, like those in the six previous editions, survived the most rigorous scrutiny—that of my students in seminars and courses in business and technical writing at La Salle University, Temple University, Rhode Island College, Centenary College of Louisiana, the Federal Reserve Bank of Philadelphia, Kroll Lindquist Avey, Philadelphia Telco Credit Union, the Board of Pensions of the United Presbyterian Church (USA), First Pennsylvania Bank and Fidelity Bank (now both Wachovia Bank), Blue Cross of Greater Philadelphia, and Philadelphia Newspapers, Inc.

For permission to reprint the selections included in this seventh edition of *Strategies*, I am happy to thank the authors, agents, and editors who handled my permissions requests with efficiency and good cheer. At La Salle University, I owe a continuing debt to my many good friends and colleagues, especially to John Baky, Joe Brogan, Jim Butler, Madeleine Dean, Gabe Fagan, Bob Fallon, Craig Franson, Perry Golia, Emery Mollenhauer, Bryan Narendorf, Steve Smith, Jack Tabor, and Lynne Texter. I am especially grateful as well to the staff of the La Salle University library, in particular to Stephen Breedlove and Nancy Tresnan in Interlibrary Loan Services.

Finally, I am indebted to the editorial and production staff at Pearson Longman, especially to my editor, Lauren Finn, and to the reviewers whom she recruited to critique the previous edition of this book: Gerald J. Alred, University of Wisconsin-Milwaukee; Cathryn Amdahl, Harrisburg Area Community College; Deborah C. Andrews, University of Delaware; George Friend, Millersville University; Miles A. Kimball, Texas Tech University; Shannah M. Whithaus, University of California, Davis.

Kevin J. Harty
Philadelphia
November 2009

Introduction

Writing consumes a substantial portion of the working day for almost all college educated workers.[1]

Ability to express ideas cogently and goals persuasively—in plain English—is the most important skill to leadership. I know of no greater obstacle to the progress of good ideas and good people than the inability to compose a plain English sentence.[2]

Whether you are planning a career in business, in industry, or in some technical field, or whether you already have such a career, you may be ill-prepared for what is perhaps the most difficult part of your job. Although you may be an excellent accountant, salesperson, manager, engineer or scientist, all of your training may not help you when you sit down to write. If this situation is the case, you are not alone in being frustrated by the writing demands of your job. Nevertheless, writing is essential to most technical and professional occupations; the ability to communicate effectively both in person and on paper can help you advance in your profession. Good writing can mean the difference between winning or losing a major sale, a pleased customer, or a challenging new position with a higher salary.

The selections in this book will help you make your letters, reports, memos, electronic communications, proposals, and other professional documents more effective. The selections represent some of the best advice veteran teachers and practitioners of business and technical writing have to offer. None of the selections, however, offers a quick cure for writing ills. There is no such cure. Like any worthwhile skill, good professional writing requires time, practice, and, most of all, discipline.

To begin with, we need to realize that there are only two kinds of professional writing:

1. clear, effective writing that meets the combined needs of the reader and the writer, and
2. bad writing.

Bad writing is unclear and ineffective; it wastes time and money. Even worse, it ignores its readers, usually raising more questions than answers.

---

[1]Paul V. Anderson, "What Survey Research Tells Us about Writing at Work," in *Writing in Nonacademic Settings*, ed. Lee Odell and Dixie Goswami (New York: Guilford, 1985), p. 30.

[2]The late John D. deButts, former Chairman, AT&T. Quoted as the epigraph to the third edition of the Bell Laboratorics' *Editorial Style Guide* (Whippany, NJ: 1979).

To be effective writers, each of us needs to develop a variety of strategies for the different writing situations we face. We must also respect writing as something more than words typed or written on the page or fed into a word processor. Writing takes thought and planning.

THREE KEY QUESTIONS

Business and technical writing situations present us with a variety of challenges. One of the ways to meet these various writing challenges is to begin by asking ourselves these three key questions:

1. Exactly who is my audience?
2. What is the most important thing I want to tell my audience?
3. What is the best way of making sure my audience understands what I have to say?

Exactly Who Is My Audience?

Whatever we write on the job, somebody—across the hall, across the city, across the country, or even across the world—will eventually read what we have written. Most likely, our readers will receive our message in their own offices or homes. Since we won't be on hand to explain anything that is unclear or that doesn't make sense, our message will have to speak for itself.

Whenever we sit down to write, we become experts, which in large part is why we are the writers and not the readers. Our readers depend on us for clear, effective writing, so that they may share in our expertise. Although this point seems obvious, business, industrial, and technical practice shows that the single most common cause of bad writing is ignoring the reader. There are any number of ways to ignore our audiences: we can talk over their heads; we can talk down to them; we can beat around the bush; we can leave out important details—and, as a result, we can undermine our credibility.

When you next sit down to write, therefore, it is important to ask yourself what you know about your audience—you must determine your audience's situation and anticipate your audience's potential reaction to your message. To cite just one example of potential confusion between the reader and the writer: Will an audience for a major sales proposal, which could include some international some clients or customers, read 02/03/10 as a date in February (by U.S. standards) or in March (by European standards)? To paraphrase the golden rule, make sure you are prepared to write unto others the way you would have them write unto you.

What Is the Most Important Thing I Want to Tell My Audience?

Whether you write one page or one hundred pages, you should be able to condense your most important idea into about 25 words. If you can't, you aren't ready to write, since you haven't figured out what you are trying to say. You may not be able to explain every reason for a decision or a proposal in 25 words, but 25 words should be enough for a statement of the decision or proposal itself. For instance, you may have several reasons for recommending that your company replace its Brand X computers with Brand Y computers. You can make the recommendation in 20 words flat:

> I recommend that we immediately replace all our Brand X computers with new Brand Y units for the reasons presented below.

In short, you can cut through all the unnecessary verbiage and come right out with your recommendation in simple, straightforward language. Then, in the body of your memo or report, you can present the relevant facts. Busy people dislike having their time wasted, and they hate surprises. So, in professional writing, the bottom line should also be the top line. Don't tell a busy reader in the last paragraph of a multipage memo or letter—or in a long e-mail—that you need a set of data next Wednesday, or that the company stands to lose a major account if you don't have that data. Let the busy reader know the date by which you need the data in the first sentence of your document.

What Is the Best Way of Making Sure My Audience Understands What I Have to Say?

Different writing situations require different strategies. After answering the first two questions, you may decide that you shouldn't write at all—that you should phone instead or make a personal visit. But once you do commit yourself to writing, you need to determine how to put the particular document together. You will need to use one strategy for good news and a different one for bad news, one for giving information and another for changing someone's mind, one for accepting a job offer and another for turning the offer down. But in each case you will need to get your main idea out as soon as possible in as few words as possible, and then later defend or elaborate on that idea as clearly and as effectively as possible.

To illustrate the importance of answering these three key questions properly, let's look at a brief excerpt from a booklet formerly used by the New York State Income Tax Bureau:

> The return for the period before the change of residence must include all items of income, gain, loss or deduction accrued to the taxpayer up to the time of his change of residence. This includes any amounts not otherwise includable in the return because of an election to report income on an installment basis.
>
> Stated another way, the return for the period prior to the change of residence must be made on the accrual basis whether or not that is the taxpayer's established method of reporting. However, in the case of a taxpayer changing from nonresident to resident status, these accruals need not be made with respect to items derived from or connected with New York sources.

How did you respond to this information? If you were a taxpayer in need of quick and concise information to solve a particular problem, you would surely be disappointed and probably even annoyed. Tax publications and forms need not be complicated; since ordinary people normally read the publications and fill out these forms, they should be written for the average taxpayer, not for a trained accountant. In fact, all professional writing should be reader-directed.

Furthermore, the result of such convoluted writing is that these two paragraphs do not fulfill their purpose; they do not tell taxpayers how to adjust their returns when changing residence. Although the grammar is correct, the message is certainly not effective. Among other faults, the writer forgot to ask, "Who is my audience?" Unfamiliar words or usages such as *includable, accrual basis,* and *election* appear without explanation. If taxpayers cannot understand such language, they will complete their returns incorrectly and cheat either themselves or the state out of money. In the end, these two paragraphs—and others like them in the tax booklet—will have missed their mark, and unnecessary complications for both taxpayers and the state will be the result.

GUIDELINES FOR EFFECTIVE WRITING

To make sure you answer the three key questions correctly, keep these guidelines in mind:

- *Put your main idea up front.* Then provide whatever background or evidence your reader needs to understand your main idea.
- *Avoid using technical terms with nontechnical readers.* If you are an accountant writing to another accountant, use all the technical terminology you need. But if you are an accountant writing to a layperson, use ordinary language that the layperson will understand. If you must use technical terms, define them carefully. Is a CD a bank product or a source for music? Does IRA stand for another bank product or a terrorist group? Different audiences may have different interpretations of these acronyms.
- *Limit the length and complexity of your sentences.* Whenever possible, try to include only one main idea in each sentence. More mechanically, try also to limit your sentences to 25 to 35 words (or about 2½ typed lines). Generally speaking, the shorter the sentences, the fewer the difficulties you and your reader will get into. To ensure that your sentences are easily understood, move the main subject and verb to the front of the sentence and cut out any unnecessary words.
- *Limit the length and content of your paragraph.* Nothing intimidates a reader more than a half-page-long block of dense prose. Rather than using one paragraph to discuss every aspect of a topic, use a separate paragraph for each aspect of your topic. In that way, you can limit your paragraphs to five or six sentences. If you really need a longer paragraph, use indentation or enumeration so that your subpoints stand out from the pack.
- *Give your reader all necessary information in a clear and unmistakable way.* If your reader needs to let you know something by June 12, tell the reader so plainly. If you want your reader to check back with you for additional information, make sure you provide your e-mail address or telephone number, and your travel or vacation schedule if you are going to be out of the office. If you are attaching or enclosing anything, specify exactly what. If your message is a follow-up to some previous correspondence or to a recurring problem, make sure you give the reader this information too.

The selections that follow suggest many ways in which you can make your professional writing more effective. They also suggest ways you can make the process more enjoyable. If you view your professional writing as a chore, its effectiveness will be limited. But the more you get into the habit of asking the three key questions before you write your memos, letters, reports, and other documents, the easier, the more effective—and the more enjoyable—writing will become for you.

Part 1

Process as Well as Product

The old adage tells us to think before we speak. We should also think before we write. Actually, we should think before we write, while we write, and after we write. Thinking is what the writing process is all about. A process approach to writing is simply a writing strategy that asks writers to make sure they carefully plan each written message, rather than simply letting words fall where they may in the hope they will somehow organize themselves effectively and make sense to their intended audience.

People in business and industry are, however, trained to think in terms of finished products, bottom lines, and deadlines, so at first they may react with skepticism—if not with antagonism—to a process that requires them to slow down and think, especially when it is 4:30 P.M. and they need to get a memo to the boss by 5:00 P.M. Sometimes, sheer momentum and adrenaline will actually help, and a writer will produce an acceptable, even an effective, document. More times than not, though, the document will fail to achieve its purpose. The writer who balked at spending an extra ten minutes thinking a document through ends up spending an additional hour writing a follow-up document to clarify what should have been clear in the first document or, even worse, to mend fences because the original document created new problems.

In the introduction, I suggested an approach to the writing process that involved having writers ask themselves three key questions:

1. Exactly who is the audience?
2. What is the most important thing they want to tell this audience?
3. What is the best way of making sure this audience understands what they have to say?

These three key questions are simply one of any number of approaches to the writing process. The essays that follow in this section of *Strategies* offer other approaches and additional insights into a process approach to writing.

Underlying such an approach is the idea that good writing for any purpose, be it produced for the world of work or not, requires careful planning. There is no magic bullet here. Spending an extra five minutes, or five hours for that matter, in writing a document will not in and of itself guarantee that document's success. What is important is how a writer spends that time. Some documents are easily roughed out in a few minutes; others may require hours—days? weeks?—of planning and drafting. Often a process approach involves more than a bit of trial and error. No one approach works all the time for all writers in all situations. As idiosyncratic as any individual approach to the writing process may be, writers for the world of work fail to pay attention to planning at their own peril.

In the first essay, John Keenan offers a five-part approach to the writing process that asks writers to consider purpose, audience, format, evidence, and organization. Michael Adelstein follows Keenan with another five-part approach to writing that lays down a schedule for any writing task: 15% worrying, 10% planning, 25% writing, 45% revising, and 5% proofreading. The number of steps involved is, of course, unimportant. Again, what is important is that there be a conscious effort to understand that, in business and technical writing, the process is as important as the goal. Keenan's approach is more open-ended, allowing writers considerable freedom in the amount of time they spend on the different steps in the writing process. While allowing for some variation among writing situations, Adelstein suggests a more regimented approach that will appeal to other writers.

Revision is essential to successful writing, and Linda Flower and John Ackerman suggest ways in which the process of revision can help writers produce more effective documents. The authors stress the need especially for writers "to translate" what they write from writer-based prose, which makes sense to them, to reader-based prose, which will ensure that their readers get the information they need in the language and form in which they need it. Again, audience is the key here— that documents need to make sense to, and meet the needs of, their intended audience seems just plain common sense. Alas, too often, common sense is absent, by accident or design, from any number of documents produced for the world of work. Can you understand the notice of change in terms for your credit card? The step-by-step procedures for assembling a piece of furniture or a child's toy? The instructions for filling in mandated forms online? Your local, state, or federal tax publications? Your apartment lease? Your cellphone agreement? And somewhat infamously, in days gone by, the directions for setting the clock on your VHS player?

Next in an often reprinted and adapted essay, John S. Harris examines the writing process from a different perspective. The fault in poor quality documents may lie as much with the managers who assign them as with those who produce them. To counter problems in the management of writing, Harris offers a project worksheet designed to facilitate efficient writing management.

Complementing the essays by Flower and Ackerman and by Harris, Jack Selzer reports on his application of methods used to study the composing processes of twelfth graders to the composing process of a single engineer based in Chicago who spends roughly half his time on the job writing. While Selzer notes that his essay offers only tentative suggestions about how technical writers should compose documents—and how college and university teachers should prepare their students for the writing demands of the world of work—his case study is a valuable example of the writing process at work in the hands of one well-educated, at times over-taxed professional. Of especial note are the somewhat surprising amounts of time that Selzer's technical writer devotes to different stages of the writing process.

What follows in this first section of *Strategies* are different discussions of the idea that it is important to take a process approach to any writing assignment in the many worlds of work. Writing is hard work. Writing takes planning. Throughout the remaining essays collected in *Strategies*, this message will be repeated in a variety of ways by experts with a variety of backgrounds and from a variety of fields, such as business, science, technology, industry, and the academy. Think before you write, while you write, and after you write—and only then send or deliver your message.

John Keenan

Using PAFEO Planning

A former technical writer for SmithKline, the late John Keenan was Professor of English at La Salle University in Philadelphia and coauthor with Kevin J. Harty of Writing for Business and Industry: Process and Product *(Macmillan, 1987).*

Surveys tell us that "lack of clarity" is the most frequently cited weakness when executives evaluate their employees' writing. But since lack of clarity results from various bad habits, it is often used as a convenient catchall criticism. Pressed to explain what they meant by lack of clarity, readers would probably come up with comments such as these:

"I had to read the damn thing three times before I got what he was driving at. At least I *think* I got his point; I'm not sure."

"I couldn't follow her line of thought."

"I'm just too busy to wade through a lot of self-serving explanation and justification. If he has something to say, why didn't he just say it without all that buildup?"

Most unclear writing results from unclear thinking. But it is also true that habits of clear writing help one to think clearly. When a writer gets thoughts in order and defines the purpose and goal, what he wants to say may no longer be exactly the same as it was originally. Sometimes the writer may even decide it is better *not* to write. Whatever the case, the work done *before* the first draft in the prewriting process and *after* the draft in the revising process is often the difference between successful communication and time-wasting confusion. . . .

THINK PAFEO

Some years ago I made up a nonsense word to help my students remember the important steps in constructing a piece of writing. It seemed to stick in their minds. In fact, I keep running into former students who can't remember my name, but remember PAFEO because it proved to be so useful. Here are the magic ingredients:

P stands for purpose
A stands for audience
F stands for format
E stands for evidence
O stands for organization.

Put together, they spell PAFEO, and it means the world to me!

PURPOSE

Put the question to yourself, "Why am I writing this?" ("Because I have to," is not a sufficient answer.) This writing you're going to do must aim at accomplishing something; you must be seeking a particular response from your reader. Suppose, for example, you're being a good citizen and writing to your congressman on a matter of interest to you. Your letter may encompass several purposes. You are writing to inform him of your thinking and perhaps to persuade him to vote for or against a certain bill. In explaining your position, you may find it useful to narrate a personal experience or to describe a situation vividly enough to engage his emotions. Your letter may therefore include the four main kinds of writing—exposition, argument, narration, and description—but one of them is likely to be primary. Your other purposes would be subordinated to your effort to persuade the congressman to vote your way. So your precise purpose might be stated: "I am writing to Congressman Green to persuade him to vote for increased social security benefits provided by House Bill 5883."

Write it out in a sentence just that way. Pin it down. And make it as precise as you can. You will save yourself a good deal of grief in the writing process by getting as clear a focus as you can on your purpose. You'll know better what to include and what to omit. The many choices that combine to form the writing process will be made easier because you have taken the time and the thought to determine the exact reason you have for writing this communication.

When you're writing something longer than a letter, like a report, you can make things easier for yourself and your reader by making a clear statement of the central idea you're trying to develop. This is your thesis. To be most helpful, it must be a complete sentence, not just the subject of a sentence. "Disappointing sales" may be the subject you are writing about, but it is not a thesis. Stating it that way won't help you organize the information in your report. But if you really say something specific about "disappointing sales," you will have a thesis that will provide a framework for development. For example:

> Disappointing sales may be attributed to insufficient advertising, poor selection of merchandise, and inadequate staffing during peak shopping hours.

The frame for the rest of the report now exists. By the time you have finished explaining how each cause contributes to the result (disappointing sales), the report is finished. Not only finished, but clear; it follows an orderly pattern. The arguments, details, illustrations, statistics, or quotations are relevant because the thesis has given you a way of keeping your purpose clearly in focus.

Of course the ideal method is to get your purpose and your thesis down before you write a first draft, but I can tell you from experience that it doesn't always work that way. Sometimes the only way to capture a thesis statement is to sneak up on it by means of a meandering first draft. When you've finished that chore, read the whole thing over and try to ambush the thesis by saying, "OK, now just what am I trying to say?" Then *say it* as quickly and concisely as you can—out loud, so you can hear how it sounds. Then try to write it down in the most precise and concise way you can. Even if you don't capture the exact thesis statement you're looking for, there's a good chance that you will have clarified your purpose sufficiently to make your next revision better.

AUDIENCE

Most of the writing the average person does is aimed at a specific reader: the congressman, the boss, a business subordinate, a customer, a supplier. Having a limited audience can be an advantage. It enables the writer to analyze the reader and shape the writing so that it effectively achieves the purpose with that particular reader or group of readers.

Here are some questions that will help you communicate with the reader:

1. How much background do I need to give this reader, considering his or her position, attitude toward the subject, and experience with this subject?
2. What does the reader need to know, and how can I best give him or her this information?
3. How is my credibility with this reader? Must I build it gradually as I proceed, or can I assume that he or she will accept certain judgments based on my interpretations?
4. Is the reader likely to agree or disagree with my position? What tone would be most appropriate in view of this agreement or disagreement?

The last question, I think, is very important. It implies that the writer will try to see the reader's point of view, will bend every effort to look at the subject the way the reader will probably look at it. That isn't easy to do. Doing it takes both imagination and some understanding of psychology. But it is worth the considerable effort it involves; it is a gateway to true communication.

Let me briefly suggest a point here that is easily overlooked in the search for better techniques of communication. It is simply this: *better writing depends on better reading*. Technique isn't everything. One cannot learn to be imaginative and understanding in ten easy lessons, but reading imaginative literature—fiction, poetry, drama—is one way of developing the ability to put yourself in someone else's place so you can see how the problem looks from that person's angle. The writer who limits reading to his or her own technical field is building walls around the imagination. The unique value of imaginative literature is the escape that it allows from the prison of the self into the experience and emotions of persons of different backgrounds. That ability to understand why a reader is likely to think and act in a certain way is constantly useful to the writer in the struggle to communicate.

FORMAT

Having thought about your purpose and your audience, consider carefully the appropriate format for this particular communication you are writing. Of course the range of choice may be limited by company procedures, but even the usual business formats allow some room for the writer to use ingenuity and intelligence.

The key that unlocks this ingenuity is making the format as well as the words work toward achieving your purpose. You can call attention to important points by the way you arrange your material on the page.

Writers sometimes neglect this opportunity, turning the draft over to the typist without taking the trouble to plan the finished page. Remember the reader, his or her desk piled high with things to be read, and try to make your ideas as clear as possible on the page as the reader glances at it.

External signals such as headings, underlining, and numerals are ways of giving the reader a quick preview. Use them when they are appropriate to your material.

Don't be afraid of using white space as a way of drawing attention to key ideas.

To see how experts use format for clarity and emphasis, take a look at some of the sales letters all of us receive daily. Note how these persuasive messages draw the reader's attention to each advantage of the product. You may not want to go that far, but the principle of using the format to save the reader's time is worth your careful consideration.

Overburdened executives are always looking for shortcuts through the sea of paper. Many admit that they cannot possibly read every report or memo. They scan, they skip, they look for summaries. A good format identifies the main points quickly and gives an idea of the organizational structure and content. If the format looks logical and interesting, readers may be lured into spending more time on your ideas. You've taken the trouble to separate the important from the unimportant, thus saving them time. The clear format holds promise of a clear analysis, and what boss can be too busy for that?

EVIDENCE

Unless you're an authority on your subject, your opinions carry only as much weight as the evidence you can marshal to support them. The more evidence you can collect before writing, the easier the writing task will be. Evidence consists of the facts and information you gather in three ways: (1) through careful observation, (2) through intelligent fieldwork (talking to the appropriate persons), and (3) through . . . research.

When you follow the evidence where it leads and form a hypothesis, you are using inductive reasoning, the scientific method. If your evidence is adequate, representative, and related to the issue, your conclusion must still be considered a probability, not a certainty, since you can never possess or weigh *all* the evidence. At some point you make the "inductive leap" and conclude that the weight of evidence points to a theory as a probability. The probability is likely to be strong if you are aware of the rules of evidence.

The Rules of Evidence

Rule 1. Look at the Evidence and Follow Where It Leads.

The trick here is not to let your own bias seduce you into selecting only the evidence you agree with. If you aren't careful, you unconsciously start forcing the evidence to fit the design that seems to be emerging. When fact A and fact B both point toward the same conclusion, there is always the temptation to *make* fact C fit. Biographer Marchette Chute's warning is worth heeding: ". . . you will never succeed in getting at the truth if you think you know, ahead of time, what the truth ought to be."

A reliable generalization ought to be based on a number of verifiable, relevant facts—the more the better. Logicians tell us that evidence supporting a generalization must be (1) known or available, (2) sufficient, (3) relevant, and (4) representative. Let's see how these apply to the generalization, "Cigarette smoking is hazardous to your health."

The evidence accumulated in animal studies and in comparative studies of smokers and nonsmokers has been published in medical journals: it is therefore known and available. Is it sufficient? The government thinks so; the tobacco industry does not. Which is more likely to have a bias that might make it difficult to follow where the evidence leads?

Tobacco industry spokesmen argue that animal studies are not necessarily relevant to human beings and point to individuals of advanced age who have been smoking since childhood as living refutations of the supposed evidence. But the number of cases studied is now in the thousands, and studies have been done with representative samplings. The individuals who have smoked without apparent damage to their health are real enough, but can they be said to be numerous enough to be representative of the usual effects of tobacco on humans? "Proof" beyond doubt lies only in mathematics, but the evidence in this example is the kind on which a sound generalization can be based.

Rule 2. Look for the Simplest Explanation that Accounts for All the Evidence.

When the lights go out, the sudden darkness might be taken as evidence of a power failure. But a quick investigation turns up other evidence that must be accounted for: the streetlights are still on; the refrigerator is still functioning. So a simpler explanation may exist, and a check of the circuit breakers or fuse box would be appropriate.

Rule 3. Look at All Likely Alternatives.

Likely alternatives in the example just discussed would include such things as burned-out bulbs, loose plugs, and defective outlets.

Rule 4. Beware of Absolute Statements.

In the complexity of the real world, it is seldom possible to marshal sufficient evidence to permit an absolute generalization. Be wary of writing general statements using words like *all, never* or *always*. Sometimes these words are implied rather than stated, as in this example:

> Jogging is good exercise for both men and women.
>
> [Because it is unqualified, the statement means *all* men and women. Since jogging is not good for people with certain health problems, this statement would be better if it said *most* or *many* men and women.]

Still, caution is always necessary. Induction has its limitations, and a hypothesis is best considered a probability subject to change on the basis of new evidence.

The other kind of reasoning we do is called deduction. Instead of starting with particulars and arriving at a generalization, deduction starts with a general premise or set of premises and works toward the conclusion necessarily implied by them. If the premise is true, it follows that the conclusion must be true. This logical relationship is called an inference. A fallacy is an erroneous or unjustified inference. When you are reasoning deductively, you can get into trouble if your premise is faulty or if the route from premise to conclusion contains a fallacy. Keep the following two basic principles in mind, and watch out for the common fallacies that can act as booby traps along the path from premise to conclusion.

Two Principles for Sound Deduction

1. The ideas must be true; that is, they must be based on facts that are known, sufficient, relevant, and representative.
2. The two ideas must have a strong logical connection.

If your inductive reasoning has been sound enough to take care of the first principle, let me warn you that the second is not so simple as it sounds. We have all been exposed to so much propaganda and advertising that distort this principle that we may have trouble recognizing the weak or illogical connection. Nothing is easier than to tumble into one of the commoner logic fallacies. As a matter of fact, no barroom argument would be complete without one of these bits of twisted logic.

Twisted Logic

Begging the question. Trying to prove a point by repeating it in different words.

> Women are the weaker sex because they are not as strong as men.
> Our company is more successful because we outsell the competition.

Non sequitur. The conclusion does not follow logically.

> I had my best sales year; the company's stock should be a big gainer this year.
> I was shortchanged at the supermarket yesterday. You can't trust these young cashiers at all.

Post hoc. Because an event happened first, it is presumed to be the cause of the second event.

> Elect the Democrats and you get war; elect the Republicans and you get a depression.

Oversimplification. Treating truth as an either-or proposition, without any degrees in between.

> Better dead than Red.
> America—love it or leave it.
> If we do not establish our sales leadership in New York, we might as well close up our East Coast outlets.

False analogy. Because of one or two similarities, two different things are assumed to be *entirely* similar.

> You can lead a horse to water but you can't make him drink; there is no sense in forcing kids to go to school.
> Giving the Canal back to Panama would be like giving the Great Lakes back to the Indians.

Seen in raw form, as in the examples, these fallacies seem easy to avoid. Yet all of us fall into them with dismaying regularity. A writer must be on guard against them whenever he or she attempts to draw conclusions from data.

ORGANIZATION

Experienced writers often use index cards when they collect and organize information. Cards can be easily arranged and rearranged. By arranging them in piles, you can create an organizational plan. Here's how you play the game:

1. You can write only one point on each card—one fact, one observation, one opinion, one statistic, one whatever.

2. Arrange the cards into piles, putting all closely related points together. All evidence related to marketing goes in one pile, all evidence related to product development goes in another pile, and so on.
3. Now you can move the piles around, putting them in sequence. What kind of sequence? Consider one of the following commonly used principles:

Chronological. From past to present to future.
Background, present status, prospects
Spatial. By location.
New England territory, Middle Atlantic, Southern
Logical. Depends on the topic.
Classification and division according to a consistent principle (divisions of a company classified according to function)
Cause and effect (useful in troubleshooting manuals)
Problem-analysis-solution. Description of problem, why it exists, what to do about it.
Order of importance. From least important to most important or from most important to least important.

The choice of sequence will depend largely on the logic of the subject matter and the needs of your audience.
4. Go through each pile and arrange the cards in an understandable sequence. Which points need to precede others in order to present a clear picture?
5. That's it! You now have an outline that is both orderly and flexible. You can add, subtract, or rearrange whenever necessary.

SUMMARY

Think PAFEO. Use this word to remind you to clarify your purpose and analyze your audience before you write. When you have a clear sense of purpose, create a thesis that will act as a frame for your ideas.

Choose a format for your communication that will help the reader identify the main points quickly.

Collect your evidence before you write by observing, interviewing, and doing library research. Use the index card system to help you organize your evidence. Keep in mind the rules of evidence before you draw conclusions. Be alert to the common logic fallacies that can easily undermine the deductive process.

Try the file card system as a way of organizing your material. Write one point on each card and then place closely related points together in a pile. Place the piles in sequence according to a principle of organization you select. Some useful organizing principles include: chronological, spatial, logical, problem-analysis-solution, and order of importance. The sequence you choose will depend on the logic of the subject matter and the needs of your audience.

Michael E. Adelstein

The Writing Process

Michael E. Adelstein was formerly Professor of English at the University of Kentucky and coauthor with W. Keats Sparrow of Business Communications *(Harcourt Brace Jovanovich, 1983).*

THE WRITING PROCESS

Their prevalent belief in the myths of genius, inspiration, and correctness prevents many people from writing effectively. If these individuals could realize that they can learn to write, that they cannot wait to be inspired, and that they must focus on other aspects besides correctness, then they can overcome many obstacles confronting them. But they should be aware that writing, like many other forms of work, is a process. To accomplish it well, people should plan on completing each one of its five stages. The time allocations may vary with the deadline, subject, and purpose, but the work schedule should generally follow this pattern:

1. Worrying—15%
2. Planning—10%
3. Writing—25%
4. Revising—45%
5. Proofreading—5%

Note that only 25% of the time should be spent in writing; the rest—75%—should be spent in getting ready for the task and perfecting the initial effort. Observe also that more time is spent in revising than in any other stage, including writing.

Stage One—Worrying (15%)

Worrying is a more appropriate term for the first operation than *thinking* because it suggests more precisely what you must do. When you receive a writing assignment, you must avoid blocking it out of your mind until you're ready to write; instead, allow it to simmer while you try to cook up some ideas. As you stew about the subject while brushing your teeth, taking a shower, getting dressed, walking to class, or preparing for bed, jot down any pertinent thoughts. You need only note them on scrap paper or the back of an envelope. But if you fail to write them down, you'll forget them.

Another way to relieve your worrying is to read about the subject or discuss it with friends. The chances are that others have wrestled with similar problems and written their ideas. Why not benefit from their experience? But if you think that there is nothing in print about the subject or a related one—either because your assignment is restricted, localized, or topical—then you should at least discuss it with friends.

Let's say, for example, that as a member of the student government on your campus, you've been asked to investigate the possibility of opening a student-operated bookstore to combat high textbook prices. During free hours, you might drop into the library to read about the retail book business and, if possible, about college bookstores. If your student government is affiliated with the National Student Association, you might write to it for information about policies and practices on other campuses. In addition, you might start talking about the problem to the manager of your college bookstore, owners of other bookstores in your community, student transfers from other schools, managers of college bookstores in nearby communities, and some of your professors. Because you might be concerned about the public relations repercussions of a student bookstore, you should propose the venture to college officials. At this point, you will have heard many different ideas. To discuss some of them, bring up the subject of a student bookstore with friends. As you talk, you will be clarifying and organizing your thoughts.

The same technique can be applied to less involved subjects, such as a description of an ideal summer job, or an explanation of a technical matter like input-output analysis. By worrying about the subject as you proceed through your daily routine, by striving to get ideas from books and people or both, and by clarifying your thoughts in conversation with friends, you will be ready for the next step. Remember: you can proceed only if you have some ideas. You must have something to write about.

Stage Two—Planning (10%)

Planning is another term for organizing or for the task that students dread so—*outlining*. You should already have had some experience with this process. Like many students, unfortunately, you may have learned only how to outline a paper after writing it. This practice is a waste of time. If you want to operate efficiently, then it follows that you will have to specialize in each of the writing stages in turn. When you force yourself simultaneously to conceive of ideas, to arrange them in logical order, and to express them in words, you cannot perform all of these complex activities as effectively as if you had concentrated on each one separately. By dividing the writing process into five stages, and by focusing on each one individually, the odds are that the result will be much better than you had thought possible. Of course you will hear about people who never plan their writing but who do well anyway, just as you may know someone who skis or plays golf well without having had a lesson. There are always some naturals who can flaunt the rules. But perhaps these people could have significantly improved their writing, golf, or skiing if they had received some formal instruction and proceeded in the prescribed manner.

An efficient person plans his work. Many executives take a few minutes before leaving the office or retiring at night to jot down problems to attend to the following day. Many vacationers list tasks to do before leaving home: stop the newspaper, turn down the refrigerator, inform the mailman, cut off the hot water, check the car, mail the mortgage payment, notify the police, and the like. Of course, you can go on vacation without planning—just as you can write without planning—but the chances are that the more carefully you organize, the better the results will be.

In writing, planning consists mainly in examining all your ideas, eliminating the irrelevant ones, and arranging the others in a clear, logical order. Whether you write a formal outline or merely jot down your ideas on scrap paper is up to you. The outline is for your benefit; follow the procedure that helps you the most. But realize that the harder you work on perfecting your outline, the easier the writing will be. As you write, therefore, you can concentrate on formulating sentences instead of also being concerned with thinking of ideas and trying to organize them. For the present, realize the importance of planning. . . .

Stage Three—Writing (25%)

When you know what you want to say and have planned how to say it, then you are ready to write. This third step in the writing process is self-explanatory. You need only dash away your thoughts, using pen, pencil, or typewriter, whichever you prefer. Let your mind flow along the outline. Don't pause to check spelling, worry about punctuation, or search for exact words. If new thoughts pop into your mind, as they often do, check them with your outline, and work them into your paper if they are relevant. Otherwise discard them. Keep going until either the end or fatigue halts you. And don't worry if you write slowly: many people do.

Stage Four—Revising (45%)

Few authors are so talented that they can express themselves clearly and effectively in a first draft. Most know that they must revise their papers extensively. So they roll up their sleeves and begin slashing away, cutting out excess verbiage, tearing into fuzzy sentences, stabbing at structural weaknesses, and knifing into obfuscation. Revision is painful: removing pet phrases and savory sentences is like getting rid of cherished possessions. Just as we dislike to discard old magazines, books, shoes, and clothes, so we hate to get rid of phrases and sentences. But no matter how distasteful the process may be, professional writers know that revising is crucial; it is usually the difference between a mediocre paper and an excellent one.

Few students revise their work well; they fail to realize the importance of this process, lack the necessary zeal, and are unaware of how to proceed. Once you understand why you seem to be naturally adverse to revision, you may overcome your resistance.

Because writing requires concentrated thought, it is about the most enervating work that humans perform. Consequently, upon completing a first draft, we are so relieved at having produced something that we tidy it up slightly, copy it quickly, and get rid of it immediately. After all, why bother with it anymore? But there's the rub. The experienced writer knows that he has to sweat through it again and again, looking for trouble, willing to rework cumbersome passages, and striving always to find a better word, a more felicitous phrase, and a smoother sentence. John Galbraith, for example, regularly . . . [wrote] five drafts, the last one reserved for inserting "that note of spontaneity" that ironically makes his work appear natural and effortless. The record for revision is probably held by Ernest Hemingway, who wrote the last page of *A Farewell to Arms* thirty-nine times before he was satisfied!

To revise effectively, you must not only change your attitude, but also your perspective. Usually we reread a paper from our own viewpoint, feeling proud of our accomplishment. We admire our cleverness, enjoy our graceful flights, and glow at our fanciful turns. How easy it is to delude ourselves! The experienced writer reads his draft objectively, looking at it from the standpoint of his reader. To accomplish this, he gets away from the paper for a while, usually leaving it until the following morning. You may not be able to budget your time this ideally, but you can put the paper aside while you visit a friend, grab a bite to eat, or phone someone. Unless you divorce yourself from the paper, you will probably be under its spell; that is, you will reread it with your mind rather than with your eyes. You will see only what you think is on the page instead of what is actually there. And you will not be able to transport yourself from your role of writer to that of critic.

Only by attacking your paper from the viewpoint of another person can you revise it effectively. You must be anxious to find fault and you must be honest with yourself. If you cannot or will not realize the weaknesses in your writing, then you cannot correct them. This textbook should open your eyes to many things that can go wrong, but above all you must *want* to find them. If you blind yourself to the bad, then your work will never be good. You must convince yourself that good writing depends on good rewriting. This point cannot be repeated too frequently or emphasized too much. Tolstoy revised *War and Peace*—one of the world's longest and greatest novels—five times. The brilliant French stylist Flaubert struggled for hours, even days, trying to perfect a single sentence. But question your professors about their own writing. Many—like me—revise papers three, four, or five times before submitting them for publication. You may not have this opportunity, your deadlines in school and business may not permit this luxury; but you can develop a respect for revision and you can devote more time and effort to this crucial stage in the writing process. . . .

Stage Five—Proofreading (5%)

Worrying, planning, writing, and revising are not sufficient. The final task, although not as taxing as the others, is just as vital. Proofreading is like a quick check in the mirror before leaving for a date. A sloppy appearance can spoil a favorable acceptance of you or your paper. If, through your fault or your typist's, words are missing or repeated, letters are transposed, or sentences juxtaposed, a reader may be perturbed enough to ignore or resist your ideas or information. Poor proofreading of an application letter can cost you a job. Such penalties may seem unfair, but we all react in this fashion. What would you think of a doctor with dirty hands? His carelessness would not only disgust you but would also raise questions about his professional competence. Similarly, carelessness in your writing antagonizes readers and raises questions in their minds about your competence. The merit of a person or paper should not depend on appearances, but frequently it does. Being aware of this possibility, you should keep yourself and your writing well groomed.

Poor proofreading results from failure to realize its importance, from inadequate time, and from improper effort. Unless you are convinced that scrutinizing your final copy is important, you cannot proofread effectively. If you realize the significance of this fifth step in the writing process, then you will not only have the incentive to work hard at proofreading but also will allow time for it in planning.

Like most things, proofreading takes time. We usually run out of time for things that we don't care about. But there's always time for what we enjoy or what is important to us. So with proofreading; lack of time is seldom a legitimate excuse for doing it badly.

But lack of technique is. To proofread well, you must forget the ideas in a paper and focus on words. Slow down your reading speed, stare hard at the black print, and search for trouble rather than trying to finish quickly. . . . Some professional proofreaders start with the last sentence and read backward to the first. Whatever technique you adopt, work painstakingly, so that a few careless errors will not spoil your efforts. If you realize the importance of proofreading, view it as one of the stages in the writing process, and labor at it conscientiously, your paper will reflect your care and concern. . . .

Each Stage Is Important

These then are the five stages in the writing process: worrying, planning, writing, revising, and proofreading. Each is vital. You need to become proficient at each of them, although, at some later point in your life, an editor or efficient secretary may relieve you of some proofreading chores. But in your career as a student and in your early business years, you will be on your own to guide your paper through the five stages. Since it is your paper, no one else will be as interested in it as you. It's your offspring—to nourish, to cherish, to coddle, to bring up, and finally, to turn over to someone else. You will be proud of it only if you have done your best throughout its growth and development.

Linda Flower and John Ackerman

Evaluating and Testing as You Revise

Both Linda Flower, a member of the faculty at Carnegie Mellon University, and John Ackerman, a member of the faculty at the University of Utah, are nationally recognized authorities on the teaching of writing.

IMAGINING A READER'S RESPONSE

Even if you have a model or text to work from, as a writer you will work hard to construct a text: generating and discarding ideas, trying to figure out your point, sketching out alternative organizations, and then trying to signal that point and structure to your reader. But the story does not end there because your various readers have to work equally hard to construct a meaning based on your text. That is, readers want to construct *in their own minds* a coherent text, with a hierarchical organization (like an issue tree) based on key points. And they need to see a purpose for reading. Readers want to know *Why read this? What is the point?* and *How is all of this connected?*—and they want to find answers as quickly as possible.

Readers begin to predict the structure of a text and its meaning as soon as they face a page. They will look for cues that the text might offer about point, purpose, and structure, but if they do not find them, they will go ahead and construct their own version of the text *and assume that is what you intended*. It may be helpful to imagine your readers as needing to *write* your text for themselves. Thus, their own goals and interests will strongly influence what they look for in a text and the meaning they make out of it. Your goal, then, as a writer is to do the best job you can to make sure a reader's process through your text and his or her understanding matches or comes close to what you intended.

Once your ideas are down in a draft of some form, **revision** lets you anticipate how readers will respond and adjust the text to get the response you hope for. **Local revision** involves editing, correcting spelling and grammar, and making local improvements in wording or sentence style. **Global revision** involves looking at the big picture, but that does not mean throwing the draft out and starting again, and it may not even take a lot of time. Global revision, however, does mean looking at the text as a whole—thinking globally about the major rhetorical decisions and plans you made—now that the draft is complete. Global revisions alter the focus, organization, argument, or detail to improve the overall text.

Revision begins with a tricky reading process, a close reading of your own text. You know from your own experience in school that readers can read for different purposes: to skim a text to prepare for class discussion and then to read more carefully for an examination. In business, because writing usually augments a transaction between people, readers look for information but they also look for how well a piece of writing is adapted to their needs. The key to your success as a reviser is your ability to read your own writing critically for different features and purposes. At the simplest level, revision is *re-vision*—the process of stepping back from one's text and seeing it anew. . . .

STRATEGY 1: LOOK FOR WRITER-BASED PROSE

Why is it that even experienced writers typically choose to draft and revise rather than write a final text in one pass? Suppose you put time into planning your paper; you followed a good model; you thought about your reader as you chose what to say. Why should your first draft not do the job? One reason is because first drafts often contain large sections of **writer-based prose.** Writer-based prose appears when writers are essentially talking to themselves, talking through a problem, exploring their own knowledge, or trying to get their ideas out. In fact, producing writer-based prose is often a smart problem-solving strategy. Instead of getting blocked or spending hours staring at a blank page trying to write a perfect text the first time through, writers can literally walk through their own memory, talking out on paper what they know. Other concerns, including what the reader needs to hear, are put on temporary hold. Writer-based prose is, in fact, a very effective strategy for searching your memory and for dealing with difficult topics or lots of information. Writer-based prose may also be the best a writer can do in a new situation. A writer facing an unfamiliar task may produce writer-based prose, uncertain of what readers expect.

Whether it is a strategy or consequence, the downside of this strategy is that the text it produces is typically focused on the writer's thinking—not the readers' questions or needs—and it often comes out organized as a narrative or a river of connections. A number of studies of writers new to organizations demonstrate the reasoning behind writer-based prose and its ill-effect. New employees write consciously and unconsciously to report their discovery process or to survey all they know. And their readers impatiently wade through the river looking for the specific ideas and information they need.

... [Figure 1] is the first draft of a progress report written by four students in an organizational psychology course who were doing a consulting project with a local organization, the Oskaloosa Brewing Company. As a reader, put yourself first in the position of Professor Charns. He is reading the report to answer three questions: As analysts, what assumptions and decisions did these students make in setting up their study? Why did they make them? And where are they in the project now? Then take on the role of the client, the company vice president who follows their progress and wants to know: O.K. What is the problem (i.e., how did they define it)? And what did they conclude? Would this draft answer these questions for either of its intended readers?

Draft 1

Group Progress Report

(1)   Work began on our project with the initial group decision to evaluate the Oskaloosa Brewing Company. Oskaloosa Brewing Company is a regionally located brewery manufacturing several different types of beer, notably River City and Brough Cream Ale. This beer is marketed under various names in Pennsylvania and other neighboring states. As a group, we decided to analyze this organization because two of our group members had had frequent customer contact with the sales department. Also, we were aware that Oskaloosa Brewing had been losing money for the past five years, and we felt we might be able to find some obvious problems in its organizational structure.

(2)   Our first meeting, held February 17th, was with the head of the sales department, Jim Tucker. Generally, he gave us an outline of the organization, from president to worker, and discussed the various departments that we might ultimately decide to analyze. The two that seemed the most promising and more applicable to the project were the sales and production departments. After a few group meetings and discussions with the personnel manager, Susan Harris, and our advisor, Professor Charns, we felt it best suited our needs and Oskaloosa Brewing's needs to evaluate their bottling department.

(3)   During the next week we had a discussion with the superintendent of production, Henry Holt, and made plans for interviewing the supervisors and line workers. Also, we had a tour of the bottling department that gave us a first hand look at the production process. Before beginning our interviewing, our group met several times to formulate appropriate questions to use in interviewing, for both the supervisors and the workers. We also had a meeting with Professor Charns to discuss this matter.

(4)   The next step was the actual interviewing process. During the weeks of March 14–18 and March 21–25, our group met several times at Oskaloosa Brewing and interviewed ten supervisors and twelve workers. Finally, during this past week, we have had several group meetings to discuss our findings and the potential problem areas within the bottling department. Also, we have spent time organizing the writing of our progress report.

1 of 2

FIGURE 1   The Oskaloosa Brewing Progress Memo, Draft 1

(5)   The bottling and packaging division is located in a separate building, adjacent to the brewery, where the beer is actually manufactured. From the brewery the beer is piped into one of five lines (four bottling lines and one canning line) in the bottling house, where the bottles are filled, crowned, pasteurized, labeled, packaged in cases, and either shipped out or stored in the warehouse. The head of this operation, and others, is production manager Phil Smith. Next in line under him in direct control of the bottling house is the superintendent of bottling and packaging, Henry Holt. In addition, there are a total of ten supervisors who report directly to Henry Holt and who oversee the daily operations and coordinate and direct the twenty to thirty union workers who operate the lines.

(6)   During production, each supervisor fills out a data sheet to explain what was actually produced during each hour. This form also includes the exact time when a breakdown occurred, what it was caused by, and when production was resumed. Some supervisors' positions are production-staff-oriented. One takes care of supplying the raw material (bottles, caps, labels, and boxes) for production. Another is responsible for the union workers' assignments each day.

These workers are not all permanently assigned to a production-line position. Workers called "floaters" are used, filling in for a sick worker or helping out after a breakdown.

(7)   The union employees are generally older than 35, some in their late fifties. Most have been with the company many years and are accustomed to having more workers per a slower moving line. . . .

2 of 2

FIGURE 1   *(Continued)*

Put yourself in the shoes of the professor. What would you look for in a progress report? According to Charns, he used this report to evaluate the group's progress: Were they on schedule; were they on task; did he need to intervene? However, he didn't need a blow-by-blow story to do that. As an evaluator he wanted to see whether they knew how to analyze an organization: Were they making good decisions (that is, decisions they could justify in this report); had they made any discoveries about this company? His needs as a reader, then, reflected his dual role as a teacher (supervisor) and an evaluator.

When we showed this draft to a manager (with comparable experience and responsibility to the Oskaloosa VP), we got a very different response. Here was a reader looking quickly for the information she wanted and building an image of the writers' business savvy based on their text. Here is part of her response as she read and thought aloud (the student text she reads is underlined):

Work began on our project with the initial group decision to evaluate . . . *OK.* Our project *What project is this? I must have a dozen "projects" I keep tabs on. And who is this group?* This beer is marketed . . . *blah, blah, I'm tempted to skim. This must be a student project. But why am I reading about the fact somebody bought a lot of beer for their frat? Maybe the next paragraph.*

Draft 2

MEMORANDUM

TO: Professor Martin Charns

FROM: Nancy Lowenberg, Todd Scott, Rosemary Nisson,
Larry Vollen

DATE: March 31, 1987

RE: Progress Report: The Oskaloosa Brewing Company

Why Oskaloosa Brewing?

Oskaloosa Brewing Company is a regionally located brewery manufacturing
several different types of beer, notably River City and Brough Cream Ale. As
a group, we decided to analyze this organization because two of our group
members have frequent contact with the sales department. Also, we were
aware that Oskaloosa Brewing had been losing money for the past five years
and we felt we might be able to find some obvious problems in its organizational structure.

Initial Steps: Where to Concentrate?

After several interviews with top management and a group discussion, we felt
it best suited our needs, and Oskaloosa Brewing's needs, to evaluate the production department. Our first meeting, held February 17, was with the head
of the sales department, Jim Tucker. He gave us an outline of the organization and described the two major departments, sales and production. He indicated that there were more obvious problems in the production
department, a belief also suggested by Susan Harris, the personnel manager.

Next Step

The next step involved a familiarization with the plant and its employees. First,
we toured the plant to gain an understanding of the brewing and bottling
processes. Next, during the weeks of March 14–18 and March 21–25, we interviewed ten supervisors and twelve workers. Finally, during the past week we
had group meetings to exchange information and discuss potential problems.

The Production Process

Knowledge of the actual production process is imperative in understanding
the effects of various problems on efficient production. Therefore, we have
included a brief summary of this process.

The bottling and packaging division is located in a separate building, adjacent
to the brewery, where the beer is actually manufactured. From the brewery
the beer is piped into one of five lines (four bottling lines and one canning
line) in the bottling house, where the bottles are filled, crowned, pasteurized,
labeled, packaged in cases, and either shipped out or stored in the warehouse.

Problems

Through extensive interviews with supervisors and union employees, we have
recognized four apparent problems within the bottling house operations.
The first is that the employees' goals do not match those of the company. . . .
This is especially apparent in the union employees, whose loyalty lies with the
union instead of the company. This attitude is well-founded, as the union ensures them of job security and benefits. . . .

FIGURE 2   The Oskaloosa Brewing Progress Memo, Draft 2

Our first meeting . . . *Ok, they saw Jim and Susan, . . . looked at bottling, . . . wrote their paper. And now they are telling me where my packaging division is located! This is like a shaggy plant tour story. They are just wasting my time. And I suppose I should say that I am also forming an image of them as rather naive, sort of bumbling around the plant, interrupting my staff with questions. I mean, what are they after? Do they have any idea of what they are doing?*

Now put yourself in the shoes of the professor. What would you look for in a progress report? How would you evaluate this group as decision makers? Have they learned anything about analyzing organizations? How would you evaluate their progress at this point? Have they made any discoveries, or are they just going through the steps?

Fortunately, this is not the draft the writers turned in to their professor or the company manager. The revised draft [as shown in Figure 2] was written after a short conference with a writing instructor who instead of offering advice, asked the writers to predict what each of their readers would be looking for. It took ten minutes to step back from their draft and to rethink it from the perspective of their professor and the Oskaloosa manager. They found that they needed global revision—a revision that kept the substance of their writer-based first draft, but transformed it into reader-based text. As you compare these two drafts, notice the narrative and survey organization in the first draft and the "I did it" focus that are often a tip-off to writer-based prose, and how they improved the second draft.

How would you characterize the differences between drafts one and two? One clear difference is the use of a conventional memo/report format to focus the reader's attention. But beyond the visual display of information, the writers moved away from narrative organization, an "I" focus, and a survey form or "textbook" pattern of organization. Watch for these three patterns as you revise.

Narrative Organization

The first four paragraphs of the first draft are organized as a narrative, starting with the phrase "Work began. . . ." We are given a story of the writers' discovery process. Notice how all of the facts are presented in terms of when they were discovered, not in terms of their implications or logical connections. The writers want to tell us what happened and when; the reader, on the other hand, wants to ask "why?" and "so what?"

A narrative organization is tempting to write because it is a prefabricated order and easy to generate. All of us walk around with stories in our head, and chronology is a common rhetorical move. Instead of creating a **hierarchical** organization among ideas or worrying about a reader, the writer can simply remember his or her own discovery process and write a story. Remember that in a hierarchical structure, such as an issue tree, the ideas at the top of the structure work as the organizing concepts that include other ideas. The alternative is often a string of ideas simply linked by association or by the order in which the writer thought about them. Papers that start out, "In studying the reasons for the current decline in our return customers, ..." are often a dead giveaway. They tell us we are going to watch the writer's mind at work and follow him or her through the process of thinking out conclusions. Following one's own associations makes the text easier to write. But another reason new employees are tempted to write narrative reports is that they were often rewarded for narratives at some point in their career *as students*. They fail to realize that in business the reader is someone who expects to *use* this text (not check off whether or not they did the assignment).

A narrative pattern, of course, has the virtue of any form of drama—it keeps you in suspense by withholding closure. But this drama is an effective strategy only if the audience is willing to wait that long for the point. Most professional and academic readers are impatient, and they tend to interpret such narrative, step-by-step structures either as wandering and confused (Is there a point?) or as a form of hedging. Narrative structures may be read as veiled attempts to hide what really happened or the writers' actual position. Although a progress report naturally involves narrative, how has Draft 2 been able to *use* the narrative to answer readers' questions?

The "I" Focus

The second feature of Draft 1 is that it is a discovery story starring the writers. Its drama, such as it is, is squarely focused on the writer: "I did/I thought/ I felt. . . ." Of the fourteen sentences in the first three paragraphs, ten are grammatically focused on the writer's thoughts and actions rather than on the issues. For example: "Work began . . . ," "We decided . . . ," Also, "we were aware . . . and we felt. . . ." Generally speaking, the reader is more interested in issues and ideas than in the fact that the writer thought them.

In pointing out the "I" focus in Draft 1, we are not saying that writers cannot refer to themselves or begin a sentence with "I," as many learned in school. Sometimes a specific reference to oneself is exactly the information a reader needs, and a reader may respond to the honesty and directness. Use "I" or "we" to make a claim or when it is an important piece of information, not just as a convenient way to start a sentence. In Draft 2, the students are clearly present as people doing the research, but the focus is on the information the reader wants to hear.

Survey Form or Textbook Organization

In the fifth paragraph of Draft 1 the writers begin to organize their material in a new way. Instead of a narrative, we are given a survey of what the writers observed. Here, the raw facts of the bottling process dictated the organization of the paragraph. Yet the client-reader already knows this, and the professor probably does not care. In the language of computer science we could say the writers are performing a "memory dump": printing out information in the exact form in which they stored it in memory. Notice how in the revised version the writers try to use their observations to understand production problems.

The problem with a survey or "textbook" pattern is that it ignores the reader's need for a different organization of the information. Suppose, for example, you are writing to model airplane builders about wind resistance. The information you need comes out of a physics text, but that text is organized around the field of physics; it starts with subatomic particles and works up from there. To meet the needs of your reader, you have to adapt that knowledge, not lift it intact from the text. Sometimes writers can simply survey their knowledge, but generally the writer's main task is to use knowledge rather than reprint it.

To sum up, in Draft 2 of the Oskaloosa report, the writers made a real attempt to write for their readers. Among other things, the report is now organized around major questions readers might have, it uses headings to display the overall organization of the report, and it makes better use of topic sentences that tell the reader what each paragraph contains and why to read it. Most important, it focuses more on the crucial information the reader wants to obtain.

Obviously this version could still be improved. But it shows the writers attempting to transform writer-based prose into reader-based prose and change their narrative and survey pattern into a more issue-centered top-to-bottom organization.

STRATEGY 2: TEST YOUR TEXT FOR A READER-BASED STRUCTURE

Reading your text for writer-based prose lets you spot places where you were still exploring ideas or talking to yourself—places that probably call for some sort of global or structural revision to make this text a reader-based document. But that does not tell you how to revise. **Reader-based prose** foregrounds and makes explicit the information a reader needs or expects to find. Reader-based prose tries to anticipate and support an active reader, one who probably will use your writing for some specific end. What do you want your reader to see, think, or do? How will your reader respond? One important approach to global revision is to look at your text as a conversation with the reader in which you set up some initial agreements and expectations and then fulfill your promises. We offer three ways to test for a reader-based structure: *testing your drafts against your initial plans, using clues that reveal this plan to a reader,* and *keeping the promises you made in your writing.*

Does Your Text Reflect Your Plans?

Texts have a way of running off by themselves. The more text you produce, the more convinced you are that your prose is complete, readable, even entertaining. This is natural given the commitment it takes to write anything, but because texts often drift away from your intentions, you need a way to keep your text honest or to realize that you have come up with a better approach. So instead of reading your text "as written" and just going with the flow, start by setting up an image of your purpose and plans in your mind's eye, then test your text against that image. Can you find any evidence of your plans in the text?

To get a good image of your plan, return to . . . your planning notes to review your plans consciously. In your mind or on paper, restate the plans *to do* and *say* that you produced prior to your current draft, and find the exact places in your text where your writing satisfies (or departs from) your plans to reach a reader. You could set the mental exercise up as a checklist [Figure 3].

Holding your draft up against the backdrop of your own plans can help you notice how well the two fit together. Did you have important goals, or good points in your notes that have just not appeared in your text yet? Did you simply forget ideas? Or did you find—as many writers do—that the act of writing was itself an inventive, generative process? Your plans may have changed as a result of writing. If that happened, what should you do? At this point, inexperienced writers often abandon their old plans and follow wherever the text seems to be taking them. However, experienced writers make another move. They go back into planning and look for possible ways to consolidate their new ideas with other old plans. They try to build a new plan that makes use of the good parts of both ideas. They use this round of planning to guide their global revisions consciously.

This strategy is obviously one you will use more than once—a kind of in-process evaluation that lets you keep checking in with your goals for writing and checking your text against the big picture of what you want it to do.

My plans for writing, to do and say were...

    The important Goals and Purposes I gave myself...
    My Key Points...
    How I wanted my Reader to respond (and what other responses I anticipated)...
    My choice of Text Conventions...
    How I planned to make all of this work together...

As a checklist, I could evaluate my writing this way:

Plans *to do* and *say*	Draft	Text Reference
Goals...	✓	----------------------------
Key points...	✓	----------------------------
Intended Response...	✓	----------------------------
Text Conventions, Models...	✓	----------------------------
Making it all work together...	????	*oops, gotta work on this!!!*

FIGURE 3 Checking Your Text Against Your Plans

Cues That Reveal Your Plans to Your Reader

Maybe you are satisfied that you have indeed <u>defined</u> a real and shared <u>problem</u> for your reader, and <u>compared</u> some <u>alternative</u> ways to respond to it, <u>supported</u> them with <u>examples</u>, while <u>proposing</u> your favored course of <u>action</u>. But will the reader recognize all of those rhetorical moves? It is possible that you "talked about" this information, but did not make your good rhetorical plan to define, compare, support and propose fully apparent or explicit.

In most pieces of writing there are two conversations going on. One is the information that the reader needs or expects to find: the recommendations that you want to make, the results of your study, the idea you are proposing, the specifics of a solution. As we shall see, this conversation is held together, usually, by a strong chain of topics and an appropriate rhetorical pattern. But the second conversation is explicitly between the writer and the reader, announcing what the reader will find, in what order, and reminding the reader of where he or she is in the text.

This second conversation is often called **metadiscourse.** *Meta-* is a Greek prefix that means "along with" or "among," and the basic strategy is to include explicit statements and cues to the reader that announce and reinforce your intentions along with your content. There are two main ways writers give such cues. One is to talk directly to the reader, inserting metacomments that preview what will come, remind, predict, or summarize. This lets the writer step back, make the plan of the text more visible, and direct traffic, by telling the reader, "In the next section I will argue that. . . ." The other kind of cues work more like traffic signals—they are the conventional words and phrases that signal transitions, or logic, or the structure of ideas. Readers often expect to find these metacomments and signalling cues in some standard places. Some common places to insert cues to the reader include:

Title, title page
Table of contents
Abstract
Introduction or first paragraphs
Headings
The beginning and end of paragraphs (i.e., topic sentences)
Entire paragraphs in between long sections

So review your text first to see if you have used enough cues to make your plan clear, and second to see if you have included cues in places readers expect to see some guidance on what to look for and how to read this document [Figure 4].

There is an endless variety of sentences and phrases that can be invented and inserted to announce and reinforce your main ideas and the progression that you want your reader to follow. To show you the power of metadiscourse and how it plays out in a text, here is an excerpt from a shareowner's letter with the

Cues that signal your plan and guide the reader:

Cues that lead the reader forward

To show addition:		*To show time:*	
Again	Moreover,	At length	And then
And	Nor,	Immediately thereafter,	Later,
And then,	Too,	Soon,	Previously,
Besides	Next,	After a few hours,	Formerly,
Equally important,	First, second, etc.	Afterwards,	First, second, etc.
Finally	Lastly,	Finally,	Next, etc.
Further,	What's more,	Then	
Furthermore,			

Cues that make the reader stop and compare

But	Notwithstanding,	Although
Yet,	On the other hand,	Although this is true,
And yet,	On the contrary,	While this is true,
However,	After all,	Conversely,
Still	For all that,	Simultaneously,
Nevertheless,	In contrast,	Meanwhile
Nonetheless,	At the same time,	In the meantime,

Cues that develop and summarize

To give examples:	*To emphasize:*	*To repeat:*	*To signal a relationship:*
For instance,	Obviously,	In brief,	Finally
For example,	In fact,	In short,	Because
To demonstrate,	As a matter of fact,	As I have said,	Yet
To illustrate,	Indeed,	As I have noted,	For instance,
As an illustration,	In any case,	In other words,	
	In any event,	That is,	

To introduce conclusions:	*To summarize:*
Hence,	In brief,
Therefore,	On the whole,
Accordingly,	Summing up,
Consequently,	To conclude,
Thus,	In conclusion,
As a result,	

FIGURE 4   Giving Cues to the Reader

Metacomment cues that announce and reinforce your intentions

To ask a question about your topic or the argument unfolding:

What series of events led to event? . . .
To answer that question . . .

To preview what will come:

In the next section, we will see how this formula applies . . .
The third paragraph will reveal how . . .

To summarize what has been said thus far:

In the preceding pages, I've described . . .
Thus far, I have argued . . .

To comment on your writing and thinking as it unfolds:

I haven't mentioned yet that . . .
I'm talking about . . .
My main point is . . .

FIGURE 4   *(Continued)*

metadiscourse highlighted [Figure 5]. We offer the original paragraph numbers with the cues underlined and the rhetorical purpose of the cues as we read them. . . .

Did You Keep Your Promises?

Your text started out with the best of intentions—a strong rhetorical plan and cues that keep your reader on track. The next test is to see if you followed through on the promises that you made. Read your text as if you were outlining its key points and promises and then look back to see if you have delivered the necessary detail. For instance:

- Your problem/purpose statement promises four main points and an extended example: Does each paragraph keep that promise? By referring back to your announced plan and delivering four main (i.e., well-developed) points in the same order that you promised?
- Your topic sentence in the seventh paragraph promises the two key instances that support a legal precedent: Does the paragraph deliver them in the order and detail necessary?

Chairman's Letter
Rhetorical Purpose/Cues

1		Often the greatest opportunities.........................
4	ties to history	Our strong 1984 results speak for themselves ......
5		Pacific Telesis Group earned $829 million ....
6	forces question	What happened? How did the corporation that many observers predicted would be the biggest loser in the AT&T breakup turn out to be one of the biggest winners?
7	links date with solution	To answer that question, you have to go back to 1980, when we developed.........................
8	signals logic	Our employees mobilized to make it work. And work it did. More specifically: ....
8c	signals order & emphasis	Third, and very important, we've built a relationship with the California Public Utilities Commission ....
	previews, emphasizes	a subject I'll return to later on in this letter............

The Future of Your Investment

34	previews	A corporation, particularly one as new as ours, must operate with a clearly articulated and widely understood vision of its future....................
37	summarizes	In the preceding pages I've described to you our strategies for deploying technology, marketing technology, and diversifying into new lines ....
38	summarizes, emphasizes	I've talked about our determination ....
	signals logic, emphasis uses authority	But there is another very significant factor I haven't mentioned. I'm talking about the people who work for the Pacific Telesis Group

FIGURE 5   Metadiscourse in the Chairman's Letter

John S. Harris

The Project Worksheet for Efficient Writing Management

John S. Harris is Professor Emeritus of English at Brigham Young University. The author of several books on technical writing, he was the founding president of the Association of Teachers of Technical Writing.

When employees produce poor quality documents, the fault may lie not with their incompetence or lack of devotion to the job, but with inadequate and unclear assignments from their project managers or publications managers. The Project Worksheet is designed to help managers give initial writing assignments, effectively manage documents during production, and evaluate finished products. The following pages describe the Worksheet and suggest ways publications managers can use it effectively.

THE PROJECT WORKSHEET

The Project Worksheet consists of a series of questions that help writers and managers consider the factors involved in planning a document. I developed the Worksheet years ago, and faculty in the technical writing program at Brigham Young University have successfully used it to teach technical writing for some years. After graduation, many of our students continue to use it in industry to plan documents and make document assignments.

PROJECT WORKSHEET

Subject _____ Title _____
Assigned by _____ Approved _____ Assignment date _____
Writer _____ Agreed to _____ Due date _____

Primary Reader:

    Technical level (education, experience, etc.):
    Position (title or organizational relationship):
    Attitude toward subject:
    Other factors:

Secondary Readers (others who may read the document):

    Technical level:
    Position:
    Attitude toward subject:
    Other factors:

Reader's Purpose:

    What should the reader know after reading?
    What should the reader be able to do after reading?
    What attitude should the reader have after reading?
    How will the reader access the material?

Writer's Purpose:

    Intellectual purpose:
    Career or monetary purpose:

Logistics:

    Sources (lab reports, library research, etc.):
    Physical size limits (if any):
    Form or medium prescribed or desirable:
    Available aids (graphics, etc.):
    Means of production:
    Outline (Preliminary):

Distribution and Disposition:

FIGURE 1   Project Worksheet

What the Writer Must Consider

The manager and writer must determine the document's intended readers, its purpose, scope, form, length, graphic aids, and sources of information.[1] They must know such things before the writing begins. Failure to consider them results in inefficient document production and poor-quality documents.

Experienced writers in an organization usually answer these planning questions intuitively or subconsciously. Or they get the answers by direct conference, by study of past documents, or through the grapevine. They then efficiently plan and write good documents.

But less-experienced writers learn the answers to the questions only by the inefficient and expensive trial-and-error method of submitting draft documents and then repeatedly amending them as management requires.

Managers—whether of engineering projects, scientific studies, or computer software documentation—can reduce the trial-and-error writing cycle by providing complete answers for such planning questions during a writing assignment conference. But managers cannot provide the answers to the planning questions without first knowing the questions and their consequences. The Project Worksheet in Figure 1 guides both writers and managers in considering the important factors in planning documents. It can, of course, be adapted for special situations. Managers may want to reformat it to allow more space for answers, and some may wish to put it into a word processor as a template. Let us first examine the Worksheet questions and then consider procedures for using the Worksheet for document management.

Housekeeping Headings

Headings such as assignment date, due date, writer, and assignment authority are self-explanatory. Still, listing them together permits the use of the Worksheet as a tracking document for projects. The *document subject* is the file subject. The *document title* may be the same, or it may be something less prosaic—especially if the document is going out of house. Thus a document subject could be *Dental Hygiene,* and the document title could be *Your Teeth: An Owner's Manual.*

Primary Reader

No factor is more important for the writer than full understanding of the nature and needs of the document's primary reader. Experienced writers know this, of course. But even they do not always know everything that management knows and believes about the readers of the projected document. Too frequently both managers and writers assume they understand who the readers will be, but they may have two quite different audiences in mind. Using the Worksheet, managers and writers can reach an understanding of this and other questions.

---

[1]Although this . . . [essay] explains how managers can use the Project Worksheet for managing documents, the books listed under Selected Readings explain how writers can use the Worksheet and other methods to design technical documents for various audiences and purposes.

Reader's Technical Level

By carefully considering the technical level of the reader, the manager and writer can decide the proper level of explanation needed. How much information does the reader already have? Are definitions of *photo-grammetry* or *perihelion* or *debentures* needed? Considering such things can help avoid losing the reader in a maze of technical jargon, or alternatively avoid alienating a reader with overly simplistic explanations. In the trade-off between those two extremes, erring on the side of simplicity is nearly always better.

Reader's Organizational Relationship

The writer must also consider whether the document will go to the executive tower or to the shop floor. Since writers often prepare documents for someone else's signature, the manager—and the writer—must consider the organizational relationship of the reader *to the document's signer*. Thus, if the document will be signed by the boss, the writer must—for the task—carefully assume the persona of the boss. Is the signer addressing superiors, subordinates, or peers? Such situations raise delicate questions, and the manager must recognize the entailed problems and pass on an understanding of those problems to the writer.

Reader's Attitude

Similarly, the attitude of the reader must be considered. Is the reader hostile to the new manufacturing procedure because it will result in downsizing her department? Or is the reader skeptical about the efficacy of new cutting-edge technology because it has not yet been proved? Or is the reader torpid and apathetic and needing a stiff jolt to see the promise—or the threat—of the subject of the document?

Other Factors

Often even more subtle factors about the reader must be considered. Some of these may overlap the preceding questions, but they may also affect the kind of document needed. Is the reader a white, conservative Republican woman of sixty, raised on an Iowa farm, or a young Afro-American male from the South Bronx, or a highly educated but condescending academic? Is the reader an Ivy-League MBA obsessed with this year's bottom line, a high school dropout production-line worker who is fearful that increased automation will eliminate jobs, a displaced homemaker with an acute case of computer anxiety, or an immigrant with limited understanding of English? Such demographic factors may require delicate adjustments in the document.

Secondary Reader

Often a secondary reader must also be considered. The company annual report may be read by both stockholders and the CEO. An advertising brochure intended for customers may also be read by the competition. An environmental impact statement may be read by both the Douglas Fir Plywood Association and the Sierra Club. A report intended for Level 2 management may have to get past a Level 3 gatekeeper. Such situations require that the writer juggle the factors of two or more audiences at once, and this requires some skill. If the readers differ in attitude, the writer must watch out for red-flag statements that may cause a secondary reader to charge. If the differences are in technical level, the secondary reader's need for more elementary explanations or more technical information can often be taken care of in footnotes, glossaries, sidebars, or appendices.

The Reader's Purpose

Organizational documents have purposes as varied as securing approval for a new manufacturing process, justifying spending public funds for a reclamation project, instructing a software purchase on how to use a spreadsheet, or easing the worries of environmentalists about the effect of a new highway near a prime trout-fishing stream. Four basic questions about the reader's purposes need consideration:

- What should the reader know after the reading?
- What should the reader be able to do after reading?
- What attitude should the reader have after reading?
- How will the reader access the information?

What Should the Reader Know after Reading?

What factual information does the reader need to obtain from the document? Does the reader need to know the percentage of radial keratotomy patients who can pass a 20/40 eye examination without glasses after the operation? The percentage of impurities remaining in palladium after the macrocycle solvent extraction process? The change in numbers of predator kills of sheep after reintroduction of wolves to the grazing range? Often the specific information the reader is to gain from the document can be presented in lists, outlines, tables, or graphs.

What Should the Reader Be Able to Do after Reading?

What the reader can *do* after reading may be quite different from what the reader *knows*. Knowing the names for the stages of mitosis is different from being able to recognize telophase through a microscope. Knowing the stoichiometric ratio for combustion of a gasoline/air mixture is different from being able to adjust a fuel-injection system to achieve the ideal mixture.

What a reader can do after reading may depend on technical skills. It may also depend on the reader's capability to make executive decisions based on the information contained in the document. Thus the reader's needs probably extend beyond gaining general information to applying specific knowledge. A reader may use the information on color changes in a chemical solution to perform titration in the assay laboratory. Or a reader may use the information on the size of natural gas reserves of the overthrust belt to decide the feasibility of building a 24-inch pipeline from Wyoming to California.

What Attitude Should the Reader Have after Reading?

Earlier the Worksheet asked about the reader's attitude before reading. Here the Worksheet asks about the attitude the writer and manager want the reader to have *after* reading the document. Do they want the reader to believe and feel that the proposed SDI weapons system is an effective deterrent to foreign aggression? Or do they want the reader to believe that it is a horrendously expensive and impractical pork-barrel boondoggle? Though such attitudes in technical documents may be based on hard data, they are nonetheless attitudes—sometimes emotionally charged attitudes—and the writer must realize that shaping those attitudes is sometimes part of the job, even a moral responsibility. The technical writer uses different tools for shaping attitudes than the politician or advertiser does, and may have a higher regard for truth, but like the politician or advertiser, the technical writer may be an attitude shaper.

And one other attitude deserves consideration: the attitude that the reader should have toward the preparer of the document. The writer wants the reader to think that the document was prepared by a credible and meticulous professional who cares about the subject, the needs of the reader, and the needs of his or her employer. Though this point may seem obvious, writers do not always automatically consider it.

How Will the Reader Access the Information?

We read novels, murder mysteries, and perhaps newspaper editorials beginning-to-end, but almost everything else, we read in some other fashion. We do not read dictionaries, phone books, repair manuals, computer documentation, or encyclopedias beginning-to-end. We often read textbooks and journal articles in a nonlinear fashion too. Sometimes the text is well designed to help us get the critical information quickly. Or, exasperatingly, the text may bury critical information in the middle of a full-page paragraph. Whatever way the text is designed, readers scan, or skip around trying to find what they want without reading every blessed word.

Realizing what information the reader wants, the writer or manager can design documents so that the information is easy to find. Information accessibility relies on such devices as

- Headings
- Outlines
- Indexes
- Graphics
- Underlining
- Sidebars
- Glosses
- Varied typefaces
- Cross-references
- Bulleted lists (like this).

USA Today uses many of these devices. The *New York Times* uses fewer. *USA Today* lacks the substance of the *Times,* but it is easier to get the news from it quickly. A similar comparison could be made between *Popular Science* and *Scientific American.* The differences in format reflect how the writers and editors anticipate the publications will be read.

The writer and manager must carefully consider whether the reader will read beginning-to-end or access pieces of data individually. The basic consideration should be the importance of the information being conveyed. The more important the information, the more accessible it should be. The document manager must help the writer anticipate *all* the ways that *all the readers* will want to access the information and require the writer to provide the machinery that will allow that access. Most writers of technical and scientific documents should pay much more attention to accessibility. Few readers of technical documents read them beginning-to-end.

Writer's Purpose

The writer's and reader's purposes for a document differ just as the buyer's and seller's purposes differ. Both have their agendas. The writer—or the manager—may want to have a project approved. The target reader may want to know if the project is feasible.

The writer probably has potential salary, prestige, and promotion purposes for writing, but may also be writing because the task is challenging or intellectually interesting. The writer and manager should decide in advance whether the project is routine and can be done rather perfunctorily, or whether it will affect the safety of the user, the prosperity of the company, the security of the nation, the preservation of the environment—or the continued employment of the writer. These questions help the writer and manager determine the priorities of the task.

Logistics

The logistics are the nuts and bolts things—such as where the information comes from, the size of the projected document, and what form the document will take. These too must be considered in advance.

Sources of Information

Will the document be based on observation, personal opinion, government reports, a literature search, engineers' notes, customer interviews, public opinion polls, laboratory tests, compilations of vendors' brochures, or what? Frequently, lead time may be required, so early consideration of sources is wise to allow tests to be run, surveys to be conducted, or publications to be ordered.

Size of Document Expected

A two-page memo will not do if a twenty-page report is expected, and a twenty-page report will not do if a two-page memo is expected. Again, the question should be resolved between the writer and the manager before the writing begins.

Form or Medium Prescribed or Desirable

The form or medium of the eventual document should also be considered in advance. Should the document follow the company style sheet? Would a film, a wall chart, a wallet card, or a video be a more useful medium? *Such choices should be made according to subject, purpose, reader (user), and cost.*

Graphic Aids Available

Would photographs or art work be useful? Are facilities available to prepare them? Is there time? Are funds available? Again, these must be considered early.

Means of Document Production

The means of production of the document also need to be considered early. Will the document be laid out on a Macintosh with PageMaker software? Will it be photocopied or multilithed? How will the means of production affect the legibility and credibility of the document, and how much will it cost?

Outline

Even at the early planning stages, the writer and manager should consider the topics to be treated, their order, and their proportion of the expected document. Such an outline can, of course, be revised during preparation.

Distribution and Disposition

How many copies will be needed? Where do they go? What happens to them? The manager and writer should consider these questions—and their many consequences—in advance. Will the document be read by the competition? Will it come back to haunt everybody ten years later? Will it be subpoenaed in court? The wise consider such things.

PROJECT PLANNING CONFERENCE

The manager and the writer must come to an agreement about a document's audience, purpose, and scope, and the logistics of its development, production, and distribution. Such negotiation is most efficient in a planning conference. Usually the manager calls the conference, but the negotiation can take a variety of forms, depending on the situation and the experience of the writers.

With an inexperienced writer, the manager may say, "Willoughby, I want you to write a proposal for my signature recommending adoption of the hyperbaric procedure. It should be addressed to Allardyce, the plant manger. He is a chemical engineer with twenty years' experience on the job. But it will also be read by Sung. She is the company comptroller and has ultimate approval power on expenditures. She is pretty conservative, but her attention to cash flow probably saved the company during the last recession."

With a more experienced writer, the manager can more inductively and democratically ask, "Kim, we need a brochure about our prefabricated forms for concrete. What ways do you see to make a brochure that will meet the needs of all of its readers?" Obviously, here the manager respects the writer's knowledge and expects useful suggestions.

Whatever the method, the manager and writer should agree upon the answers, write them down—Yes, and *sign off—each keeping a copy.* Such a signed-off Worksheet is then a kind of contract agreed to by both parties, and both can feel more secure with it. The manager is now more secure knowing that the assignment is clearly understood, and the writer is more secure knowing what is expected.

POSTCONFERENCE MANAGEMENT

Obviously other factors may arise during the writing. The manager may receive new data, or the writer may see new ways to deal with the problems. Depending on their impact on the document, such things may require additional conferences and a renegotiating of the specifications.

As needed, the manager may discreetly ask about the progress of the document, or may even ask to see sections in draft. However, if the initial assignment has been done carefully, a responsible and skilled writer should be able to produce a sound document with little intermediate prodding.

The writer properly attaches the Project Worksheet to the draft form of the document when submitting it. Then the manager checks to see if it fulfills the assignment. If it does, the manager approves it for production.

Quite often, however, problems appear. Of these, failures to match the assignment are the most obvious, and the manager can ask for a rewrite to make the document match the specifications. The most common problem seems to be a failure to consider adequately the technical levels of all the readers.

Or it may become clear that the specifications need changing. If for good reasons they do need changing, the manager can change them and ask that the new specifications be followed, but the manager who has agreed to the original specifications is less likely to make such changes capriciously or arbitrarily. If lessening the power to make arbitrary changes seems to take the fun out of being boss, then the manager should recognize that the resultant empowerment of the writer is not only enlightened and trendy, but also pragmatically effective.

OTHER APPLICATIONS

If the writer's manager does not make such detailed assignments, the writer obviously can still use the Project Worksheet for planning. Or the writer can use the Worksheet to initiate a conference and negotiate with the manager. We have found that managers are often impressed when writers request such conferences and demonstrate through their questions—the Worksheet questions—that they have a clear understanding of the situation.

The Worksheet is also effective in negotiating contracts in freelance writing assignments, or as an assignment device between editor and writer. In the university, a professor can make writing assignments following the Worksheet questions. Or a sharp student can use the questions to clarify a vaguely given assignment. And many problems of master's theses and doctoral dissertations would be avoided if candidates and supervising professors negotiated the specifications for theses and dissertations through the Worksheet.

In much technical writing, the most important work is the planning done before the first words of the document are written. If managers will use the Project Worksheet approach to document management, their writers will work more efficiently and produce better documents.

SELECTED READINGS

Anderson, P. V. (ed.), *Teaching Technical Writing: Teaching Audience Analysis and Adaptation*, ATTW Anthology No. 1, Association of Teachers of Technical Writing, St. Paul, Minnesota, 1980.

Caernarven-Smith, P., *Audience Analysis and Response*, Firman Technical Publications, Pembroke, Massachusetts, 1983.

Mathes, J. C., and D. Stevenson, *Designing Technical Reports: Writing for Audiences in Organizations* (2nd Edition), Macmillan, New York, 1991.

Pearsall, T., *Audience Analysis for Technical Writing*, Glencoe Press, Beverly Hills, California, 1969.

Souther, J. W., and M. L. White, *Technical Report Writing* (2nd Edition), John Wiley & Sons, New York, 1977.

Spilka, R., Orality and Literacy in the Workplace: Process- and Text-Based Strategies for Multiple-Audience Adaptation. *Journal of Business and Technical Communication*, 4:1, pp. 44–67, 1990.

Jack Selzer

The Composing Process
of an Engineer

Jack Selzer is Professor of English at Pennsylvania State University where he teaches courses in rhetoric and composition and scientific and technical writing.

Since Janet Emig over a decade ago investigated *The Composing Processes of Twelfth-Graders*, many researchers have studied various aspects of writers' composing habits. However, because it has mostly considered only unskilled beginning writers, student writers working in academic contexts, or professional writers like novelists or journalists, that research has had relatively little impact on the teaching of technical writing.[1] Little work has been done on the composing strategies of people who call themselves engineers or scientists, not writers or students; little study has been devoted to people who compose within the limitations of the workplace. Although as a profession we know *what* scientists and engineers write at work, we know far less about *how* they plan, arrange, write, and rewrite on the job. As a result, teachers of technical writing have been unable to teach students reliable ways to succeed under the special and dynamic circumstances presented by on-the-job writing.

PROCEDURES

To begin to overcome these difficulties, I decided to investigate in detail the composing processes of a single engineer. My subject was Kenneth E. Nelson, an experienced engineer in Chicago who spends roughly half of his time on the job writing various proposals, reports, and correspondence. Educated at the University of Illinois at Chicago Circle and at Northwestern, Nelson specializes in transportation. Presently he manages the Chicago office of Henningson, Durham, and Richardson (HDR), one of the nation's largest "design, systems, and sciences" firms, and directs the highway, airport, and environmental studies undertaken there.[2]

To find out how Nelson writes at work, I adopted and adapted methods suggested by Emig and by Cooper and Odell's *Research on Composing*.[3] Most basically, I collected and examined all the interim written materials that contributed to several of his finished products—jottings, notes, outlines, plans, drafts, revisions. I did not ask Nelson to compose aloud for me, even though protocol analysis is commonly used to investigate writing processes, for composing aloud can be extremely unnatural, artificial, and obtrusive, especially in Nelson's work environment.[4] Instead, I asked Nelson to respond in detail, on a tape recorder, before and after he finished each writing session, to a long series of written questions that I had devised concerning the conduct and length of each session. In addition, I visited Nelson at work to observe him writing and to determine what I could about the effects of Nelson's physical environment. After those visits, I interviewed Nelson at considerable length about things I had observed, about comments he had made on the tapes, and about the principles and attitudes that shape his habits; and I suggested a series of changes (major and minor, substantial and stylistic) in his work in order to prompt him to explain and defend his choices. I even looked at his revisions of his coworkers' work to get a sense of his stylistic habits. Finally, I followed Nelson's writing as it proceeded through the documents comprising an entire engineering project, from the original "Qualifications Statement" (a sort of preliminary proposal used in transportation engineering to select those eligible for a formal project proposal), to the proposal and presentation required to win a contract for the project, to the project's progress reports, technical memos, and final report. Thus, I was able to observe how Nelson composes in different situations and how he re-uses some documents to shape others in the course of a project.

RESULTS

While Nelson's composing habits are in some ways fairly conventional—he performs distinct planning, arranging, writing, and revising activities—I found that he places special emphasis on planning and arranging at the expense of revision. In addition, I learned—unexpectedly—that his writing process is in many ways more linear than recursive.

Planning and Inventing

While he is planning his writing, Nelson behaves like most other writers: he determines his purpose, and then invents and selects content to carry out that purpose.

Although Nelson never makes the formal, written "statements of purpose" recommended by some textbooks, he still determines his purpose rather efficiently. Since he nearly always writes in response to a specific request (e.g., a client's request for a proposal; requirements for progress reports and final reports) and since he writes certain kinds of documents again and again, his consideration of purpose has become ingrained, almost second nature. Thus, according to his tape-recorded comments, Nelson has a clearly persuasive aim when he writes proposals and recommendations, and an informative goal for technical memos and progress reports. He also knows from experience that in some cases he might have to juggle several purposes—a persuasive recommendation report might have particular parts that must inform; a proposal must "look good" aesthetically if it is to accomplish its larger persuasive end.[5]

But if arriving at a purpose is a relatively routine part of Nelson's writing process, his invention procedures are anything but routine. For except when he writes unimportant or very routine items, especially correspondence, Nelson takes as much time to invent content as a professional writer. For the reports and proposals that occupy most of his writing time, Nelson spends up to 80% of his time inventing and arranging! Not only that, over the years Nelson has devised an impressive repertoire of techniques that enable him to invent the material he needs for each document.

For example, Nelson analyzes his audience's needs carefully not when he is making stylistic choices later in his writing process but when he wants to generate content. Because Nelson knows that his audiences will approve or reject his proposals or judge reports useful or deficient, he thinks about their needs at the very beginning of the writing process. He considers past associations with clients or telephone conversations with them to stimulate his thinking. While inventing content for a proposal related to an airport-development project in Waukegan, for instance, Nelson mulled over a four-page RFQ (Request for Qualifications) for over two hours, thinking about his audience's criteria and considering how he could adapt his company's resources for such a client. Similarly, when he wrote the final report for the project, his preliminary notes show that he considered his audience's technical background and the ways his report would be used, while he was considering what to include. By the end of a project, Nelson often knows readers so personally that meeting their needs is not difficult. Nelson is so aware of how he might adapt content for his primary audience that he only rarely and in minor ways considers secondary audiences (such as persons in his office) or possible future uses of his reports.

In addition to audience analysis, Nelson uses other tactics to stimulate invention. Sometimes, if the project is important enough and if it involves his specialty, he visits the Northwestern University library to review the literature on a given topic. Far more often, though, he consults with colleagues. Either he speaks with advisors on the telephone (a third of the Waukegan Airport proposal, for example, was developed from two phone calls to the Omaha office) or he engages his coworkers in formal and informal conversations. The sessions amount to a sort of communal brainstorming procedure. Moreover, Nelson exploits more individual brainstorming activities. It is not clear if Nelson uses some kind of private heuristic to develop ideas or if he might have developed a mental checklist of some sort from his past experience with certain documents that unconsciously guides his brainstorming. What is clear is that he notes ideas on paper until his memory is exhausted.

Further, Nelson jogs his memory by reviewing previously completed documents. Past letters, old proposals, and completed reports, especially on related projects or for the same client, suggest what might be included in present documents. In fact, Nelson often borrows sentences, paragraphs, sections—even graphics—from past documents and incorporates them into new proposals, reports, and correspondence. Nearly half of one proposal that I saw came directly from past documents: from a company brochure came part of the introduction; from several past proposals he lifted sections of justification; from files he got standard certification data, supporting documents, resumes, and several graphics. In addition, he re-uses consecutively any documents related to the same project. For instance, once HDR redesigned some roads and a railroad underpass in Franklin Park, near Chicago. The project itself required nineteen tasks (surveys, technical descriptions, and summaries of technical work), seven technical memos (each when a significant step was completed), and a series of progress reports. When it came to writing the final report, Nelson essentially incorporated all those interim documents, adapted the project proposal into an introduction, added conclusions and recommendations, and tidied up, and his final report was finished.

In short, Nelson relies on an impressive array of invention procedures—analyzing audiences, reading, consulting colleagues, brain storming, and reviewing previously written documents. Nelson uses such techniques in no particular order. Nor does he use each one every time he writes. Nevertheless, these techniques mutually reinforce each other and serve Nelson well as he searches for the content he needs in a given situation. Then, at last, after his invention stage is well advanced, Nelson begins to review his material to see how much is necessary to satisfy his needs—and to see if he can keep the length of his document down. Of course, the process of selection has gone on unconsciously throughout the invention process. But now, especially because Nelson believes that most reports and proposals contain far too much material, he consciously tries to let rhetorical considerations determine what he will include. Consequently, he reviews his purpose and audience again, eliminates extraneous material, and commits himself to the details most appropriate to his aim.

One last point. Once Nelson has invented and selected his ideas, he rarely adds more to them later. After he has invented and selected the materials relevant to a writing task, he arranges them—and doesn't look back.

Arrangement

Several students of the writing process have argued that arrangement is less important to writers than some teachers believe.[6] Except when he composes the most routine correspondence, however, Nelson follows a particular procedure for arranging ideas; as he told me in one interview, he does not "see how anyone could write anything of any length or any importance without an outline."

The intricacy, tidiness, and formality of Nelson's outlines are interesting features of his writing process. Nelson divides the material he has generated and selected into groups and subgroups. While he uses no numbers, letters, Roman numerals, or the like, he does use dots, indentations, and headings to indicate coordinate and subordinate relationships. For anything likely to require more than four or five pages of written text, he uses separate sheets of paper for each major heading. If the outline is for a proposal, letter, or progress report, he completes the outline before he begins; if the outline is for a final report, he begins it early in the engineering operation and then revises it as necessary throughout the project. But while such revisions in the outline are possible before he begins a draft, almost never will Nelson modify his plan after he has begun to write. For to Nelson writing presupposes an outline; it is not much of an exaggeration to say that he cannot write without one.

Nelson follows well-established principles in arranging entire documents, individual segments, and particular subsections and paragraphs. As you might expect by now, his arrangements are most of all determined by audience. When he organized the Waukegan Airport Qualifications Statement, for instance, his seven sections conformed exactly with the seven criteria suggested in the RFQ; even within several of those sections, he ordered references, accounts of past projects, and personnel according to their relative importance to his audience. Nelson is also aware of the emphasis inherent in first and final positions in a document and of the relationship between general and specific information. If Nelson cannot determine his audience's preference for the arrangement of a proposal or report, he will adopt his firm's conventional format.[7] Finally, "writer preferences" on some occasions account for some of Nelson's orderings; at times he orders material so that he can keep better control of it as a writer.

When I commented on the detail of his outlines, Nelson showed me some of his engineering plans: a Critical Path Diagram showed how the redesign of a city street would proceed from initial study to final design; and a Project Task Flow detailed how a transit plan would move from preliminary studies, literature reviews, and transit rider surveys to preliminary plans, public hearings, and revisions to final recommendations and implementation. Perhaps detailed plans for writing complex documents come naturally to professionals who must plan and coordinate complicated engineering tasks.[8]

Drafting

Given such attention to planning and arrangement, and given his re-use of previously written documents, it should not be surprising that Nelson's actual writing of a draft proceeds smoothly and efficiently, nor that he spends relatively little time drafting—less than 20% of the total time he spends in composing, on the average. Nelson typically sits at a desk in a quiet office, takes up a pen and a pad of white, lined paper (he does not type or use word-processing equipment), and produces a rough draft.

Because he has detailed plans and outlines and is ready to incorporate previously written documents, Nelson composes each unit very efficiently, pausing and rescanning much less frequently than the writers observed by Perl, Pianko, and Stallard. My observations and Nelson's remarkably clean drafts showed that once Nelson writes a sentence he seldom reconsiders it. Instead, he pushes forward with confidence so that whole drafts of proposals and whole chapters of reports can be completed at one sitting. For one short proposal I observed, Nelson composed over 1200 words of his own and incorporated two other documents into his draft in less than two hours. Only one paragraph, three sentences, and three other single words in that draft were at all reconsidered, scratched out, and redrafted before the next sentence was composed. While not every one of his drafts goes so smoothly, and while it is possible that he "rehearses" at least some sentences before writing them, the evidence I saw suggests strongly that Nelson is a confident, efficient—and linear—composer.

The principles that guide Nelson's drafts are extremely conventional and conservative. He composes each section or chapter around discrete beginnings, middles, and ends, and announces the purpose of paragraphs in a topic sentence or in a paragraph's first few words. Because he believes that long paragraphs are hard to read, Nelson writes short ones that "give the reader a chance to breathe." (The representative samples that I analyzed from proposals, technical memos, and reports had a mean length of just 77 words, with a high of 138 and a low of 52.) The same motive explains his sentences: in the documents I examined, they averaged between eighteen and twenty-one words in length—and between 71% and 90% were grammatically simple! Nelson builds length by means of prepositions and participles rather than by adding clauses. He uses colons only to introduce lists and *never* uses semicolons or dashes because he is afraid of misusing them. He consciously avoids contractions and personal pronouns (except in correspondence) because he believes that his writing demands a formal rhetorical stance. Only occasionally does Nelson strive to achieve stylistic effects, to "sound good" (especially through the skillful use of a parallel series), for he has little time to concentrate on the non-utilitarian. He strives for diction that is simple, denotative, and non-technical, since most of his writing goes to readers outside his organization.

Revision

After Nelson completes a rough draft, his secretary types it for him with spacing generous enough to permit revisions. But although Nelson revises all but the least important communications, he subordinates revision to—and separates it from—other activities in his writing process. While professional writers like those studied by Donald Murray, Nancy Sommers, and others revise extensively as they plan, invent, draft, and redraft,[9] revision takes up less than 5% of Nelson's time and consists of little more than superficial editing. As Nelson has become a more confident and competent writer, and as he comes to spend more time planning, his drafts have needed less revision. Moreover, the time he can spend on revision is limited by competing demands on his time and that of his secretary. Thus, in the Qualifications Statement for the Waukegan Airport, for example, Nelson made only minor revisions and only in nine of the 107 sentences. He removed contractions; simplified diction; deleted unnecessary words in two sentences; and edited the manuscript carefully, correcting spelling and commas. I never saw Nelson add material or reorganize it when he was revising. If for academic and professional writers revision is a messy, recursive matter of discovering and shaping what one wants to say, for Nelson revising is a rather clean matter of polishing a rough draft that already approximates his intentions.

CONCLUSIONS AND DISCUSSION

It is impossible to come to reliable conclusions about the writing process of engineers on the basis of a single case study. Nevertheless, some observations based on Nelson's composing habits are worth making, if only to direct further research and to suggest some new directions in pedagogy, especially if we keep in mind Cooper and Odell's point that all research in composing by its very nature "is tentative, subject to continual revision."[10]

The most striking thing about Nelson's composing habits is how closely they approximate the habits of the professional writers and skilled academic writers whose composing processes have been studied by other researchers. Nelson writes alone, not as part of a team. Except for the most common memos and correspondence, he spends as much time planning as many professional writers, despite the pressures and time limitations imposed on him at work. He invents content in detail and through various schemata of invention. He arranges material carefully. He consciously shapes his style. His composing process always includes a distinct, if brief, revision stage. Thus, if Nelson's habits are like those of other engineers, it may in technical writing courses be worth attending to the writing process in much the same way that it is attended to in other courses. That means that instead of ignoring invention and planning, as nearly all technical writing texts now do, teachers might direct students to various ways of developing, selecting, and arranging content. It means that technical writing teachers might begin to modify students' writing processes (not just correct their products) by examining their students' plans, outlines, rough drafts, and revisions. Since engineering and science are themselves processes, engineers and scientists are as likely as any students to respond to courses that also approach writing as a process.

However, some important differences between Nelson's composing habits at work and the habits of other writers need consideration, too. Several researchers have inveighed against what Sondra Perl has called "the fallacy of reducing the composing process to a simple linear scheme" of prewriting, writing, and revising; they have argued that composing is more accurately described as a recursive set of optional actions than as a sequence of linear stages.[11] Yet the linear model of composing does seem to describe accurately the writing habits of Kenneth Nelson. For him, writing activities fall into mutually exclusive and consecutive stages: rarely does he begin to arrange or draft before his inventing and global planning are completed; rarely does he invent or revise while he writes his first draft; rarely does revision include anything but final editing. Whether his linearity is a personal quirk or a characteristic of on-the-job writers in general or engineers in particular must be determined by further research. In the meantime, it may be appropriate to describe the writing process of engineers as more linear than recursive. It may also be appropriate in teaching prospective engineers to emphasize principles and techniques of arrangement and, by contrast, to regard revision as the least important activity in the engineer's writing process.

In addition, if we can judge from Nelson, an engineer's techniques for invention differ in important ways from the techniques for invention employed by other writers. Since engineers may do less private brainstorming than group brainstorming, teachers might explore ways to incorporate group invention into their technical writing courses. Since engineers seem to consider the needs of their audience as they invent, analysis of audience might be incorporated into an expanded invention segment of a course in technical writing, instead of being considered a separate step, as it now is in textbooks. Finally, since invention in technical writing makes heavy use of previously written documents and graphics, especially ones composed by the writer or his co-workers in earlier stages of a particular project, technical writing courses might teach students to adapt and re-use previously written material—for example, by requiring students to simulate all the stages of an entire project cycle, from proposals and progress reports to technical memos, descriptions, and final reports.

Such suggestions about the conduct of technical writing courses must remain suggestions and not firm recommendations, however, until we know more about the composing processes of engineers. Additional research on composing might reveal how Nelson, his firm, and his subdiscipline are and are not typical. It might show how his composing habits are more efficient or less efficient than those of his colleagues. It might suggest that some tasks call for very different composing habits and skills than others, or it might imply that technical writers should develop *several* composing styles that they can call upon in different composing situations. One thing seems certain, however: only when more research is completed will teachers know better how to prepare students for the kind of writing they will do at work.

NOTES

1. Janet Emig, *The Composing Processes of Twelfth-Graders*, NCTE Research Report No. 13 (Urbana, IL: National Council of Teachers of English, 1971). See also especially Lester Faigley and Stephen Witte, "Analyzing Revision," *College Composition and Communication*, 32 (December, 1981), 400–14; Linda Flower and John Hayes, "The Cognition of Discovery: Defining a Rhetorical Problem," *College Composition and Communication*, 31 (February, 1980), 21–32, and "Problem-Solving Strategies and the Writing Process," *College English*, 39 (December, 1977), 449–61; Sondra Perl, "The Composing Processes of Unskilled College Writers," *Research in the Teaching of English*, 13 (December, 1979), 317–36; Sharon Pianko, "A Description of the Composing Processes of College Freshman Writers," *Research in the Teaching of English*, 13 (February, 1979), 5–22; Nancy Sommers, "Revision Strategies of Student Writers and Experienced Adult Writers," *College Composition and Communication*, 31 (December, 1980), 378–88; and Charles Stallard, "An Analysis of the Writing Behavior of Good Student Writers," *Research in the Teaching of English*, 8 (Fall, 1974), 206–19.

2. A few more details about Nelson may be relevant. Thirty-four years old, Nelson has lived most of his life near Chicago, where he attended public schools through twelfth grade, took college preparatory classes, but "wrote very little"

(he reports) before college. He attended Iowa State University in 1966–67, where he took Freshman English, his only writing course in college but one which had an enormous impact on his writing. He also credits his M.A. thesis director at Northwestern with inspiring him to take special pride in his writing. Like many engineers, Nelson recognizes the importance of good writing to his work. He sometimes even volunteers to do the writing associated with a project instead of some of the technical work, and he enjoys publishing professional articles on engineering, even though such articles do little to advance his career. Except for those articles, Nelson says, the writing he does at work is typical of the writing done by most engineers at a similar career stage within his particular engineering sub-discipline.

3. Emig, *Composing Processes;* Charles R. Cooper and Lee Odell, ed., *Research on Composing: Points of Departure* (Urbana, IL: National Council of Teachers of English, 1978).

4. Flower and Hayes describe protocol analysis and the results it can generate in "Identifying the Organization of Writing Processes" and "The Dynamics of Composing: Making Plans and Juggling Constraints," both in *Cognitive Processes in Writing,* ed. Lee W. Gregg and E. R. Steinberg (Hillsdale, NJ: Erlbaum, 1980), pp. 3–50. A good introduction to the effects of researchers on the phenomena they study is in Eugene Webb, et al. *Unobtrusive Measures* (Chicago: Rand-McNally, 1966). For a critique of protocol analysis as a research tool, see Faigley and Witte, p. 412.

5. C. H. Knoblauch, in "Intentionality and the Writing Process: A Case Study," *College Composition and Communication,* 31 (May, 1980), 153–59, has also discussed how writers at work juggle multiple aims.

6. Janet Emig, for example, has shown that arrangement occupies little of the time of student writers and that even professional writers often do little detailed arranging, especially if their material is narrative, descriptive, or lyric. See *Composing Processes,* pp. 20–24.

7. The pressure to conform to "company practice" is greater at some engineering firms than at others. Nelson's present employer decides only very minor details about his writing—e.g., abbreviations, resume formats, report covers. On the other hand, Nelson has also worked for companies that allowed him much less autonomy, companies that "second guessed" (Nelson's term) nearly every writing decision he made, even minor stylistic decisions.

8. The Critical Path Diagram and the Project Task Flow are remarkably analogous to models of the writing process. In fact, when I talk to my students about the writing process, I compare it to the processes engineers go through in the course of an engineering project—gathering data, planning, designing, implementing, evaluating.

9. Donald Murray, "Write Before Writing," *College Composition and Communication,* 29 (December, 1978), 375–81, and "Internal Revision: A Process of Discovery," in Cooper and Odell, pp. 85–103; Sommers, "Revision Strategies." For more work on revision, see Faigley and Witte; Perl; John D. Gould, "Experiments on Composing Letters: Some Facts, Some Myths, and Some Observations,"

in *Cognitive Processes in Writing;* and Ellen Nold, "Revising: Toward a Theory," unpublished paper delivered at the Conference on College Composition and Communication, Minneapolis, April, 1979.

10. Cooper and Odell, p. xiv.

11. Sondra Perl, "Understanding Composing," *College Composition and Communication,* 31 (December, 1980), 363–69. See also Nancy Sommers, "Revision Strategies" and "Response to Sharon Crowley," *College Composition and Communication,* 29 (May, 1978), 209–11; and Linda Flower and John Hayes, "A Cognitive Process Theory of Writing," *College Composition and Communication,* 32 (December, 1981), 365–87.

Part 2

Problems with Language

In Lewis Carroll's *Through the Looking Glass,* Humpty Dumpty and Alice have the following exchange:

> "When *I* use a word," Humpty Dumpty said, in a rather scornful tone, "it means just what I choose it to mean—nothing more or less."
> "The question is," said Alice, "whether you *can* make words mean so many different things."

After reading some examples of business and technical writing, it is easy to suspect that Humpty Dumpty has been promoted to project manager—or even company president.

It is not always clear why business and technical writers get themselves into the problems with language that they do. At times, they mistakenly assume that their readers will know what they are talking about, or that their goal is to impress rather than inform their readers. At other times, they simply imitate their superiors or model their documents after those in the files, as if the filing cabinet were a repository for sacred writings handed down from on high.

To solve problems with language, business and technical writers must remember their readers and then be guided by two principles:

- they should write everything as clearly, straightforwardly, and simply as possible; and
- they should write in a manner or style with which they would be comfortable speaking.

These two principles will help writers avoid problems with jargon, gobbledy-gook, legalese, and sexist and biased language. They will also serve as a guide in selecting the appropriate style for different writing situations.

Jargon is simply technical language unique to a profession or an occupation. It only becomes a problem when writers use it in writing to an audience without the necessary background or training to understand it. A systems engineer writing to another systems engineer could rightly assume that the following passage would make sense to his or her reader:

> If you are using a CONFIG.SYS file to modify version 2.0 of the Personal Computer DOS, you may want to create a CONFIG.SYS file to use with the program instead of the AUTOEXEC.BAT file.

Unfortunately, this passage comes from an introductory computer manual.

Jargon in the extreme becomes gobbledygook, mindless gibberish akin to double-talk and characterized by pretentiousness. For example, the host of a popular television game show tells contestants who are losing that they are in "a deficit situation"; ordinary No. 2 pencils become, on the requisition forms of some bureaucrats, "writing implements, standard issue"; politicians wary of angering voters call tax increases "revenue enhancements" and "misspeak themselves" rather than lie when they are caught making false claims or leveling inaccurate charges against their opponents; "turn out the lights when you leave" becomes "illumination is required to be extinguished upon vacation of the premises"; the threat that "anyone caught smoking on the premises will be dealt with accordingly" may at first cause someone to think twice before lighting up, but, in the final analysis, we may well wonder just what the threat is really supposed to mean.

Gobbledygook also includes words and phrases that writers mistakenly think sound the way business and technical writing should sound. They may be in vogue or out of date, but either way, they have unfortunately come to be viewed by some writers as examples of good professional writing practice. People no longer meet for discussions—they "interface"—and every issue about which they interface has "parameters," "viable" and otherwise. Some of these same people see nothing wrong with beginning their letters as follows:

> Pursuant to yours of the twelfth, enclosed herewith please find our check in the amount of $24.95.

Subsequently in the same letter, they "are pleased to advise that," and they go on to refer to data "hereunder discussed" or "above referenced."

Legalese is an overreliance on legal terminology—or legal *sounding* terminology—when Plain English will serve the reader and the writer as well.

Sexist or biased language is linguistic discrimination usually, although not exclusively, against women and groups that are perceived to be minorities. Just as all managers are not men, so all secretaries are not women. Common sense, sensitivity to audience and language, and fairness can help writers avoid sexism and bias.

Problems in any of these areas can be exacerbated in international business settings. As the world grows smaller thanks to technical advances in communication, audiences grow larger and much more complex. An American automobile manufacturer learned the hard way that marketing a model called "Nova" to customers who spoke Spanish was a potentially no-win situation since, in Spanish, *nova* can mean "doesn't go or run."

The essays in this section of *Strategies* address further the issues touched upon in these introductory comments. The first three selections are classic pieces, still invaluable in the advice that their authors offer.

Stuart Chase, a veteran of many years' work as a consultant to various federal agencies, sends up gobbledygook, the linguistic overkill that is all too common in the writing of government officials, bureaucrats, lawyers, and, sadly, even academics (who especially should know better).

Two essays that originally appeared in the *Harvard Business Review* follow Chase's discussion to suggest how style and tone are important in any piece of writing for the world of work. In the first essay, John S. Fielden argues that, to get their messages across, successful writers vary their style to suit each situation with which they deal. In the second essay, Marvin H. Swift, noting that for most people writing takes real effort, discusses how improvements in thinking go hand in hand with improvements in style and in tone to produce a well-focused message.

Diversity in the workplace has lead to a need for diversity in language in writing for the world of work. At one time, it seemed all executives were men, and all their assistants were women. Changes in the composition of the workforce in terms of gender have led to changes in the use of language to reflect such changes in the workplace. Guidelines developed at the University of Wisconsin offer business and technical writers some suggestions on how to avoid language that stereotypes or denigrates men as well as women.

Finally, given the increasingly global focus of business and industry and the problems that can accompany doing business in an ever-expanding international market, Gwyneth Olofsson, who heads an international training and consulting firm based in Sweden, discusses almost two dozen letters drawn from the global workplace in which international communication can very quickly turn into international miscommunication.

Stuart Chase

Gobbledygook

Stuart Chase worked for many years as a consultant to various government agencies; his other books include The Tyranny of Words *(1938) and* Democracy Under Pressure *(1945).*

[Editor's note: Chase's essay first appeared in 1953, and so the author uses the "generic he," the standard for pronoun usage at the time. Today, as the guidelines from the University of Wisconsin reprinted later in this section of *Strategies* make clear, such usage should be avoided. Chase's discussion and advice are, nonetheless, still invaluable to writers today.]

Said Franklin Roosevelt, in one of his early presidential speeches: "I see one-third of a nation ill-housed, ill-clad, ill-nourished." Translated into standard bureaucratic prose his statement would read:

> It is evident that a substantial number of persons within the Continental boundaries of the United States have inadequate financial resources with which to purchase the products of agricultural communities and industrial establishments. It would appear that for a considerable segment of the population, possibly as much as 33.3333* of the total, there are inadequate housing facilities, and an equally significant proportion is deprived of the proper types of clothing and nutriment.

*Not carried beyond four places.

This rousing satire on gobbledygook—or talk among the bureaucrats—is adapted from a report[1] prepared by the Federal Security Agency in an attempt to break out of the verbal squirrel cage. "Gobbledygook" was coined by an exasperated Congressman, Maury Maverick of Texas, and means using two, or three, or ten words in the place of one, or using a five-syllable word where a single syllable would suffice. Maverick was censuring the forbidding prose of executive departments in Washington, but the term has now spread to windy and pretentious language in general.

---

[1]This and succeeding quotations from FSA report by special permission of the author, Milton Hall.

"Gobbledygook" itself is a good example of the way a language grows. There was no word for the event before Maverick's invention; one had to say: "You know, that terrible, involved, polysyllabic language those government people use down in Washington." Now one word takes the place of a dozen.

A British member of Parliament, A. P. Herbert, also exasperated with bureaucratic jargon, translated Nelson's immortal phrase, "England expects every man to do his duty":

> England anticipates that, as regards the current emergency, personnel will face up to the issues, and exercise appropriately the functions allocated to their respective occupational groups.

A New Zealand official made the following report after surveying a plot of ground for an athletic field:[2]

> It is obvious from the difference in elevation with relation to the short depth of the property that the contour is such as to preclude any reasonable developmental potential for active recreation.

Seems the plot was too steep.

An office manager sent this memo to his chief:

> Verbal contact with Mr. Blank regarding the attached notification of promotion has elicited the attached representation intimating that he prefers to decline the assignment.

Seems Mr. Blank didn't want the job.

> A doctor testified at an English trial that one of the parties was suffering from "circum-orbital haematoma."

Seems the party had a black eye.

In August 1952 the U.S. Department of Agriculture put out a pamphlet entitled:

> "Cultural and Pathogenic Variability in Single-Condial and Hyphaltip Isolates of Hemlin-Thosporium Turcicum Pass."

Seems it was about corn leaf disease.

On reaching the top of the Finsteraarhorn in 1845, M. Dollfus-Ausset, when he got his breath, exclaimed:

> The soul communes in the infinite with those icy peaks which seem to have their roots in the bowels of eternity.

Seems he enjoyed the view.

A government department announced:

> Voucherable expenditures necessary to provide adequate dental treatment required as adjunct to medical treatment being rendered a pay patient in in-patient status may be incurred as required at the expense of the Public Health Service.

Seems you can charge your dentist bill to the Public Health Service. Or can you?

---

[2]This item and the next two are from the piece on gobbledygook by W. E. Farbstein, *New York Times*, March 29, 1953.

LEGAL TALK

Gobbledygook not only flourishes in government bureaus but grows wild and lush in the law, the universities, and sometimes among the literati. Mr. Micawber was a master of gobbledygook, which he hoped would improve his fortunes. It is almost always found in offices too big for face-to-face talk. Gobbledygook can be defined as squandering words, packing a message with excess baggage and so introducing semantic "noise." Or it can be scrambling words in a message so that meaning does not come through. The directions on cans, bottles, and packages for putting the contents to use are often a good illustration. Gobbledygook must not be confused with double talk, however, for the intentions of the sender are usually honest.

I offer you a round fruit and say, "Have an orange." Not so an expert in legal phraseology, as parodied by editors of *Labor:*

> I hereby give and convey to you, all and singular, my estate and interests, right, title, claim and advantages of and in said orange, together with all rind, juice, pulp and pits, and all rights and advantages therein . . . anything hereinbefore or hereinafter or in any other deed or deeds, instrument or instruments of whatever nature or kind whatsoever, to the contrary, in any wise, notwithstanding.

The state of Ohio, after five years of work, has redrafted its legal code in modern English, eliminating 4,500 sections and doubtless a blizzard of "where-ases" and "hereinafters." Legal terms of necessity must be closely tied to their referents, but the early solons tried to do this the hard way, by adding synonyms. They hoped to trap the physical event in a net of words, but instead they created a mumbo-jumbo beyond the power of the layman, and even many a lawyer, to translate. Legal talk is studded with tautologies, such as "cease and desist," "give and convey," "irrelevant, incompetent, and immaterial." Furthermore, legal jargon is a dead language; it is not spoken and it is not growing. An official of one of the big insurance companies calls their branch of it "bafflegab." Here is a sample from his collection.[3]

> One-half to his mother, if living, if not to his father, and one-half to his mother-in-law, if living, if not to his mother, if living, if not to his father. Thereafter payment is to be made in a single sum to his brothers. On the one-half payable to his mother, if living, if not to his father, he does not bring in his mother-in-law as the next payee to receive, although on the one-half to his mother-in-law, he does bring in the mother or father.

You apply for an insurance policy, pass the tests, and instead of a straightforward "here is your policy," you receive something like this:

> This policy is issued in consideration of the application therefore, copy of which application is attached hereto and made part hereof, and of the payment for said insurance on the life of the above-named insured.

---

[3]Interview with Clifford B. Reeves by Sylvia F. Porter, *New York Evening Post*, March 14, 1952.

ACADEMIC TALK

The pedagogues may be less repetitious than the lawyers, but many use even longer words. It is a symbol of their calling to prefer Greek and Latin derivatives to Anglo-Saxon. Thus instead of saying: "I like short clear words," many a professor would think it more seemly to say: "I prefer an abbreviated phraseology, distinguished for its lucidity." Your professor is sometimes right, the longer word may carry the meaning better—but not because it is long. Allen Upward in his book *The New Word* warmly advocates Anglo-Saxon English as against what he calls "Mediterranean" English, with its polysyllables built up like a skyscraper.

Professional pedagogy, still alternating between the Middle Ages and modern science, can produce what Henshaw Ward once called the most repellent prose known to man. It takes an iron will to read as much as a page of it. Here is a sample of what is known in some quarters as "pedageese":

> Realization has grown that the curriculum or the experiences of learners change and improve only as those who are most directly involved examine their goals, improve their understandings and increase their skill in performing the tasks necessary to reach newly defined goals. This places the focus upon teacher, lay citizen and learner as partners in curricular improvement and as the individuals who must change, if there is to be curriculum change.

I think there is an idea concealed here somewhere. I think it means: "If we are going to change the curriculum, teacher, parent, and student must all help." The reader is invited to get out his semantic decoder and check on my translation. Observe there is no technical language in this gem of pedageese, beyond possibly the word "curriculum." It is just a simple idea heavily ototververbalized.

In another kind of academic talk the author may display his learning to conceal a lack of ideas. A bright instructor, for instance, in need of prestige may select a common sense proposition for the subject of a learned monograph—say, "Modern cities are hard to live in"—and adorn it with imposing polysyllables: "Urban existence in the perpendicular declivities of megalopolis . . ." et cetera. He coins some new terms to transfix the reader—"mega-decibel" or "stratocosmopolis"—and works them vigorously. He is careful to add a page or two of differential equations to show the "scatter." And then he publishes, with 147 footnotes and a bibliography to knock your eye out. If the authorities are dozing, it can be worth an associate professorship.

While we are on the campus, however, we must not forget that the technical language of the natural sciences and some terms in the social sciences, forbidding as they may sound to the layman, are quite necessary. Without them, specialists could not communicate what they find. Trouble arises when experts expect the uninitiated to understand the words; when they tell the jury, for instance, that the defendant is suffering from "circumorbital haematoma."

Here are two authentic quotations. Which was written by a distinguished modern author, and which by a patient in a mental hospital? You will find the answer at the end of [this selection].

1. Have just been to supper. Did not knowing what the woodchuck sent me here. How when the blue blue blue on the said anyone can do it that tries. Such is the presidential candidate.
2. No history of a family to close with those and close. Never shall he be alone to be alone to be alone to be alone to be alone to lend a hand and leave it left and wasted.

REDUCING THE GOBBLE

As government and business offices grow larger, the need for doing something about gobbledygook increases. Fortunately the biggest office in the world is working hard to reduce it. The Federal Security Agency in Washington,[4] with nearly 100 million clients on its books, began analyzing its communication lines some years ago, with gratifying results. Surveys find trouble in three main areas: correspondence with clients about their social security problems, office memos, official reports.

Clarity and brevity, as well as common humanity, are urgently needed in this vast establishment which deals with disability, old age, and unemployment. The surveys found instead many cases of long-windedness, foggy meanings, clichés, and singsong phrases, and gross neglect of the reader's point of view. Rather than talking to a real person, the writer was talking to himself. "We often write like a man walking on stilts."

Here is a typical case of long-windedness:

> *Gobbledygook as found:* "We are wondering if sufficient time has passed so that you are in a position to indicate whether favorable action may now be taken on our recommendation for the reclassification of Mrs. Blank, junior clerk-stenographer, CAF 2, to assistant clerk-stenographer, CAF 3?"
>
> *Suggested improvement:* "Have you yet been able to act on our recommendation to reclassify Mrs. Blank?"

Another case:

> Although the Central Efficiency Rating Committee recognizes that there are many desirable changes that could be made in the present efficiency rating system in order to make it more realistic and more workable than it now is, this committee is of the opinion that no further change should be made in the present system during the current year. Because of conditions prevailing throughout the country and the resultant turnover in personnel, and difficulty in administering the Federal programs, further mechanical improvement in the present rating system would require staff retraining and other administrative expense which would seem best withheld until the official termination of hostilities, and until restoration of regular operations.

The FSA invites us to squeeze the gobbledygook out of this statement. Here is my attempt:

---

[4]Now the Department of Health and Human Services.

> The Central Efficiency Rating Committee recognizes that desirable changes could be made in the present system. We believe, however, that no change should be attempted until the war is over.

This cuts the statement from 111 to 30 words, about one-quarter of the original, but perhaps the reader can do still better. What of importance have I left out?

Sometimes in a book which I am reading for information—not for literary pleasure—I run a pencil through the surplus words. Often I can cut a section to half its length with an improvement in clarity. Magazines like *The Reader's Digest* have reduced this process to an art. Are long-windedness and obscurity a cultural lag from the days when writing was reserved for priests and cloistered scholars? The more words and the deeper the mystery, the greater their prestige and the firmer the hold on their jobs. And the better the candidate's chance today to have his doctoral thesis accepted.

The FSA surveys found that a great deal of writing was obscure although not necessarily prolix. Here is a letter sent to more than 100,000 inquirers, a classic example of murky prose. To clarify it, one needs to *add* words, not cut them:

> In order to be fully insured, an individual must have earned $50 or more in covered employment for as many quarters of coverage as half the calendar quarters elapsing between 1936 and the quarter in which he reaches age 65 or dies, whichever first occurs.

Probably no one without the technical jargon of the office could translate this; nevertheless, it was sent out to drive clients mad for seven years. One poor fellow wrote back: "I am no longer in covered employment. I have an outside job now."

Many words and phrases in officialese seem to come out automatically, as if from lower centers of the brain. In this standardized prose people never *get* jobs, they "secure employment"; *before* and *after* become "prior to" and "subsequent to"; one does not *do*, one "performs"; nobody *knows* a thing, he is "fully cognizant"; one never *says*, he "indicates." A great favorite at present is "implement."

Some charming boners occur in this talking-in-one's-sleep. For instance:

> The problem of extending coverage to all employees, regardless of size, is not as simple as surface appearances indicate.
> Though the proportions of all males and females in ages 16–45 are essentially the same . . .
> Dairy cattle, usually and commonly embraced in dairying . . .

In its manual to employees, the FSA suggests the following:

Instead of	Use
give consideration to	consider
make inquiry regarding	inquire
is of the opinion	believes
comes into conflict with	conflicts
information which is of a confidential nature	confidential information

Professional or office gobbledygook often arises from using the passive rather than the active voice. Instead of looking you in the eye, as it were, and writing "This act requires . . .," the office worker looks out of the window and writes: "It is required by this statute that . . ." When the bureau chief says, "We expect Congress to cut your budget," the message is only too clear; but usually he says, "It is expected that the departmental budget estimates will be reduced by Congress."

> GOBBLED: "All letters prepared for the signature of the Administrator will be single spaced."
> UNGOBBLED: "Single space all letters for the Administrator." (Thus cutting 13 words to 7.)

Only People Can Read

The FSA surveys pick up the point . . . that human communication involves a listener as well as a speaker. Only people can read, though a lot of writing seems to be addressed to beings in outer space. To whom are you talking? The sender of the officialese message often forgets the chap on the other end of the line.

A woman with two small children wrote the FSA asking what she should do about payments, as her husband had lost his memory. "If he never gets able to work," she said, "and stays in an institution would I be able to draw any benefits? . . . I don't know how I am going to live and raise my children since he is disable to work. Please give me some information. . . ."

To this human appeal, she received a shattering blast of gobbledygook, beginning, "State unemployment compensation laws do not provide any benefits for sick or disabled individuals . . . in order to qualify an individual must have a certain number of quarters of coverage . . ." et cetera, et cetera. Certainly if the writer had been thinking about the poor woman he would not have dragged in unessential material about old-age insurance. If he had pictured a mother without means to care for her children, he would have told her where she might get help—from the local office which handles aid to dependent children, for instance.

Gobbledygook of this kind would largely evaporate if we thought of our messages as two way—in the above case, if we pictured ourselves talking on the doorstep of a shabby house to a woman with two children tugging at her skirts, who in her distress does not know which way to turn.

Results of the Survey

The FSA survey showed that office documents could be cut 20 to 50 percent, with an improvement in clarity and a great saving to taxpayers in paper and payrolls.

A handbook was prepared and distributed to key officials.[5] They read it, thought about it, and presently began calling section meetings to discuss

___
[5] By Milton Hall.

gobbledygook. More booklets were ordered, and the local output of documents began to improve. A Correspondence Review Section was established as a kind of laboratory to test murky messages. A supervisor could send up samples for analysis and suggestions. The handbook is now used for training new members; and many employees keep it on their desks along with the dictionary. Outside the Bureau some 25,000 copies have been sold (at 20 cents each) to individuals, governments, business firms, all over the world. It is now used officially in the Veterans Administration and in the Department of Agriculture.

The handbook makes clear the enormous amount of gobbledygook which automatically spreads in any large office, together with ways and means to keep it under control. I would guess that at least half of all the words circulating around the bureaus of the world are "irrelevant, incompetent, and immaterial"—to use a favorite legalism; or are just plain "unnecessary"—to ungobble it.

My favorite story of removing the gobble from gobbledygook concerns the Bureau of Standards at Washington. I have told it before but perhaps the reader will forgive the repetition. A New York plumber wrote the Bureau that he had found hydrochloric acid fine for cleaning drains, and was it harmless? Washington replied: "The efficacy of hydrochloric acid is indisputable, but the chlorine residue is incompatible with metallic permanence."

The plumber wrote back that he was mighty glad the Bureau agreed with him. The Bureau replied with a note of alarm: "We cannot assume responsibility for the production of toxic and noxious residues with hydrochloric acid, and suggest that you use an alternate procedure." The plumber was happy to learn that the Bureau still agreed with him.

Whereupon Washington exploded: "Don't use hydrochloric acid; it eats hell out of the pipes!"[6]

---

[6]Note: The second quotation on page 61 comes from Gertrude Stein's *Lucy Church Amiably*

John S. Fielden

"What Do You Mean You Don't Like My Style?"

When he wrote this essay for the Harvard Business Review, *John S. Fielden was Professor of Management Communications at the University of Alabama. With his colleague Ronald Dulek, he coauthored a series of books on effective business writing.*

In large corporations all over the country, people are playing a game of paddleball—with drafts of letters instead of balls. Volley after volley goes back and forth between those who sign the letters and those who actually write them. It's a game nobody likes, but it continues, and we pay for it. The workday has no extra time for such unproductiveness. What causes this round robin of revision?

Typos? Factual misstatements? Poor format? No. *Style* does. Ask yourself how often you hear statements like these:

- "It takes new assistants about a year to learn my style. Until they do, I have no choice but to bounce letters back for revision. I won't sign a letter if it doesn't sound like me."
- "I find it difficult, almost impossible, to write letters for my boss's signature. The boss's style is different from mine."

In companies where managers primarily write their own letters, confusion about style also reigns. Someone sends out a letter and hears later that the reaction was not at all the one desired. It is reported that the reader doesn't like the writer's "tone." A colleague looks over a copy of the letter and says, "No wonder the reader doesn't like this letter. You shouldn't have said things the way you did. You used the wrong style for a letter like this." "Style?" the writer says. "What's wrong with my style?" "I don't know" is the response. "I just don't like the way you said things."

Everybody talks about style, but almost nobody understands the meaning of the word in the business environment. And this lack of understanding hurts both those who write letters for another's signature and those who write for themselves. Neither knows where to turn for help. Strunk and White's marvelous book *The Elements of Style* devotes only a few pages to a discussion of style, and that concerns only literary style.[1] Books like the Chicago *Manual of Style*[2] seem to define style as all the technical points they cover, from abbreviations and capitalizations to footnotes and bibliographies. And dictionary definitions are usually too vague to be helpful.

Even such a general definition as this offers scant help, although perhaps it comes closest to how business people use the word:

Style is "the way something is said or done, as distinguished from its substance."[3]

Managers signing drafts written by subordinates, and the subordinates themselves, already know that they have trouble agreeing on "the way things should be said." What, for instance, is meant by "way"? In trying to find that way, both managers and subordinates are chasing a will-o'-the-wisp. There *is* no magical way, no perfect, universal way of writing things that will fend off criticism of style. There is no one style of writing in business that is appropriate in all situations and for all readers, even though managers and subordinates usually talk and behave as if there were.

But why all the confusion? Isn't style really the way we say things? Certainly it is. Then writing style must be made up of the particular words we select to express our ideas and the types of sentences and paragraphs we put together to convey those ideas. What else could it be? Writing has no tone of voice or body gesture to impart additional meanings. In written communication, tone comes from what a reader reads into the words and sentences used.

Words express more than *denotations*, the definitions found in dictionaries. They also carry *connotations*. In the feelings and images associated with each word lies the capacity a writing style has for producing an emotional reaction in a reader. And in that capacity lies the tone of a piece of writing. Style is largely a matter of tone. The writer uses a style; the reader infers a communication's tone. Tone comes from what a reader reads into the words and sentences a writer uses.

In the business environment, tone is especially important. Business writing is not literary writing. Literary artists use unique styles to "express" themselves to a general audience. Business people write to particular persons in particular situations, not so much to express themselves as to accomplish particular purposes, "to get a job done." If a reader doesn't like a novelist's tone, nothing much can happen to the writer short of failing to sell some books. In the business situation, however, an offensive style may not only prevent a sale but may also turn away a customer, work against a promotion, or even cost you a job.

While style can be distinguished from substance, it cannot be divorced from substance. In business writing, style cannot be divorced from the circumstances

---

[1] William Strunk, Jr. and E.B. White, *The Elements of Style* (New York: Macmillan, 1979).

[2] *Manual of Style* (Chicago: University of Chicago Press, 1969).

[3] *The American Heritage Dictionary of the English Language* (Boston: American Heritage and Houghton Mifflin, 1969).

under which something is written or from the likes, dislikes, position, and power of the reader.

> **A workable definition of style** in business writing would be something like this: Style is that choice of words, sentences, and paragraph format which by virtue of being appropriate to the situation and to the power positions of both writer and reader produces the desired reaction and result.

WHICH STYLE IS YOURS?

Let's take a case and see what we can learn from it. Assume that you are an executive in a very large information-processing company. You receive the following letter:

Mr.(Ms.) Leslie J. Cash
XYZ Corporation
Main Street
Anytown, U.S.A.

Dear Leslie:

As you know, I respect your professional opinion highly. The advice your people have given us at ABC Corporation as we have moved into a comprehensive information system over the past three years has been very helpful. I'm writing to you now, however, in my role as chairman of the executive committee of the trustees of our hospital. We at Community General Hospital have decided to establish a skilled volunteer data processing evaluation team to assess proposals to automate our hospital's information flow.

I have suggested your name to my committee. I know you could get real satisfaction from helping your community as a member of this evaluation team. Please say yes. I look forward to being able to count on your advice. Let me hear from you soon.

Frank J. Scalpel
Chairman
Executive Committee
Community General Hospital
Anytown, U.S.A.

If you accepted the appointment mentioned in this letter, you would have a conflict of interest. You are an executive at XYZ, Inc. You know that XYZ will submit a proposal to install a comprehensive information system for the hospital. Mr. Scalpel is the vice president of finance at ABC Corp., a very good customer of yours. You know him well since you have worked with him on community programs as well as in the business world.

I can think of four typical responses to Scalpel's letter. Each says essentially the same thing, but each is written in a different business style:

Response 1

Mr. Frank J. Scalpel
Chairman, Executive Committee
Community General Hospital
Anytown, U.S.A.

Dear Frank,

As you realize, this litigious age often makes it necessary for large companies to take stringent measures not only to avoid conflicts of interest on the part of their employees but also to preclude even the very suggestion of conflict. And, since my company intends to submit a proposal with reference to automating the hospital's information flow, it would not appear seemly for me to be part of an evaluation team assessing competitors' proposals. Even if I were to excuse myself from consideration of the XYZ proposal, I would still be vulnerable to charges that I gave short shrift to competitors' offerings.

If there is any other way that I can serve the committee that will not raise this conflict-of-interest specter, you know that I would find it pleasurable to be of service, as always.

Sincerely,

Response 2

Dear Frank,

Your comments relative to your respect for my professional opinion are most appreciated. Moreover, your invitation to serve on the hospital's data processing evaluation team is received with gratitude, albeit with some concern.

The evaluation team must be composed of persons free of alliance with any of the vendors submitting proposals. For that reason, it is felt that my services on the team could be construed as a conflict of interest.

Perhaps help can be given in some other way. Again, please be assured that your invitation has been appreciated.

Sincerely,

Response 3

> Dear Frank,
>
> Thank you for suggesting my name as a possible member of your data processing evaluation team. I wish I could serve, but I cannot.
>
> XYZ intends, naturally, to submit a proposal to automate the hospital's information flow. You can see the position of conflict I would be in if I were on the evaluation team.
>
> Just let me know of any other way I can be of help. You know I would be more than willing. Thanks again for the invitation.
>
> Cordially,

Response 4

> Dear Frank,
>
> Thanks for the kind words and the invitation. Sure wish I could say yes. Can't, though. XYZ intends to submit a sure-fire proposal on automating the hospital's information. Shouldn't be judge and advocate at the same time!
>
> Any other way I can help, Frank—just ask. Thanks again.
>
> Cordially,

What do you think of these letters?

Which letter has the style you like best? Check off the response you prefer.

Response   1   2   3   4
               ❑   ❑   ❑   ❑

Which letter has the style resembling the one you customarily use? Again, check off your choice.

Response   1   2   3   4
               ❑   ❑   ❑   ❑

Which terms best describe the style of each letter? Check the appropriate boxes.

Response 1	❑ Colorful ❑ Dull	❑ Passive ❑ Forceful	❑ Personal ❑ Impersonal
Response 2	❑ Colorful ❑ Dull	❑ Passive ❑ Forceful	❑ Personal ❑ Impersonal
Response 3	❑ Colorful ❑ Dull	❑ Passive ❑ Forceful	❑ Personal ❑ Impersonal
Response 4	❑ Colorful ❑ Dull	❑ Passive ❑ Forceful	❑ Personal ❑ Impersonal

Let's compare reactions

Now that you've given your reactions, let's compare them with some of mine.

Response 1 seems cold, impersonal, complex. Most business people would, I think, react somewhat negatively to this style because it seems to push the reader away from the writer. Its word choice has a cerebral quality that, while flattering to the reader's intelligence, also parades the writer's.

Response 2 is fairly cool, quite impersonal, and somewhat complex. Readers' reactions will probably be neither strongly positive nor strongly negative. This style of writing is "blah" because it is heavily passive. Instead of saying "I appreciate your comments," it says "Your comments are most appreciated"; instead of "I think that my services could be construed as a conflict of interest," it says "It is felt that my services could be construed. . . ." The use of the passive voice subordinates writers modestly to the back of sentences or causes them to disappear.

This is the impersonal, passive style of writing that many with engineering, mathematics, or scientific backgrounds feel most comfortable using. It is harmless, but it is certainly not colorful; nor is it forceful or interesting.

Response 3 illustrates the style of writing that most high-level executives use. It is simple; it is personal; it is warm without being syrupy; it is forceful, like a firm handshake. Almost everybody in business likes this style, although lower-level managers often find themselves afraid to write so forthrightly (and, as a result, often find themselves retreating into the styles of responses 1 and 2—the style of 1 to make themselves look "smart" to superiors and the style of 2 to appear unbossy and fairly impersonal). Persons who find response 2 congenial may feel a bit dubious about the appropriateness of response 3. (Although I have no way of proving this judgment, I would guess that more readers in high positions—perhaps more owner-managers—would like response 3 than would readers who are still in lower positions.)

Response 4 goes beyond being forceful; it is annoyingly self-confident and breezy. It is colorful and conversational to an extreme, and it is so intensely personal and warm that many business people would be offended, even if they were very close acquaintances of Frank Scalpel's. "It sounds like an advertising person's chitchat," some would probably say.

STRATEGY IS PART OF STYLE

As you compared your responses with mine, did you say, "What difference does it make which style *I* like or which most resembles *my* customary style? What matters is which style will go over best with Mr. Scalpel in this situation"? If you did, we're getting somewhere.

Earlier, when we defined business writing style, some may have wanted to add, "And that style should sound like me." This was left out for a good reason. Circumstances not only alter cases; they alter the "you" that it is wise for your style to project. Sometimes it's wise to be forceful; at other times it's suicidal. Sometimes being sprightly and colorful is appropriate; at other times it's ludicrous. There are times to be personal and times to be impersonal.

Not understanding this matter of style and tone is why the big corporation game of paddleball between managers and subordinates goes on and on. The subordinate tries to imitate the boss's style, but in actuality—unless the boss is extremely insensitive—he or she has no single style for all circumstances and for all readers. What usually happens is that after several tries, the subordinate writes a letter that the boss signs. "Aha!" the subordinate says. "So that's what the boss wants!" And then the subordinate tries to use that style for all situations and readers. Later, the superior begins rejecting drafts written in the very style he or she professed liking before. Both parties throw up their hands.

This volleying is foolish and wasteful. Both superior and subordinate have to recognize that in business writing, style cannot be considered apart from the given situation or from the person to whom the writing is directed. Expert writers select the style that fits a particular reader and the type of writing situation with which they are faced. In business, people often face the following writing situations:

Positive situations.
Saying yes or conveying good news.

Situations where some action is asked of the reader.
Giving orders or persuading someone to do as requested.

Information-conveying situations.
Giving the price of ten widgets, for example.

Negative situations.
Saying no or relaying bad news.

In each of these situations, the choice of style is of strategic importance.

In positive situations, a writer can relax on all fronts. Readers are usually so pleased to hear the good news that they pay little attention to anything else. Yet it is possible for someone to communicate good news in such a cold, impersonal, roundabout, and almost begrudging way that the reader becomes upset.

Action-request situations involve a form of bargaining. In a situation where the writer holds all the power, he or she can use a forceful commanding style. When the writer holds no power over the reader, though, actions have to be asked for and the reader persuaded, not ordered. In such cases, a forceful style will not be suitable at all.

In information-conveying situations, getting the message across forcefully and straightforwardly is best. Such situations are not usually charged emotionally.

In negative situations, diplomacy becomes very important. The right style depends on the relative positions of the person saying no and the person being told no.

For instance, if you were Leslie Cash, the person in the example at the beginning of the article whom Frank Scalpel was inviting to serve on a hospital's evaluation team, you would be in a situation of having to say no to a very important customer of your company. You would also be in a doubly sensitive situation because it is unlikely that Mr. Scalpel would fail to recognize that he is asking you to enter a conflict-of-interest situation. He is probably asking you *anyway*.

Therefore, you would not only have to tell him no, but you would have to avoid telling him that he has asked you to do something that is highly unethical. In this instance, you would be faced with communicating two negative messages at once or else not giving Scalpel any sensible reason for refusing to serve.

SUIT YOUR STYLE TO THE SITUATION

Now that we've thought about the strategic implications of style, let's go back to look at each of the responses to Scalpel's request and ask ourselves which is best.

Do we *want* to be personal and warm? Usually yes. But in this situation? Do we want to communicate clearly and directly and forcefully? Usually yes. But here? Do we want to appear as if we're brushing aside the conflict, as the third response does? Or do we want to approach that issue long-windedly, as in the first response, or passively, as in the second? What is the strategically appropriate style?

In the abstract, we have no way of knowing which of these responses will go over best with Mr. Scalpel. The choice is a matter of judgment in a concrete situation. Judging the situation accurately is what separates successful from unsuccessful executive communicators.

Looking at the situation with strategy in mind, we note that in the first response, the writer draws back from being close, knowing that it is necessary to reject not only one but two of the reader's requests. By using legalistic phraseology and Latinate vocabulary, the writer lowers the personal nature of the communication and transforms it into a formal statement. It gives an abstract, textbooklike response that removes the tone of personal rejection.

The very fact that response 1 is difficult to read and dull in impact may be a strategic asset in this type of negative situation. But if in this situation a subordinate presented response 1 to you for your signature, would it be appropriate for you to reject it because it is not written in the style *you* happen to *like* best in the abstract—say, the style of response 3?

Now let's look at response 2. Again, we see that a lack of personal warmth may be quite appropriate to the situation at hand. Almost immediately, the letter draws back into impersonality. And by using the passive constantly, the writer avoids the need to say "I must say no." Furthermore, the term *construed* reinforces the passive in the second paragraph. This term is a very weak but possibly a strategically wise way of implying that *some* persons (*other* people, not the writer) could interpret Scalpel's request as an invitation to participate in an improper action. Now we can see that, instead of seeming dull and lacking in personal warmth as it did in the abstract, response 2 may be the type of letter we would be wise to send out, that is, when we have taken the whole situation into careful consideration and not just our personal likes and dislikes.

The third response, and to even greater extent the fourth, have styles that are strategically inappropriate for this situation. In fact, Scalpel might well regard the colorful style of the fourth response as highly offensive. Both responses directly and forcefully point out the obvious conflict, but by being so direct each runs the risk of subtly offending him. (The third response is "you can see the position of conflict I'd be in if I were on the evaluation team," and the fourth is "Shouldn't be judge and advocate at the same time!") We could make a pretty strong argument that the direct, forceful, candid style of the third response and the breezy, warm, colorful, intensely personal "advertising" style of the fourth response may both prove ineffectual in a delicate, negative situation such as this.

WHAT EFFECT DO YOU WANT?

At this point, readers may say, "All right. I'm convinced. I need to adjust my style to what is appropriate in each situation. And I also need to give directions to others to let them know how to adjust their styles. But I haven't the foggiest notion of how to do either!" Some suggestions for varying your writing style follow. I am not implying that a communication must be written in one style only. A letter to be read aloud at a colleague's retirement party, for instance, may call not only for a warm, personal style but for colorfulness as well. A long analytic report may require a passive, impersonal style, but the persuasive cover letter may call for recommendations being presented in a very forceful style.

For a forceful style

This style is usually appropriate only in situations where the writer has the power, such as in action requests in the form of orders or when you are saying no firmly but politely to a subordinate.

- Use the active voice. Have your sentences do something to people and to objects, not just lie there having things done to them; have them give orders: "Correct this error immediately" (you-understood is the subject) instead of "A correction should be made" (which leaves the reader wondering, made by whom).
- Step up front and be counted:
  "I have decided not to recommend you for promotion" instead of "Unfortunately, a positive recommendation for your promotion is not forthcoming."
- Do not beat around the bush or act like a politician. If something needs to be said, say it directly.
- Write most of your sentences in subject-verb-object order. Do not weaken them by putting namby-pamby phrases before the subject:
  "I have decided to fund your project" instead of "After much deliberation and weighing of the pros and cons, I have decided to fund your project."
- Do not weaken sentences by relegating the point or the action to a subordinate clause:
  If your point is that your company has won a contract, say "Acme won the contract, although the bidding was intense and highly competitive," not "Although Acme won the contract, the bidding was intense and highly competitive."
- Adopt a tone of confidence and surety about what you say by avoiding weasel words like:
  "Possibly," "maybe," "perhaps."
  "It could be concluded that. . . ."
  "Some might conclude that. . . ."

For a passive style

This style is often appropriate in negative situations and in situations where the writer is in a lower position than the reader.

- Avoid the imperative—never give an order:
  Say "A more effective and time-conserving presentation of ideas should be devised before our next meeting" as opposed to "Do a better job of presenting your ideas at our next meeting. Respect my time and get right to the point."
- Use the passive voice heavily because it subordinates the subject to the end of the sentence or buries the subject entirely. The passive is especially handy when you are in a low-power position and need to convey negative information to a reader who is in a higher position (an important customer, for instance):
  Say "Valuable resources are being wasted" instead of "Valuable resources are being wasted by your company" or, even worse, "You are wasting valuable resources."
- Avoid taking responsibility for negative statements by attributing them to faceless, impersonal "others":
  Say "It is more than possible that several objections to your proposed plans might be raised by some observers" or "Several objections might be raised by those hostile to your plans" instead of "I have several objections to your plans."
- Use weasel words, especially if the reader is in a high-power position and will not like what you are saying.
- Use long sentences and heavy paragraphs to slow down the reader's comprehension of sensitive or negative information.

For a personal style

This style is usually appropriate in good-news and persuasive action-request situations.

- Use the active voice, which puts you, as the writer, at the front of sentences:
  "Thank you very much for your comments" or "I appreciated your comments" instead of "Your comments were very much appreciated by me" or the even more impersonal "Your comments were very much appreciated."
- Use persons' names (first names, when appropriate) instead of referring to them by title:
  "Bill James attended the meeting" instead of "Acme's director attended the meeting."
- Use personal pronouns—especially "you" and "I"—when you are saying positive things:
  "I so much appreciate the work you've done" as opposed to "The work you've done is appreciated."
- Use short sentences that capture the rhythm of ordinary conversation:
  "I discussed your proposal with Frank. He's all for it!" as opposed to "This is to inform you that your proposal was taken up at Friday's meeting and that it was regarded with favor."
- Use contractions ("can't," "won't," "shouldn't") to sound informal and conversational.

- Direct questions to the reader:
  "Just ask yourself, how would your company like to save $10,000?"
- Interject positive personal thoughts and references that will make the reader know that this letter is really to him or her and not some type of form letter sent to just anyone.

For an impersonal style

This style is usually appropriate in negative and information-conveying situations. It's always appropriate in technical and scientific writing and usually when you are writing to technical readers.

- Avoid using persons' names, especially first names. Refer to people, if at all, by title or job description:
  "I would like to know what you think of this plan" instead of "What do you think of this, Herb?"
  "Our vice president of finance" or "the finance department," not "Ms. Jones."
- Avoid using personal pronouns, especially "you" and "I" ("we" may be all right because the corporate we is faceless and impersonal):
  "The logistics are difficult, and the idea may not work" instead of "I think you have planned things so that the logistics are difficult and your idea may not work."
  "We wonder if the idea will work" rather than "I don't think the idea will work."
- Use the passive voice to make yourself conveniently disappear when desirable:
  "An error in the calculations has been made" instead of "I think your calculations are wrong."
- Make some of your sentences complex and some paragraphs long, avoid the brisk, direct, simple-sentence style of conversation.

For a colorful style

Sometimes a lively style is appropriate in good-news situations. It is most commonly found in the highly persuasive writing of advertisements and sales letters.

- Insert some adjectives and adverbs:
  Instead of "This proposal will save corporate resources," write "This (hard-hitting) (productivity-building) (money-saving) proposal will (easily) (surely) (quickly) (immediately) save our (hard-earned) (increasingly scarce) (carefully guarded) corporate resources."
- If appropriate, use a metaphor (A is B) or a simile (A is like B) to make a point:
  "Truly this program is a *miracle* of logical design." "Our solution strikes at the very *root* of Acme's problems." "This program is like *magic* in its ability to. : . ."

For a less colorful style

By avoiding adjectives, adverbs, metaphors, and figures of speech, you can make your style less colorful. Such a style is appropriate for ordinary business writing and also results from:

- Blending the impersonal style with the passive style.
- Employing words that remove any semblance of wit, liveliness, and vigor from the writing.

Please bear in mind that these six styles are not mutually exclusive. There is some overlap. A passive style is usually far more impersonal than personal and also not very colorful. A forceful style is likely to be more personal than impersonal, and a colorful style is likely to be fairly forceful. Nevertheless, these styles are distinct enough to justify talking about them. If we fail to make such distinctions, style becomes a catchall term that means nothing specific. Even if not precise, these distinctions enable us to talk about style and its elements and to learn to write appropriately for each situation.

DISCUSS NEEDS FIRST

What conclusions can we draw from this discussion? Simply that, whether you write your own letters or have to manage the writing of subordinates, to be an effective communicator, you must realize that:

1. Each style has an impact on the reader.
2. Style communicates to readers almost as much as the content of a message.
3. Style cannot be isolated from a situation.
4. Generalizing about which style is the best in all situations is impossible.
5. Style must be altered to suit the circumstances.
6. Style must be discussed sensibly in the work situation.

These conclusions will be of obvious help to managers who write their own letters. But what help will these conclusions be to managers who direct assistants in the writing of letters? In many instances, writing assignments go directly to subordinates for handling. Often, manager and assistant have no chance to discuss style strategy together. In such cases, rather than merely submitting a response for a signature, the subordinate would be wise to append a note: e.g., "This is a very sensitive situation, I think. Therefore, I deliberately drew back into a largely impersonal and passive style." At least, the boss will not jump to the conclusion that the assistant has written a letter of low impact by accident.

When they do route writing assignments to assistants, superiors could save much valuable time and prevent mutual distress if they told the subordinates what style seemed strategically wise in each situation. Playing guessing games also wastes money.

And if, as is often the case, neither superior nor subordinate has a clear sense of what style is best, the two can agree to draft a response in one style first, and if that doesn't sound right, to adjust the style appropriately.

Those who write their own letters can try drafting several responses to tough but important situations, each in a different style. It's wise to sleep on them and then decide which sounds best.

Whether you write for yourself or for someone else, it is extremely unlikely that in difficult situations a first draft will be signed by you or anyone else. Only the amateur expects writing perfection on the first try. By learning to control your style and to engineer the tone of your communications, you can make your writing effective.

SUCH STUFF AS STYLE IS MADE ON

**To Frank A. Nichols, Secretary,
Concord Free Trade Club**

Hartford, March 1885
Dear Sir:

I am in receipt of your favor of the 24th inst., conveying the gratifying intelligence
that I have been made an honorary member of the Free Trade Club of Concord,
Massachusetts, and I desire to express to the Club, through you, my grateful sense
of the high compliment thus paid me.

It does look as if Massachusetts were in a fair way to embarrass me with kind-
nesses this year. In the first place a Massachusetts Judge has just decided in open
court that a Boston publisher may sell not only his own property in a free and
unfettered way, but may also as freely sell property which does not belong to him
but to me—property which he has not bought and which I have not sold. Under
this ruling I am now advertising that judge's homestead for sale; and if I make as
good a sum out of it as I expect I shall go on and sell the rest of his property.

In the next place, a committee of the public library of your town has condemned
and excommunicated my last book [*Adventures of Huckleberry Finn*], and doubled its
sale. This generous action of theirs must necessarily benefit me in one or two additional ways. For instance, it will deter other libraries from buying the book and you
are doubtless aware that one book in a public library prevents the sale of a sure
ten and a possible hundred of its mates. And secondly it will cause the purchasers
of the book to read it, out of curiosity, instead of merely intending to do so after
the usual way of the world and library committees; and then they will discover, to
my great advantage and their own indignant disappointment, that there is nothing
objectionable in the book, after all.

And finally, the Free Trade Club of Concord comes forward and adds to the splen-
did burden of obligations already conferred upon me by the Commonwealth of
Massachusetts, an honorary membership which is more worth than all the rest
since it endorses me as worthy to associate with certain gentlemen whom even
the moral icebergs of the Concord library committee are bound to respect.

May the great Commonwealth of Massachusetts endure forever, is the heartfelt
prayer of one who, long a recipient of her mere general good will, is proud to
realize that he is at last become her pet. . . .

Your obliged servant
S. L. Clemens

To the gas company

Hartford, February 1, 1891
Dear Sirs:

Some day you will move me almost to the verge of irritation by your chuckle-headed Goddamned fashion of shutting your Goddamned gas off without giving any notice to your Goddamned parishioners. Several times you have come within an ace of smothering half of this household in their beds and blowing up the other half by this idiotic, not to say criminal, custom of yours. And it has happened again to-day. Haven't you a telephone?

Ys
S. L. Clemens

Marvin H. Swift

Clear Writing Means Clear Thinking Means...

Marvin H. Swift had a distinguished career teaching business and technical communications at the General Motors Institute.

If you are a manager, you constantly face the problem of putting words on paper. If you are like most managers, this is not the sort of problem you enjoy. It is hard to do, and time consuming; and the task is doubly difficult when, as is usually the case, your words must be designed to change the behavior of others in the organization.

But the chore is there and must be done. How? Let's take a specific case.

Let's suppose that everyone at X Corporation, from the janitor on up to the chairman of the board, is using the office copiers for personal matters; income tax forms, church programs, children's term papers, and God knows what else are being duplicated by the gross. This minor piracy costs the company a pretty penny, both directly and in employee time, and the general manager—let's call him Sam Edwards—decides the time has come to lower the boom.

Sam lets fly by dictating the following memo to his secretary:

```
To: All Employees
From: Samuel Edwards, General Manager
Subject: Abuse of Copiers
```

It has recently been brought to my attention that many of the people who are employed by this company have taken advantage of their positions by availing themselves of the copiers. More specifically, these machines are being used for other than company business.

Obviously, such practice is contrary to company policy and must cease and desist immediately. I wish therefore to inform all concerned—those who have abused policy or will be abusing it—that their behavior cannot and will not be tolerated. Accordingly, anyone in the future who is unable to control himself will have his employment terminated.

If there are any questions about company policy, please feel free to contact this office.

Now the memo is on his desk for his signature. He looks it over; and the more he looks, the worse it reads. In fact, it's lousy. So he revises it three times, until it finally is in the form that follows:

To: All Employees
From: Samuel Edwards, General Manager
Subject: Use of Copiers

We are revamping our policy on the use of copiers for personal matters. In the past we have not encouraged personnel to use them for such purposes because of the costs involved. But we also recognize, perhaps belatedly, that we can solve the problem if each of us pays for what he takes.

We are therefore putting these copiers on a pay-as-you-go basis. The details are simple enough . . . . . .

Samuel Edwards

This time Sam thinks the memo looks good, and it *is* good. Not only is the writing much improved, but the problem should now be solved. He therefore signs the memo, turns it over to his secretary for distribution, and goes back to other things.

FROM VERBIAGE TO INTENT

I can only speculate on what occurs in a writer's mind as he moves from a poor draft to a good revision, but it is clear that Sam went through several specific steps, mentally as well as physically, before he had created his end product:

- He eliminated wordiness.
- He modulated the tone of the memo.
- He revised the policy it stated.

Let's retrace his thinking through each of these processes.

Eliminating wordiness

Sam's basic message is that employees are not to use the copiers for their own affairs at company expense. As he looks over his first draft, however, it seems so long that this simple message has become diffused. With the idea of trimming the memo down, he takes another look at his first paragraph:

It has recently been brought to my attention that many of the people who are employed by this company have taken advantage of their positions by availing themselves of the copiers. More

specifically, these machines are being used for other than company business.

He edits it like this:

> *Item:* "recently"
> *Comment to himself:* Of course; else why write about the problem? So delete the word.
>
> *Item:* "It has been brought to my attention"
> *Comment:* Naturally. Delete it.
>
> *Item:* "the people who are employed by this company"
> *Comment:* Assumed. Why not just "employees"?
>
> *Item:* "by availing themselves" and "for other than company business"
> *Comment:* Since the second sentence repeats the first, why not coalesce?

And he comes up with this:

> Employees have been using the copiers for personal matters.

He proceeds to the second paragraph. More confident of himself, he moves in broader swoops, so that the deletion process looks like this:

> Obviously, such practice is contrary to company policy and ~~must cease and desist immediately. I wish therefore to inform all concerned those who have abused policy or will be abusing it that their behavior cannot and will not be tolerated. Accordingly, anyone in the future who is unable to control himself will have his employment terminated.~~ (will result in dismissal.)

The final paragraph, apart from "company policy" and "feel free," looks all right, so the total memo now reads as follows:

> To: All Employees
> From: Samuel Edwards, General Manager
> Subject: Abuse of Copiers
>
> Employees have been using the copiers for personal matters. Obviously, such practice is contrary to company policy and will result in dismissal.
>
> If there are any questions, please contact this office.

Sam now examines his efforts by putting these questions to himself:

> *Question:* Is the memo free of deadwood?
> *Answer:* Very much so. In fact, it's good, tight prose.
> *Question:* Is the policy stated?
> *Answer:* Yes—sharp and clear.
> *Question:* Will the memo achieve its intended purpose?
> *Answer:* Yes. But it sounds foolish.
> *Question:* Why?
> *Answer:* The wording is too harsh; I'm not going to fire anybody over this.
> *Question:* How should I tone the thing down?

To answer this last question, Sam takes another look at the memo.

Correcting the tone

What strikes his eye as he looks it over? Perhaps these three words:

- Abuse . . .
- Obviously . . .
- . . . dismissal . . .

The first one is easy enough to correct: he substitutes "use" for "abuse." But "obviously" poses a problem and calls for reflection. If the policy is obvious, why are the copiers being used? Is it that people are outrightly dishonest? Probably not. But that implies the policy isn't obvious; and whose fault is this? Who neglected to clarify policy? And why "dismissal" for something never publicized?

These questions impel him to revise the memo once again:

```
To: All Employees
From: Samuel Edwards, General Manager
Subject: Use of Copiers

Copiers are not to be used for personal matters. If there are
any questions, please contact this office.
```

Revising the policy itself

The memo now seems courteous enough—at least it is not discourteous—but it is just a blank, perhaps overly simple, statement of policy. Has he really thought through the policy itself?

Reflecting on this, Sam realizes that some people will continue to use the copiers for personal business anyhow. If he seriously intends to enforce the basic policy (first sentence), he will have to police the equipment, and that raises the question of costs all over again.

Also, the memo states that he will maintain an open-door policy (second sentence)—and surely there will be some, probably a good many, who will stroll in and offer to pay for what they use. His secretary has enough to do without keeping track of affairs of that kind.

Finally, the first and second sentences are at odds with each other. The first says that personal copying is out, and the second implies that it can be arranged.

The facts of organizational life thus force Sam to clarify in his own mind exactly what his position on the use of copiers is going to be. As he sees the problem now, what he really wants to do is put the copiers on a pay-as-you-go basis. After making that decision, he begins anew:

```
To: All Employees
From: Samuel Edwards, General Manager
Subject: Use of copiers

We are revamping our policy on the use of copiers . . . . . .
```

This is the draft that goes into distribution and now allows him to turn his attention to other problems.

THE CHICKEN OR THE EGG?

What are we to make of all this? It seems a rather lengthy and tedious report of what, after all, is a routine writing task created by a problem of minor importance. In making this kind of analysis, have I simply labored the obvious?

To answer this question, let's drop back to the original draft. If you read it over, you will see that Sam began with this kind of thinking:

- "The employees are taking advantage of the company."
- "I'm a nice guy, but now I'm going to play Dutch uncle."
- ∴ "I'll write them a memo that tells them to shape up or ship out."

In his final version, however, his thinking is quite different:

- "Actually, the employees are pretty mature, responsible people. They're capable of understanding a problem."
- "Company policy itself has never been crystallized. In fact, this is the first memo on the subject."
- "I don't want to overdo this thing—any employee can make an error in judgment."
- ∴ "I'll set a reasonable policy and write a memo that explains how it ought to operate."

Sam obviously gained a lot of ground between the first draft and the final version, and this implies two things. First, if a manager is to write effectively, he needs to isolate and define, as fully as possible, all the critical variables in the writing process and scrutinize what he writes for its clarity, simplicity, tone, and the rest. Second, after he has clarified his thoughts on paper, he may find that what he has written is not what has to be said. In this sense, writing is feedback and a way for the manager to discover himself. What are his real attitudes toward that amorphous, undifferentiated gray mass of employees "out there"? Writing is a way of finding out. By objectifying his thoughts in the medium of language, he gets a chance to see what is going on in his mind.

In other words, *if the manager writes well, he will think well*. Equally, the more clearly he has thought out his message before he starts to dictate, the more likely he is to get it right on paper the first time round. In other words, *if he thinks well, he will write well*.

Hence we have a chicken-and-the-egg situation: writing and thinking go hand in hand; and when one is good, the other is likely to be good.

Revision sharpens thinking

More particularly, rewriting is the key to improved thinking. It demands a real openmindedness and objectivity. It demands a willingness to cull verbiage so that ideas stand out clearly. And it demands a willingness to meet logical contradictions head on and trace them to the premises that have created them. In short, it forces a writer to get up his courage and expose his thinking process to his own intelligence.

Obviously, revising is hard work. It demands that you put yourself through the wringer, intellectually and emotionally, to squeeze out the best you can offer. Is it worth the effort? Yes, it is—if you believe you have a responsibility to think and communicate effectively.

University of Wisconsin–Extension Equal Opportunities Program Office and Department of Agricultural Journalism

A Guide to Nonsexist Language

With a little thought, you can use accurate, lively, figurative language in your classrooms, publications, columns, newsletters, workshops, broadcasts and telecommunications—and still represent people fairly. Breaking away from sexist language and traditional patterns can refresh your style.

You can follow two abbreviated rules to check material for bias: Would you say the same thing about a person of the opposite sex? Would you like it said about you? That's the bottom line. Use your own good sense on whether a joke, comment or image is funny—or whether it unfairly exploits people and perpetuates stereotypes.

Most fairness rules improve communication. Use explicit, active words; give concrete examples, specifics and anecdotes to demonstrate facts; present your message in context of the "big picture"; draw your reader in; use parallel forms; present a balanced view; and avoid clichés and generalizations that limit communication. Balanced language rules also guide you to choose or create balanced visual images.

Good communication respects individual worth, dignity, integrity and capacity. It treats people equally despite their sex, race, age, disability, socioeconomic background or creed. And it expresses fairness and balance. To communicate effectively, use real people, describe their unique characteristics and offer specific information. Using stereotypes or composites stifles communication and neglects human potential.

Routinely using male nouns and pronouns to refer to all people excludes more than half the population. There have been many studies that show that when the generic "he" is used, people in fact think it refers to men, rather than men *and* women. Making nouns plural to ensure plural pronouns can help you avoid using the singular "generic" male pronoun.

Many professional titles and workplace terms exclude women and unfairly link men with their earning capacity, while others patronize and subordinate women. Such nongeneric titles reinforce assumptions restricting women and men to stereotypical roles, inaccurately identify people, and give false images of people and how they live and work.

As a communicator, teacher or illustrator, you can help correct and eliminate irrelevant and inaccurate concepts about what it means to be male or female, black or white, young or old, rich or poor, healthy or disabled, or to hold a particular belief.

Editing, publishing and style manuals recognize the need for creating accurate, quality messages without slighting anyone and are beginning to prescribe standards for writing and evaluating manuscripts that represent people without stereotyping them.

Colleges and universities may want to develop their own booklets on nonsexist communication. For example, Franklin and Marshall College (PA) and Michigan State University have developed their own materials on bias-free language.

PRONOUNS: EACH PERSON, TO THE BEST OF HER OR HIS ABILITY

1. *Address Your Reader*
   No. If he studies hard, a student can make the honor roll.

   Yes. If you study hard, you can make the honor roll.

2. *Eliminate the Pronoun*
   No. Each nurse determines the best way she can treat a patient.

   Yes. Each nurse determines the best way to treat a patient.

3. *Replace Pronouns with Articles*
   No. A careful secretary consults her dictionary often.

   Yes. A careful secretary consults a dictionary often.

4. *Use Plural Nouns and Pronouns*
   No. Teach the child to walk by himself.

   Yes. Teach children to walk by themselves.

   He is expanding his operation.

   They are expanding their operation.

   Everyone needs his own space.

   All people need their own space.

5. *Alternate Male and Female Pronouns Throughout Text*
   No. The baby tries to put everything he finds in his mouth.

   Yes. The baby tries to put everything she finds in her mouth.

6. *Use Both Pronouns and Vary Their Order*
   No. A worker with minor children should make sure his will is up to date.

   Yes. A worker with minor children should make sure her or his will is up to date.

7. *Use Specific, Genderless Nouns*
   No. The average man on the street speaks his mind on the issues.

   Yes. The average voter speaks out on political issues.

8. *Substitute Job Titles or Descriptions*
   No. He gave a test on Monday.

9. *Repeat the Noun or Use a Synonym*
   No. The professor who gets published frequently will have a better chance when he goes before the tenure board.

Yes. The professor gave a test on Monday.

Yes. The professor who gets published frequently will have a better chance when faculty tenure is granted.

(*Note:* We don't recommend using "their" to refer to a singular noun.)

(*Note:* Nations, battleships, gas tanks and other objects have no gender.)

TITLES: PEOPLE WORKING

Replace Language Stereotyping Men

No	Yes
Businessman/men	Business person/people, people in business, executive, merchant, industrialist, entrepreneur, manager
Cameraman	Camera operator, photographer
Chairman	Chairperson, chair, moderator, group leader, department head, presiding officer
Congressmen	Members of Congress, Representatives, congressmen and congresswomen
Craftsman	Craftsperson, artisan
Deliveryman/boy	Delivery driver/clerk, porter, deliverer, courier, messenger
Draftsman	Drafter
Fireman	Firefighter
Foreman	Supervisor
Guys	Men, people
Headmaster	Principal
Kingpin	Key person, leader
Lumberman	Wood chopper, tree/lumber cutter
Male nurse	Nurse

Manhole/cover	Sewer hole, utility access/cover
Man-hours	Labor, staff/work hours, time
Man-made	Manufactured, handbuilt, hand made, synthetic, simulated, machine-made
Night watchman	Night guard, night watch
Policeman	Police officer, detective
Pressman	Press operator
Repairman, handyman	Repairer (Better: plumber, electrician, carpenter, steam fitter's apprentice)
Salesman/men	Salespeople, salesperson(s), sales agent(s), sales associate(s), sales representative(s), sales force
Spokesman	Representative, spokesperson, advocate, proponent
Sportsman	Sports/outdoor enthusiast (Better: hunter, fisher, canoer)
Sportsmanship	Fair play
Statesman	Political leader, public servant, diplomat
Statesmanship	Diplomacy
Steward/stewardess	Flight attendant
Weatherman	Weather reporter, meteorologist
Workmen	Workers

Replace Titles Stereotyping Women

No	Yes
Authoress	Author
Aviatrix	Pilot, aviator
Career girl/woman	Professor, engineer, mathematician, administrative assistant
Coed	Student
Gal, Girl, Girl Friday	Woman, secretary, assistant, aide (Better: full name)

Housewife, lady of the house	Homemaker, consumer, customer, shopper, parent
Lady/female doctor, lawyer	Doctor, lawyer
Little lady, better half	Spouse, partner
Maid, cleaning lady	Houseworker, housekeeper, custodian
Poetess	Poet
Sculptress	Sculptor
Usherette	Usher
Waitress	Wait person, waiter
Working wife/mother	Worker

Replace Stereotypical Adjectives and Expressions

No	Yes
Act like a lady and think like a man	Act and think sensitively and clearly
Act like a gentleman/man	Be polite, brave, keep your chin up
Dear Sir	Dear Madam or Sir, Dear Personnel Officer/Director, Dear Executive/Manager (Better: name)
Fatherland	Homeland, native land
Founding fathers	Pioneers, colonists, patriots, forebears, founders
Gentleman's agreement	Informal agreement, your word, oral contract, handshake
Lady luck	Luck
Ladylike, girlish, sissy, effeminate	Tender, cooperative, polite, neat, fearful, weak, illogical, inactive (Both male and female characteristics)
Layman, layman's terms	Lay, common, ordinary, informal, nontechnical
Maiden name	Birth name
Maiden voyage	First/premiere voyage
Male chauvinist	Chauvinist

Male ego	Ego
Man-sized	Husky, sizable, big, large, voracious
Man-to-man defense,/talk	Player-to-player, person-to-person, face-to-face, one-to-one
Manly, tomboy	Courageous, strong, vigorous, adventurous, spirited, direct, competitive, physical, mechanical, logical, rude, active, messy, self-confident (Both female and male characteristics)
Mother doing dishes, father reading the paper	Men and women doing dishes, women and men reading the paper (Note: Also applies to visual images)
Mother Nature, Father Time	Nature, time
Mothering, fathering	Parenting, child-rearing
Motherly	Protective, supportive, kind
Unwed mother	Mother
Woman did well for a woman/ as well as a man	Woman did well, woman performed competently
Woman's/man's work	Avoid (Too broad; use specifics)
Women's page	Lifestyle, living section

Gwyneth Olofsson

International Communication and Language

Gwyneth Olofsson owns Communico, an international training and consulting firm based in Sweden.

English has become the *lingua franca* of the business world, and people from Amsterdam to Zanzibar use it every day as a "tool of the trade." They also spend a lot of time and money trying to eliminate their language mistakes, not realizing that the fewer they make the more dangerous the errors are likely to become, because people aren't expecting them. Furthermore, just because someone has mastered the grammar and vocabulary of a language and pronounces it better than some native speakers does not mean he or she *uses* it in the same way.

Communication is not only about what the words mean in the dictionary, it's also about how you string them together. There is, after all, a certain difference between "Do that job tomorrow," "I'd appreciate it if you did that job tomorrow," and "Do that job tomorrow or I'll have your guts for garters," even if all three phrases are designed to achieve the same end. Those of us who are native English speakers have a responsibility not to use expressions that are likely to confuse non-native speakers (e.g., "Have you cottoned on, or do I have to spell that out to you?"). We also have to ensure that when "born" English speakers encounter a communication style that seems brusque, unfriendly, or arrogant in someone whose native language is not English, they will not assume that this is a true reflection of this person's personality or intention. It may well be that the speaker hasn't mastered the many nuances of words and body language that a native speaker interprets without even thinking about it. So in an unfamiliar culture, newcomers may find themselves wondering if the downcast eyes that accompany a statement are a sign of modesty or dishonesty.

Recently I ran an intercultural simulation, one part of which involved a group of ten British participants "learning" to be members of a fictitious culture. This made-up culture valued touch, and as part of the exercise participants were encouraged to touch each other at every opportunity, especially when communicating with each other. The simulation was a nightmare for everyone involved. The older male members of the group in particular found it extremely difficult to touch their colleagues at all. It wasn't surprising. Their physical contact with non-family members over the last forty years had been limited to a handshake with customers and a quick elbow in the ribs from strangers on a crowded subway, so to learn to communicate with colleagues in a tactile way that is the norm for millions of people in Latin America or Africa was just too much of a challenge.

Communication is about your facial expression, gestures, and actions. This was brought home to me a few years ago when a young family moved in to the next farm. My Swedish husband was born and brought up on a farm located on an island off the Swedish coast, and the new family had moved there from an outlying island and had two young children, as we did.

The four kids started to play together one day and were having a wonderful time when it started to rain. I went out and asked them, in Swedish, if they wanted to come into the house to play. The two new children looked at me and said nothing, then suddenly turned tail and ran as fast as they could in the direction of their home.

I couldn't make any sense of this, but when I went in and told my husband what had happened he showed no surprise. Without looking up from his newspaper he said, "They've gone home to ask their mother if they can come in." I was amazed. How did he know? He'd never even met them. But sure enough, in a couple of minutes there was a knock at the door and there they stood. Thinking about it, there were two things that surprised me. The first was that the two children hadn't said a word when I'd asked them a question, and the second was that my husband had understood the whole situation without even having seen what had happened.

The explanation was, of course, that he and the two children shared the same cultural roots. He had grown up, as they had, in a community where everyone knew everyone else; a homogenous community where people understood what their neighbors would do before they did it. If you grow up in a society like this you don't need to spell things out. Communication takes place without words because the situation is familiar and is governed by a set of unwritten rules that everyone understands.

If, on the other hand, you look at a country with an entirely different profile, like the U.S., for example, a relatively new country where enormous numbers of people immigrated from other cultures, communication patterns developed quite differently. With high levels of mobility as thousands of people headed west across the continent, individuals were forced to get to know one another quickly and establish their own rules as they went along. It's clear that in such a situation good communication skills were vital, because you couldn't expect the people you met to share your background or assumptions, so your communications with your peers had to be clear, unambiguous, and explicit. This explains why today many people in the U.S. have a very different communication style than the natives of the small island off the west coast of Sweden—and many other places where people have known each other all their lives.

MORAL

The way we communicate, and what we do or do not say, may be entirely mystifying to people from other cultures, even though we believe we have made ourselves perfectly clear.

WHAT TO SAY AND HOW TO SAY IT

Even those of us who pride ourselves on being direct don't always say what we mean. If English speakers were to phone a colleague's secretary and ask "Is David in?" we would be surprised if she answered, "Yes" and put the phone down. We assume she would answer the question we *didn't* ask, "May I speak to David?"

Different cultures have different attitudes to directness. I remember a time several years ago when I was in England and having problems with my car. I drove to a garage, parked the car in front, and went inside to report the problem. There was a long line, and as I waited a truck driver came in and addressed the woman waiting behind me in a broad Newcastle accent. "Thanks for moving your car, pet. The other wife just walked away and blocked me in."

In fact, "the other wife" was me. I hadn't seen the truck arrive behind me, and by leaving my car where I did had managed to block his exit. We're talking here about a Newcastle-upon-Tyne truck driver, with tattoos, beer belly, and shaven head, wearing a T-shirt with a picture of a man, not unlike himself, strangling a big snake. But because of the way he had been brought up, this poor guy could not bring himself to speak to me directly and tell me I was blocking his exit, but had to speak to the woman behind me to give him a pretext to tell the world of my stupidity. I mean, it wasn't as if he looked like he was afraid of conflict or had spent his formative years at Eton with Prince William learning how to conduct himself correctly in court circles. But somewhere in his cultural soft-wiring he'd learned that in certain situations, and addressing a certain type of person (e.g., a middle-aged woman, as opposed to a young man), he should use an indirect communication style.

Your own personal communication style will be affected by many factors. Obviously, the culture you come from plays a large part, as does your own native language. Even climate may have a role to play in how we express ourselves. One interesting (although not entirely serious) observation on this theme was made by the English writer Ford Madox Ford who wrote, "You cannot be dumb [silent] when you live with a person, unless you are an inhabitant of the North of England or the State of Maine." As someone with roots in the North of England I don't know if I can agree wholeheartedly with his conclusion that the colder the climate, the more taciturn the people. However, he's not alone in his conclusion: in both Italy and France the people of the south regard those in the cooler north as reserved and antisocial.

Other considerations affect both what we say and how we say it. For example, the CEO of a large corporation might mutter to a few friends over a drink at the club. "Well, guys, we really made a balls up of the last year's sales, didn't we?" However, he probably wouldn't make the same comment at the annual general meeting (although it might wake up the shareholders). He is more likely to say, "Due to circumstances beyond our control, our sales performance in the last year was disappointing." No matter where we come from, we all know that how we speak depends on the audience we are speaking to.

And speaking of audiences, if you gave a presentation and asked for questions, would you be pleased or worried if there weren't any? Would you take the silence to mean that you had made your point so clearly that everyone understood everything or as a warning sign that trouble was brewing? Would you assume that the audience had found your talk so boring they'd all dropped off to sleep? Or would [you] expect questions to emerge later during the informality of the coffee break? It depends, among other things, on whether the audience was comfortable with silence and whether they came from a culture where asking questions in public is about losing face. Or perhaps they all came from the State of Maine or the North of England. . . .

Letters 1–2

Many of us ask questions if we don't understand something. However, in some cultures this is not a step to be taken lightly.

Asking Questions   Letter 1

From the U.S. about **MEXICO**

The company is introducing a complicated new process in one of its workshops in Mexico. We know it's difficult, and we have a training and support package we can offer if needed. I strongly suspect that they're having problems down there, but we haven't received a single request for advice or support. Why not?

As you know the process is a complicated one, why don't you provide the support package automatically instead of waiting for a request? Admitting you need help can be a difficult thing to do no matter what culture you come from. Questions of prestige and fear of losing face can mean that people are unwilling to expose themselves to possible criticism. Also, if in your culture you have learned that good employees know all the answers, you may well hesitate to tell your bosses that you don't! This problem can be compounded if headquarters is located abroad, especially in a country that is bigger or richer than your own; this can make national sensitivities even worse.

He Asked What?   Letter 2

From CANADA about **CHINA**

> I enjoyed my trip to China, but I was very surprised by some questions business acquaintances I hardly knew asked me. Two questions they asked me during a meal were how much my watch cost and how old my wife was. (I'm just glad she wasn't there to hear it!)

It's odd what different cultures regard as acceptable questions. In France and many other European countries, they regard the North American exchange of personal information (Do you have any children? What do you do in your free time?) as rather intrusive, though the French will quite happily discuss matters of religion, which are regarded as taboo by, for example, many people from the Middle East. Canadians and North Americans, of course, simply see such inquiries as a friendly way of building a relationship, and they expect to answer the same questions themselves. At the same time, North Americans usually find questions about money and age too personal to ask business acquaintances. However, for many Chinese, whether in China or elsewhere in Asia, and for people in the Middle East these questions form part of ordinary conversation and are just one way of getting to know you better. Indeed, such questions are seen as a natural way to show you're interested in your new acquaintance. People in countries as far apart as China, India, and Mexico might even think it rather unfriendly if people they met did *not* show any interest in their personal concerns.

Letters 3–4

The way people communicate with each other at work is affected by the structure of the organization they work for and by the expectations of fellow employees.

Communication Stop   Letter 3

From SWEDEN about **GERMANY**

> I work for a multinational company and am involved in a project that requires a lot of technical input. I contacted a German colleague I'd met at a conference for a little help. When I spoke to him on the phone he was quite pleased to help us, but the next day my manager got an e-mail from the German guy's boss saying that my colleague was too busy to help me.

I think the problem here is that you didn't use the "correct" channels of communication, according to the German company, anyway. In Germany, and indeed in the majority of European and American companies, the manager wants to be informed of what his or her department members are doing, as it's an important part of his or her role to co-ordinate their efforts. What you should have done first was to contact the manager and ask if you could approach your German colleague for some assistance. Not doing so might be interpreted by his or her manager as very rude, and even a bit underhanded.

I understand that you come from a country, Sweden, where it's the norm to delegate an enormous amount of power to non-managerial staff and give them a high degree of independence, especially if they are technical specialists. However, this is certainly not the case in most countries, which tend to be much more hierarchical. Indeed, most managers from the U.K. to the United Arab Emirates, by way of the U.S., would want to be informed of such an approach to a subordinate.

I suggest your manager make a formal request to his German counterpart asking if you may contact the specialist. You should include a description of the kind of questions to be tackled, and a description of the benefits your project will make to the company. And be *very* polite. After all, you are asking the manager for a favor—to be allowed to use the valuable time of one of the department's members.

Communication Breakdown   Letter 4

From NEW ZEALAND about **FRANCE**

> We're having real problems with our French subsidiary. We want a couple of departments in the French head office to collaborate in preparing a program for some visiting customers who want to see production operations. Naturally, this will involve consultation with the factory staff to see what is practicable. However, arrangements seem to be at a standstill. We can't understand what the problem can be.

What you have asked your French managers to do is to communicate in ways they may not be used to. First, you are asking your managers to operate across departmental boundaries; hence, it's not clear who is responsible for what. Second, they are being asked to communicate across hierarchical boundaries, because the managers will not be able to arrange a trip to see production facilities without some collaboration and discussion with the factory personnel.

The French, as well as Latin American and Southern European business cultures, tend to have very clear hierarchies where each person's responsibilities are spelled out. The same applies to cultures with a Confucian heritage like Japan, China, and South Korea, where respect is awarded to age, education, and rank in the company. The French also have rather compartmentalized communication patterns, and information is not freely shared as a matter of course, but tends to remain the property of those higher up the ladder. "Knowledge is power" is the name of the game, and one likely to hinder interdepartmental collaboration. Your culture (which is more tolerant of uncertainty) is more like that of the Scandinavians, the British, and Irish in your belief in a free flow of information, but many other cultures find this difficult to deal with. You are more likely to get a positive result if you give *one* of the managers responsibility for arranging the visit, and instruct him or her to involve the factory in the plans.

Letters 5–6

You may like to have things out in the open, or prefer to leave them unsaid.

A Major Error   Letter 5

*From MEXICO about **GERMANY***

We have a new German manager who is making himself extremely unpopular here. He has introduced a new quality control system that is complicated and takes time to learn. Inevitably mistakes are made. However, when he finds an error, he seems to delight in pointing this out to the person involved in front of everyone. Several people are already thinking of handing in their notices.

Your new manager is certainly not trying to offend people intentionally. In his own direct way, a way shared by U.S. Americans who also believe that it is better to "tell it like it is," he might even be trying to help by identifying the problem. He obviously does not understand that Mexicans regard this very direct approach as fault-finding, confrontational, and aggressive. Mexicans, like most Central and South Americans and East Asians, are skilled at avoiding confrontations and situations that involve a loss of face, but this is still something your new manager has to learn. Until he does, try not to take his criticism personally.

No No   Letter 6

*From the U.S. about **INDONESIA***

I found it very difficult working in Indonesia because I couldn't get a straight answer to a straight question, and this often led to misunderstandings. As far as I could see, they often said yes when they meant no. Why?

Most Indonesians find it hard to give a straightforward *no* to a request. If you ask for something to be done that is difficult or even impossible your Indonesian colleague, instead of saying *no* or *sorry,* may say instead that he will try. Also, a promise to do something that keeps getting postponed can be another indirect way of refusing a request. There is no intention to deceive, but simply a wish to avoid situations leading to open disagreement or disappointment that would cause you to lose face. And bear in mind that people from cultures with this indirect communication style are perfectly well understood by each other. They are simply tuned in to "reading between the lines" in a way you are not.

This communication pattern is not confined to Indonesia. In countries as far away from Indonesia as Pakistan, India, and Japan the word *no* is regarded as impolite and is rarely heard in a business context. In Mexico and South America, too, politeness and diplomacy are valued as useful ways of avoiding conflict.

But bear in mind that speakers of English can be indirect sometimes too. If invited to a party they don't want to attend, the vast majority of English speakers will say they have a cold rather than admit that they're planning to spend the evening in front of the TV. This is just another variation on the "white lie" theme, and as such is remarkably similar to the indirect response you mentioned in your question.

Letters 7–9

It's easy to create the wrong impression if you choose an inappropriate communication style—and what is inappropriate is in the ear of the listener.

Aggressive   Letter 7

From SWEDEN about FRANCE

I find it extremely difficult to discuss business with the French. It is impossible to talk about things with them calmly and sensibly. They are very critical of any ideas that they have not originated themselves, but take any criticism of their own plans personally and get angry.

If you come from a country like Sweden, where open conflict is frowned on, you may find the French debating style very aggressive. For the French, a love of words is combined with a liking for verbal combat, and they are used to organizing their case logically and presenting their arguments with force and conviction, not necessarily because they believe in them, but because they consider that it is through argument and counter-argument that you will eventually arrive at the truth or the best solution to a problem. And if you don't, the debate has been an enjoyable chance to flex your intellectual muscles anyway!

However, the bad feelings that may result from such spectacular clashes will usually quickly be forgotten, which is also hard for people from more low-key cultures to understand. Of course, the French are not alone in their love of discussion. Greeks, Israelis, Argentineans, and Poles all enjoy a good debate too, and North Americans and Australians are no shrinking violets when it comes to putting their points forward. For the French and Australians in particular, debate is a way of taking the measure of a new acquaintance.

In your particular case, at a meeting with the French you should emphasize the most important points of your argument and repeat them patiently. Don't get tied up with details or try to score debating points. Instead, focus on the most important points you want to achieve and keep the meeting focused on them. Be very well prepared, and if in a corner, be ready to use a weapon to which the French have no defense—silence.

Patronizing Pommie   Letter 8

From AUSTRALIA about the U.K.

We have a new boss from the U.K. with one of the most affected upper-class English accents I have ever heard. Every time he opens his mouth I can just see him at the Queen's garden party in a tuxedo and top hat. I just can't take him seriously, and I wonder how he expects to communicate with the other guys in the company.

For historical reasons an upper-class English accent in Australia is associated with money and power, and the use and misuse of both. Australia is a proud new multiethnic country and many Aussies find reminders of their colonial past, that includes the accent of the former ruling class, embarrassing and even painful.

But it's true that this particular type of British accent (RP, which is short for Received Pronunciation) is linked to a certain powerful social group in a way that different U.S. regional accents are not. It also continues to be an accent that dominates the boardrooms of many companies. Even in England itself people with strong regional accents may associate RP with snobbery and privilege, which is why younger members of the upper classes try to tone it down a bit. But give your boss a chance. It would be unfair to judge how well he's likely to do his job on the basis of his vowel sounds!

Just Making Conversation   Letter 9

From BRITAIN about JAPAN

> I met several Japanese businesspeople who visited Britain recently, and I tried to be pleasant and help them relax. I told a few jokes that seemed to go down well, but I later heard that they hadn't been appreciated. Yet at the time everyone laughed!

Your mistake was to treat your visitors as if they were from your own country. I'm sure this was done from the best of motives, but it is a mistake to assume that every culture shares the same kind of humor. Just because your Japanese visitors laughed didn't necessarily mean that they found your joke funny—people from different cultures tend to laugh at different things. Research about what people of different nationalities find funny concluded that the Irish, British, Australians, and New Zealanders thought that jokes involving word play were funniest. Canadians and U.S. Americans preferred jokes where there was a sense of superiority—either because a person looked stupid or was made to look stupid by another person. Many European countries, like France, Denmark, and Belgium, liked rather surreal jokes and jokes about serious topics like death and illness.

You don't say whether you told your jokes during a business meeting or after work in the pub. However, in many countries humor is confined to non-work situations, and joking in an important meeting, for example, is seen as a sign that you are not treating the subject (or the individual) with respect. This would certainly apply to Germany and Finland as well as Japan, where humor when business matters were being discussed would be regarded as inappropriate. And of course it might well be that your visitors didn't understand your English but did not want to lose face by showing it, because even if you are fluent in a foreign language, jokes are always the last things you understand.

Finally, you need to know that people from East Asian countries as widely apart as Japan, South Korea, and Thailand may laugh if embarrassed or nervous as well as when they're happy.

Letters 10–11

Rudeness may be what the listener hears, rather than what the speaker intends.

Rude, or Just Informal?   Letter 10

*From DENMARK about **DENMARK***

> In Denmark we tend to communicate in an informal way and consequently leave out
> titles like "Mr." or "Dr." We also like to communicate directly rather than "beating about
> the bush." But I know this isn't the case in other cultures and wondered just how rude
> we are perceived to be.

It depends where you're going and who you're meeting. In Northern Europe,
Australia, and the U.S., communication styles are quite relaxed and informal, and
people take pride in talking to both manual workers and top managers in more or
less the same way. They also tend to be rather pragmatic in their understanding of
what language is for—generally it's to get things done. So they say clearly what
they mean so the message comes over loud and clear. This group won't regard
your informal and direct style as at all rude.

In other cultures, however, what you say may be secondary to how you say
it, and the British, along with the Arabs and people from many Asian cultures,
put a lot of weight on how the message is delivered. Words are regarded as an
important way of establishing and building relationships, not simply a tool for
getting things done. If your "tone" is wrong and you are perceived as rude, people from these cultures can take offense, and, for example, not using the right titles for an individual can be regarded as a sign of disrespect.

As a general rule, it's better to err on the side of formality when communicating with people of other nationalities, even if you've worked together for
quite some time. Words define your relationship with an individual, and if you
want to ensure that the relationship is one of mutual respect, your communication style must reflect that.

Let Me Finish!   Letter 11

*From SOUTH AFRICA about **ITALY***

> I travel often in Italy and in other Mediterranean countries, and I find it very irritating
> to be constantly interrupted. What can I do to stop this?

The short answer is—not a lot. What you as a South African would call a
rude interruption, nationals from Southern European countries may regard as
perfectly acceptable. They may instead see an interruption as an expression of interest and involvement in what the speaker is saying and in his or her ideas. In
short, in countries such as Italy, if you wait for a pause in the conversation in order to present your own point of view, you'll never open your mouth! You'll find
that the nationals of these countries interrupt each other too, so don't take it
personally. This is because silence does not have an important role in the communication patterns of most Latin countries. Indeed, the tempo of conversation
may simply be too fast to allow for a pause between speakers.

If you are interrupted in the middle of a presentation, don't show annoyance
but say that you'll deal with the points raised at the end of your talk; don't let

yourself be thrown off track. If the interruption occurs in the middle of an informal meeting, accept that this is regarded as a legitimate way of raising relevant points and practice your debating skills.

Letters 12–13

When to remain silent is a decision we make almost unconsciously when operating in our own culture. But in another culture this decision may be interpreted in a way we don't expect.

Stuck Dumb   Letter 12

From POLAND about SOUTH KOREA

During my recent trips to South Korea I have built up a good relationship with an engineer of about my own age who works in my own area of expertise. He speaks good English, and we have had a number of informal meetings where we've made tentative decisions about some technical developments. However, when his boss is present he hardly ever opens his mouth, even though this manager has to use an interpreter and does not have a technical background.

It is quite usual in South Korea, and neighboring Japan, that a younger employee will be quiet in front of older managers as a sign of respect. It would be regarded as immodest to display his superior knowledge of English or the technical matter at hand in front of his boss. This manager will not be directly involved in the technical side of things, but will want to know a little about you personally and see you "in action" so he can come to some conclusion about whether you and the company you represent are likely to make good working partners.

Small Talk Versus Silence   Letter 13

From FINLAND about the U.K.

We hear a lot about the importance of "small talk" when doing business with the British. But if you don't have anything particular to say, why should you keep on talking? Surely it makes more sense to keep your mouth shut.

In cultures where conversation is an art form, as in France and Italy, a firmly shut mouth may be equated with a firmly shut mind. You may be regarded as rude if you are not prepared to make an effort to get to know your counterparts on a personal rather than simply on a business level. However, you are not the only one to find this need for "small talk" difficult. In addition to Finns, Swedes and Norwegians also have a problem with it. In your cultures silence is accepted as a part of conversation in a way it is not in many others (although the Japanese are more like you in their acceptance of silence). To many Europeans and Americans, general social conversation is a prelude to more serious discussions and is regarded as a way of getting to know your colleague before you get down to brass tacks.

If you are stuck about what to talk about, non-controversial topics are best to start with. In 1758, Samuel Johnson wrote, "It is commonly observed that when two Englishmen meet, their first talk is of the weather." Some things just don't change, and not only the English find this subject a useful "icebreaker" with strangers. Other useful subjects are the journey to the meeting, sports, and questions about your visitor's hometown or area, but the real secret is to relax and allow yourself to show you are interested in your partner and what he or she has to say. Feel free to ask questions, as long as they don't get *too* personal. People usually enjoy talking about themselves. Neither should you be afraid to talk about yourself and your own interests. Conversation is like dancing the tango (surprisingly, perhaps, this is very popular in Finland) in that it needs practice. It also requires sensitivity to what your "partner" is feeling and anticipation of the next move.

Letter 14

Giving presentations at home can be bad enough, but speaking to people of other cultures can be even harder.

Political Correctness   Letter 14

From AUSTRALIA about the US

> I've just returned from the U.S. where I gave a number of lectures on a technical matter. During one of my talks I used the expression "to call a spade a spade." One of my listeners raised his hand and said that he found the expression offensive—he had taken it as a racist comment! Is this political correctness run wild?

To put it bluntly, yes it is. The expression "to call a spade a spade" simply means to describe something truthfully and honestly. However, in the U.S. *spade* is a derogatory term for a black person; it comes from the expression "as black as the ace of spades." Your listener obviously confused the two.

When you speak in public on any subject, it is simple good manners to ensure that what you say does not unintentionally offend any particular group, hurt their feelings, or show them disrespect, especially if this group has been given a hard time by society at large over the years; women, black people, homosexuals, and handicapped people are some groups that spring to mind. It's obvious that people belonging to these groups are just as deserving of consideration and courtesy as the traditional top dogs—white heterosexual able-bodied males.

However, this respect for the dignity of others should not stop you from getting your own message across. The term *political correctness* has unfortunately come to be associated with a "holier than thou" attitude, and some North Americans use it to beat less politically correct fellow citizens over the head. Luckily, it is primarily a North American phenomenon, but one that the rest of us should be aware of when we have contact with Canadians or U.S. Americans.

IN A NUTSHELL: *What to say and how to say it*

Global Business Standards

Good small talk topics:

Weather is always safe, although boring, especially in countries that don't have a lot!

Sports are usually safe too, unless the city or country has suffered a spectacular defeat in the national sport recently.

The art and cultural history of the country is usually safe (but watch out for any historical discussion that can lead to a political debate.)

Global Warnings

No swearing in your own or any other language.

Keep humor to a minimum until you are sure your partners/guests laugh at the same things as you.

Don't comment negatively about another culture—especially on religion, politics, or sexual matters. (Occasionally requests for information on the first two may be interpreted favorably, but be careful.)

- **Argentina:** People like to express opinions and love to debate. Voices may be louder than elsewhere in South America. (See Letters 4, 5, 6, 7, 11, and 13.)
- **Australia:** People enjoy talking and debating. There is an informal style of communication that is not based on hierarchy. (See Letters 7, 8, 9, 10, and 14.)
- **Austria:** Communication within companies is inhibited by departmental and hierarchical boundaries. There is a direct yet formal communication style. May be an adversarial approach to debate among peers. (See Letter 3.)
- **Belgium:** Communication within companies is inhibited by departmental and hierarchical boundaries. French speakers' adversarial style in discussions may appear very negative or aggressive. Flemish speakers are more low-key. (See Letters 3 and 9.)
- **Brazil:** Relatively personal questions (in more reserved cultures) about income, age, and so on are acceptable. Emotions are expressed openly. (See Letters 4, 5, 6, 11, and 13.)
- **Canada:** There are different communication styles depending on whether you are in English- or French-speaking Canada. (See U.K. and France.) (See Letters 2, 7, 9, and 14.)
- **China:** Personal questions about income, age, and so on are acceptable. Ordinary conversations can be loud and may sound unintentionally rude or angry. (See Letters 2, 4, and 5.)
- **Denmark:** Informal communication style is the norm. (See Letters 4, 9, and 10.)

- **Finland:** Small talk is not usual. Silence is accepted. The verbal style is very quiet and restrained. (See Letters 4, 9, and 10.)
- **France:** Communication within companies is inhibited by departmental and hierarchical boundaries. Adversarial style in discussions may appear to outsiders to be very negative or aggressive. (See Letters 2, 3, 4, 7, and 9.)
- **Germany:** Communication within companies may be inhibited by departmental and hierarchical boundaries. There is a direct yet formal communication style. Adversarial style in discussions may appear very negative or aggressive. Negative messages are given directly; tact is not a priority. (See Letters 3, 5, and 9.)
- **Hong Kong:** Personal questions about income, age, and so on are acceptable. Ordinary conversations can be loud, and may sound unintentionally rude or angry. (See Letters 2, 4, and 5.)
- **India:** Personal questions about income, age, and so on are acceptable. In these "high context" cultures a straight *no* is regarded as rude. Explanations and communication styles may be indirect. (See Letters 2 and 6.)
- **Indonesia:** Quiet, calm polite conversation style is the norm. This is also appreciated in others. (See Letters 2, 5, and 6.)
- **Italy:** Overlapping conversational style is the norm. Interruptions are not regarded negatively. Emotions are expressed openly. (See Letters 3, 4, 11, and 13.)
- **Japan:** Deference to senior and older colleagues (when present) may inhibit Japanese from communicating. Self-consciousness about their English may be another inhibiting factor. There is an oblique and indirect communication style and modesty is important. A straight *no* is regarded as rude. (See Letters 4, 5, 6, 9, 12, and 13.)
- **Mexico:** There is an indirect communication style. Direct confrontation is avoided. It's important to "save face." (See Letters 1, 2, 4, 5, 6, 11, and 13.)
- **Netherlands:** People have a rather blunt and straightforward speaking style and are quite informal.
- **Norway:** There is an informal and direct communication style. Silence is an accepted part of communication. (See Letters 4, 10, and 13.)
- **Poland:** People enjoy debate and discussions. Politeness and formality are quite important. (See Letter 7.)
- **Russia:** The first response to any question is usually *no*, but persistence is often rewarded. It is important for Russians not to lose face in discussions. They may show disagreement or anger quite openly.
- **Saudi Arabia:** Ordinary conversations can be loud and may sound unintentionally rude or angry to outsiders. Emotions are expressed openly. (See Letters 2 and 10.)
- **South Africa:** Lots of sports analogies (from rugby, cricket, etc.) used. Different ethnic groups use different communication styles. (See Letter 11.)
- **South Korea:** When getting to know you, people may ask personal questions, but they are not intending to be rude. (See Letters 5, 9, and 12.)
- **Spain:** A straight *no* is regarded as rude. Explanations and communication styles may be indirect. (See Letters 3, 4, 11, and 13.)
- **Sweden:** Communication across hierarchical boundaries is common. Written communication in English may sound brusque, even rude, because of first

language interference. Silence is an accepted part of communication. (See Letters 3, 4, 7, 10, and 13.)

- **Switzerland:** Humor has little place in business. German speakers will not make small talk, but French and Italian speakers will.
- **Taiwan:** See China.
- **Thailand:** There is a very tactful communication style, and heated debates are not popular. (See Letters 5 and 9.)
- **Turkey:** People may be reluctant to say *no*. It is more important to be polite than to be accurate or clear. (See Letters 3 and 4.)
- **U.K.:** Small talk is an important social skill. Humor is used widely to defuse tension and to create positive social contacts. People are judged according to how they use language. An oblique style, including understatement or irony, may be used. (See Letters 3, 4, 8, 9, 10, and 13.)
- **U.S.:** Political correctness (and good manners) means that you should be very careful how you express yourself. This applies to all references to gender, age, race, religion, or sexual orientation. Communication is generally direct and explicit. (See Letters 1, 2, 3, 5, 6, 7, 9, 10, and 14.)
- **Venezuela:** People like to debate but rarely admit they are wrong or do not know something. (See Letters 4, 5, 6, 11, and 13.)

A GLOBAL LANGUAGE?

There are over 400 million speakers of English as a first language in the world, with about the same number of people using it as a second language. However, over 700 million people speak one of the many dialects of Chinese. The world also contains almost 300 million Spanish speakers, and about 180 million speakers of Hindi and Arabic, respectively. (And undoubtedly included in these figures are a good few thousand gifted people who speak *all* these languages.)

However, English speakers can take comfort from statistics that say 75 percent of the world's mail, telexes, and cables are in English, that it is the medium for 80 percent of the information stored on the world's computers, and that it is the language of over half the world's technical and scientific periodicals. In fact, it can be said with justice that English is on the way to becoming the first truly global language.

The need for a language in which people from Siberia to Santiago can communicate directly with each other has long been acknowledged, and the establishment of artificial languages such as Esperanto has tried unsuccessfully to fulfill this need. Now, due to a series of accidents of history, it looks as if English is likely to step into the breach. But if a language is "global," it is no longer the exclusive property of its native speakers. Indeed, it is claimed that there is a European variety of English, sometimes called *Euro-English*, which is already evolving, and some people believe that it will eventually become the European language of business. It even has an official name: English as a lingua franca in Europe (ELFE). This version of English regards as acceptable some "mistakes" that most teachers of the language spend their careers trying to eradicate. For example, "He goes to work every day at 8:00 o'clock" would be accepted as correct, as the meaning of the sentence remains clear.

Some academics believe that this modified version of English, which would turn increasingly to continental Europe rather than to the U.S. or the U.K. for its standards of correctness and appropriateness, is the future. Whether that is true remains to be seen, but whatever happens, the message is clear: English is a useful tool for international communication, but it is no longer the exclusive property of people who speak it as a first language.

And what about this privileged group: Those of us who by an accident of birth have learned to speak the global language of business and industry without effort? Can we just rest on our laurels in the knowledge that our customers, suppliers, and even our employers will communicate with us in *our* native language, rather than in *theirs*?

That might be a mistake. I know of at least one international company of management consultants that will not employ anyone who does not speak at least one foreign language fluently. The reason given is that each language gives you a new perspective on the world, and if you are going to work with people not from your own culture you need to be able to shift away from your "native" perceptions from time to time, because language affects how you think.

Letters 15–16

It's inevitable that when speaking English as a foreign language you will make mistakes, and these mistakes can take many forms.

Rude Writers   Letter 15

From SPAIN about **SWEDEN**

In the office where I work we have often had visitors from Sweden, and we've been very impressed both by their English and by their pleasant and friendly manners. However, we have received some letters from these very same people lately and have been amazed by the poor standard of their English and by the tone of the letters, which we find rather arrogant.

You'll be wiser to trust your first impressions. There's a major difference between how we speak and how we write, and whether we're using our native language or someone else's. For example, Swedish children learn English from about the age of eight and quickly become fluent and accurate speakers, but there isn't the same emphasis on written skills (the reverse is true in Japan and South Korea, where writing is prioritized).

When they write in their own language, Swedes are often very informal and rather blunt; this reflects their egalitarian approach to their fellow citizens. When they transpose this style into written English they can unintentionally sound very rude, especially as there isn't a Swedish equivalent for *please* as there is, for example, in Spanish (*por favor*).

It is often difficult to establish the right "tone" in written communication when body language and tone of voice are missing from the communication equation. I have noticed when people from French-, Arabic-, and Spanish-speaking countries write to me, although the grammar and vocabulary may be less than perfect, the tone is extremely polite and rather more formal than letters and e-mails from the U.S. or the U.K. This is because the writers are imitating the more formal and courteous written styles of their own languages and transposing them to English.

Misunderstandings such as you describe, which arise from the tone of a letter or written material, are often the result of "first language interference" and can be hard to identify and correct. It's easier if you make the wrong impression during a face-to-face encounter, because then you get immediate feedback from your listener's body language or facial expression.

The moral is that when writing in any language you should be more formal than when you're speaking, and most importantly, ensure that the tone of the letter is polite and friendly. This is hard to do in a foreign language, but it is even more important than getting the grammar or vocabulary right. If you feel that you cannot judge the tone of your letter yourself, try to get a native speaker to read it before sending it off to ensure that you're not going to offend anyone by appearing less charming than you actually are!

Thin Skin   Letter 16

*From the NETHERLANDS about **FRANCE***

> I made a mistake the other day when a French visitor used a wrong word when he was speaking English. He told a group of us when we arrived at this office to "Please sit down, and I'll enjoy you in a minute." We Dutch laughed a little about this, and thought he would too, for we know him well and have always worked well together. However, he was extremely offended. We are sorry for our tactlessness but also surprised at his sensitivity.

His reaction is not hard to account for. There is a lot of prestige involved in how well you speak a foreign language, and if the corporate language is English but it isn't your native language, you can feel threatened if you are concerned that your English isn't up to standard. And when people feel threatened, they can become both defensive and aggressive. Speaking a foreign language means that, like it or not, you have to give a public display of how well you command one of the most important tools of your profession, and that can be a nerve-wracking experience.

The standard of English in the Netherlands and in Northern Europe is extremely high, and this fact may have made your French colleague's reaction worse. Until relatively recently the French have not taken English-language learning seriously (although they have not been as bad as the British and Americans about learning foreign languages). He may have been able to accept a native speaker's superiority, but to have another non-native speaker laughing at his errors was humiliating.

Letters 17–18

There are many countries with more than one national language and most nations have linguistic minorities. To forget these facts is to show an unacceptable degree of ignorance of the culture you are dealing with.

One Country—Two Languages   Letter 17

From BRAZIL about CANADA

> I'll be going to Quebec soon but speak only English. How important is it to be able to speak French as well?

I'd take at least a few lessons in French if you intend to do a lot of business in Canada, for this is one country where English is not regarded simply as an efficient tool for international business communication. Instead, it's regarded by some of its French-speaking citizens as a symbol of the oppression by the English-speaking majority of the French-speaking minority.

Canada is divided into ten different provinces, and they have both French and English as their official languages. Today you will find both languages on maps, tourist brochures, and product labels. Historically there has been friction between the French-speaking Québécois and the English-speaking people who have surrounded them for centuries. The Québécois have seen French speakers in other provinces become assimilated into the English-speaking culture, and they take great pains to preserve their language and culture so the same thing doesn't happen to them. So if Quebec is your destination I suggest learning as much French as possible before departure, both as a goodwill gesture and as a survival measure in case you meet some of the Québécois who can't or won't speak English. But be warned: The French they speak in Canada is not the same as that spoken in France, and even some of the English you hear in Québec may be unfamiliar, as many French words have been incorporated into the English they speak there.

One Country—Several Languages   Letter 18

From AUSTRALIA about BELGIUM

> I will probably be traveling to Belgium in the near future. I speak elementary French and my native language is English. Will that be enough?

A lot depends on where in Belgium you are going, for despite its small size and population of around 10 million, there are two completely different languages spoken. In Flanders, the northern part of the country, the people speak Flemish, which is a variation of Dutch, and all employers in Flanders are required by law to use Flemish in the workplace.

In Wallonia, the southern part of the country, they speak French, as do many of the inhabitants of Brussels. For Belgians, which language they speak is very much a part of their national identity. The situation in the country is made even more complicated because many Walloons cannot speak Flemish and some Flemish people are reluctant to speak French! However, in the capital about a quarter of the residents are non-Belgian, so there English is increasingly accepted. Be grateful that English is your native language, because it can be regarded as a sort of "neutral territory" outside the political and historical issues that otherwise make the language question in Belgium such a hot potato.

Letters 19–20

There are many different "Englishes," two of which are described here.

British versus U.S. English   Letter 19

From FRANCE about the U.S.

> I've recently come back from the U.S. where I attended a conference. One lecture dealt with different human resources issues, and I was surprised to hear the term *attrition* used in this context. The only time I've heard it before is in war of *attrition,* meaning a war involving total destruction of the enemy. When I got home I checked in my English dictionary and found *attrition* means "the state of wearing away." I'm none the wiser!

I'm not surprised. This is an excellent example of what George Bernard Shaw meant when he wrote "England and America are two countries separated by the same language." I imagine you learned British English rather than American, and there is a little area where the two don't correspond. Don't be alarmed: *Attrition* doesn't refer to a particularly drastic (and permanent) way of getting rid of unwanted staff! It's a human resources term describing the process by which people leave their jobs at a company when they move to another position, retire, decide to study, and so on and are not replaced. The term for the same phenomenon in England is *natural wastage* (which most Americans think sounds like some sort of sewerage system).

Don't blame your dictionary. Apart from the British-English and American-English differences, the English language is in a constant state of change and dictionaries cannot possibly keep up with all developments.

"International English" for Presentations   Letter 20

*From the U.S. about **the Rest of the World***

> I'm used to giving presentations in the U.S., but I will soon be going abroad for the first time. I'll be presenting information in a number of different countries where I guess most people do not speak English as their first language. Are there any changes I should make to my presentations to adapt them?

Speaking to non-native English speakers certainly requires extra thought, although in certain parts of Asia, for example, Singapore and Hong Kong, which are former British colonies, people may speak English as a first language.

To give a clear message speak slowly and clearly and pause often. In addition, use a tape recorder or ask someone not from your own hometown to establish whether you have a strong accent and if you do, try to tone it down. It's important to be confident and believe in what you are presenting, but make sure you don't come over as too loud (aggressive) or too relaxed (casual). In the more restrained cultures of Eastern Asia or Northern Europe you could appear to be trying to dominate your audience.

To give non-English native speakers a chance to absorb the key facts, repeat your main points in different ways. Try not to use sports metaphors. Violent metaphors are also inappropriate, especially in cultures that value gentle and controlled behavior, so don't use phrases like "bite the bullet," "twist your arm," or "ride roughshod over someone."

If you want your listeners to understand you, avoid the latest buzzwords, idioms, and slang. The use of initials and abbreviations can also be confusing, so use the full form instead. Two more things: don't use even the mildest swear words, and be careful in your use of humor.

It would also be wise to avoid using hand gestures to illustrate a point as they may not be interpreted the same way internationally. One example would be the way a Mexican speaker brought a presentation to a speedy halt in the U.K. by indicating the number two by two raised fingers with the back of his hand facing the audience. He had inadvertently told his British audience to f*** off.

What you *should* do is to make sure that you take plenty of visual material, as this can remove the need for words, and clarify points for people whose native language is not English. Another idea is to distribute written information (in English or the home language) before the meeting so participants have time to read it and translate it if necessary. Remember that it is hard work listening to a foreign language, so keep your presentation shorter than you would at home and make sure you have lots of breaks. This also gives people the chance to ask you questions, something they may not wish to do in front of a large audience if their English is shaky, or if they feel such questions would entail a loss of face by revealing they haven't followed everything you have said.

And a final word of advice: If you don't already speak a foreign language, start to learn one. It will give you an insight into what your Asian colleagues are up against.

Letter 21

Native speakers of English have an enormous business advantage, but they should not misuse it, or they will cause resentment.

Sensitive Speakers Sought   Letter 21

From MEXICO about the U.K., the U.S., AUSTRALIA, etc.

> Why can't native English-speakers show a little more sensitivity in their dealings with non-English speakers? They often use their superiority in the language to dominate meetings, and if there are two or more present they speak far too fast and use words and expressions we are not familiar with.

Your question is a useful reminder to everyone who has English as his or her first language. People who speak no foreign languages themselves, and this includes many British and American people, often forget what a strain it is listening to a foreign tongue, and when speaking to foreigners they make no concessions when it comes to their choice of words. Not only that, they forget that their listeners may have learned to speak British RP (Received Pronunciation) or Network Standard American English at school and are not used to strong regional accents. Ironically, it's when non-native speakers speak really good English that the worst problems arise, for it's then that Aussies, Kiwis, or Brits forget they're talking to a foreigner and speak in exactly the same way they would to someone from back home, while their poor listeners struggle to keep up.

One of the most important things for native speakers to remember is to listen. Don't treat a person's silence as a sign for you to continue to speak, but wait. Your colleague has to formulate his or her ideas in a foreign language, and that takes time.

Letters 22–23

As long as there are different languages there will inevitably be problems with translation.

Language Mistake   Letter 22

From SOUTH KOREA about BRAZIL

> My company employed an agency to translate our material for the Brazilian market. We'd already sent away the material when we discovered that it had been written in Spanish and not Portuguese. Our Brazilian agents have told us that it's useless and they require new material. Are the languages really so different?

As well as being the language of Brazil, Portuguese is widely spoken in Venezuelan cities, and elsewhere in South America that Spanish isn't the primary language. It was lucky that your agents spotted the mistake before the material was printed, for national language forms a vital part of national identity, and not respecting this is asking for trouble. Spanish and Portuguese are closely related languages but they are far from being identical, and Brazilians dislike foreigners who do not appreciate this fact. I can imagine that a similar assumption about the inter-changeability of Swedish, Norwegian, and Danish or the different Chinese languages would cause the same sort of resentment. You really have no choice but to recall the Spanish version and provide a Portuguese version as quickly as possible. If you are interested in doing business in Brazil it would be wise to show an interest in, and a certain background knowledge of, the country so you avoid "putting your foot in it" again. You can consult appropriate books, and the Internet is a great source of useful information.

Interpreters   Letter 23

From MEXICO about **JAPAN**

> I'm going to be traveling to Japan with a small group of other managers. We don't speak Japanese and were wondering if we should take an interpreter with us, which would be very expensive, or if we can ask the Japanese firm if they can arrange one for us.

It depends on how much money is at stake. If you're hoping to build a solid long-term relationship that is going to earn your company a fat profit, then it's worth thinking about developing a working relationship with a fluent Japanese speaker (preferably a native speaker) who is bicultural as well as bilingual and knows what your company does.

You can hire an interpreter from an agency in Japan, but then you'd have to make sure you allowed sufficient time in Japan to get to know each other before you met your potential partners. She (most Japanese translators are female) needs to know in advance what ground the talks are going to cover so she can prepare herself. She also needs to become familiar with the communication style of the person or people she's translating for. One more thing: if you do decide to hire an interpreter in Japan, book her well in advance as there are not many Japanese-Spanish translators, and you may have to accept a Japanese-English substitute.

Asking the Japanese company to provide an interpreter may not be a good idea, because even though you can be quite sure she will translate the Japanese side's message correctly (she will probably know their business very well), there's no guarantee your message is going to be expressed as you intended. For example, she may not want to take on the responsibility of delivering a message from you that will not please her fellow citizens. They may not have heard the expression "Don't shoot the messenger," but many interpreters are only too familiar with the meaning behind it.

To minimize the possibilities of misunderstandings, have a written summary of the points you are going to make at the meeting translated and distributed *before* the meeting, and get a written summary of the proceedings translated into Japanese shortly *after* the meeting.

IN A NUTSHELL: *A Global Language?*

Global Business Standards

For native English speakers: learn at least one foreign language as well as you can.
For non-native English speakers: learn English as well as you can.
For everyone: learn a few words of the language of any country you visit and of any foreign visitor you are going to meet.

- **Argentina:** The official language is Spanish, but it is influenced somewhat by Italian. (See Letters 15 and 22.)
- **Australia:** The language is influenced by both British and American English, but it has a distinctive accent and a special Aussie vocabulary. (See Letter 21.)
- **Austria:** German is spoken with a distinctive accent.
- **Belgium:** Official languages are Flemish (similar to Dutch), French, and German. The language spoken is closely tied to a person's ethnicity, and group loyalty is strong. (See Letters 15 and 18.)
- **Brazil:** Portuguese is spoken here—not Spanish like most of the rest of South America. (See Letters 15 and 22.)
- **Canada:** There are two official languages: English and French. The language spoken is closely tied to a person's ethnicity, and group loyalty is strong. (See Letters 15, 17, and 21.)
- **China:** The official spoken language is Mandarin, a language based on tones. It is also the only form of written language. In some provinces people speak one of four major dialects, but these aren't understood by speakers of the other dialects. (See Letter 20.)
- **Denmark:** Danish is almost indistinguishable to Norwegian in written form. Norwegians, Danes, and Swedes can often understand each other.
- **Finland:** The language is similar to Hungarian (!). In some areas Finns also speak Swedish.
- **France:** You are judged according to how well you speak French, and your command of the language is seen as an indicator of your education and intelligence. There is a big difference between using the familiar *tu* (informal) and the more formal *vous*. (See Letters 15 and 16.)
- **Germany:** There is a big difference between using the familiar *Du* and the formal *Sie*.
- **Hong Kong:** English, Cantonese, and Mandarin are widely spoken. (See Letter 20.)
- **India:** There are eighteen official languages and about as many dialects distributed geographically (e.g., Hindi, Punjabi, and Gujarati, and Urdu, which is spoken mostly by Muslim minority). English is widely spoken by educated people. Many people are bilingual or multilingual.

- **Indonesia:** There are more than 300 ethnic languages. Bahasa Indonesia, the major unifying language, is adapted from Bhasa Melayu (Malay). (See Letter 20.)
- **Italy:** About 60 percent of Italians speak a dialect, which may be impossible for other Italians to understand. The vast majority also speaks standard Italian.
- **Japan:** Spoken Japanese and Chinese are quite different. Basic literacy requires mastery of three alphabets, one of which is derived from Chinese and contains about two thousand characters. (See Letters 20 and 23.)
- **Mexico:** Spanish is spoken by 98 percent of the population. (See Letters 15 and 21.)
- **Netherlands:** Dutch is spoken. It is almost identical to Flemish, which is spoken in Belgium. It is also the ancestor of South Africa's Afrikaans. The Dutch are some of the best speakers of English as a foreign language in the world. (See Letter 16.)
- **Norway:** There are two distinct and rival versions of Norwegian. Norwegian is almost indistinguishable to Danish in written form. Norwegians, Danes, and Swedes can often understand each other.
- **Poland:** Polish is a Slavic language, but unlike Russian, it uses the Latin script.
- **Russia:** Russian uses the Cyrillic alphabet. Words are pronounced as they are spelled. Russian is spoken by most people, but Russia is made up of about a hundred ethnic groups, many with their own languages.
- **Saudi Arabia:** Arabic is the official language of the country and is widely spoken in the whole region. (See Letter 15.)
- **South Africa:** There are eleven official languages. English, Afrikaans (related to Dutch), and Zulu are the main ones.
- **South Korea:** Compared to Chinese and Japanese, the alphabet is easy to learn. Foreign (English) words are readily integrated into Korean. There is much pressure on young Koreans to learn English. (See Letters 20 and 22.)
- **Spain:** The Castilian dialect is the accepted standard. There are also three regional languages. Catalan (as well as Castilian) is spoken widely in Barcelona, Spain's second-largest city. There are some differences from the Spanish of Latin America. (See Letter 15.)
- **Sweden:** A sharp intake of breath can mean *yes*. Norwegians, Danes, and Swedes can often understand each other. (See Letter 15.)
- **Switzerland:** There are four official languages and most Swiss speak at least two fluently. The result of the most recent census shows the breakdown of first language speakers as follows: (Swiss) German 63.9%, French 19.5%, Italian 6.6%, Romansh 0.5%, others 9.5%.
- **Taiwan:** Mandarin is the official language, but 70 percent of the population speaks Southern Fujianese, often called Taiwanese. They do not use the modernized Chinese script currently used in China.
- **Thailand:** Like Chinese, Thai is a tonal language. The written script is based on ancient Indian languages. Fellow Thais usually understand regional and ethnic dialects. (See Letter 20.)

- **Turkey:** Turkey is an oral culture. What is said and heard is taken more seriously than what is written.
- **U.K.:** Differences between British and American English may lead to misunderstandings. (See Letters 15, 19, 20, and 21.)
- **U.S.:** Differences between British and American English may lead to misunderstandings. Spanish is widely spoken by Latin American immigrants in southern states and California. (See Letters 15, 19, 20, and 21.)
- **Venezuela:** Spanish is spoken. There is a distinctive Venezuelan accent, and some specifically Venezuelan vocabulary exists. In major cities Portuguese is quite common. (See Letters 15 and 22.)

Part 3

Business and Technical Correspondence

Traditionally, business and technical correspondence has taken two forms: the letter and the memo. More recently, it has assumed a third electronic form, e-mail. This electronic innovation has brought with it a myriad of issues, most of which unfortunately remain unresolved. There has increasingly been plenty of discussion of, but little agreement about, the etiquette of e-mail—or netiquette.

In the past, business and technical correspondence *seemed* easier on some levels: letters went to people outside of the company; memos, to people inside the company. Letters were advertisements for writers and their companies. Memos provided a record of decisions made and actions taken within a department of a company.

Letters and memos announce or reaffirm policies, confirm decisions and conversations, and send or request information. Some letters and memos are routine; others concern pressing issues. In either case, letters and memos require careful writing.

Given the volume of correspondence many companies produce, it is easy for business and technical writers to be tempted to use shortcuts when writing. Looking for a shortcut can, however, court danger if the shortcut involves relying on form responses or copies of previous—though not necessarily good examples of—similar correspondence.

There is nothing wrong with form messages be they letters, memos or e-mail, as long as such correspondence is appropriate to the given writing situation.

A simple message reminding customers of bills past due or transmitting attached data is often an effective and time-efficient way to communicate—provided such messages are appropriate to the situations and audiences with which they are used.

The danger with form messages is that they can become a crutch that writers depend on even in situations in which they are inappropriate. Such misuse of form letters, memos, and e-mails can create new problems for writers. Writers may have to send a follow-up message to fix what they tried to do in the first piece of correspondence. Or worse, they might have to send *several* follow-up messages.

A process approach to business and technical correspondence will help determine when form messages are appropriate and when something more original is required. The careful use of the writing process can also make follow-ups unnecessary.

The advent of electronic correspondence would seem to offer a boon to business and technical writers, but every silver lining has its cloud. The ease with which electronic correspondence can be transmitted has led some writers to become more casual—if not careless and sloppy—in their electronic correspondence than they would be in producing correspondence in the more traditional forms of letters and memos.

Electronic correspondence can be sent efficiently and effectively within and outside companies and businesses to multiple audiences, even those across the globe. At the same time, a misstatement, a mistake, or an unintended slight can suddenly be transmitted to a very large global audience—an audience at times even much larger than the original, intended audience—making the writer look foolish, or worse, look foolish to a large body of readers. Just ask an internationally known electronics retailer that decided to lay off a number of employees using the following e-mail message:

> The workforce reduction notification is currently in progress. Unfortunately your position is one that has been eliminated.

Forgetting for a moment that such a message is no way to handle employee dismissals, this e-mail was subsequently posted on the worldwide Web by someone, picked up by the newswires, and soon turned into a major international public relations fiasco for the company.

As I indicated earlier, there is yet no established or generally adopted etiquette for electronic correspondence. In the absence of such etiquette, writers would be wise to be conservative in such correspondence, adhering closely to the rules and principles that work so well for letters and memos. Whether the product is a letter, a memo, or an electronic message, a process approach is the safest approach for a writer to take.

The selections in this part of *Strategies* follow a decidedly process-oriented approach to business and technical correspondence in all forms. Sharon J. Gerson and Steven M. Gerson begin this section of *Strategies* with an overview of when to use which form of written communication for what purposes. The Gersons use the term "communication channel" in distinguishing when it is appropriate to use memos, when it is better to use letters, and when it is safe to rely on e-mail and other forms of electronic communication, such as instant messaging.

Readers in the world of work are impatient with people who waste their time, and David V. Lewis offers some suggestions on how to write to people effectively and efficiently; he shows business writers how to save their readers' time while also selling themselves and the organizations and companies that they represent through their correspondence.

Saying "no" is, of course, always difficult and presents special problems for writers. As Allan A. Glatthorn suggests, writers can say "no" in their correspondence and still keep clients, make friends, or even develop further business contacts. Complementing the initial essay in this section of *Strategies*, John S. Fielden and Ronald E. Dulek then suggest a model for efficient professional writing, no matter what form the writing may take.

Sharon J. Gerson and Steven M. Gerson

The Importance of Memos, Letters, and E-mail

Sharon J. Gerson and Steven M. Gerson are noted educators, authors, and consultants in the field of business communication.

WHICH COMMUNICATION CHANNEL SHOULD YOU USE?

Memos, letters, and e-mail messages are three common types of communication channels. [Table 1 shows the significance of e-mails, memos, and letters in the workplace.] Other communication channels include reports, Web sites, blogs, PowerPoint presentations, oral communication, and instant messages. When should you write an e-mail message instead of a memo? When should you write a memo instead of a letter? Is an instant message appropriate to the situation? You will make these decisions based on your audience (internal or external), the complexity of your topic, the speed with which your message can be delivered, and security concerns.

For example, e-mail is a convenient communication channel. It is easy to write a short e-mail message, which can be sent almost instantaneously to your audience at the click of a button. However, e-mail might not be the best communication channel to use. If you are discussing a highly sensitive topic such as a pending merger, corporate takeover, or layoffs, an e-mail message would be less secure than a letter sent in a sealed envelope.

You might need to communicate with employees working in a manufacturing warehouse. Not all of these employees will necessarily have an office or access to a computer. If you sent an e-mail message, how would they access this correspondence? A memo posted in the break room would be a better choice of communication channel.

THE DIFFERENCES AMONG MEMOS, LETTERS, AND E-MAIL

To clarify the distinctions among memos, letters, and e mail, review Table 1.

TABLE I Memos versus Letters versus E-mails

Characteristics	Memos	Letters	E-mail
Destination	Internal: correspondence written to colleagues within a company.	External: correspondence written outside the business.	Internal *and* external: correspondence written to friends and acquaintances, coworkers within a company, and clients and vendors.
Format	Identification lines include "Date," "To," "From," and "Subject," The message follows.	Includes letterhead address, date, reader's address, salutation, text, complimentary close, and signatures.	Identification lines: To and subject. The Date and From are computer generated. Options include cc (complimentary copy), Ref (reference), and Distribution (other recipients of the e-mail message).
Audience	Generally high tech or low tech, mostly business colleagues.	Generally low tech and lay readers, such as vendors, clients, stakeholders, and stockholders.	Multiple readers due to the internal and external nature of e-mail.
Topic	Generally topics related to internal corporate decisions; abbreviations and acronyms often allowed.	Generally topics related to vendor, client, stakeholder, and stockholder interests; abbreviations and acronyms usually defined.	A wide range of diverse topics determined by the audience.
Complexity and Length of Communication	Memos usually are limited to a page of text. If you need to write longer correspondence and develop a topic in more detail, you might consider using a different communication channel, such as a short report.	Letters usually are limited to a page of text, though you might write a two- or three-page report using a letter format. If you need to develop a topic in greater detail than can be conveyed in one to three pages, you might want to use a different communication channel, such as a longer, formal report.	An effective e-mail message usually is limited to one viewable screen (requiring no scrolling) or two screens. E-mail, generally, is not the best communication channel to use for complex information or long correspondence. If your topic demands more depth than can be conveyed in a screen or two, you might want to write a report instead.

(Continued)

Characteristics	Memos	Letters	E-mail
Tone	Informal due to peer audience.	More formal due to audience of vendors, clients, stakeholders, and stockholders.	A wide range of tones due to diverse audiences. Usually informal when written to friends, informal to coworkers, more formal to management.
Attachments or Enclosures	Hard-copy attachments can be stapled to the memo. Complimentary copies (cc) can be sent to other readers.	Additional information can be enclosed within the envelope. Complimentary copies can be sent to other readers.	Computer word processing files, HTML files and Web links, PDF files, RTF files, or downloadable graphics can be attached to e-mail. Complimentary copies (cc) can be sent to other readers. Size of these files is an issue, because large documents can crash a reader's system. A good rule is to limit files to 750 kilobytes (K).
Delivery Time	Determined by a company's in-house mail procedure.	Determined by the destination (within the city, state, or country). Letters could be delivered within 3 days but may take more than a week.	Often instantaneous, usually within minutes. Delays can be caused by system malfunctions or excessively large attachments.
Security	If a company's mail delivery system is reliable, the memo will be placed in the reader's mailbox. Then, what the reader sees on the hard-copy page will be exactly what the writer wrote. Security depends on the ethics of coworkers and whether the memo was sent in an envelope.	The U.S. Postal Service is very reliable. Once the reader opens the envelope, he or she sees exactly what the writer wrote. Privacy laws protect the letter's content.	E-mail systems are not secure. E-mail can be tampered with, read by others, and sent to many people. E-mail stays within a company's computer backup system and is the property of the company. Therefore, e-mail is not private.

FAQs: Memos vs. E-Mail

Q: Why write a memo? Haven't memos been replaced by e-mail?

A: E-mail is rapidly overtaking memos in the workplace, but employees still write memos for the following reasons.

1. Not all employees work in offices or have access to computers. Many employees who work in warehouses or in the field cannot easily access an e-mail account. They must depend on hard-copy documentation like memos.
2. Not all companies have e-mail. This may be hard to believe in the twenty-first century, but still it's a fact. These companies depend on hard-copy documentation like memos.
3. Many unions demand that hard-copy memos be posted on walls, in break rooms, in offices, and elsewhere, to ensure that all employees have access to important information. Sometimes, unions even demand that employees initial the posted memos, thus acknowledging that the memos have been read.
4. Some information cannot be transmitted electronically via e-mail. A bank we've worked with, for example, sends hard-copy cancelled checks as attachments to memos. They cannot send the actual cancelled check via e-mail.
5. E-mail messages are easy to disregard. We get so many e-mail messages (many of them spam) that we tend to quickly delete them. Memos, in contrast, make more of an official statement. People might take hard-copy memos more seriously than e-mail messages.

MEMOS

Reasons for Writing Memos

Memos are an important means by which employees communicate with each other. Memos, hard-copy correspondence written within your company, are important for several reasons.

First, you will write memos to a wide range of readers. This includes your supervisors, coworkers, subordinates, and multiple combinations of these audiences. Memos usually are copied (cc: complimentary copies) to many readers, so a memo sent to your boss could be read by an entire department, the boss's boss, and colleagues in other departments.

Because of their frequency and widespread audiences, memos could represent a major component of your interpersonal communication skills within your work environment.

Furthermore, memos are very flexible and can be written for many different purposes:

- **Documentation**—expenses, incidents, accidents, problems encountered, projected costs, study findings, hirings, firings, reallocations of staff or equipment
- **Confirmation**—a meeting agenda, date, time, and location; decisions to purchase or sell; topics for discussion at upcoming teleconferences; conclusions arrived at; fees, costs, or expenditures

- **Procedures**—how to set up accounts, research on the company intranet, operate new machinery, use new software, apply online for job opportunities through the company intranet, create a new company Web site, or solve a problem
- **Recommendations**—reasons to purchase new equipment, fire or hire personnel, contract with new providers, merge with other companies, revise current practices, or renew contracts
- **Feasibility**—studying the possibility of changes in the workplace (practices, procedures, locations, staffing, equipment, or missions/visions)
- **Status**—daily, weekly, monthly, quarterly, biannually, yearly statements about where you, the department, or the company is regarding many topics (sales, staffing, travel, practices, procedures, or finances)
- **Directive (delegation of responsibilities)**—informing subordinates of their designated tasks
- **Inquiry**—asking questions about upcoming processes or procedures
- **Cover**—prefacing an internal proposal, long report, or other attachments

Criteria for Writing Memos

Memos contain the following key components.

- Memo identification lines—Date, To, From, and Subject
- Introduction
- Discussion
- Conclusion
- Audience recognition
- Appropriate memo style and tone

Figure 1 shows an ideal, all-purpose organizational template that works well for memos, letters, and e-mail.

Introduction: A lead-in or overview stating *why* you are writing and *what* you are writing about.

Discussion: Detailed development, made accessible through highlighting techniques, explaining *exactly what*

-
-
-

Conclusion: State *what* is next, *when* this will occur, and *why* the date is important.

FIGURE I   All-Purpose Template for Memos, Letters, and E-mail

The memo checklist will give you the opportunity for self-assessment and peer evaluation of your writing. Input from peers can be an important way for you to gauge the response to your memo, determine if content should be added or deleted, and check for correctness.

MEMO CHECKLIST

___ 1. Does the memo contain identification lines (Date, To, From, and Subject)?

___ 2. Does the subject line contain a topic and a focus?

___ 3. Does the introduction clearly state
- Why this memo has been written?
- What topic the memo is discussing?

___ 4. Does the body explain exactly what you want to say?

___ 5. Does the conclusion
- Tell when you plan a follow-up or when you want a response?
- Explain why this dated action is important?

___ 6. Are highlighting techniques used effectively for document design?

___ 7. Is the memo concise?

___ 8. Is the memo clear,
- Achieving specificity of detail?
- Answering reporter's questions?

___ 9. Does the memo recognize audience,
- Defining acronyms or abbreviations where necessary for various levels of readers (high tech, low tech and lay)?

___ 10. Did you avoid grammatical errors? Errors will hurt your professionalism. . . .

FAQs: Letters vs. E-Mail

Q: Why write a letter? Haven't letters been replaced by e-mail?

A: Though e-mail is quick, it might not be the best communication channel, for the following reasons.

1. E-mail might be too quick. In the workplace, you will write about topics that require a lot of thought. Because e-mail messages can be written and sent quickly, people too often write hurriedly and neglect to consider the impact of the message.

2. E-mail messages tend to be casual, conversational, and informal. Not all correspondence, however, lends itself to this level of informality. Formal correspondence related to contracts, for example, requires the more formal communication channel of a letter. The same applies to audience. You might want to write a casual e-mail to a coworker, but if you were writing to the president of a company, the mayor of a city, or a foreign dignitary, a letter would be a better, more formal choice of communication channel.

3. E-mail messages tend to be short. For content requiring more detail, a longer letter would be a better choice.

4. We get so many e-mail messages a day that they are easy to disregard—even easy to delete. Letters carry more significance. If you want to ensure that your correspondence is read and perceived as important, you might want to write a letter instead of an e-mail.

5. Letters allow for a "greater paper trail" than e-mail. Most employees' e-mail inboxes fill up quickly. To clean these inboxes up, people tend to delete messages that they don't consider important. In contrast, hard-copy letters are wonderful documentation.

LETTERS

Reasons for Writing Letters

Letters are external correspondence that you send from your company to a colleague working at another company, a vendor, a customer, a prospective employee, and stake-holders and stockholders. Letters leave your work site (as opposed to memos, which stay within the company).

Because letters are sent to readers in other locations, your letters not only reflect your communication abilities but also are a reflection of your company. This section provides letter components, formats, criteria, and examples to help you write . . . [various] kinds of letters:. . . .

Essential Components of Letters

Your letter should be typed or printed on $8\frac{1}{2} \times 11$ inch paper. Leave 1 to $1\frac{1}{2}$ inch margins at the top and on both sides. Choose an appropriately businesslike font (size and style), such as Times New Roman or Arial (12 point). Though "designer fonts," such as Comic Sans and Shelley Volante, are interesting, they tend to be harder to read and less professional.

Your letter should contain the essential components shown in Figure 2.

Writer's Address. This section contains either your personal address or your company's address. If the heading consists of your address, then you will include your street address, the city, state, and zip code. The state may be abbreviated with the appropriate two-letter abbreviation.

If the heading consists of your company's address, you will include the company's name, street address, and city, state, and zip code.

Date. Document the month, day, and year when you write your letter. You can write your date in one of two ways: May 31, 2008 or 31 May 2008. Place the date one or two spaces below the writer's address.

Reader's Address. Place the reader's address two lines below the date.

- Reader's name (If you do not know the name of this person, begin the reader's address with a job title or the name of the department.)
- Reader's title (optional)
- Company name
- Street address
- City, state, and zip code

Salutation. The traditional salutation, placed two spaces beneath the reader's address, is *Dear* and your reader's last name, followed by a colon (Dear Mr. Smith:).

You can also address your reader by his or her first name if you are on a first-name basis with this person (Dear John:). If you are writing to a woman and are

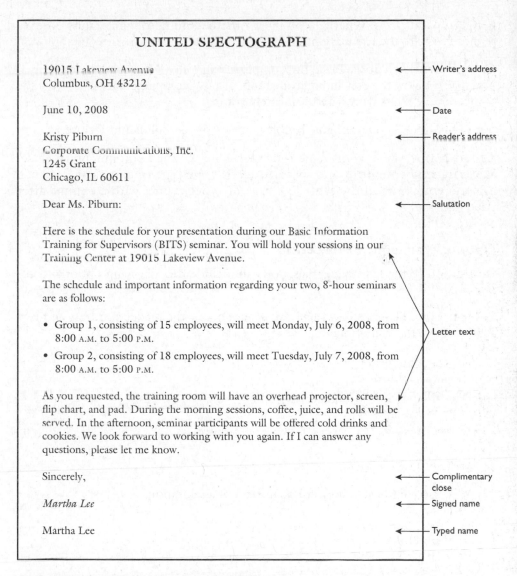

FIGURE 2   Essential Letter Components

unfamiliar with her marital status, address the letter *Dear Ms. Jones*. However, if you know the woman's marital status, you can address the letter accordingly (Dear Miss Jones *or* Dear Mrs. Jones:).

Letter Body. Begin the body of the letter two spaces below the salutation. The body includes your introductory paragraph, discussion paragraph(s), and concluding paragraph. The body should be single spaced with double spacing between paragraphs. Whether you indent the beginning of paragraphs or leave them flush with the left margin is determined by the letter format you employ.

Complimentary Close. Place the complimentary close, followed by a comma, two spaces below the concluding paragraph. Typical complimentary closes include "Sincerely," "Yours truly," and "Sincerely yours."

Signed Name. Sign your name legibly beneath the complimentary close.

Typed Name. Type your name four spaces below the complimentary close. You can type your title one space beneath your typed name. You also can include your title on the same line as your typed name, with a comma after your name.

Optional Components of Letters

In addition to the letter essentials, you can include the following optional components.

Subject Line. Place a subject line two spaces below the reader's address and two spaces above the salutation.

Dr. Ron Schaefer
Linguistics Department
Southern Illinois University
Edwardsville, IL 66205

Subject: Linguistics Conference Registration Payment

Dear Dr. Schaefer:

You also could use a subject line instead of a salutation.

Linguistics Department
Southern Illinois university
Edwardsville, IL 66205

Subject: Linguistics Conference Registration Payment

A subject line not only helps readers understand the letter's intent but also (if you are uncertain of your reader's name) avoids such awkward salutations as "To Whom It May Concern," "Dear Sirs," and "Ladies and Gentlemen." In the simplified format, both the salutation and the complimentary close are omitted, and a subject line is included.

New-Page Notations.   If your letter is longer than one page, cite your name, the page number, and the date on all pages after page 1. Place this notation either flush with the left margin at the top of subsequent pages or across the top of subsequent pages. (You must have at least two lines of text on the next page to justify another page.)

Left margin, subsequent page notation   Across top of subsequent pages

Mabel Tinjaca   Mabel Tinjaca   2   May 31, 2008
Page 2
May 31. 2008

Writer's and Typist's Initials. If the letter was typed by someone other than the writer, include both the writer's and the typist's initials two spaces below the typed signature. The writer's initials are capitalized, the typist's initials are typed in lowercase, and the two sets of initials are separated by a colon. If the typist and the writer are the same person, this notation is not necessary.

Sincerely,

W. T. Winnery

WTW: mm

Enclosure Notation. If your letter prefaces enclosed information, such as an invoice or report, mention this enclosure in the letter and then type an enclosure notation two spaces below the typed signature (or two spaces below the writer and typist initials). The enclosure notation can be abbreviated "Enc."; written out as "Enclosure"; show the number of enclosures, such as "Enclosures (2)"; or specify what has been enclosed—"Enclosure: January Invoice."

Copy Notation. If you have sent a copy of your letter to other readers, show this in a copy notation. A complimentary copy is designated by a lowercase "cc." List the other readers' names following the copy notation. Type the copy notation two spaces below the typed signature or two spaces below either the writer's and typist's initials or the enclosure notation.

Sincerely,

Brian Altman
Enclosure: August Status Report
cc: Marcia Rittmaster and Larry Rochelle

Formatting Letters

Three common types of letter formats include full block (Figure 3), full block with subject line (Figure 4), and simplified (Figure 5) [pp. 130–132]. Two popular and professional formats used in business are full block and full block with subject line. With both formats, you type all information at the left margin without indenting

1 to 1 1/2 inch
margins on all
sides of the letter

State Health Department

1890 Clark Road
Jefferson City, MO 67220

2–4 spaces above
and below the
date

June 6, 2008

Dale McGraw, Manager
Elmwood Mobile Home Park
Elmwood, MO 64003

2–4 spaces above
and below the
salutation

Dear Mr. McGraw:

Single space
within the
paragraphs.
Double space
between the
paragraphs.

On April 19, 2008, Ryan Duran and I, environmental specialists from the Health Department, conducted an inspection of the Elmwood Mobile Home Park Wastewater Treatment Facility. The purpose was to assess compliance with the following: the state's Clean Water Law, Clean Water Commission regulations, and your facility's plan for pollution control. The inspection also would allow the state to promote proper operation of Wastewater Facilities and to provide technical assistance where needed to the Elmwood Mobile Homes management.

Though the Elmwood Mobile Home pollution control plan had expired in 2007, a consent judgment was issued by the state's Attorney Generals Office. The county court stipulated a timeline for correction by connection to an available sewer system. Your mobile home park's wastewater system has continually discharged to the Little Osage River. A copy of the abatement order, which requires that monthly discharge monitoring reports (DMRs) be submitted by the 28th of the month following the reporting periods, is attached. All DMRs for the previous twelve months have been received, and reported pollution parameters are not within limits. Due to the plant's performance, the stream was placed on the 2000, 303 (d) stream for impairment by the Elmwood Mobile Home.

As part of the inspection, a review of the facility's DMR was conducted. Twenty-four-hour composite samples were collected using a composite sampler. Attached are the results of the 24-hour composite samples collected on April 20, 2008. Every one of the problems documented is an infraction that must be addressed.

Within 30 days of receipt of this letter, please submit to the Health Department written documentation describing steps taken to correct each of the concerns identified in the attachments. Also include engineering reports, and submit a timeframe to eliminate the problems. Thank you for your cooperation.

2 spaces before
"Sincerely"

Sincerely,

4 spaces between
"Sincerely" and
the typed signature

Harvey Haddix
Environmental Manager

Attachment

FIGURE 3   Full Block Format

State Health Department
1890 Clark Road   Jefferson City, MO 67220

June 6, 2008

Dale McGraw, Manager
Elmwood Mobile Home Park
Elmwood, MO 64003

Subject: Pollution Control Inspection

Dear Mr. McGraw:

On April 19, 2008, Ryan Duran and I, environmental specialists from the Health Department, conducted an inspection of the Elmwood Mobile Home Park Wastewater Treatment Facility. The purpose was to assess compliance with the following: the state's Clean Water Law, Clean Water Commission regulations, and your facility's plan for pollution control. The inspection also would allow the state to promote proper operation of Wastewater Facilities and to provide technical assistance where needed to the Elmwood Mobile Homes management.

Though the Elmwood Mobile Home pollution control plan had expired in 2007, a consent judgment was issued by the state's Attorney Generals Office. The county court stipulated a timeline for correction by connection to an available sewer system. Your mobile home park's wastewater system has continually discharged to the Little Osage River. A copy of the abatement order, which requires that monthly discharge monitoring reports (DMRs) be submitted by the 28th of the month following the reporting periods, is attached. All DMRs for the previous twelve months have been received, and reported pollution parameters are not within limits. Due to the plant's performance, the stream was placed on the 2000, 303 (d) stream for impairment by the Elmwood Mobile Home.

As part of the inspection, a review of the facility's DMR was conducted. Twenty-four-hour composite samples were collected using a composite sampler. Attached are the results of the 24-hour composite samples collected on April 20, 2008. Every one of the problems documented is an infraction that must be addressed.

Within 30 days of receipt of this letter, please submit to the Health Department written documentation describing steps taken to correct each of the concerns identified in the attachments. Also include engineering reports, and submit a timeframe to eliminate the problems. Thank you for your cooperation.

Sincerely,

Harvey Haddix
Environmental Manager

Attachment

FIGURE 4   Full Block Format with Subject Line

State Health Department
1890 Clark Road
Jefferson City, MO 67220

June 6, 2008

Dale McGraw, Manager
Elmwood Mobile Home Park
Elmwood, MO 64003

Subject: Pollution Control Inspection

On April 19, 2008, Ryan Duran and I, environmental specialists from the Health Department, conducted an inspection of the Elmwood Mobile Home Park Wastewater Treatment Facility. The purpose was to assess compliance with the following: the state's Clean Water Law, Clean Water Commission regulations, and your facility's plan for pollution control. The inspection also would allow the state to promote proper operation of Wastewater Facilities and to provide technical assistance where needed to the Elmwood Mobile Homes management.

Though the Elmwood Mobile Home pollution control plan had expired in 2007, a consent judgment was issued by the state's Attorney Generals Office. The county court stipulated a timeline for correction by connection to an available sewer system. Your mobile home park's wastewater system has continually discharged to the Little Osage River. A copy of the abatement order, which requires that monthly discharge monitoring reports (DMRs) be submitted by the 28th of the month following the reporting periods, is attached. All DMRs for the previous twelve months have been received, and reported pollution parameters are not within limits. Due to the plant's performance, the stream was placed on the 2000, 303 (d) stream for impairment by the Elmwood Mobile Home.

As part of the inspection, a review of the facility's DMR was conducted. Twenty-four-hour composite samples were collected using a composite sampler. Attached are the results of the 24-hour composite samples collected on April 20, 2008. Every one of the problems documented is an infraction that must be addressed.

Within 30 days of receipt of this letter, please submit to the Health Department written documentation describing steps taken to correct each of the concerns identified in the attachments. Also include engineering reports, and submit a timeframe to eliminate the problems. Thank you for your cooperation.

Harvey Haddix
Environmental Manager

Attachment

FIGURE 5   Simplified Format Omitting "Dear . . ." and "Sincerely"

paragraphs, the date, the complimentary close, or signature. The full block with subject line differs only with the inclusion of a subject line.

Another option is the simplified format. This type of letter layout is similar to the full block format in that all text is typed margin left. The two significant omissions include no salutation ("Dear _____:") and no complimentary close ("Sincerely,"). Omitting a salutation is useful in the following instances:

- You do not know your reader's name (NOTE: Avoid the trite salutation, "To Whom It May Concern:")
- You are writing to someone with a nongender-specific name (Jesse, Terry, Stacy, Chris, etc.) and you do not know whether to use "Mr.," "Mrs.," or "Ms." . . .

The Administrative Management Society (AMS) suggests that if you omit the salutation, you also should omit the complimentary close. Some people feel that omitting the salutation and the complimentary close will make the letter cold and unfriendly. However, the AMS says that if your letter is warm and friendly, these omissions will not be missed. More importantly, if your letter's content is negative, beginning with "Dear" and ending with "Sincerely" will not improve the letter's tone or your reader's attitude toward your comments. . . .

LETTERS CHECKLIST

___ 1. **Letter Essentials:** Does your letter include the eight essential components (writer's address, date, recipient's address, salutation, text, complimentary close, writer's signed name, and writer's typed name)?

___ 2. **Introduction:** Does the introduction state *what* you are writing about and *why* you are writing?

___ 3. **Discussion:** Does your discussion clearly state the details of your topic depending on the type of letter?

___ 4. **Highlighting/Page Layout:** Is your text accessible? To achieve reader-friendly ease of access, use headings, boldface, italics, bullets, numbers, underlining, or graphics (tables and figures). These add interest and help your readers navigate your letter.

___ 5. **Organization:** Have you helped your readers follow your train of thought by using appropriate modes of organization? These include chronology, importance, problem/solution, or comparison/contrast.

___ 6. **Conclusion:** Does your conclusion give directive action (tell what you want the reader to do next and when) and end positively?

___ 7. **Clarity:** Is your letter clear, answering . . . [the reader's] questions and providing specific details that inform, instruct, or persuade?

___ 8. **Conciseness:** Have you limited the length of your words, sentences, and paragraphs?

___ 9. **Audience Recognition:** Have you written appropriately to your audience? This includes avoiding biased language, considering the multicultural/cross-cultural nature of your readers, and your audience's role (supervisors, subordinates, coworkers, customers, or vendors). Have you created a positive tone to build rapport?

___ 10. **Correctness:** Is your text grammatically correct? Errors will hurt your professionalism. . . .

E-MAIL

Why Is E-mail Important?

E-mail (electronic mail) is different from hard-copy memos and letters in many ways. The primary difference is that people read online text differently than they read hard-copy text. E-mail has become a predominant means of routine correspondence. Many companies are "geared to operate with e-mail," creating what the Harvard Business school calls "e-mail cultures" for the following reasons ("The Transition to General Management." Harvard Business School. 1998. November 12, 2002. www.hbs.edu/gm/index.html).

Time. "Everything is driven by time. You have to use what is most efficient" (Carolyn Miller, et al. "Communication in the Workplace." *Center for Communication in Science, Technology, and Management.* October 1996, 10). The primary driving force behind e-mail's prominence is time. E-mail is quick. Whereas a posted letter might take several days to deliver, e-mail messages can be delivered within seconds.

FAQs: Professionalism in E-Mail Messages

Q: E-mail messages are just casual communication, right? So writing an e-mail message is easy, isn't it, since you don't have to worry about grammar or correct style?

A: Nothing could be further from the truth. E-mail might be your major means of communication in the workplace. Therefore, you must pay special attention to correctness.

Listen to what managers at an engineering company say about e-mail messages:

- "Most business communication is now via e-mail. Business e-mail needs to be almost as formal and as carefully written as a letter because it is a formal and legal document. Never send an e-mail that you would not be comfortable seeing on the front page of a newspaper, because some day you may."
- "I see more and more new hires wanting to rely on e-mail. It is a totally ineffective way to resolve many issues on an engineering project. But they seem to feel it is OK for almost any communication. I suspect the general acceptance by their peers for this form of communication has led them to mistakenly assume the same is true for a business setting."
- "Many young people tend to be very 'social' in e-mails. Your employer owns your e-mails written on your work computers. They are NOT private. They can be used not only against you, but against your firm in court. For example, if I send an e-mail to a coworker that states in it somewhere what a lousy job Frank is doing on the such-and-such project and that project goes bad, it is possible that e-mail could end up in court and be used against my employer. In my mind all I was doing was venting my frustrations to an understanding friend and co-worker. But, in reality, I am creating a permanent record of anything I say."

Steven M. Gerson, et al. ("Core Competencies." Survey. Prentice Hall. 2004)

Convenience. With wireless communication, you can send e-mail from note-books to handhelds. Current communication systems combine a voice phone, personal digital assistant, and e-mail into a package that you can slip into a pocket or purse. Then, you can access your e-mail messages anywhere, anytime.

Internal/External. E-mail allows you to communicate internally to coworkers and externally to customers and vendors. Traditional communication channels, like letters and memos, have more limited uses. Generally, letters are external correspondence written from one company to another company; memos are internal correspondence transmitted within a company.

Cost. E-mail is cost effective because it is paper free. With an ability to attach files, you can send many kinds of documentation without paying shipping fees. This is especially valuable when considering international business.

Documentation. E-mail provides an additional value when it comes to documentation. Because so many writers merely respond to earlier e-mail messages, what you end up with is a "virtual paper trail" (Miller, 15). When e-mail is printed out, often the printout will contain dozens of e-mail messages, representing an entire string of dialogue. This provides a company an extensive record for future reference. In addition, most companies archive e-mail messages in backup files.

Reasons for Writing E-mail Messages

E-mail is used to convey many types of information in business and industry. You can write an e-mail message to accomplish any of the following purposes.

- **Directive**—inform a subordinate or a team of employees to complete a task.
- **Cover/transmittal**—inform a reader or readers that you have attached a document, and list the key points that are included in the attachment.
- **Documentation**—report on expenses, incidents, accidents, problems encountered, projected costs, study findings, hiring, firings, and reallocations of staff or equipment.
- **Confirmation**—inform a reader about a meeting agenda, date, time, and location; decisions to purchase or sell; topics for discussion at upcoming teleconferences; conclusions arrived at; fees, costs, or expenditures.
- **Procedures**—explain how to set up accounts, research on the company intranet, operate new machinery, use new software, apply online for job opportunities through the company intranet, create a new company Web site, or solve a problem.
- **Recommendations**—provide reasons to purchase new equipment, fire or hire personnel, contract with new providers, merge with other companies, revise current practices, or renew contracts.
- **Feasibility**—study the possibility of changes in the workplace (practices, procedures, locations, staffing, or equipment).
- **Status**—provide a daily, weekly, monthly, quarterly, biannual, or yearly report about where you, the department, or the company is regarding a topic of your choice (class project, sales, staffing, travel, practices, procedures, or finances).
- **Inquiry**—ask questions about upcoming processes, procedures, or assignments.

Techniques for Writing Effective E-mail Messages

To convey your messages effectively and to ensure that your e-mail messages reflect professionalism, follow these tips for writing e-mail.

Recognize Your Audience. E-mail messages can be sent to managers, coworkers, subordinates, vendors, and customers, among other audiences. Your e-mail readers will be high tech, low tech, and lay people. Thus, you must factor in levels of knowledge.

If an e-mail message is sent internationally, you also might have to consider your readers' language. Remember that abbreviations and acronyms are not universal. Dates, times, measurements, and monetary figures differ from country to country. . . . In addition, your reader's e-mail system might not have the same features or capabilities that you have. Hard-copy text will look the same to all readers. E-mail platforms, such as in AOL, Outlook, Juno, HotMail, and Yahoo, display text differently. To communicate effectively, recognize your audience's level of knowledge, unique language, and technology needs.

Identify Yourself. Identify yourself by name, affiliation, or title. You can accomplish this either in the "From" line of your e-mail or by creating a signature file or .sig file. This .sig file acts like an online business card. Once this identification is complete, readers will be able to open your e-mail without fear of corrupting their computer systems.

Provide an Effective Subject Line. Readers are unwilling to open unsolicited or unknown e-mail, due to fear of spam and viruses. In addition, corporate employees receive approximately 50 e-mail messages each day. They might not want to read every message sent to them. To ensure that your e-mail messages are read, avoid uninformative subject lines, such as "Hi," "What's New," or "Important Message." Instead, include an effective subject line, such as "Subject: Meeting Dates for Tech Prep Conference."

Keep Your E-mail Message Brief. E-readers skim and scan. To help them access information quickly, "Apply the 'top of the screen' test. Assume that your readers will look at the first screen of your message only" (Mary Munter, et al. "Business E-Mail: Guidelines For Users." *Business Communication Quarterly* 66 (March 2003): 31). Limit your message to one screen (if possible).

Organize Your E-mail Message. Successful writing usually contains an introductory paragraph, a discussion paragraph or paragraphs, and a conclusion. Although many e-mail messages are brief, only a few sentences, you can use the introductory sentences to tell the reader why you are writing and what you are writing about. In the discussion, clarify your points thoroughly. Use the concluding sentences to tell the reader what is next, possibly explaining when a follow-up is required and why that date is important.

Use Highlighting Techniques Sparingly. Many e-mail packages will let you use highlighting techniques, such as boldface, italics, underlining, computer-generated bullets and numbers, centering, font color highlighting, and font color changes. Many other e-mail platforms will not display such visual enhancements. To avoid having parts of the message distorted, limit your highlighting to asterisks (*), numbers, double spacing, and all-cap headings.

Proofread Your E-mail Message. Errors will undermine your professionalism and your company's credibility. Recheck your facts, dates, addresses, and numerical information before you send the message. Try these tips to help you proofread an e-mail message.

- Type your text first in a word-processing package, such as Microsoft Word.
- Print it out. Sometimes it is easier to read hard-copy text than text online. Also, your word-processing package, with its spell check and/or grammar check, will help you proofread your writing.

Once you have completed these two steps (writing in Word or WordPerfect and printing out the hard-copy text), copy and paste the text from your word-processing file into your e-mail.

Make Hard Copies for Future Reference. Making hard copies of all e-mail messages is not necessary because most companies archive e-mail. However, in some instances, you might want to keep a hard copy for future reference. These instances could include transmissions of good news. For example, you have received compliments about your work and want to save this record for your annual job review. You also might save a hard copy of an e-mail message regarding flight, hotel, car rental, or conference arrangements for business-related travel.

Be Careful When Sending Attachment. When you send attachments, tell your reader within the body of the e-mail message that you have attached a file; specify the file name of your attachment and the software application that you have used (HTML, PowerPoint, PDF, RTF [rich text format], Word, or Works); and use compression (Zip) files to limit your attachment size. Zip files are necessary only if an attachment is quite large.

Practice Netiquette. When you write your e-mail messages, observe the rules of "netiquette."

- **Be courteous.** Do not let the instantaneous quality of e-mail negate your need to be calm, cool, deliberate, and professional.
- **Be professional.** Occasionally, e-mail writers compose excessively casual e-mail messages. They will lowercase a pronoun like "i," use ellipses (. . .) or dashes instead of more traditional punctuation, use instant messaging shorthand language such as "LOL," or "BRB," and depend on emoticons ☺☹. These e-mail techniques might not be appropriate in all instances. Don't forget that your e-mail messages represent your company's professionalism. Write according to the audience and communication goal.
- **Avoid abusive, angry e-mail messages.** Because of its quick turnaround abilities, e-mail can lead to negative correspondence called flaming. Flaming is sending angry e-mail, often TYPED IN ALL CAPS. . . .

E-MAIL CHECKLIST

___ 1. Does the e-mail use the correct address?

___ 2. Have you identified yourself? Provide a "sig" (signature) line.

___ 3. Did you provide an effective subject line? Include a *topic* and a *focus*.

___ 4. Have you effectively organized your e-mail?

Consider including the following:

- Opening sentence(s) telling *why* you are writing and *what* you are writing about.
- Discussion unit with itemized points telling *what exactly* the e-mail is discussing.
- Concluding sentence(s), *summing up* your e-mail message or telling your audience what to do next

___ 5. Have you used highlighting techniques sparingly?

- Avoid boldface, italics, color, or underlining.

- Use asterisks (*) for bullets, numbers, and double spacing for access.

___ 6. Did you practice netiquette?

- Be polite, courteous, and professional.
- Don't flame.

___ 7. Is the e-mail concise?

___ 8. Did you identify and limit the size of attachments?

- Tell your reader(s) if you have attached files and what types of files are attached (PPT, PDF, RTF, Word, etc.).
- Limit the files to 750 K.

___ 9. Does the memo recognize audience?

- Define acronyms or abbreviations where necessary.
- Consider a diverse audience (factoring in issues, such as multiculturalism or gender).

___ 10. Did you avoid grammatical errors?

INSTANT MESSAGING

E-mail could be too slow for today's fast-paced workplace. Instant messaging (IM) could replace e-mail in the workplace within the next five years. Studies suggest IM pop-ups are already providing businesses many benefits.

Benefits of Instant Messaging

Following are benefits of instant messaging.

- Increased speed of communication.
- Improved efficiency for geographically dispersed workgroups.
- Collaboration by multiple users in different locations.
- Communication with colleagues and customers at a distance in real time, such as the telephone.
- Avoidance of costly long distance telephone rates (Note: Voice-over IP [VoIP] services, which allow companies to use the Internet for telephone calls, could be more cost efficient than IM.)
- More "personal" link than e-mail.
- Communication channel that is less intrusive than telephone calls.

- Communication channel that allows for multitasking (With IM, you can speak to a customer on the telephone or via an e-mail message and *simultaneously* receive product updates from a colleague via IM.)
- Quick way to find out who is in the office, out of the office, available for conversation, or unavailable due to other activities. [Jeff Hoffman. "Instant Messaging in the Workplace." *Intercom* (February 2004): 16-17; Deb Shinder. "Instant Messaging: Does It Have a Place in Business Networks?" *WindowSecurity.com.* June 8, 2005. i.e. www.windowsecurity.com/articles/Instant-Messaging-Business-Networks.html.]

Challenges of Instant Messaging

For business purposes, IM is so new that corporate standards have not been formalized. Software companies have not yet redesigned IM home versions for the workplace. This leads to numerous potential problems, including security, archiving, monitoring, and the following (Hoffman 2004; Shinder 2005):

- **Security issues.** This is the biggest concern. IM users are vulnerable to hackers, electronic identity theft, and uncontrolled transfer of documents. With unsecured IM, a company could lose confidential documents, internal users could download copyrighted software, or external users could send virus-infected files.
- **Lost productivity.** Use of IM on the job can lead to job downtime. First, we tend to type more slowly than we talk. Next, the conversational nature of IM leads to "chattiness." If employees are not careful, or monitored, a brief IM conversation can lead to hours of lost productivity.
- **Employee abuse.** IM can lead to personal messages rather than job-related communication with coworkers or customers.
- **Distraction.** With IM, a bored colleague easily can distract you with personal messages, online chats, and unimportant updates.
- **Netiquette.** As with e-mail, due to the casual nature of IM, people tend to relax their professionalism and forget about the rules of polite communication. IM can lead to rudeness or just pointless conversations.
- **Spim.** IM lends itself to "spim," instant messaging spam—unwanted advertisements, pornography, pop-ups, and viruses.

Techniques for Successful Instant Messaging

To solve potential problems, consider these 10 suggestions.

1. **Choose the correct communication channel.** Use IM for speed and convenience. If you need length and detail, other options—e-mail messages, memos, reports, letters—are better choices. In addition, sensitive topics or bad news should never be handled through IM. These deserve the personal attention provided by telephone calls or face-to-face meetings.
2. **Document important information.** For future reference, you must archive key text. IM does not allow for this. Therefore, you will need to copy and paste IM text into a word-processing tool for long-term documentation.

3. **Summarize decisions.** IM is great for collaboration; however, all team members might not be online when decisions are made. Once conclusions have been reached that affect the entire team, the designated team leader should e-mail everyone involved. In this e-mail, the team leader can summarize key points, editorial decisions, timetables, and responsibilities.
4. **Tune in, or turn off.** The moment you log on, IM software tells everyone who is active online. Immediately, your IM buddies can start sending messages, IM pop-ups can be distracting. Sometimes, in order to get your work done, you might need to turn off your IM system. Your IM product might give you status options, such as "on the phone," "away from my desk," or "busy." Turning on IM could infringe upon your privacy and time. Turning off might be the answer.
5. **Limit personal use.** Your company owns the instant messaging in the workplace. IM should be used for business purposes only.
6. **Create "buddy" lists.** Create limited lists of IM users, including legitimate business contacts (colleagues, customers, and vendors).
7. **Avoid public directories.** This will help ensure that your IM contacts are secure and business related.
8. **Disallow corporate IM users from installing their own IM software.** A company should require standardized IM software for safety and control.
9. **Never use IM for confidential communication.** Use another communication channel if your content requires security.
10. **Use IM software that allows you to archive and record IM communications.** As with e-mail, IM programs can let systems administrators log and review IM conversations. Some programs create reports that summarize archived information and let users search for text by keywords or phrases. These systems are perfect for future reference (Hoffman 2004; Shinder 2005).

David V. Lewis

Making Your Correspondence Get Results

When he wrote this essay, David V. Lewis was in-house consultant in sales and management training with Western Company of North America in Fort Worth, Texas.

If you turn out an average of five letters a day, you'll produce nearly twice as many words during the year as the typical professional writer.

These letters reflect *your* attitude—and obviously your organization's—toward customers. Realizing this, many progressive organizations train key people in the art of writing readable, results-getting letters. For example, the New York Life Insurance Company produces more than a million letters a year and uses its correspondence as a public relations tool.

"Anyone who writes a letter for New York Life holds a key position in our organization," says Nathan Kelne, vice president of the company. "By the letters our people write, they help determine how the public feels toward our company, and toward the life insurance business as a whole. Since they are instrumental in shaping the personality of the company, they are in a very real sense public relations writers."

For example, before New York Life launched its companywide letter-writing courses, here's how one of its executives tried to explain to a beneficiary the way the death claim was to be paid on a $3,000 policy:

> The monthly income per $1,000 under option 10 years certain is $7.93 per $1,000 total face amount of insurance, which total is $3,000.

Fortunately, the beneficiary was able to cut through the jargon. He replied:

> As I understand your letter, you seem to be saying that I should receive a monthly check for the amount of $23.79 for at least 10 years.

But another policyholder's response to a similarly bewildering letter is more typical:

> Please tell me what you want me to do, and I'll be glad to do it.

Some universally proven principles that can help you sell yourself and your company to the public will now be examined.

WRITE FOR . . . [THE READER], NOT TO . . . [THE READER]

General Foods is an organization that believes strongly in creating a favorable image through its correspondence. The public relations people came across this letter signed by a marketing executive and ready for mailing:

```
Dear Sir:
    Enclosed please find a questionnaire which we are sending to
all our retail contacts in this state.
    Will you please answer this as soon as possible? It's very
important that we have an immediate reply. We're delaying final
plans for our retail sales program in this area until we get
answers to the questionnaire.
    With thanks in advance, we are,

                                        Gratefully yours, . . .
```

The letter is clear and to the point; it *does* communicate readily. But there's a major flaw. It points out benefits the company will receive instead of suggesting how the program will help the recipient. The letter is writer- rather than reader-oriented.

Psychologists say that each of us is basically interested in himself or herself. We want to know "what's in it for me?" Once you routinely approach letter writing from this point of view, you'll find yourself telling your readers in specific terms how the letter will benefit them.

The questionnaire letter was rewritten this way:

```
Dear Sir:
    Enclosed is a questionnaire on our proposed retail sales pro-
gram. Your advance opinion on how this new plan would help you
and others will be very useful in our evaluation of the program.
    If you will fill out and return this questionnaire as soon as
possible, we can let you and other retail contacts in this area
know promptly of changes in the present program. Thank you.

                                        Very truly yours, . . .
```

The revised version asks for your advance opinion, suggests how quick action might help you and *others*, and promises to let you know promptly of changes. There's also another improvement. The tired and outdated "With thanks in advance" has been replaced by a modern "Thank you."

The best way to persuade your readers to your point of view is to show them that it will be worth their while to do so. This rule holds true for just about every successful letter, sermon, sales presentation, or advertisement. A good sales letter, for example, is much like a good ad in that it attempts to dramatize benefits to the reader.

What does it take to get—and hold—a reader's attention? The most power-ful letters appeal to basic needs and emotions rather than to purely logical rea-sons. Mainly, management people want to know how to save time, money, and effort. Show them how your product or service can help them do one or more of these things, and you're likely to get their attention.

With effort, almost any letter can be oriented to the reader, even the usually hard-to-write collection letter. Here's such a specimen, written almost entirely from the writer's point of view:

```
Dear Sir:
    Our records show that you are three months delinquent in pay-
ment of your bill for $37.50.
    Perhaps this is an oversight on your part. Otherwise we can-
not understand why you have not taken care of this obligation.

                                        Very truly yours, . . .
```

Keeping the reader's self-esteem in mind, the letter could have been rewritten this way:

```
Dear Sir:
    We know you'll want to take care of your small past-due account
for $37.50. This will help you to maintain the fine credit you
have built up with us over the years.

                                        Sincerely, . . .
```

To help develop the "you" attitude, put yourself in your reader's shoes, then write from his or her point of view. Once you've developed this attitude, you'll automati-cally start telling your readers what's in it for them. Instead of saying, "I wish to thank you," you'll write, "Thank you." Instead of writing, "We'd like to have your business," you'll write, "You'll find our service can help your business in many ways."

PERSONALIZE YOUR LETTERS
(THERE'S POWER IN PRONOUNS)

Some years ago, many would have considered this letter to have been perfectly proper and very effective:

```
Gentlemen:
    Enclosed herewith are the subject documents which were re-
quested in yours of the 10th. The documents will be duly re-
viewed and an opinion rendered as to their relevancy in the
involved litigation.

                                        Very truly yours, . . .
```

The letter *was* all right—back in the horse-and-buggy days! Phrases like "enclosed herewith," "duly received," and "involved litigation" would have marked the writer as learned. But the executive who makes a habit of writing like that today is generally regarded as an anachronism.

Current usage calls for clear, to-the-point letters, written mostly in conversational language. Like good conversation, your letters should generally be friendly, filled with personal references, and almost always informal in tone and language. Here's how the horse-and-buggy letter might have been rewritten by the modern executive:

Dear Sam:
   Here are the documents you asked for. I'll look them over and let you know if we can use them in our lawsuit.

                      Cordially, . . .

When experts write a letter, even a form letter, they generally try to make it sound as personal as possible. Almost always, it contains a sprinkling of personal pronouns. In orienting your letter to the reader, fill it with "you," "your," and "yours." Use "I" and "me" sparingly.

Here's a case in point, a letter sent out by a mortgage company (emphasis added by the author):

Dear Mr. Jones:
   We want to thank you for your query about *our* new mortgage insurance plan.
   We are enclosing a pamphlet which outlines benefits of *our* new policy and gives testimonials from some of *our* policyholders.
   We would like very much to enroll you within the next 30 days, since we are offering a special low premium rate as *our* introductory offer.

                    Very truly yours, . . .

The repeated use of *we* and *our* clearly shows the letter is written with the mortgage company's interests at heart. But notice how substituting *you* and *yours* orients the letter to the reader's interest. (Emphasis has again been added by the author.)

Dear Mr. Jones:
   Thank *you* for *your* recent inquiry about our new mortgage insurance plan.
   You'll find that the enclosed pamphlet outlines benefits of the policy in detail. *You'll* also probably be interested in the testimonials furnished by some policyholders.
   If *you* sign up within the next 30 days, *you'll* be able to take advantage of special premiums we're offering on an introductory basis. Thank you.

                    Cordially, . . .

The word is out now in enlightened business circles. Companies are telling their executives to regard every letter as a personal contact: to write your own way, to develop your own style (within bounds), to make your letter distinctively *you*.

MASTERING TONE (YOUR PERSONALITY IN PRINT)

Writing a "rejection letter" that leaves the recipient's self-esteem intact and preserves his or her goodwill is a difficult task. It requires tact, diplomacy, and empathy—all of which must be effected through appropriate *tone*. For example, here's the way one banker turned down a builder, a long-time customer:

> Dear Mr. Jones:
> We regret to inform you that your request for an additional loan in the amount of $250,000 must be rejected. It was the judgment of the loan committee that, with your present commitment, such a loan would present too much of a risk for us.
> Naturally, we look forward to doing business with you on your existing commitment.
>
> Sincerely, ...

What's wrong: Tone, mainly—the *way* the rejection is phrased. It deflates the reader's ego and makes it virtually certain the builder will do his banking elsewhere in the future.

True, the rejection was "justified." But why not let the reader down more gently and leave the door open for future business? For example:

> Dear Mr. Jones:
> One of the most distasteful tasks we have is to turn down a loan application, particularly when it is from a regular and respected customer like you.
> We know you'll be disappointed, and so are we. We share your excitement about your plans to expand the Roseland Project, and hope that circumstances will later warrant our working with you on this and other projects.
> However, the current economic outlook, combined with your delinquent status on your existing loan, makes your new loan application a questionable venture for us at the present time.
> We will be glad to work with you in any way we can to resolve your current financial problems, and we look forward to helping you meet your future financial commitments.
>
> Sincerely, ...

The two letters say the same thing, but in vastly different ways. Suffice it to say that tone is as important to a letter as good muscle tone is to an athlete. A negatively phrased letter can have the same effect as an abrasive personality. As one New York Life executive put it:

> By its very nature, the "no" letter is a turndown and leaves the reader unsatisfied. Yet there are ways to soften the blow, and one of the best is simple candor. So, if you must say "no," state the reason first: "Currently there are no vacancies in that department. Therefore, I cannot offer you a position with the company at this time."
> A "no" response often requires positive alternatives if they are appropriate (for example, "Although, for the reasons mentioned, I cannot do as you ask, may I suggest that ...").

You have to be more diplomatic and more sensitive if you're to have any chance of salvaging your reader's goodwill or ego.

And that really is your goal in an effective "no" letter—to tell your readers something they don't want to hear in a way that compels understanding and, ideally, acceptance.

Unfortunately, tone requirements vary not only from person to person, but from one situation to another. For example, you would ordinarily use fast-paced, persuasive prose for a sales-promotion letter. In writing to a highly regarded law firm, you might use a slightly more "dignified" approach. If you're writing for a service-type organization, you might use a middle-of-the-road approach, as the government does.

Government letter writers are told to strive for a tone of "simple dignity," to make letters brief and to the point, and to avoid gobbledygook. "Don't act as if you're the only game in town," they're told. "On the other hand, don't bow and scrape just because you're a service organization."

Poor letters start with poor thinking on the part of the writer. Negative thoughts lead to negative words—and before you know it, there goes the old ball game. Here's a letter from a manager of a department store to a customer who complained that an appliance she had recently bought didn't work. (Negative words have been italicized by the author.)

> Dear Sir:
>
> I am in receipt of your letter in which you *state* that the hair dryer you purchased from us recently *failed* to meet the warranty requirements.
>
> You *claim* that the dryer *failed* to do the things *you say* our salesman promised it would do.
>
> Possibly *you misunderstood* the salesman's presentation. Or perhaps *you failed to follow instructions* properly. We *positively* know of no other customer who has made a similar complaint about the dryer. The feeling is that it will do all that is stated *if properly used*.
>
> However, we are willing to make some concessions for the *alleged* faulty part. We will allow you to return it; however, *we cannot* do so *until* you sign the enclosed card and return it to us.
>
> Very truly yours,...

The tone is unmistakably negative. "State" and "failed to meet" in the opening paragraph imply there's some doubt that the claim is valid. In the second paragraph, "you say" suggests the salesman didn't make the statement at all.

Such phrases as "you misunderstood," "you failed to follow instructions," and "if properly used" tell you in so many words that you're not too bright. And to wrap it up, the writer uses the negative "we cannot... until" instead of the positive "we will... as soon as."

Most letters aren't this negative, of course. But it doesn't take much to offend. Any of these negative words or phrases, in themselves, could have spoiled the tone of an otherwise effective letter.

If you've been guilty of taking a negative approach, study the following examples. In each case, the negative thought (emphasis added by the author) has been converted into a positive one.

Negative	Since you *failed* to say what size you wanted, we cannot send you the shirts.
Positive	You'll receive the shirts within two or three days after you send us your size on the enclosed form.
Negative	We *cannot* pay this bill in one lump sum as you requested.
Positive	We can clear up the balance in six months by paying you in monthly installments of $20.
Negative	We're sorry we *cannot* offer you billboard space for $200.
Positive	We can offer you excellent billboard space for $300.
Negative	We are *not* open on Saturday.
Positive	We are open from 8 A.M. to 8 P.M. daily, except Saturday and Sunday.

Negative words aren't the only cause of poor letter tone. Many letters are made more or less "neutral" by mechanical, impersonal, or discouraging language. Here's an example of each fault with a preferred alternative:

Interpersonal	Many new names are being added to our list of customers. It is always a pleasure to welcome our new friends.
Personal	It's a pleasure to welcome you as our customer, Mr. Jones. We will make every effort to serve you well.
Mechanical	This will acknowledge yours of the 10th requesting a copy of our company's annual report. A copy is enclosed herewith.
Friendly	Thanks for requesting a copy of our annual report, which is enclosed. We hope you will find it helpful.
Discouraging	Since we have a shortage of personnel at this time, we won't be able to process your order until the end of the month.
Encouraging	We should have more help shortly, which will enable us to get to your order by the end of the month.

Ideally, the tone of your letter should reflect the same ease in conversation that you enjoy when talking about your favorite hobby, business, or pastime.

HOW TO WRITE (MORE) THE WAY YOU TALK

This letter was sent out by a large department store. Imagine yourself as the recipient.

```
Dear Sir:
   We are in receipt of yours of July 10 and contents have been
duly noted.
```

As per your request, we are forwarding herewith copies of our new fall brochure. Thanking you in advance for any business you will be so gracious as to do with us,

Yours truly, . . .

Conversational? Of course not. Who uses such language as "We are in receipt of . . . ," "duly noted . . . ," and "as per your request"? Practically no one. People just don't talk that way. Most of these phrases went out with the Model-T—or should have.

Face to face, the writer probably would have said, "Here's the fall brochure you requested. Let me know if we can serve you." It says the same thing, in less space, and without all the fuss.

Some business and professional people still feel it isn't quite proper to write conversationally, mainly because they have seen so much stilted business writing. But many progressive companies are telling their people to communicate in plain English, using only those technical terms that are absolutely necessary. As one executive of a major company said, "The best letters are more than just stand-ins for personal contact. They bridge any distance by the friendly way they have of talking things over person to person." And this from a U.S. Navy bulletin: "At best, writing is a poor substitute for talking. But the closer our writing comes to conversation, the better our exchange of ideas will be."

The consensus clearly is that informal, natural business writing is *in;* stilted business writing is *out.*

One word of caution about writing (more) the way you talk. Since World War II, readability experts have urged business people to "write more the way they talk" or "write as they talk."

Detractors have soft-pedaled the idea, claiming that most conversation is rambling, often incoherent, and frequently a bit too earthy. These are valid objections, but they miss the point. You're not being asked to write *exactly* the way you talk. Rather, you're being asked to bridge the gap between the spoken and the written word—to narrow the difference in the way you would *give* an order verbally and the way you would *write* that same order in a memo. Naturally, writing requires more restraint than speech, and the writer must normally use fewer words. But you can do these things and still capture the tone and cadence of spoken English.

The first step in making your correspondence more conversational is to rid your vocabulary of worn-out business phrases. Here are some of the more flagrant offenders. They were stylish once, but they've done their duty and need to be honorably discharged.

Old Hat	Conversational
At a later date	Later
If this should prove to be the case	If this is the case
This will acknowledge receipt of	Thank you for
Attached herewith please find	Here is; Enclosed is
We shall advise you accordingly	We'll let you know

Old Hat	Conversational
Due to the fact that	Because
With regard to	About
Please notify the writer as to	Please let me know
Enclosed please find a stamped envelope	I've enclosed a stamped envelope
We are submitting herewith a duplicate copy	Here is a copy
In compliance with your request	Here is
We are submitting herewith our check in the amount of $75	Here is our check for $75
We beg to advise (acknowledge) that	[Begging is unnecessary]
The information will be duly recorded	We'll record the information
The subject typewriter	This typewriter
In compliance with your request	As you requested
We will ascertain the facts and advise accordingly	We'll let you know
The writer wishes to state	[Just say it]

This list is far from complete but you get the idea. Once you're mentally geared to writing more conversationally, you'll detect many other clichés. Try to eliminate them.

Contractions will also make your writing more conversational. They play a part—a very large part—in almost everyone's everyday conversation. Even your most learned associate doesn't say, "We shall endeavor to be there at eight o'clock"; he's more likely to say, "We'll try to be there at eight o'clock." Instead of saying, "I am going to the ball game," he'll probably say, "I'm going to the ball game." It takes less effort to say, "You needn't bother to call," than to say, "You need not bother to call." Contractions tend to make the spoken words flow more smoothly. That's why they make writing appear more natural.

Probably the most common contractions are here's, there's, where's, what's, let's, haven't, hasn't, hadn't, won't, wouldn't, can't, couldn't, mustn't, don't, doesn't, didn't, aren't, isn't, and weren't. Then there are the pronoun contractions: I'll, I'm, I'd, I've, he's, he'll, he'd, and so forth.

Using these and other contractions when they facilitate the flow of words will do much to give your writing a quality of spontaneity and warmth. But they must be used with discretion. Using too many contractions can sometimes make your writing too informal. And used in the "wrong" place, they might not "sound right." Indeed, the key is whether the contraction sounds right when the sentence is read.

Take this section from the Gettysburg Address: "But in a larger sense, we cannot dedicate, we cannot consecrate, we cannot hallow this ground." The passage would undoubtedly have lost its historic tone if *can't* had been used instead of cannot.

On the other hand, the advertising slogan "We'd rather fight than switch" would lose some of its punch if phrased, "We would rather fight than switch." Appropriate usage depends on how the contraction makes the sentence sound when it's read aloud.

Next time you get ready to write a letter, ask yourself, "How would I say this if I were talking to the person?" Then go ahead and write in that vein.

Allan A. Glatthorn

"I Have Some Bad News for You"

A consultant in management communications and the author of more than thirty books on writing, Allan A. Glatthorn is retired senior faculty member in the Teaching of Writing Program at the University of Pennsylvania.

One of the most difficult letters or memos to write is the one containing bad news. A subordinate requests a salary increase which you cannot grant. A community organization asks for a contribution which you do not wish to make. An unqualified applicant asks for an appointment to discuss a position with your company, and you do not wish to take the time. You decide to have to dismiss a good worker because declining business mandates cutbacks. In each case you have some unpleasant news to deliver—but you wish to deliver it in a way that does not offend or alienate. How do you accomplish this difficult task? Let me offer some general guidelines and then explain the specific techniques.

The first guideline is to remind you that the successful manager is people-sensitive, able to empathize with others. When you receive a request, you stand in the shoes of the petitioner. You realize, to begin with, that from the standpoint of the asker there are no foolish requests. People ask for things that they need, that they believe they are entitled to, that they hope to receive. And you also realize that there is really no good way to break bad news. No matter how empathic and tactful you may be, your bad news will inevitably cause disappointment and will often cause distress.

The second guideline derives from the first: remember that bad news is best delivered face to face. People getting bad news have some strong needs. They want an opportunity to express their negative feelings. They want the chance to press the request or appeal the decision. They want to explore the reasons more fully to be sure that there is no hidden message. These needs can best be met in a face-to-face meeting. So if you have bad news to give to an employee or a valued client, the best method is to confer with the individual, deliver the bad news in person, and then, if desirable, follow up with a written statement for the record. Don't avoid the unpleasant confrontation by writing a memo, hoping that the petitioner will go away quietly.

Finally, remember that everyone values honesty and forthrightness, especially when being disappointed. Typically, the receiver of bad news is inclined to be cynical, often resenting your attempts to be tactful and politic. You therefore should be sure that your desire to soften the blow does not beguile you into distorting the truth. Explain as tactfully as possible the real reasons for the bad news, instead of offering lame excuses.

With these general guidelines in mind, you should be able to send two kinds of "bad news" messages: the indirect and the direct.

THE INDIRECT BAD NEWS MESSAGE

The indirect message of bad news uses the soft and gentle approach. It tries to cushion the blow by burying the bad news in the middle of the letter or memo, surrounded by positive expressions of appreciation. You send the indirect message under one or more of these circumstances:

- You want further contact with the petitioner.
- You want to project the image of a caring individual.
- You believe that the petitioner won't be able to handle a more direct statement.

The formula is a simple one: THANKS . . . BECAUSE . . . SORRY . . . THANKS.

Thanks

You begin with a positive statement. You express appreciation for the idea offered, the interest expressed, the petition received. Here's how an indirect bad news letter from an insurance company begins:

> Thank you very much for your recent inquiry about our automobile insurance coverage. We are pleased that you have considered transferring your account to our company.

Because

You then continue with the reasons for the bad news. The strategy here is that stating the reasons first cushions the shock, preparing the reader for the bad news to come. Remember to use reasons that will make sense to the petitioner and that will at least project an image of sincerity. If at all possible, state reasons that will depersonalize the rejection, as the next paragraph of that letter does:

> In order to keep our premiums as low as possible, we find it necessary to accept only a small number of new accounts. And in fairness to our present customers, we accept applications only from those whose claims records are comparable to those of drivers we presently insure.

Sorry

You next present the bad news itself, but you state it in a positive fashion. If you can suggest an alternative, do so. If you can find a way to leave the door open, make that clear—but do not give false hopes. Notice how the insurance letter continues:

> Even though we would like to include you among our insured drivers, we will not be able to do so at the present time. It seems to us that your best choice at this time is to remain with your present company. If your claims record improves during the coming year, we would be happy to have you reapply for coverage with us.

Thanks

The indirect message of bad news closes with another expression of appreciation—and ends on a positive note, as this example illustrates:

> We do appreciate your considering our company. And we hope you will be able to reapply under more positive circumstances.

Figure 1 shows another example of this formula at work.

```
To: Bill Harkins
From: Joanne Clemens
Subject: Flex-Time Proposal
Date: February 19,1985     File: A-342

    Bill, thanks very much for forwarding your proposal for
a flex-time schedule for your department. I appreciate the
creative energy—I can always count on getting good ideas
from you.
    Our data suggest that flex time would result in an uneven
distribution of worker hours at a time when uniformity seems
desirable. As you are aware, the recent increase in customer
demand is presenting us with the right kind of problem: our
people and equipment are working at maximum capacity. My expe-
rience with other companies using flex time indicates that our
productivity would suffer if we instituted it now.
    And my concern for maintaining productivity makes me re-
luctant to implement your excellent suggestion now. However,
I have asked our personnel department to review the data. Be-
cause of my respect for your leadership, I want to give all of
your ideas the most careful consideration.
    Thanks again for taking the time to share your ideas with
me. I appreciate your developing a very sound proposal at a
time when I know you are quite busy.
```

FIGURE 1   The Indirect Bad News Message

THE DIRECT MESSAGE OF BAD NEWS

The direct message is a tough no-nonsense statement. While courteous, it gets right to the point and does not try to bury the bad news. It would be used under one or more of these circumstances:

- You want to slam the door shut, discouraging any other request from that petitioner.
- You want to project an image of toughness and directness.
- You are addressing an individual who prefers forthrightness and equates indirectness with softness or dishonesty.

The formula for the direct message is THANKS . . . SORRY . . . BECAUSE . . . THANKS. It uses the same ingredients as the indirect message, but it changes the order. And the language is less subtle and more direct.

Thanks

You begin with a courteous expression of appreciation, since courtesy is expected even in the most direct communication. So a firm and direct letter rejecting an applicant might begin like this:

> Thank you for your letter and resume. We appreciate your interest in joining Mutual Life.

Sorry

The direct message moves quickly to the bad news, to be sure that the message is heard as intended. The bad news is stated forthrightly—but without offending. So the rejection letter continues:

> Unfortunately, we do not have a position available that would match your qualifications, and it seems unlikely that such a position will develop in the future.

Because

Now the reasons come, after the bad news has been delivered. The reasons are stated directly but not offensively, as in this example:

> We have found that our most successful middle-level managers are those who have had the benefit of working with Mutual in a variety of nonmanagerial positions. We therefore tend to promote from within and do not encourage applications for managerial positions from those who have not previously worked with us.

Thanks

The message ends courteously—but the door is firmly closed. There must be no mistake about it: the news is bad. So the rejection letter ends like this:

> We hope you will be able to find employment with a company that can make use of your excellent qualifications, and we do appreciate your interest in applying with us.

The successful manager projects both people-sensitivity and toughness. The indirect message emphasizes sensitivity; the direct message affirms the toughness.

John S. Fielden and Ronald E. Dulek

How to Use Bottom-Line Writing in Corporate Communications

When they wrote this article, John S. Fielden and Ronald Dulek were Professors of Management Communications at the University of Alabama. Jointly, they also authored a series of books on effective business writing.

Every top executive complains about "wordy" memos and reports. From Eisenhower to Reagan, stories have circulated about their refusal to read any memo longer than one page. The CEO of one of the largest companies in the United States actually demands reports so short they can be typed on a three-by-five card. And J. P. Morgan is reputed to have refused audience to anyone who could not state his purpose on the back of a calling card.

"Don't be wordy!" "Be brief, brief, brief!" "Be succinct!" One writing expert after another exhorts business people with these slogans. And who will disagree?

We do.

As a result of an in-depth study of the writing done at the division headquarters of a very large and successful company, we are absolutely convinced that advice such as "Be brief!" is not only useless, it does not even address itself to the real writing problem.

What causes trouble in corporate writing is not the length of communications (for most business letters, memos, and reports are short), but a lack of efficiency in the organizational pattern used in these communications. And, as you will see, it is for the most part a lack of organizational efficiency on the part of writers that is often deliberate, or, if not consciously deliberate, so deeply ingrained in their behavioral programming that it causes an irresistible impulse to beat around the bush.

Put simply, people organize messages backwards, putting their real purpose last. But people read frontwards and need to know the writer's purpose immediately. That purpose is what we eventually came to call the message's bottom line.

At the beginning of the study we wondered, why do people write backwards? One possibility is that they are writing histories of their mental processes as they think their way through a problem. Since their conclusion could only be arrived at after analysis, the report therefore would state its conclusions last. But if that were the reason, it would only be analytical memos and reports that would be organized backwards.

Such was not the case in the study we did. Almost *all* memos and reports put their purpose last. Why? We determined to study the problem to see if we could design a cure for such blatantly inefficient writing.

COMPREHENSION IS THE KEY

In the division headquarters we worked with, 9,000,000 (internal and external) messages of all types are distributed annually. Our study began with an intense analysis of a sample of 2,000 letters, memos, and reports randomly drawn from company files. The typical communication was one page. Only in rare cases did any memo or report exceed three pages. These various documents were well-written in the sense of being above average in terms of mechanical correctness and aptness of word choice.

Yet only one in twenty of these communications was organized efficiently. Below is one of the actual memos we analyzed (disguised, of course). Look at your watch before you read it. Keep a record of how many times you have to read it before you really *comprehend* its message, and how long it takes to understand the report's purpose.

Memo A

The Facilities people have been working on consolidating HQ Marketing Functions into the new building at Pebble Brook. As presently envisioned, Marketing Research will remain in its current location but be provided with additional space for expansion. The following functions will be moved into the new facility—Business Analysis, Special Applications, and Market Planning. It is expected that Public Sector will be relocated in a satellite location. The above moves will consolidate all of Marketing into the Pebble Brook location with the exception noted above.

Attached is a preliminary outline of the new building by floor and whom it will house. I am interested in knowing if this approach is in agreement with your thoughts.

This memo seems brief on the surface. It contains only 115 words. But let's measure brevity not by words but by the length of time it takes a reader to comprehend a message.

We feel that if you were really the addressee, you would have had to read this memo twice. Why? Because you didn't know *why* you were reading it until the last paragraph. Once you discover the purpose—that you are being asked to approve a plan—you want to reread the memo to see if you do, in fact, agree with the moves. The memo suddenly (and, unfortunately, at its end) informed you that you were on the hook. Obviously, there is a big difference between the way you will read a memo containing information of general (and casual) interest and one which requires you to make a decision involving the physical moving and reshuffling of hundreds of powerful and sensitive people. Yet organizationally this memo as presented does not show even a foggy awareness of this difference.

Now read the revision. Notice how your comprehension time would have dropped significantly had you received this revision instead of the original.

Memo B

Attached is a preliminary outline—by floor—of the new building at Pebble Brook and a statement of whom it will house. I am interested in knowing if this approach is in agreement with your thinking.

Our suggestion is that we make the following changes:

1. Business Analysis, Special Applications, and Market Planning will. . . .
2. Public Sector will be. . . .
3. Marketing Research will remain. . . .

In terms of comprehension, the revision lets you know right away that you are expected to make a decision. Whether or not you would mull over that decision, we cannot tell. But we do know this: in terms of actual time expended in comprehending what is being asked of the reader, Memo B can be comprehended in one-third the time required by Memo A. And, if we measure brevity in terms of comprehension time, rather than number of words, Memo B produces a 66 percent savings in comprehension time.

We learned immediately in our study that comprehension time drops dramatically when a memo states its purpose—why it is being written for the reader—at the very beginning.

Confirm this point by reading Memo C, another disguised memo drawn from the division headquarters. Time your comprehension as before.

Memo C

The first of a series of meetings of the Strategic Marketing planning group will be held on Thursday, September 7, from 1 to 4 P.M. in Conference Room C. These important meetings are for the purpose of monitoring and suggesting changes in overall market strategies and product support. Attached is a list of those managers who should attend on a regular basis. These managers should specifically be prepared to review alternative strategies for the new product line. The purpose of this reminder is to ask your help in encouraging attendance and direct participation by your representatives. Please have them contact Frank Persons for any further information and to confirm their attendance.

Now read Memo D and compare comprehension time once again.

Memo D

Please encourage those of your managers whose names are listed on the attachment to attend regularly and directly participate in the meetings of the Strategic Marketing Planning group.

The next meeting is to be held on Thursday, September 7, from 1 to 4 P.M. in Conference Room C.

Please have your representative(s):

1. Contact Frank Persons for any further information and to confirm attendance.
2. Be prepared specifically to review alternative strategies for the new F-62 line
3. Be ready to discuss changes in overall market strategies and product support.

Memo D is obviously more efficient. Why? Not only because it begins by stating its purpose but also because it itemizes the actions requested of the reader, organizing them in an easy-to-digest checklist. The original gives extensive background about the meetings but buries the requested action in a fat paragraph. Most readers would have to read the original at least twice just to be able to ferret out exactly what is being asked of them.

The time being saved, of course, seems insignificant on communications as short as Memos A and C. But consider how significant the savings would be corporate-wide if every manager's comprehension time in reading all messages could be reduced by even a small percentage.

HIGH COST OF COMPREHENSION

A recent study done by International Data Corporation states that managers in information industries spend an astonishing 60 percent of their time reading and writing; professionals spend 50 percent.[1] If cost accounted, how much would, say, a 20 percent to 30 percent savings in reading and writing time amount to for companies in this industry alone? The possibilities are arresting.

We made some cost estimates for the communications undertaken by the division headquarters we studied. The 9,000,000 messages distributed annually by the division headquarters included, of course, all sorts of mailings and multiple copies of such things as new product announcements, price changes, and the like, often running into the thousands of copies. Therefore, it was not fair to assume all 9,000,000 messages mailed were individually composed. Instead, we determined through conservative estimates that 12 percent of the 9,000,000 mailings were individual communications. And for each of these we will assume, for the purpose of this article, the ridiculously low figure of $10 to be the cost of creating, typing, and distributing. Based on these estimates, the minimum total composition cost for this one divisional headquarters would be $10,800,000 a year (see Table 1).

TABLE I   Estimated Division Headquarters Writing Costs

Number of messages sent annually	9,000,000
Percent individually composed	12%
Total individually composed	1,800,000
Composition cost (per message)	$10
Minimum total composition cost	$10,800,000

[1] *Automated Business Communications: The Management Workstation.* (Framingham, Mass.. International Data Corporation, 1981): 21.

But writing time is, of course, only part of the story. What about the cost of comprehending all 9,000,000 of these messages? For while we estimate that only 12 percent of these messages were individually composed (that is, not copies), all 9,000,000 messages were presumably intended to be read. Again, in an attempt to dramatize through understatement, we will use a low salary figure: $20,000 per year. You can, of course, substitute the actual salary and other figures for your own company and determine for yourself at least roughly the magnitude of your company's reading costs.

As Table 2 shows, we approximated the division's minimum reading costs to be over $4,500,000. Of course, this figure is bound to be far below actual costs. Not only are our salary estimates unrealistically low, but we haven't taken into account the fact that many of the documents were read by multiple readers. In fact, many memos urged recipients to pass information on to colleagues and subordinates.

TABLE 2   Estimated Division Headquarters Reading Costs

Low-median salary	$20,000
	$10/hour
	17¢/minute
Average* reading time	3 minutes
Reading cost per document	$0.51
Reading cost for 9,000,000 messages	$4,590,000

*Assumed that some messages read in depth; some not given more than a glance; some barely looked at.

USING DIRECT PATTERNS

While these dollar figures were somewhat astonishing and the possibilities of dollar savings enticing, the company under study evidenced the greater concern about the waste of productivity involved in such inefficient communications having become the norm. The specter of hard-working employees' time being wasted by an inundation of inefficiently organized memos and letters was distressing. The company asked us to teach people how to report in a "bottom-line" fashion. Therefore, we taught people to tell readers immediately what was their purpose in writing and what they expected of the reader, if anything. If people had no purpose in writing, they probably shouldn't write in the first place. If they didn't expect anything of the reader and were just offering possibly useful information, we told them to say so right away.

In short, we were teaching people to use a direct organizational pattern. We were urging them to eschew the circuitous pattern in which writers, because of some sensitivity (real or imagined), withhold their purpose and do not let their readers know why they are being written to and what is being asked of them until their minds have been conditioned to accept the points the writers are trying to get across.

Obviously, there is nothing wrong with a circuitous organizational pattern in certain circumstances. But in this company, and we suspect in many other companies across the country, the circuitous pattern has become the norm for all types of communication in all situations.

Just ask yourself: how sensible is it to always write backwards, in a way that is just the opposite of how people comprehend information? Look at one more illustrative letter from our study:

Memo E

This is in reference to the letter sent you by Joe Smith of ABC Materials, Inc.

Mr. Smith requested information available from Product Analysis Reports (PAR's). As soon as information was made available to me from this source, I orally relayed the response to Mr. Smith.

Making use of the Planning Application Model, I was able to respond to Mr. Smith's request for further information about potential new products of possible interest to ABC. It was not until I received the copy of Mr. Smith's letter that I was aware that the data provided for him was not sufficient.

I have used all the resources that I am aware of to resolve Mr. Smith's concerns. Mr. Smith has informed me he is more than satisfied with the work done and considers the project completed. He has also announced an intention of doing further business with us.

Attached are copies of all the requests that I've been asked to submit during the six months that I have been assigned to this account. Also attached is a copy of an ABC analysis, submitted by my predecessor, which related to one of the items referenced in his letter. Upon request, I will forward copies of all of the relevant analysis that are in my files.

Where's the bottom line? What's this writer trying to get across? Isn't it the following?

Memo F

I have reviewed and acted upon the letter sent to you by Joe Smith of ABC Materials. Mr. Smith has informed me he is more than satisfied with the work done and considers the project completed. He has also announced an intention of doing further business with us.

Here in some detail are the steps I have taken for Mr. Smith. . . .

Since what this writer is reporting is good news, the communication is not sensitive. There's no need to report this information as circuitously as we might well be tempted to do if we had bungled the situation with Mr. Smith and had lost his business.

What percentage of all communications would you estimate to fall into the sensitive category that may call for a circuitous organizational pattern? Ten percent is the outer limit of possibility, unless one has a specialized job such as handling complaints, writing sales letters, dealing with shareholders, or the like. Why, then, upon analyzing these 2,000 sample letters, memos, and reports from this corporate division, did we find that almost all documents were organized circuitously? Why, in this extremely well-managed and successful company, was it the exceedingly rare letter or memo that did not bury its purpose somewhere in the third or fourth paragraph, and most frequently in the last sentence?

At the time, we had no idea of the etiology of the disease, but we felt we had a simple cure. We would tell people how to organize their thoughts so that the bottom line of their message would be immediately highlighted and promptly presented in everything they wrote. To facilitate this goal, we invented a series of bottom-line reporting principles which, if followed, would enable writers to communicate in a direct, straightforward, no-nonsense fashion in all situations that were not fraught with sensitivity. This would, we thought, save writing time and expense (see Table 3).

TABLE 3   Principles of Bottom-Line Reporting

Principle 1:	State your purpose first unless there are overriding reasons for not doing so.
Principle 2:	State your purpose first, even if you believe your readers need a briefing before they can fully understand the purpose of your communication.
Principle 3:	Present information in order of its importance to the reader.
Principle 4:	Put information of dubious utility or questionable importance to the reader into an appendix or attachment.
Principle 5:	In persuasive situations, where you do not know how your reader will react to what you ask for, state your request at the start in all cases except:
	a. Those where you don't (or barely) know the reader, and to ask something immediately of a relative (or absolute) stranger would probably be perceived as being "pushy."
	b. Those where the relationship between you and your reader is not close or warm.
Principle 6:	Think twice before being direct in negative messages upward.

And readers, too, would benefit—instead of having to search through a memo to find out what purpose the writer had in writing to them and what the writer wanted or expected them to do, they could look at the first paragraph and see the answer to these vital questions. Moreover, if the purpose and topic seemed irrelevant to their interests or needs, they could reject reading it, or merely give it a glance. Significant reading time and dollar savings should certainly result.

The program was instituted throughout the division. Did it work? Yes, in terms of getting the principles across and in terms of getting intellectual acceptance of these principles.

But getting emotional commitment to these principles was quite another story. We sensed in discussions that writers' commitment to being circuitous was not merely a bad habit. It was something else, something that was so ingrained that forcing personnel to be direct actually caused disquiet in many people. What could have been the reason?

PROGRAMMING FOR INEFFICIENCY

Obviously, people who work in large organizations were not born there. They have come to those organizations programmed by their social upbringing and by their educational experiences. And both of these earlier programmings strongly contribute to resistance to bottom-line reporting.

Social Upbringing

People seldom are conscious of how their social upbringing programs them to be indirect. Yet almost every sensitive social situation reinforces the wisdom of being circuitous, of not being direct. Aren't most brief answers to sensitive questions regarded as brusqueness or curtness, as being short with someone?

It begins early. The children are asked, "Do you want to go to Aunt Alice's house?" The children answer, honestly and directly, "No!" Unacceptable! The children are scolded and soon learn to beat around the bush the next time, all the while searching for some plausible excuse to forestall the visit. It is not surprising that as adults, the same children, when asked by the boss, "What do you think of my new plan? Think it'll work?" think twice before responding, "No!"

Educational Programming

Having been thoroughly programmed by their families that being direct is being impolite, the children now go to school. Here they soon learn that a twenty-page term report gets a high grade; a two-page report gets a low grade. A five-page answer to a test question is good; a one-paragraph answer is bad. Regardless of what teachers may profess, they invariably give extra credit for "effort." And effort is most easily measured by numbers of words or by pounds of pages. A premium is placed on long-windedness, and long-windedness is achieved by being circuitous rather than direct.

Indoctrination into Anxiety

On their first jobs in a large organization, young people are naturally nervous. They are very concerned that whatever they write or say not make people upset. They are also very concerned about "getting good grades." Therefore, they fall back upon the same behavior that was rewarded in school. They are going to do everything possible not to look lazy. They are going to be thorough in everything they write. Every chance to write a report to a superior is a chance to write that blockbuster of a term paper that could not fail to impress the boss. They are going to get that "A."

The fact that young people enter organizations at the bottom provides a final step in their programming for being circuitous and indirect. Everybody knows that writing *up* in an organization is far different from writing *down*. When young people enter an organization, the only direction they *can* write is up. Therefore, all the early experiences received in corporations consist of writing situations where they have to write information to people who are in fact, or may someday be, their superiors. Naturally, they become very uneasy.

Now let's suppose the company institutes a program to encourage personnel to be more direct. Imagine yourself as that newly hired young person in the organization. Are you going to believe any program suggesting that you be blunt and direct in your upward or lateral communications, when your entire lifetime programming has proved to you over and over again that bluntness is all too frequently suicidal? No chance!

Young people may give lip service to such a program, but in any real-life situation in which they feel threatened (in actuality, almost all situations) they will avoid coming to the point with an almost religious passion. And in negative or sensitive situations, the last thing they are going to do is state their purposes and requests directly.

By contrast, their higher level superiors, having enjoyed years of power positions in the hierarchy (from whence they could write down to anyone in any fashion they pleased), take a far different view of writing. The superiors now pride themselves on directness and bewail long-windedness on the part of their subordinates. But the subordinates' desires for self-preservation (reinforced by all their preorganizational programming) force them to give lip service at best to corporate attempts to "get to the point."

And, let's face it, in the corporate pyramid almost everybody is somebody's subordinate and, perhaps because of files, one never knows who is going to read what has been written. Therefore, circuitous writing is partly the habit of a lifetime and partly CYA.

WHAT YOUR ORGANIZATION CAN DO

Is a cure then impossible? Is inefficient, circuitous writing simply to be endured and its costs in lost productivity and wasted dollars merely written off?

No; a cure for inefficient writing is possible. But a thorough organization-wide cure requires that:

- People recognize and reject their social and educational programming for being circuitous in all non-sensitive writing situations. This deprogramming is the responsibility of the individual.
- People learn to write efficiently; that is, learn to organize their messages in such a way as to make it easy (and fast) for readers to comprehend the message. Teaching the bottom-line principles will impart this skill. But implementing the bottom-line principles requires strong high-level management support.
- People must develop the self-confidence necessary to send bottom-line messages upward in nonsensitive (or slightly sensitive) messages. A long-range cure depends to a great extent on attitude, on reducing the tensions inherent in superior subordinate communications. Most writing insecurities stem from real, not imagined, failures on the part of superiors to communicate clearly and unequivocally their willingness to accept bottom-lined messages from subordinates.

Higher level executives have to appreciate how threatening directness can be to subordinates. Superiors, therefore, need to be persuaded not only to have the following credo taped to the wall above their desks but also communicated to all subordinates with whom they relate:

The Superior's Credo

1. I will ask all subordinates to be direct in their messages to me and I will not become angry if subordinates do so politely—even when those thoughts run counter to mine.

2. I will recognize and appreciate subordinates' attempts to conserve my time (and other readers' time) in all memos and reports they write to me, or for my signature.
3. I will work out with subordinates some general understanding of how much detail I require in various circumstances.
4. I will make clear to subordinates that I judge their communications not by length and weight, but by directness and succinctness.
5. And when I myself report up in the organization, I will be as direct as I expect my subordinates to be.

Once senior executives have adopted and put this credo into practice, all subordinates should recognize that there is now no excuse for them not to live by the following credo:

The Subordinate's Credo

1. I will have the courage (in all but the most sensitive or negative situations) to state at the beginning of messages my purpose in writing, exactly what information I am trying to convey, and/or precisely what action(s) I want my reader to take (if possible, itemized in checklist form for easy comprehension).
2. My readers, especially if they are my superiors, are extremely busy. I must not waste their time by making them read unnecessary undigested detail any more than I would waste their time chattering on in a face-to-face interview.
3. I will make a judgment as to how much my readers need to know in order to take the action required by the communication.
4. If I am in doubt as to whether specific information is necessary to my readers, I will either put this information in summary form in attachments, or tell readers that I stand ready to offer more information if so requested.
5. I will avoid the arsenal of the con man. If I want something of a superior, I will ask for it forthrightly.

Part 4

Reports and Other Longer Documents

Nearly everyone in business and industry writes reports. The word *report* is really just a generic term for a variety of documents that vary in form and purpose. Some reports are purely informative; others are persuasive or argumentative. Reports can be simple checklists, or they can take the form of interoffice memos and e-mails, letters to clients, or more full-blown documents that are the results of weeks, if not months, of effort.

Business and technical writing practice sometimes distinguishes between formal and informal reports. Formal reports generally follow a multi-part format and are used primarily to present the results of a detailed project. Such a project often involves a considerable outlay of capital plus time and effort. The format for a formal report may mandate a cover letter or a memo of transmittal attached to a bound document consisting of an abstract, a table of contents, a glossary, an introduction, a detailed discussion of all aspects of the topic, a set of conclusions and recommendations, and pages and pages of attachments.

Informal reports tend to be shorter documents. Their formats are less complex, consisting only of such essential items as an introduction, a discussion, a set of conclusions, and, where appropriate, a list of recommendations.

To ensure that their reports are useful, writers should take the same kind of process approach that they would use when writing any other business or technical document. They should plan their reports carefully from the start so that they can clearly define and stick to their intended purpose—whether that purpose be to provide information, to analyze information and draw conclusions, or to make recommendations.

Because they are often action-oriented, reports require writers to analyze their audience—or audiences—carefully. By virtue of their length, some reports can intimidate readers who need to know the information they contain.

A classification of the kinds of audiences that business and technical writing address, which Thomas Pearsall first delineated in his *Audience Analysis for Technical Writing* (1969), is especially relevant to the audiences for reports. Those audiences can include any, or all, of the following:

- the layperson
- the executive
- the expert
- the technician
- the operator.

Each brings a different background and a different set of needs to his or her reading of a report that writers must take into account if they hope to produce an effective document. In general, using abstracts and visual aids to supplement the contents of both formal and informal reports will make those reports more accessible to larger groups of readers of varying degrees of expertise.

Proposals are in some ways simply specialized reports, although they can be written in letter, memo, or e-mail form as well. The primary purpose of a proposal is to persuade readers to do something. Sales letters and requests for adjustments are two fairly simple proposals. Internal proposals, which are aimed at changing policies and procedures within an organization, and external proposals, such as documents seeking grants or funding, are more complex persuasive documents. Because proposals aim at convincing an audience to act in a way the writer wants, a process approach can help lead writers to a successful proposal.

This section of *Strategies* begins with an essay by J. C. Mathes and Dwight W. Stevenson that returns to a familiar theme in this anthology: the importance of audience analysis. Mathes and Stevenson offer a detailed examination of the problem of audience analysis and a solution to that problem designed to meet the needs of the several audiences that reports in particular, and other business and technical documents in general, address.

Writing done for the world of work may less and less be a solitary activity. Proposals, statements of goals, reports, legal briefs, and other business and technical documents may in their final form be the work of diverse hands. Nancy Allen, Dianne Atkinson, Meg Morgan, Teresa Moore, and Craig Snow report on their research into so-called "collaborative writing" on-the-job. In such writing situations, the group dynamic can influence the process and the outcome of the writing task. Admitting that their study was both preliminary and exploratory, the authors nonetheless highlight an increasingly popular method for the production of longer documents for the world of work, one that offers advantages but raises new issues in meeting the demands and requirements of on-the-job writing situations.

Vincent Vinci then offers what amounts to a checklist that business and technical report writers, whether they work independently or collaboratively, can use as a last step in an effective writing process.

Supposedly a picture is worth a thousand words. Sheryl Lindsell-Roberts modifies that adage slightly to suggest a *pixel* is also worth a thousand words by offering some no nonsense advice on when to use graphics instead of text and how to link graphics to text when both are needed. As an addendum to Lindsell-Roberts's discussion on how to use graphics effectively, Darrell Huff, in a timeless piece, suggests—tongue-in-cheek—ways writers can misuse graphics and statistics to manipulate the truth and to inflate their prose, how they can, in short, lie with statistics. Behind Huff's piece lies a concern with the ethics of business communication, a concern more and more to the fore in the world of business.

The next essay in this section of *Strategies* addresses persuasive writing, often a hallmark of a business or technical report. In particular, David W. Ewing discusses the different strategies writers need to persuade rather than to inform their readers.

Turn on the television or radio, read a newspaper, get updates on current events on your computer, and the news is discouragingly the same: Ponzi schemes of unimaginable proportions, corruption, ethical violations, malfeasance in public office, major corporations ruined by the greed of those who run them, high-flying—and even higher spending—executives, and bankrupt pension funds and companies. Ethical behavior seems more and more to be a concept foreign to public, business, and even, alas, academic life.

But business and technical writers have very real moral and ethical obligations. Dan Jones delivers a final word on ethics with brief discussion of the relationship among ethics, writing style, and editing. Jones begins with a definition of ethics as it applies to technical prose, then offers "the ten commandments of computer ethics," and concludes by quoting from the ethical guidelines of the Society for Technical Communication (STC).

J. C. Mathes and Dwight W. Stevenson

Audience Analysis:
The Problem and a Solution

J. C. Mathes and Dwight W. Stevenson are both Professors Emeriti of Technical Communications in the College of Engineering at the University of Michigan.

Every communication situation involves three fundamental components: a writer, a message, and an audience. However, many report writers treat the communication situation as if there were only two components: a writer and his message. Writers often ignore their readers because writers are preoccupied with their own problems and with the subject matter of the communication. The consequence is a poorly designed, ineffective report.

As an example, a student related to the class her first communication experience on a design project during summer employment with an automobile company. After she had been working on her assignment for a few weeks, her supervisor asked her to jot him a memo explaining what she was doing. Not wanting to take much time away from her work and not thinking the report very important, she gave him a handwritten memo and continued her technical activities. Soon after, the department manager inquired on the progress of the project. The supervisor immediately responded that he had just had a progress report, and thereupon forwarded the engineer's brief memo. Needless to say, the engineer felt embarrassed when her undeveloped and inadequately explained memo became an official report to the organization. The engineer thought her memo was written just to her supervisor, who was quite familiar with her assignment. Due to her lack of experience with organizational behavior, she made several false assumptions about her report audience, and therefore about her report's purpose.

The inexperienced report writer often fails to design his report effectively because he makes several false assumptions about the report writing situation. If the writer would stop to analyze the audience component, he would realize that:

1. It is false to assume that the person addressed is the audience.
2. It is false to assume that the audience is a group of specialists in the field.
3. It is false to assume that the report has a finite period of use.
4. It is false to assume that the author and the audience always will be available for reference.
5. It is false to assume that the audience is familiar with the assignment.
6. It is false to assume that the audience has been involved in daily discussions of the material.
7. It is false to assume that the audience awaits the report.
8. It is false to assume that the audience has time to read the report.

Assumptions one and two indicate a writer's lack of awareness of the nature of his report audience. Assumptions three, four, and five indicate his lack of appreciation of the dynamic nature of the system. Assumptions six, seven, and eight indicate a writer's lack of consideration of the demands of day by day job activity.

A report has value only to the extent that it is useful to the organization. It is often used primarily by someone other than the person who requested it. Furthermore, the report may be responding to a variety of needs within the organization. These needs suggest that the persons who will use the report are not specialists or perhaps not even technically knowledgeable about the report's subject. The specialist is the engineer. Unless he is engaged in basic research, he usually must communicate with persons representing many different areas of operation in the organization.

In addition, the report is often useful over an extended period of time. Each written communication is filed in several offices. Last year's report can be incomprehensible if the writer did not anticipate and explain his purpose adequately. In these situations, even within the office where a report originated, the author as well as his supervisor will probably not be available to explain the report. Although organizational charts remain unchanged for years, personnel, assignments, and professional roles change constantly. Because of this dynamic process, even the immediate audience of a report sometimes is not familiar with the writer's technical assignment. Thus, the report writer usually must design his report for a dynamic situation.

Finally, the report writer must also be alert to the communication traps in relatively static situations. Not all readers will have heard the coffee break chats that fill in the details necessary to make even a routine recommendation convincing. A report can arrive at a time when the reader's mind is churning with other concerns. Even if it is expected, the report usually meets a reader who needs to act immediately. The reader usually does not have time to read through the whole report; he wants the useful information clearly and succinctly. To the reader, time probably is the most important commodity. Beginning report writers seldom realize they must design their reports to be used efficiently rather than read closely.

The sources of the false assumptions we have been discussing are not difficult to identify. The original source is the artificial communication a student is required to perform in college. In writing only for professors, a student learns to write for audiences of one, audiences who know more than the writer knows, and audiences who have no instrumental interests in what the report contains. The subsequent source, on the job, is the writer's natural attempt to simplify his task. The report writer, relying upon daily contact and familiarity, simply finds it easier to write a report for his own supervisor than to write for a supervisor in a different department. The writer also finds it easier to concentrate upon his own concerns than to consider the needs of his readers. He finds it difficult to address complex audiences and face the design problems they pose.

AUDIENCE COMPONENTS AND PROBLEMS THEY POSE

To write a report you must first understand how your audience poses a problem. Then you must analyze your audience in order to be able to design a report structure that provides an optimum solution. To explain the components of the report audience you must do more than just identify names, titles, and roles. You must determine who your audiences are as related to the purpose and content of your report. "Who" involves the specific operational functions of the persons who will read the report, as well as their educational and business backgrounds. These persons can be widely distributed, as is evident if you consider the operational relationships within a typical organization.

Classifying audiences only according to directions of communication flow along the paths delineated by the conventional organizational chart, we can identify three types of report audiences: *horizontal, vertical,* and *external.* For example, in the organization chart in Figure 1, *Part of Organization Chart for Naval Ship Engineering Center,*[1] horizontal audiences exist on each level. The Ship Concept Design Division and the Command and Surveillance Division form horizontal audiences for each other. Vertical audiences exist between levels. The Ship Concept Design Division and the Surface Ship Design Branch form vertical audiences for each other. External audiences exist when any unit interacts with a separate organization, such as when the Surface Ship Design Branch communicates with the Newport News Shipbuilding Company.

What the report writer first must realize is the separation between him and any of these three types of audiences. Few reports are written for horizontal audiences within the same unit, such as from one person in the Surface Ship Design Branch to another person or project group within the Surface Ship Design Branch itself. Instead, a report at least addresses horizontal audiences within a larger framework, such as from the Surface Ship Design Branch to the Systems Analysis Branch. Important reports usually have complex audiences, that is, vertical and horizontal, and sometimes external audiences as well.

An analysis of the problems generated by horizontal audiences—often assumed to pose few problems—illustrates the difficulties most writers face in all

---

[1] A reference in H. B. Benford and J. C. Mathes, *Your Future in Naval Architecture,* Richards Rosen, New York, 1968.

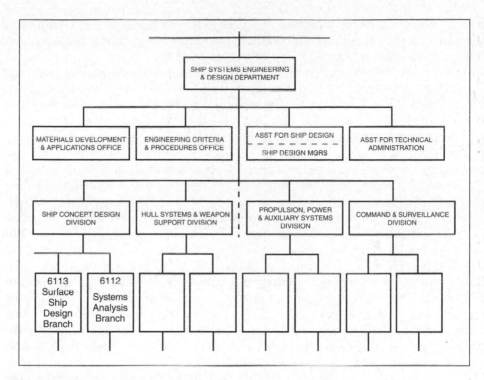

FIGURE I   Part of Organization Chart for Naval Ship Engineering Center

report writing situations. A systems engineer in the Systems Analysis Branch has little technical education in common with the naval architect in the Surface Ship Design Branch. In most colleges he takes only a few of the same mathematics and engineering science courses. The systems engineer would not know the wave resistance theory familiar to the naval architect, although he could use the results of his analysis. In turn, the naval architect would not know stochastics and probability theory, although he could understand systems models. But the differences between these audiences and writers go well beyond differences in training. In addition to having different educational backgrounds, the audiences will have different concerns, such as budget, production, or contract obligations. The audiences will also be separated from the writer by organizational politics and competition, as well as by personality differences among the people concerned.

When the writer addresses a horizontal audience in another organizational unit, he usually addresses a person in an organizational role. When addressed to the role rather than the person, the report is aimed at a department or a group. This means the report will have audiences in addition to the person addressed. It may be read primarily by staff personnel and subordinates. The addressee ultimately may act on the basis of the information reported, but at times he serves only to transfer the report to persons in his department who will use it. Furthermore, the report may have audiences in addition to those in the department addressed. It may be forwarded to other persons elsewhere, such as lawyers and comptrollers. The report travels routinely throughout organizational paths, and will have unknown or unanticipated audiences as well.

Consequently, even when on the same horizontal organizational level, the writer and his audience have little in common beyond the fact of working for the same organization, of having the same "rank" and perhaps of having the same educational level of attainment. Educational backgrounds can be entirely different; more important, needs, values, and uses are different. The report writer may recommend the choice of one switch over another on the basis of cost-efficiency analysis; his audiences may be concerned for business relationships, distribution patterns, client preferences, and budgets. Therefore, the writer should not assume that his audience has technical competence in the field, familiarity with the technical assignment, knowledge of him or of personnel in his group, similar value perspectives, or even complementary motives. The differences between writer and audience are distinctive, and may even be irreconcilable.

The differences are magnified when the writer addresses vertical audiences. Reports directed at vertical audiences, that is, between levels of an organization chart, invariably have horizontal audience components also. These complex report writing situations pose significant communication problems for the writer. Differences between writer and audience are fundamental. The primary audiences for the reports, especially informal reports, must act or make decisions on the basis of the reports. The reports thus have only instrumental value, that is, value insofar as they can be used effectively. The writer must design his report primarily according to how it will be used.

In addition to horizontal audiences and to vertical audiences, many reports are also directed to external audiences. External audiences, whether they consist of a few or many persons, have the distinctive, dissimilar features of the complex vertical audience. With external audiences these features invariably are exaggerated, especially those involving need and value. An additional complication is that the external audience can judge an entire organization on the basis of the writer's report. And sometimes most important of all, concerns for tact and business relationships override technical concerns.

In actual practice the writer often finds audiences in different divisions of his own company to be "external" audiences. One engineer encountered this problem in his first position after graduation. He was sent to investigate the inconsistent test data being sent to his group from a different division of the company in another city. He found that the test procedures being used in that division were faulty. However, at his supervisor's direction he had to write a report that would not "step on any toes." He had to write the report in such a manner as to have the other division correct its test procedures while not implying that the division was in any way at fault. An engineer who assumes that the purpose of his report is just to explain a technical investigation is poorly prepared for professional practice.

Most of the important communication situations for an engineer during his first five years out of college occur when he reports to his supervisor, department head, and beyond. In these situations, his audiences are action-oriented line management who are uninterested in the technical details and may even be unfamiliar with the assignment. In addition, his audiences become acquainted with him professionally through his reports; therefore, it is more directly the report than the investigation that is important to the writer's career.

Audience components and the significant design problems they pose are well illustrated by the various audiences for a formal report written by an engineer on the development of a process to make a high purity chemical, as listed in Figure 2, *Complex Audience Components for a Formal Report by a Chemical Engineer on a Process to Make a High Purity Chemical.* The purpose of the report was to explain the process; others would make a feasibility study of the process and evaluate it in comparison to other processes.

The various audiences for this report, as you can determine just by reading their titles, would have had quite different roles, backgrounds, interests, values, needs, and uses for the report. The writer's brief analysis of the audiences yielded the following:

> He could not determine the nature of many of his audiences, who they were, or what the specifics of their roles were.

> His audiences had little familiarity with his assignment.

> His report would be used for information, for evaluation of the process, and for evaluation of the company's position in the field.

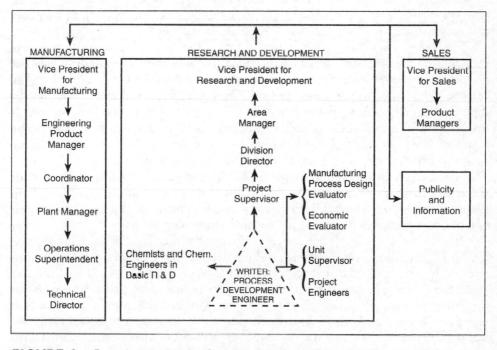

FIGURE 2   Complex Audience Components for a Formal Report by a Chemical Engineer on a Process to Make a High Purity Chemical

Some of his audiences would have from a minute to a half hour to glance at the report, some would take the report home to study it, and some would use it over extended periods of time for process analysis and for economic and manufacturing feasibility studies.

The useful lifetime of the report could be as long as twenty years.

The report would be used to evaluate the achievements of the writer's department.

The report would be used to evaluate the writing and technical proficiencies of the writer himself.

This report writer classified his audiences in terms of the conventional organization chart. Then to make them more than just names, titles, and roles he asked himself what they would know about his report and how they would use it. Even then he had only partially solved his audience problem and had just begun to clarify the design problems he faced. To do so he needed to analyze his audiences systematically.

A METHOD FOR SYSTEMATIC AUDIENCE ANALYSIS

To introduce the audience problem that report writers must face, we have used the conventional concept of the organization chart to classify audiences as *horizontal, vertical,* and *external.* However, when the writer comes to the task of performing an instrumentally useful audience analysis for a particular report, this concept of the organization and this classification system for report audiences are not very helpful.

First, the writer does not view from outside the total communication system modeled by the company organization chart. He is within the system himself, so his view is always relative. Second, the conventional outsider's view does not yield sufficiently detailed information about the report audiences. A single bloc on the organization chart looks just like any other bloc, but in fact each bloc represents one or several human beings with distinctive roles, backgrounds, and personal characteristics. Third, and most importantly, the outsider's view does not help much to clarify the specific routes of communication, as determined by audience needs, which an individual report will follow. The organization chart may describe the organization, but it does not describe how the organization functions. Thus many of the routes a report follows—and consequently the needs it addresses—will not be signaled by the company organization chart.

In short, the conventional concept of report audiences derived from organization charts is necessarily abstract and unspecific. For that reason a more effective method for audience analysis is needed. In the remaining portion of this . . . [selection], we will present a three-step procedure. The procedure calls for preparing an egocentric organization chart to identify individual report readers, characterizing these readers, and classifying them to establish priorities. Based upon an egocentric view of the organization and concerned primarily with what report readers need, this system should yield the information the writer must have if he is to design an individual report effectively.

Prepare an Egocentric Organization Chart

An egocentric organization chart differs from the conventional chart in two senses. First, it identifies specific individuals rather than complex organizational units. A bloc on the conventional chart may often represent a number of people, but insofar as possible the egocentric chart identifies particular individuals who are potential readers of reports a writer produces. Second, the egocentric chart categorizes people in terms of their proximity to the report writer rather than in terms of their hierarchical relationship to the report writer. Readers are not identified as organizationally superior, inferior, or equal to the writer but rather as near or distant from the writer. We find it effective to identify four different degrees of distance as is illustrated in Figure 3, *Egocentric Organization Chart*. In this figure, with the triangle representing the writer, each circle is an individual reader identified by his organizational title and by his primary operational concerns. The four degrees of distance are identified by the four concentric rings. The potential readers in the first ring are those people with whom the writer associates daily. They are typically those people in his same office or project group. The readers in the second ring are those people in other offices with whom the writer must normally interact in order to perform his job. Typically, these are persons in adjacent and management groups. The readers in the third ring are persons relatively more distant but still within the same organization. They are distant management, public relations, sales, legal department, production, purchasing, and so on. They are operationally dissimilar persons. The readers in the fourth ring are persons beyond the organization. They may work for the same company but in a division in another city. Or they may work for an entirely different organization.

Having prepared the egocentric organization chart, the report writer is able to see himself and his potential audiences from a useful perspective. Rather than

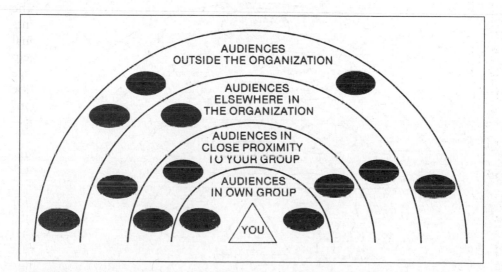

FIGURE 3   Egocentric Organization Chart

seeing himself as an insignificantly small part of a complex structure—as he is apt to do with the conventional organizational chart—the writer sees himself as a center from which communication radiates throughout an organization. He sees his readers as individuals rather than as faceless blocs. And he sees that what he writes is addressed to people with varying and significant degrees of difference.

A good illustration of the perspective provided by the egocentric organization chart is the chart prepared by a chemical engineer working for a large corporation, Figure 4, *Actual Egocentric Organization Chart of an Engineer in a Large Corporation*. It is important to notice how the operational concerns of the persons even in close proximity vary considerably from those of the development engineer. What these people need from reports written by this engineer, then, has little to do with the processes by which he defined his technical problems.

The chemical engineer himself is concerned with the research and development of production processes and has little interest in, or knowledge of, budgetary matters. Some of the audiences in his group are chemists concerned with production—not with research and development. Because of this they have, as he said, "lost familiarity with the technical background, and instead depend mostly on experience." Other audiences in his group are technicians concerned only with operations. With only two years of college, they have had no more than introductory chemistry courses and have had no engineering courses.

Still another audience in his group is his group leader. Rather than being concerned with development, this reader is concerned with facilities and production operations. Consequently, he too is "losing familiarity with the technical material." Particularly significant for the report writer is that his group leader in

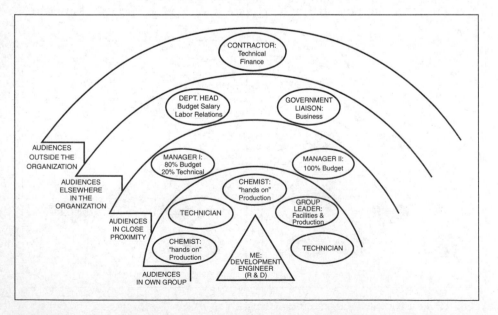

FIGURE 4   Actual Egocentric Organization Chart of an Engineer in a Large Corporation

his professional capacity does not use his B.S.Ch.E. degree. His role is that of manager, so his needs have become administrative rather than technical.

The concerns of the chemical engineer/report writer's audiences in close proximity to his group change again. Instead of being concerned with development or production operations, these audiences are primarily concerned with the budget. They have little technical contact, and are described as "business oriented." Both Manager I and Manager II are older, and neither has a degree in engineering. One has a Ph.D. degree in chemistry, the other an M.S. degree in technology. Both have had technical experience in the lab, but neither can readily follow technical explanations. As the chemical engineer said, both would find it "difficult to return to the law."

The report writer's department head and other persons through whom the group communicates with audiences elsewhere in the organization, and beyond it, have additional concerns as well as different backgrounds. The department head is concerned with budget, personnel, and labor relations. The person in contact with outside funding units—in this case, a government agency—has business administration degrees and is entirely business oriented. The person in contact with subcontractors has both technical and financial concerns.

Notice that when this writer examined his audiences even in his own group as well as those in close proximity to him, he saw that the natures, the backgrounds, and especially the operational concerns of his audiences vary and differ considerably. As he widened the scope of his egocentric organization chart, he knew less and less about his audiences. However, he could assume they will vary even more than those of the audiences in close proximity.

Thus, in the process of examining the audience situation with an egocentric organization chart, a report writer can uncover not only the fact that audiences have functionally different interests, but also the nature of those functional differences. He can proceed to classify the audiences for each particular report in terms of audience needs.

Preparation of the egocentric organization chart is the first step of your procedure of systematic audience analysis. Notice that this step can be performed once to describe your typical report audience situation but must be particularized for each report to define the audiences for that report. Having prepared the egocentric chart once, the writer revises his chart for subsequent reports by adding or subtracting individual audiences.

Characterize the Individual Report Readers

In the process of preparing the egocentric organization chart, you immediately begin to think of your individual report readers in particular terms. In preparing the egocentric chart discussed above, the report writer mentioned such items as a reader's age, academic degrees, and background in the organization as well as his operational concerns. All of these particulars will come to mind when you think of your audiences as individuals. However, a systematic rather than piecemeal audience analysis will yield more useful information. The second step of audience analysis is, therefore, a systematic characterization of each person identified in the egocentric organization chart. A systematic characterization is made in terms of *operational, objective,* and *personal* characteristics.

The *operational characteristics* of your audiences are particularly important. As you identify the operational characteristics for a person affected by your report, try to identify significant differences between his or her role and yours. What are his professional values? How does he spend his time? That is, will his daily concerns and attitudes enable him to react to your report easily, or will they make it difficult for him to grasp what you are talking about? What does he know about your role, and in particular, what does he know or remember about your technical assignment and the organizational problem that occasioned your report to come to him? You should also consider carefully what he will need from your report. As you think over your entire technical investigation, ask yourself if that person will involve staff personnel in action on your report, of if he will in turn activate other persons elsewhere in the organization, when he receives the report. If he should, you must take their reactions into account when you write your report.

In addition, you should ask yourself, "How will my report affect his role?" A student engineer recently told us of an experience he had during summer employment when he was asked to evaluate the efficiency of the plant's waste treatment process. Armed with his fresh knowledge from advanced chemical engineering courses, to his surprise he found that, by making a simple change in the process, the company could save more than $200,000 a year. He fired off his report with great anticipation of glowing accolades—none came. How had his report affected the roles of some of his audiences? Although the writer had not considered the report's consequences when he wrote it, the supervisor, the manager, and related personnel now were faced with the problem of accounting for their waste of $200,000 a year. It should have been no surprise that they were less than elated over his discovery.

By *objective characteristics* we mean specific, relevant background data about the person. As you try to identify his or her educational background, you may note differences you might have otherwise neglected. Should his education seem to approximate yours, do not assume he knows what you know. Remember that the half-life of engineering education today is about five years. Thus, anyone five to ten years older than you, if you are recently out of college, probably will be only superficially familiar with the material and jargon of your advanced technical courses. If you can further identify his past professional experiences and roles, you might be able to anticipate his first-hand knowledge of your role and technical activities as well as to clarify any residual organizational commitments and value systems he might have. When you judge his knowledge of your technical area, ask yourself, "Could he participate in a professional conference in my field of specialization?"

For *personal characteristics,* when you identify a person by name, ask yourself how often the name changes in this organizational role. When you note his or her approximate age, remind yourself how differences in age can inhibit communication. Also note personal concerns that could influence his reactions to your report.

A convenient way to conduct the audience analysis we have been describing and to store the information it yields is to use an analysis form similar to the one in Figure 5, *Form for Characterizing Individual Report Readers* [p. 180]. It may be a little time-consuming to do this the first time around, but you can establish a file of audience characterizations. Then you can add to or subtract from this file as an individual communication situation requires.

One final point: This form is a means to an end rather than an end in itself. What is important for the report writer is that he thinks systematically about the questions this form raises. The novice usually has to force himself to analyze his audiences systematically. The experienced writer does this automatically.

Classify Audiences in Terms of How They Will Use Your Report

For each report you write, trace out the communication routes on your egocentric organization chart and add other routes not on the chart. Do not limit these routes to those specifically identified by the assignment and the addresses of the report. Rather, think through the total impacts of your report on the organization. That is, think in terms of the first, second, and even some third-order consequences of your report, and trace out the significant communication routes involved. All of these consequences define your actual communication.

When you think in terms of consequences, primarily you think in terms of the uses to which your report will be put. No longer are you concerned with your technical investigation itself. In fact, when you consider how readers will use your report, you realize that very few of your potential readers will have any real interest in the details of your technical investigation. Instead, they want to know the answers to such questions as "Why was this investigation made? What is the significance of the problem it addresses? What am I supposed to do with the results of this investigation? What will it cost? What are the implications—for sales, for production, for the unions? What happens next? Who does it? Who is responsible?"

It is precisely this audience concern for nontechnical questions that causes so much trouble for young practicing engineers. Professionally, much of what the engineer spends his time doing is, at most, of only marginal concern to many of his audiences. His audiences ask questions about things which perhaps never entered his thoughts during his own technical activities when he received the assignment, defined the problem, and performed his investigation. These questions, however, must enter into his considerations when he writes his report.

Having defined the communication routes for a report you now know what audiences you will have and what questions they will want answered. The final step in our method of audience analysis is to assign priorities to your audiences. Classify them in terms of how they will use your report. In order of their importance to you (not in terms of their proximity to you), classify your audiences by these three categories:

- *Primary audiences*—who make decisions or act on the basis of the information a report contains.
- *Secondary audiences*—who are affected by the decisions and actions.
- *Immediate audiences*—who route the report or transmit the information it contains.

NAME: TITLE:

A. OPERATIONAL CHARACTERISTICS:
    1. His role within the organization and consequent value system:

    2. His daily concerns and attitudes:

    3. His knowledge of your technical responsibilities and assignment:

    4. What he will need from your report:

    5. What staff and other persons will be activated by your report
        through him:

    6. How your report could affect his role:

B. OBJECTIVE CHARACTERISTICS:
    1. His education—levels, fields, and years:

    2. His past professional experiences and roles:

    3. His knowledge of your technical area:

C. PERSONAL CHARACTERISTICS:
    Personal characteristics that could influence his reactions—age,
    attitudes, pet concerns, etc.

FIGURE 5   Form for Characterizing Individual Report Readers

The *primary audience* for a report consists of those persons who will make decisions or act on the basis of the information provided by the report. The report overall should be designed to meet the needs of these users. The primary audience can consist of one person who will act in an official capacity, or it can consist of several persons representing several offices using the report. The important point here is that the primary audience for a report can consist of persons from any ring on the egocentric organization chart. They may be distant or in close proximity to the writer. They may be his organizational superiors, inferiors, or equals. They are simply those readers for whom the report is primarily intended. They are the top priority users.

In theory at least, primary audiences act in terms of their organizational roles rather than as individuals with distinctive idiosyncracies, predilections, and values. Your audience analysis should indicate when these personal concerns are likely to override organizational concerns. A typical primary audience is the decision maker, but his actual decisions are often determined by the evaluations and recommendations of staff personnel. Thus the report whose primary audience is a decision maker with line responsibility actually has an audience of staff personnel. Another type of primary audience is the production superintendent, but again his actions are often contingent upon the reactions of others.

In addition, because the report enters into a system, in time both the line and staff personnel will change; roles rather than individuals provide continuity. For this reason, it is helpful to remember the words of one engineer when he said, "A complete change of personnel could occur over the lifetime of my report." The report remains in the file. The report writer must not assume that his primary audience will be familiar with the technical assignment. He must design the report so that it contains adequate information concerning the reasons for the assignment, details of the procedures used, the results of the investigation, and conclusions and recommendations. This information is needed so that any future component of his primary audience will be able to use the report confidently.

The *secondary audience* for a report consists of those persons other than primary decision makers or users who are affected by the information the report transmits into the system. These are the people whose activities are affected when a primary audience makes a decision, such as when production supervision has to adjust to management decisions. They must respond appropriately when a primary audience acts, such as when personnel and labor relations have to accommodate production line changes. The report writer must not neglect the needs of his secondary audiences. In tracing out his communication routes, he will identify several secondary audiences. Analysis of their needs will reveal what additional information the report should contain. This information is often omitted by writers who do not classify their audiences sufficiently.

The *immediate audience* for a report are those persons who route the report or transmit the information it contains. It is essential for the report writer to identify his immediate audiences and not to confuse them with his primary audiences. The immediate audience might be the report writer's supervisor or another middle management person. Yet usually his role will be to transmit information rather than to use the information directly. An information system has numerous persons who transmit reports but who may not act upon the information or who may not be affected by the information in ways of concern to the report writers. Often, a report is addressed to the writer's supervisor, but except for an incidental memo report, the supervisor serves only to transmit and expedite the information flow throughout the organizational system.

A word of caution: at times the immediate audience is also part of the primary audience; at other times the immediate audience is part of the secondary audience. For each report you write, you must distinguish those among your readers who will function as conduits to the primary audience.

As an example of these distinctions between categories of report audiences, consider how audiences identified on the egocentric organization chart, Figure 4 [p. 176], can be categorized. Assume that the chemical engineer writes a report on a particular process improvement he has designed. The immediate audience might be his Group Leader. Another would be Manager I, transmitting the report to Manager II. The primary audiences might be Manager II and the Department Head; they would ask a barrage of nontechnical questions similar to those we mentioned a moment ago. They will decide whether or not the organization will implement the improvement recommended by the writer. The Department Head also could be part of the secondary audience by asking questions relating to labor relations and union contracts. Other secondary audiences, each asking different questions of the report, could be:

> The person in contact with the funding agency, who will be concerned with budget and contract implications.

> The person in contact with subcontractors, determining how they are affected.

> The Group Leader, whose activities will be changed.

> The "hands on" chemist, whose production responsibilities will be affected.

> The technicians, whose job descriptions will change.

In addition to the secondary audiences on the egocentric organization chart, the report will have other secondary audiences throughout the organization—technical service and development, for example, or perhaps waste treatment.

At some length we have been discussing a fairly detailed method for systematic audience analysis. The method may have seemed more complicated than it actually is. Reduced to its basic ingredients, the method requires you, first, to identify all the individuals who will read the report, second, to characterize them, and third, to classify them. The *Matrix for Audience Analysis*, Figure 6, is a convenient device for characterizing and classifying your readers once you have identified them. At a glance, the matrix reveals what information you have and what information you still need to generate. Above all, the matrix forces you to think systematically. If you are able to fill in a good deal of specific information in each cell (particularly in the first six cells), you have gone a long way towards seeing how the needs of your audiences will determine the design of your report.

Types of audiences \ Characteristics	Operational	Objective	Personal
Primary	①	④	⑦
Secondary	②	⑤	⑧
Immediate	③	⑥	⑨

FIGURE 6   Matrix for Audience Analysis

   We have not introduced a systematic method for audience analysis with the expectation that it will make your communication task easy. We have introduced you to the problems you must account for when you design your reports—problems you otherwise might ignore. You should, at least, appreciate the complexity of a report audience. Thus, when you come to write a report, you are less likely to make false assumptions about your audience. To develop this attitude is perhaps as important as to acquire the specific information the analysis yields. On the basis of this attitude, you now are ready to determine the specific purpose of your report.

Nancy Allen, Dianne Atkinson, Meg Morgan, Teresa Moore, and Craig Snow

---

What Experienced Collaborators Say about Collaborative Writing

The authors were all members of the faculty at Purdue University when they conducted the research that led to this article.

Heightened interest in writing on the job has uncovered, almost by accident, another writing issue of recent and growing concern: collaborative writing. For several years researchers have been aware that collaborative writing exists in the professional setting. In 1982 Faigley and Miller, for example, surveyed 200 professionals about their on-the-job writing and learned that 73.5% of these professionals wrote collaboratively on the job (561).

However, in spite of this established frequent occurrence of collaboration, most writing research has concentrated on other aspects of on-the-job writing. Writing instructors interested in collaboration have had to glean facts from research directed toward other topics. As a result, the information we have about collaborative writing is fragmentary and unfocused.

One recent source of information is Odell and Goswami's collection of studies of non-academic writing. Although none of these studies explored collaborative writing as its primary focus, many revealed secondarily the collaborative nature of writing on the job. In one study from this collection, Paul Anderson cites several surveys that reveal the predominance of collaborative writing on the job (50-51), reconfirming Faigley and Miller's finding. Anderson also notes that many kinds of collaboration occur under many different circumstances.

Odell's own article in the collection concerns a study to "investigate some of the relations between organizational contexts and writing" (250). Yet much of the article describes the specific interactions between a legislative analyst and the agency attorney, as the analyst prepares to write a document on a piece of legislation. Odell points out that the agency where both worked "encouraged discussion and collaboration not only on this sort of topic, but on others as well, as part of the process of inquiry" (260).

A final example from the Odell and Goswami collection, Paradis, Dobrin, and Miller's article on writing at Exxon, also reveals instances of collaboration. In this study, collaborative writing is most apparent in the authors' descriptions of how a document "cycles" from the staff person who researches and drafts it to the supervisor who edits the draft. At a luncheon meeting with younger staff members, the writing researchers learned that "those who did not interact with supervisors at the planning stage of the writing process generally had trouble at the editorial stage" (294). (Readers might also want to see other articles in this collection, such as Couture, *et al.* and Lauerman, *et al.,* for further incidental information on collaborative writing.)

Because, as with Odell and Goswami, the uncovering of collaborative-writing settings has been peripheral to most writing research available to date, little specific information on collaborative-writing processes emerges. From these studies we gain little sense of the details or range of variation in the processes collaborative writers use, few clearly articulated reasons for employing a collaborative effort as opposed to an individual effort, and no coherent evaluation of collaboration from the writers themselves.

Some of these omissions are overcome in the Doheny-Farina ethnographic study of writing in an "emerging" software company. Although the focus of this study is again broader than collaborative writing, Doheny-Farina does trace the history of a collaboratively written business plan as it moves through the organization. He reports that critical decisions affecting the philosophy and direction of the company were made as the president and vice presidents discussed a draft of this business plan.

However, only Ede and Lunsford have focused their research efforts on collaboration. In 1983 they published an article relating their own experiences writing together. Then in 1986, after an initial survey using a questionnaire mailed to 530 members of six professional organizations, they explored the nature of collaborative writing in greater detail through on-site visits. The results of these studies provide the only detailed information now available on collaboration. (See both Ede and Lunsford under References for specific 1986 citations.)

It is clear from the studies cited that collaborative writing can include a range of activities:

- a supervisor's assignment of a document that is researched and drafted by a staff member but carefully edited by the supervisor (Paradis, Dobrin, and Miller)
- collaborative planning of a document that is drafted and revised by an individual (Odell)
- individual planning and drafting of a document that is revised collaboratively (Doheny-Farina)

- a peer's critiquing of a co-worker's draft (Anderson)
- the coauthoring of a document (Ede and Lunsford)

It is also clear that using the term "collaborative writing" to describe all these very different writing activities raises questions as to how to interpret research results, such as Faigley and Miller's. In fact, a panel entitled "The Role of Collaboration in the Writing Process: Three Perspectives" at the 1986 Conference on College Composition and Communication included three presentations by four well-known researchers (Gere, Hilgers, Lunsford, and Ede), all describing completely different collaborative-writing situations.

The range of possible collaborative-writing situations reflects the range in discussions of collaborative learning and writing at a more philosophical and theoretical level. Mason, concerned with what he perceived as authoritarian and ineffective pedagogies in British schools, based his pedagogy on a learning philosophy that emphasized groups of students working together to solve problems. Mason encouraged the use of this group approach "to get something done about the state of the world" (125).

Bruffee recently articulated a philosophical base for his previously described pedagogy ("Collaborative Learning" 635-52). He called upon the works of Oakeshott, Vygotsky, Kuhn, and Rorty to focus on the connections between human thought and conversation, on knowledge as socially derived belief, and on normal and abnormal discourse. Bruffee, however, in his early applications of collaborative learning, centered his concern on peer-group editing of individually written drafts. In this kind of group work, the single author is free to accept or reject the peers' advice.

Wiener makes a distinction between this sort of "group work" and collaboration. He asserts that consensus is necessary to create a truly collaborative situation (55). That is, individuals must share power in making decisions that can be accepted by the group as a whole. Without consensus as a criterion for decision making, individuals retain all power and responsibility just as if they were solitary writers.

Other studies of "collaboration" in the classroom also discuss it as "group work" rather than as "consensus." Gere and Abbott limit their inquiry into collaboration to include only peer responses to individually written drafts; Gebhardt calls for peer response throughout the writing process, in planning as well as revision, but these responses are still directed toward individually written work. Although Clifford calls for a collaborative pedagogy, he discusses groups of students working together in non-consensual situations.

Only a few recent studies offer pedagogies that involve group consensus. Goldstein and Malone (1985) describe a classroom methodology in which groups of students design a single shared document. O'Donnell, *et al.,* in an empirical study comparing group and individual performances on a writing task, demonstrate the effectiveness of consensus-based writing groups in producing a better document at the college level. Finally, Daiute, in a case study, suggests the kinds of learning that can occur when students in elementary school engage in a collaborative-writing task. Although consensus operated within these three collaborative situations, its effects on group writing are not explored.

Two problems emerge from reviewing this research. First, very little detail is known about collaborative-writing processes in general. Second, many studies have covered a wide range of activities without focusing on the special characteristics of collaboration involving group authorship. Clearly there is a need for an in-depth study of the features of collaborative writing in the meaning discussed by Wiener: a situation in which decisions are made by consensus.

It is this kind of collaboration that interested us as researchers. We wanted to investigate collaboration as it existed in the activities of experienced collaborators on the job—professional people who had worked together throughout the planning, drafting, and revising activities of a single document. We chose, therefore, to examine what we felt were the most interesting and unstudied aspects of collaborative writing. We looked for answers to these questions:

- What kinds of people form collaborative-writing groups and what kinds of tasks do they undertake?
- What are the writing processes used by experienced collaborators?
- What significant group processes emerge in collaborative-writing groups?
- How do experienced collaborators feel about the costs and rewards of collaboration?

METHODS

Our objective was to conduct an exploratory study of the experiences of active collaborative writers from the business and professional worlds. To get at the detailed nature of their processes, we sought qualitative responses to open questions in interviews with professionals who had collaborated on a wide range of projects. The following paragraphs describe the specific methods used to reach this objective.

Participants

Study participants were recruited by the researchers to represent a wide range of collaborative settings and projects. The sample of respondents, therefore, was purposive and non-random. A total of 20 respondents were interviewed, 14 men and 6 women, who reported on 14 separate collaborative projects. Most respondents were from the Midwest, though one was from New York and one from Washington state. Collaborators who were also writers by profession were excluded from the list, as they were considered to form a separate group that may or may not perform in the same manner as general writers from the business and professional worlds. Table 1 [p. 188] lists the professional areas represented in the sample and the number of respondents drawn from each area. No potential respondent refused to participate in this study.

In order to obtain detailed descriptions and varied perspectives of group interactions and processes, all five members of one group (a group of teachers)

TABLE I   Professional Areas of Respondents

Area	Number Interviewed
Small Business	I
University Teaching	7
Scientific Research within a University	4
Scientific Research within a Corporation	2
Government Agency	2
Community Service	3
Law Firm	I

were interviewed. These interviews resulted in a large number of teachers being included as respondents.

Structured Interview Form

A structured interview form was developed to assure complete and comparable coverage of each collaborative project. Initial questions elicited demographic information about the respondent and his or her professional position. Subsequent questions concerned the membership of the collaborative group, the roles played and contributions made by various group members, the writing process used, and the nature and frequency of group interaction. Final questions asked for respondents' evaluations of the document produced and of the experience as a whole. The majority of the interview questions were open-ended, and prompts were used to encourage detailed description.

Respondent Interviews

Each respondent was interviewed in person by one or a pair of the researchers, using the structured interview form. Each interview lasted for approximately two hours and was audio tape recorded and later transcribed. Respondents were asked to recount a "particularly memorable" collaborative-writing experience. The interviewers did not define "particularly memorable," nor did they ask the respondents to explain why they chose a particular experience as their subject.

During the interviews, respondents were encouraged to formulate observations, evaluations, and conclusions concerning any aspect of their collaborative-writing project and to illustrate these observations with specific details. All interviews were conducted between February and September of 1985.

Two of the experimenters also observed and tape recorded several meetings of the group of university teachers preparing a textbook.

Analysis

Analysis of the interview transcripts proceeded in two stages. In the first stage, the relatively closed-ended questions elicited basic demographic profiles of the group members and collaborative projects: the who, what, where, when, and why.

These profiles provided information about the variety of people who participated in these collaborative projects and the range of problems addressed.

In the second stage, respondents' detailed observations of the processes and evaluations were collated. These responses provided information on the operation of the collaborative process, the nature of collaborative interactions, respondents' likes and dislikes concerning collaboration, and respondents' suggestions for making collaborative projects rewarding.

RESEARCH FINDINGS

The results of this study provide some answers to our research questions. Because of the small sample interviewed, these answers are not complete, but the information obtained in this study allows us to draw some tentative conclusions concerning the people, tasks, and processes involved in collaborative writing. These results are presented according to the two approaches used in our analysis. Demographic information and information about the collaborative process is presented first, followed by the respondents' observations on the collaborative process itself.

Demographic Information

Range of Tasks and Group Affiliations

Our respondents reported that during their professional careers they had worked in groups on a wide variety of written-communication tasks, covering almost every kind of document written professionally. When asked to describe an especially memorable project in detail, they chose to report on proposals, books, articles, goals statements, reports, and legal briefs. The distribution of these tasks among groups and the organizational affiliation of each group are shown in Table 2 [p. 190].

The tasks our respondents chose to report on were ones which they felt were "successful." That is, the respondents ranked themselves as "satisfied" or "very satisfied" with the document produced and with the experience as a whole. In their discussions, three respondents also mentioned some experiences with unsatisfactory collaborations, but they did not choose those projects to describe in detail. The projects they did describe encompassed a fairly broad range of tasks.

Diversity of Group Membership

We found that groups varied, from those whose members had little in common except the collaborative project to those whose very similarities had brought them together. There were also many gradations between "different" and "similar" groups.

Nine of the groups we studied were made up of members whose backgrounds, training, and specialties differed. Consequently, individual members of these groups brought diverse skills to their projects. Group A, for example,

TABLE 2 Writing Tasks and Group Affiliations

Writing Task	Number of Interviews	Number of Projects	Group Identifier & Affiliation
Proposals	4	4	(A) Small Business
			(B) University
			(C) Government
			(D) Corporation
Books	7	3	(E) University*
			(F) University
			(G) University
Articles	3	2	(H) University
			(I) University*
Goal Statements	2	2	(J) Community
			(K) Corporation
Reports	3	2	(L) Community*
			(M) Government
Legal Briefs	1	1	(N) Partnership
Totals	20	14	

More than one group member interviewed.

comprised a medical doctor, a pharmacologist, and a business manager, all of whom were partners in a small business. The members of Group B all came from the same university department, but each had a different specialty, and one had had very different training and experience from the other two. Both of these groups prepared proposals for the National Institutes of Health (NIH), and the members represented the different areas of expertise necessary for the research each group planned to conduct.

Other groups showed similar variety in their membership. One corporate group, Group K, included managers from each of the five divisions of a corporation that would work on the same project. The five members of a volunteer community-task force, Group L, represented residents with varied occupations from several social sectors of the same community; the qualification they shared for involvement in this project was that of being a concerned parent. Group H included members living in California, Indiana, and Mexico, who performed research in different but related areas.

Five groups were made up of members who had similar training and professional interests. The tasks they engaged in did not require diverse specialties but instead were large tasks, some of which had strict time deadlines.

Though some projects required breadth of skills and others were more focused, this difference was not necessarily reflected in the *general* project type. Proposals, textbooks, professional articles, and reports were prepared both by groups whose members had diverse skills and by those whose members had similar skills. Both goals statements were prepared by groups whose members had diverse skills, and the legal brief was prepared by a group whose members had similar skills.

Task Restrictions

The restrictions imposed by the form and content requirements of the final documents for these writing tasks varied. Most respondents began their tasks knowing the type of document they were to write and its general format, but they were reasonably free as to the content. Groups A and B, however, were following the NIH guidelines for proposals and consequently had very specific format and content-area requirements. Group L, preparing a report for a local school board, was least restricted. They had no format instructions at all and, in fact, knew very little about appropriate report format in general. Their instructions were simply to present recommendations to their board.

Information About the Collaborative Process

Group Writing Processes

All groups reported handling the planning activities for the document as a whole before working on subparts. No group planned and completed one section of their document before proceeding to the next section. The two goal statements and one report were maintained as a single writing task throughout the groups' entire projects and were not divided into subparts.

Respondents reported that the major and most satisfying collaborative effort usually took place at the beginning of a project, while group members planned the document. In this phase, members of most groups met to discuss the project's goals and the document's purpose, content, organization, and audience.

The initial period of group planning was most often followed by periods of relatively independent materials research and drafting, during which individuals worked alone. In fact, members of 10 of the 14 groups reported that actual words-on-paper drafting was always an individual effort. Some respondents reported that attempts at group drafting produced only frustration.

Six groups (B, C, E, F, G, and M) divided the drafting task, with individual members drafting the sections most familiar to them or falling within their areas of expertise. This approach was the most common among the writers we interviewed. Groups D and H followed another common approach in which one member produced a working draft after considerable group planning. The other members then commented extensively on the draft, and they discussed their comments as a group. One member of Group J used notes he had taken during group discussions to produce a draft for the group. Everyone then commented on the latest draft at subsequent meetings. In one corporate group, K, each member drafted a complete version of the entire goals statement, and succeeding group meetings involved coming to agreement on one combined version. These discussions sometimes became quite heated. In the small-business group, A, the head of the company roughed out a complete draft, which was then turned over to the other two group members. They filled in their special areas, and one of them assumed responsibility for all stylistic editing. They seldom met as a group to discuss changes or additions, feeling that changes in one section did not affect the others.

Group L began drafting together, but haggled over words and sentences, so that they were unable to get any completed ideas on paper. After a few abortive tries, the group asked one member with some writing experience to do the drafting. At each subsequent meeting, that member listened to and made notes of the discussions, took his notes home, and translated them into a rough draft, following a process similar to that of Group J. He then brought his draft and notes back to the group, who haggled over his interpretation, as well as his prose. Although this method didn't eliminate all the group's writing problems, it did provide a completed draft, and the members reported being quite satisfied with this approach.

Two members of Group E attempted composing some sections together but found that their styles were so different that they were not able to compose well together. They agreed to divide their tasks and compose separately; each then commented freely on the other's sections for revision.

The members of Group G tape recorded their brainstorming sessions and used transcriptions of these tapes to prepare drafts, dividing the sections between them. Occasionally they would compose small amounts of text together orally during their taping sessions (their entire introduction was drafted in this way), but most of their composing was done individually, using the brainstorming transcripts as notes. They exchanged drafts for comments and revision until both authors were satisfied with all parts.

Initial drafts of legal briefs were usually prepared by individuals in Group N's law firm, but our respondent chose to tell us about a collaborative experience that was unusual for him. Because the scope of this particular task was large, he worked with a collaborator. They divided the research, and each prepared outlines of separate sections. Then, using past similar briefs as references, they began composing their brief together, sentence by sentence. As sections were completed, secretaries prepared word-processor copies for them to use in revision. During this stage, one would revise while the other worked on a new section. They sat at opposite ends of a table, taking turns with the actual hand writing or dictating, for a period of a few days, working until 2 or 3 a.m. and once overnight, until a complete draft was finished. The draft was then reviewed and revised both within this firm and by other firms associated with the case. The respondent estimated that the brief might have gone through 50 drafts by the time it reached its final form.

Only one group, Group I, reported composing together on a fairly regular basis, word by word, sentence by sentence. The two members of this group have written several articles together, and in their typical process, either one of them can be responsible for producing a working draft. They then work very closely on revision, often composing sentences together. They reported that their finished documents reflect such a melding of their writing that neither can identify who wrote what words, nor do they remember which of them wrote the working drafts for many of their papers. These group members write articles individually on other subjects but write together on the area in which their interests overlap. They have neighboring offices and have been writing together successfully for 15 years. One of their publications has been cited over 2000 times in the past 10 years.

As these reported writing processes show, revision, like planning, was a group activity for our respondents, and it often involved renewed planning. As group members went over a draft, they were stimulated to think of new ideas for their document and to change some of their old ideas. As a result, revision was both global and detailed. In one instance, the members of Group F changed the entire organization of their book after they decided that their initial partial drafts "didn't work." In another instance, a member of Group E remembered trying to "informalize" the style of one writer to match the style of others in the group. The actual presence of a draft also focused group members' attention on the written word, and many respondents reported stylistic and wording changes. One member of Group F noted that changes were made concerning "clarity of exposition." The 50 revisions of the legal brief mentioned above changed that document from more than 100 pages to 68.

Group Interaction

Members interacted extensively during the early stages of a project to set goals, design research plans, generate alternative solutions, discuss past experiences, divide work, and draw conclusions from their research on the project problem. These interactions occurred for all groups without correlation to the drafting procedure eventually used by the group. Most occurred face to face, but some respondents' interactions occurred through telephone conversations or via computer modem.

Some respondents reported this initial planning interaction to be the most rewarding part of collaboration. One respondent from Group E said, "It's easier as a writer to get a sense of audience and purpose because you have to articulate those things and you have to make decisions about them."

While actual drafting was often done individually, all groups again reported extensive interaction concerning revision. As was shown by several of the examples described above, these interactions concerned revisions at all levels.

We found three aspects of group interaction that were particularly interesting and deserve separate elaboration: the ability of the group to act as a first-line audience, the role of conflict, and group interaction via computers.

Group as First-line Audience. For the groups in our sample, the intended readers were usually members of outside organizations: granting agencies, judges, fellow professionals, students, and boards of directors. Consequently, group interaction was sometimes centered around group members consciously or unconsciously assuming the role of audience for the document. Members of the collaborative groups often discussed problems in the document that they thought intended readers might perceive later, trying to clear up those problems in advance. The respondent from Group F expressed his concern with "clarity of exposition" explicitly as a concern for their intended readers. He thought his collaborator "might have taken certain things for granted because of his background that . . . were not clear enough to a person with a slightly different background." The members of Group B purposely played the roles of proposal evaluators in one of their meetings. One researcher from Group H, describing the cost and benefit of this aspect of group work, said, "You have to have people who are willing to challenge things that are very dear to you, even if it becomes personally hurtful. If it isn't going to stand up to that kind of challenge, then maybe it isn't going to stand up."

Group Conflict. Group conflict, which many people fear may occur, did occur in all our respondents' groups, ranging from a relatively minor conflict over the use of a particular term to major conflicts over research conclusions. Our respondents indicated a range of tolerance for group conflict, referring to it in terms that went from the "least satisfying" aspect of collaboration or "painful but necessary" to "exhilarating." One experienced academic researcher said, "It's easier to become creative when you work with somebody and have them confront you . . . and you do the same to them" (Group F). Another collaborator, an academic researcher from Group H, suggested that instead of calling the process collaborative writing, it should be called "collaborative fighting." He added:

> Most of the conflicts I've been involved in in the end have been productive. In the interim, they have had all sorts of negative effects—self doubts, doubts about other people, and all sorts of things. I've had my stomach turned in knots a couple of dozen times by this guy [his associate] because of the way in which he marks up my manuscripts, but then I also know that although I may take it personally, I'm gonna get over that, and I'm gonna be able to deal with it; and in the long run probably two thirds to three fourths of the comments he made—if I'm gonna implement them in some fashion—are gonna make that into a better paper. So it checks and balances in a way.

This same respondent remembered a battle with an associate over a paper they were co-authoring with a graduate student. The two senior collaborators shouted at each other while the graduate student cowered in a corner. The battle was uncomfortable, but it settled issues and "helped make that paper a classic."

Not all conflicts were handled this directly. One respondent from Group E reported that conflicts over "sensitive matters" were resolved outside of group meetings.

The respondent from Group F not only supported the advantages that can result from conflict but also saw conflict as a necessary part of collaboration. While he agreed that mutual respect between collaborators was important, he also believed that too much respect would prevent members from challenging one another and would thereby lessen the group's creativity. He said:

> What's interesting is in many of these collaborations you have as much disrespect for the other person as you have respect. And it's necessary. In fact, I think that's a very important ingredient of creative work—lack of respect—because if you have total respect for other people and you're totally awed by them, it is impossible to go beyond them. So

you have to entertain this notion that they are screwballs at some level, and they are wedded to their notions, . . . they're in their own ruts as you are in your own, and that's a very healthy viewpoint.

Computer-Aided Interaction. Three groups used the computer to replace face-to-face interaction. Two of these groups communicated over long distances via a modem, sharing planning activities and drafts. These groups have been collaborating since the mid-seventies, initially either meeting face-to-face at conferences or using the telephone. A third group, A, used the computer differently. The group leader roughed out his ideas for the entire draft of their document on the computer, storing it on disk; then the other two members individually filled in their contributions in specialized sections. The three members rarely met as a group to discuss their document, even though they were partners in the same business and worked part of the time in the same building.

Group Decision Making

The group members we interviewed shared decision-making power in two ways. First, any one person in these groups could object to any decision made in the group or even decisions made by the group leader. Second, they shared decision-making power only within this specific group and for their collaborative task. The power they shared in the collaborative context did not extend to other contexts.

For our respondents' groups, an individual member's decision-making power and behavior were not dependent on leadership style within the group. In Group E, a group with a relatively autocratic leader, members still felt free to suggest ideas, make changes, and generally voice their opinions. In Group B, a group with a more democratic leader, one of the three members went along with the leader's decision when it was accepted by the third group member, even though he didn't agree.

Within these groups, the right to question a decision did not mean the right to change a decision. As in the example just mentioned, the decisions made within these groups were ones that all members could accept, even though they might not entirely agree with them. Our respondents reported a strong sense of commitment for themselves and their fellow group members toward completing the project. This commitment encouraged the groups to move forward with "acceptable" decisions when absolute agreement could not be reached.

Group Leadership

Most of these groups were organized around group leaders who provided a central point for organizing the details of running the group, such as calling meetings and setting completion dates for subtasks. In nine groups the leadership position was assumed because of seniority or rank. In two groups the leader was appointed by the larger organization under which this group operated. Leadership in one group rotated, depending upon time available or idea initiation. Two groups operated with no leader. Though the majority of groups clearly reflect a tendency toward structure through leadership, the two groups with no leader show that leadership structure is not essential.

Respondents' Observations on Collaboration

The writers we interviewed found the benefits of collaboration to be worth the costs. Although our respondents mentioned costs of time, of energy, and sometimes of ego, they stated that the documents they produced were definitely better than those any one of them could have produced alone. As mentioned earlier, these collaborators rated themselves as "satisfied" or "very satisfied" with these collaborative experiences and with the documents they produced. Of course, this positive result would not be true for all collaborations. Because these collaborators chose to tell us about successful experiences, their evaluations were necessarily skewed.

The costs of collaboration mentioned most often were time and ego. All respondents felt that collaboration required large amounts of time. Though the respondent in Group N reported composing sentences with his partner in this collaboration, he said that he would not do this again because it was "too time-consuming." The respondents' concern with ego prompted the collaborator from Group G to advise others who might participate in collaboration to "check your ego at the door." He said that collaborators should be "confident in their own abilities and yet able to take criticism." He felt this was the hardest part of collaboration.

All of these respondents recommended collaboration, at least for large or complex projects. They reported either that their group document was better than a document any one of them could have done alone or that the document couldn't have been done at all by one person.

DISCUSSION

The results of this research suggest three important points that merit elaboration: the functions of conflict within collaborative groups, the features that distinguish the kind of collaboration in which a group produces a single document, and the basic types of collaborative groups found within this sample, based on the advantage that group work offered for each task.

Functions of Conflict

The statements from our respondents that conflict contributed to their creativity and to the quality of their final document are supported by other work done on group decision-making and creativity. Janis found that failure to allow for the development and expression of opposing views within the group could produce such defective decision-making that the overall value of group effort was lost. The pejorative term "group think" has been widely used to characterize situations in which excessive group cohesiveness or a strong hierarchy, such as exists in military contexts, suppresses opposing opinion. In such cases groups tend to echo the opinions of the group leader and lose the advantage of varied perspectives.

In fact, a group's effectiveness may depend upon its ability to preserve various viewpoints. Weick presents an insightful discussion of the importance of "doubt" in the group decision making process. He cautions groups to avoid coming too quickly to premature decisions about actions to be taken (220). Our respondents certainly reaffirm these studies by attesting to the importance of including all viewpoints.

Rothenberg's work on "Janusian thinking" provides an analogy for the value of diverse opinions to group creativity. Rothenberg claimed that the dissonance caused by holding opposing or inconsistent perspectives simultaneously generated innovative, hence creative, resolutions ("Creative Contradictions" 55). Though this condition exists only occasionally for individuals, it is a natural part of group work. Members of a group never have exactly the same perspective on any subject and, as our respondents told us, their perspectives are often divergent or conflicting. When the group can tolerate some disharmony and work through divergent opinion to reach a consensus, their work is enhanced. The constraint of unanimity placed on juries, in which any individual can block a decision that he or she cannot accept, is an example of the protection of minority opinion in order to achieve high-quality decisions. Excellent reviews of research on small-group decision-making, group problem solving, and conflict can be found in Abelson and Levy, Kelley and Thibaut, and Putnam, respectively.

Distinguishing Shared-Document Collaboration

By collating details from our respondents' descriptions of their collaborative-writing experiences, we observed that these collaborations, all of which involved co- or group authorship, repeatedly exhibited three distinguishing features:

- production of a shared document
- substantive interaction among members
- shared decision-making power over and responsibility for the document

These features can be reflected in a wide range of group behaviors and in connection with varied tasks. The groups we studied did, indeed, differ considerably from each other in how they interacted and shared power. Yet each exhibited these three features. We believe, therefore, that this combination of features can be used to distinguish this type of collaboration, which we call "shared-document collaboration," from other types of collaboration.

Shared Document

As the most salient feature of this form of collaborative writing, "shared document" refers to the emergence of one document, a product of an agreed-upon insight, from the collaborative experience. Though this feature may seem obvious, its importance should not be slighted. It is because the group shares the goal of producing a single document that they have a unity of focus and engage in consensus to reach decisions.

This feature distinguishes this kind of collaborative effort from collaborations found in many classrooms, where peer feedback on individually written documents is encouraged. In such classroom situations, the collaborative effort is directed toward helping an individual student achieve a personal understanding or insight which will then contribute to that student's individually-authored document. Shared-document collaboration always involves a single document produced by more than one person.

Substantive Interaction

This feature means that collaborators may make contributions that affect their document at all levels, from stylistic details to global organization and content. This feature, then, distinguishes shared-document collaboration from situations in which an editor or supervisor simply assigns a project to a subordinate. The editor or supervisor may lay out the purposes and constraints of the project, which the subordinate will follow, but without interaction on these issues, these people are not shared-document collaborators.

Most interactions in shared-document collaboration typically take place at the beginning and end of the project. During their interactions the group often functions as a first-line audience, and conflict plays an important part in the group experience. The interactions do not always occur face-to-face but may involve written comments and technological media. The key point of this feature is that the communication is two-way and interactive, not just superior to subordinate.

Shared Decision-Making Power and Responsibility

All members of a shared-document collaborative group have power within the group's decision-making process and share responsibility for the resulting document. This feature means that individual members are not free to make final decisions affecting the document without consulting the group but instead must go through the group process. Each member's responsibility for the document, then, results naturally from involvement in decisions that were made as the document was produced.

This feature distinguishes shared-document collaboration from situations in which someone might critique a draft of a colleague's article. Since the author is free to accept or reject the advice, such critiquing does not constitute shared-document collaboration. Also because of this feature, a research assistant or lab assistant would not be considered as a shared-document collaborator unless he or she had sufficient status to share decision-making power concerning the final draft.

This definition of shared-document collaboration is exploratory in nature but nevertheless places some definitive boundaries upon this kind of collaborative-writing experience. The first feature is specific, the last two include a range of activities within the definition's boundaries. For example, there could be more or less interaction of a particular kind or within different activities of the writing process. Also, there could be more or less power exerted, or responsibility placed or assumed. The results of this research have only begun to point the way toward an identification and analysis of these dimensions.

Group Typology

Each of the groups in our sample was formed because a group offered some particular advantage in accomplishing the task. We found that these group advantages fell into three categories:

- The size of the task and/or the time limits imposed upon it required the labor of more than one person.
- The scope of the task required or benefited from more than one area of expertise.
- The task included as one of its primary goals the melding of divergent perspectives.

These three kinds of group advantages, to which we have assigned the descriptive labels "labor intensive," "specialization," and "synthesis," formed the bases around which the groups in our sample were organized. Table 3 shows how many groups of each type we interviewed and what collaborative tasks these groups accomplished.

TABLE 3   Group Classifications and Tasks

Group Type	Tasks Performed
Labor-Intensive Groups (N = 5)	Legal Brief Proposal Textbook Article
Specialization Groups (N = 6)	Proposal Textbook
Synthesis Groups (N = 3)	Goal Statement Report

None of the groups we looked at was a pure example of any one of these group types. Most of them shared the qualities of at least two types, if not all three. By looking closely at the kinds of contributions members made to a group and the kind of final document they produced, however, we were able to classify each group according to its dominant characteristics.

The general nature of the task did not automatically dictate a particular group structure and, as the table shows, proposals and textbooks were prepared by both labor-intensive and specialization groups. Instead, the particular goals of the group members interacted with the nature of the specific task and outside restrictions to determine the advantages group work would offer to a task. The following paragraphs describe each group type more clearly, with examples drawn from the sample groups.

Labor Intensive

These groups were formed primarily to enlist a number of people in performing a large task within a limited time period. These groups used the "divide and conquer" approach of separating their major projects into more manageable subtasks. Members of these groups were able to perform more than one of the possible subtasks that came out of the larger project. That is, once the task had been divided into more manageable units, any given unit could have been performed by more than one of the group members.

Jobs within these groups were chosen by members or assigned by the group leader. Group E, for example, prepared a large textbook following this organizational pattern. Although the possibility exists that one member of the group could have produced the text working alone, it would not have been produced within the same time period.

Specialization

These groups formed in order to draw on multiple areas of expertise that were required for their document or that would improve their document. For example, Group A needed the special knowledge of a medical doctor, a pharmacologist, and a business expert in preparing a major grant proposal. Group F produced a textbook that contained sections on different technical areas requiring different areas of expertise. Members of the specialization groups planned together and challenged points on one another's drafts in all areas, but they could not exchange jobs within the group, as members of labor-intensive groups could. Each member had a specific task according to that member's specialized skill. The documents they produced reflected a broader range of expertise than the range any one could have provided alone.

Synthesis

These groups were formed to meld divergent perspectives into a solution acceptable to the whole group or to an outside group. These groups represented both a variation of perspectives and an actual conflict of opinion. For example, Group J was composed of members that had been in conflict over the goals for a community center. Their final document provided a goals statement that would help direct activities at the center and, in the process of preparing that goals statement, they resolved the differences in community viewpoints.

Both the document and the synthesis were important results of their collaboration. One corporate group, K, used their collaborative-writing task as a team-building exercise, also making synthesis a major outcome of their work.

QUESTIONS FOR FUTURE RESEARCH

Because this study was exploratory, the sample size was small, providing only partial answers to our questions concerning shared-document collaboration. These partial answers do, however, indicate directions future research might take to help us learn more specific information about shared-document collaboration and how it is practiced in particular settings.

Respondents in this study reported on "successful" collaborations. Although a few respondents made incidental references to collaborations with which they were not satisfied, we made no attempt to systematically investigate "failed" collaborations. A study of such "failed" instances and their causes would be especially useful to corporations and organizations that encourage collaboration.

This study indicated that a range of leadership styles exists in collaborative groups. Further study that directly examined leadership could help us learn what sort of leadership techniques are most productive in the collaborative setting and whether leadership styles correlate with writing tasks or group membership.

We found that more than one group type and writing process could be used for the same writing task. Task restrictions may, however, impose limits on collaboration that would become apparent only in the study of a large number of cases. As researchers and teachers, we need to know how the task itself affects the collaborative-writing process.

Similarly we need to know more about how the new technologies are affecting shared-document collaboration. Some researchers are studying the effects of using word processors on individual writers and on peer-group editing. More study needs to be devoted to technology's effects on writers producing a shared document.

The sample used in this study contained a high percentage of respondents who had academic affiliations. More in-depth information is needed on shared-document collaborations in business, industry, government, and the military. When more is known about these collaborative processes, interesting comparisons might be made of the similarities and differences between collaboration that occurs within an organizational setting and the more autonomous collaborations of groups that are loosely associated with organizations or are entirely independent.

A correlated topic that needs study is the interaction between the hierarchy of the organization and the hierarchy of collaborative-group members. We have no systematic study, for example, of the effects of corporate structure on the processes or creative insight of collaborative-writing groups. We can only draw inferences from the more general research on creativity and small-group work.

Information drawn from studies on any of these topics would find immediate use in classrooms and in the business and professional worlds. We hope that the results of this exploratory research will point the way toward such future work.

REFERENCES

Abelson, Robert P., and Ariel Levi. "Decision Making and Decision Theory." *Handbook of Social Psychology*. Ed. Gardner Lindzey and Elliot Aronson. 3rd ed. Vol. 1. Hillsdale, NJ: Lawrence Erlbaum, 1985. 2 vols. 231–310.

Anderson, Paul V. "What Survey Research Tells Us about Writing at Work." *Writing in Nonacademic Settings*. Ed. Lee Odell and Dixie Goswami. New York: Guilford Press, 1985. 3–83.

Bruffee, Kenneth A. "Collaborative Learning and the 'Conversation of Mankind.'" *College English* 46 (1984): 635–52.

——. "The Way Out." *College English* 33 (1972): 456–80.

Clifford, John. "Composing in Stages: The Effects of a Collaborative Pedagogy." *Research in the Teaching of English* 15 (1982): 37–53.

——. "Teaching Composing Collaboratively." *Arizona English Bulletin* 22 (1980): 95–98.

Couture, Barbara, *et al.* "Building a Professional Writing Program through a University-Industry Collaborative." *Writing in Nonacademic Settings*. Ed. Lee Odell and Dixie Goswami. New York: Guilford Press, 1985. 391–426.

Daiute, Collette. "Do 1 and 1 Make 2?: Patterns of Influence by Collaborative Authors." *Written Communication* 3 (1986): 382–408.

Doheny-Farina, Stephen. "Writing in an Emerging Organization: An Ethnographic Study." *Written Communication* 3 (1986):158–84.

Ede, Lisa, and Andrea Lunsford. "Let Them Write . . . Together." *English Journal* forthcoming.

——. "Collaborative Learning: Lessons from the World of Work." *Writing Programs Administrator* forthcoming.

——. "Why Write . . . Together?" *Rhetoric Review* 2 (1983): 150–57.

Faigley, Lester, and Thomas Miller. "What We Learn from Writing on the Job." *College English* 44 (1982): 557–69.

Gebhardt, Richard. "Teamwork and Feedback: Broadening the Base of Collaborative Writing." *College English* 42 (1980): 69–74.

Gere, Anne Ruggles. "Collaborating in Writing Groups: An Historical Perspective." Conference on College Composition and Communication. New Orleans, March 1986.

Gere, Anne Ruggles, and Robert D. Abbott. "Talking about Writing: The Language of Writing Groups." *Research in the Teaching of English* 19 (1985): 362–81.

Goldstein, Jone Rymer, and Elizabeth L. Malone. "Using Journals to Strengthen Collaborative Writing." *Bulletin of the Association for Business Communication* 47 (1985): 24–29.

Hilgers, Thomas. "The Development of Collaborative Writing Skills: From 'I Like' to 'They Like.'" Conference on College Composition and Communication. New Orleans, March 1986.

Janis, Irving R. *Victims of Groupthink*. Boston: Houghton Mifflin, 1972.

Kelley, Harold H., and John W. Thibaut. "Group Problem-Solving." *Handbook of Social Psychology*. Ed. Gardner Lindzey and Elliot Aronson. 2nd ed. Vol 4. Reading, MA: Addison-Wesley, 1969. 4 vols. 1–101.

Lauerman, David A., *et al.* "Workplace and Classroom: Principles for Designing Writing Courses." *Writing in Nonacademic Settings*. Ed. Lee Odell and Dixie Goswami. New York: Guilford Press, 1985. 427–50.

Lunsford, Andrea, and Lisa Ede. "Collaboration in Writing on the Job: A Research Report." Conference on College Composition and Communication. New Orleans, March 1986.

——. "Singular Texts/Plural Authors." Multidisciplinary Studies in Composition Seminar, Purdue University. West Lafayette. IN, May 1986.

Mason, Edwin. *Collaborative Learning*. New York: Agathon Press, 1972.

Odell. Lee. "Beyond the Text: Relations between Writing and Social Context." *Writing in Nonacademic Settings*. Ed. Lee Odell and Dixie Goswami. New York: Guilford Press, 1985. 249–80.

O'Donnell, Angela, *et al.* "Cooperative Writing." *Written Communication* 2(1985): 307–15.

Paradis, James. David Dobrin, and Richard Miller. "Writing at Exxon ITD: Notes on the Writing Environment of an R & D Organization." *Writing in Nonacademic Settings*. Ed. Lee Odell and Dixie Goswami. New York: Guilford Press, 1985. 281–307.

Putnam, Linda. "The Role of Conflict in Group Decision Making" *Group Decision-making and Communication Processes*. Ed. R. Hirokawa and M.S. Poole. Beverly Hills, CA: Sage Publications, 175–96.

Rothenberg, Albert. "Creative Contradictions." *Psychology Today* June, 1979: 55–62.

——. "The Process of Janusian Thinking in Creativity." *Archives of General Psychiatry* 24 (1971): 195–205.

Weick, Karl E. *The Social Psychology of Organizing*. 2nd ed. Reading, MA: Addison-Wesley, 1979.

Wiener, Harvey. "Collaborative Learning in the Classroom: A Guide to Evaluation." *College English* 48 (1986): 52–61.

Vincent Vinci

Ten Report Writing Pitfalls: How to Avoid Them

Vincent Vinci was Director of Public Relations for Lockheed Electronics when he wrote this article.

The advancement of science moves on a pavement of communications. Chemists, electrical engineers, botanists, geologists, atomic physicists, and other scientists are not only practitioners but interpreters of science. As such, the justification, the recognition and the rewards within their fields result from their published materials.

Included in the vast field of communications is the report, a frequently used medium for paving the way to understanding and action. The engineering manager whose function is the direction of people and programs receives and writes many reports in his career. And therefore the need for technical reports that communicate effectively has been internationally recognized.

Since scientific writing is complicated by specialized terminology, a need for precision and the field's leaping advancement, the author of an engineering report can be overwhelmed by its contents. The proper handling of contents and communication of a report's purpose can be enhanced if the writer can avoid the following 10 pitfalls.

PITFALL 1: IGNORING YOUR AUDIENCE

In all the forms of communications, ignoring your audience in the preparation of a report is perhaps the greatest transgression. Why? All other forms of communication, such as instruction manuals, speeches, books and brochures, are directed to an indefinable or only partially definable audience. The report, on the other hand, is usually directed to a specific person or group and has a specific purpose. So, it would certainly seem that if one knows both the "who" and the "why," then a report writer should not be trapped by this pitfall.

But it is not enough to know the who and why, you need to know "how." To get to the how, let's assume that the reader is your boss and has asked you to write a trip report. You are to visit several plants and report on capital equipment requirements. Before you write the first word, you will have to find out what your boss already knows about these requirements. It is obvious that he wants a new assessment of the facilities' needs. But, was he unsatisfied with a recent assessment and wants another point of view, or is a new analysis required because the previous report is outdated—or does he feel that now is the time to make the investment in facilities so that production can be increased over the next five years? That's a lot of questions, but they define both the who and why of your trip and, more importantly, your report.

By this time you may get the feeling that I am suggesting you give him exactly what he wants to read. The answer is yes and no. No, I don't mean play up to your boss's likes and dislikes. I do mean, however, that you give him all the information he needs to make a decision—the pros and the cons.

I mean also that the information be presented in a way that he is acclimated to in making judgments. For example, usually a production-oriented manager or executive (even the chief executive) will think in terms of his specialty. The president of a company who climbed the marketing ladder selling solvents will think better in marketing terms. Therefore, perhaps the marketing aspects of additional equipment and facilities should be stressed. You should also be aware that if you happen to be the finance director, your boss will expect to see cost/investment factors too.

A simple method for remembering, rather than ignoring, your audience is to place a sheet of paper in front of you when you start to write your report. On the paper have written in bold letters **WHO, WHY** and **HOW,** with the answers clearly and cogently defined. Keep it in front of you throughout the preparation of your report.

PITFALL 2: WRITING TO IMPRESS

Nothing turns a reader off faster than writing to impress. Very often reports written to leave a lasting scholarly impression on top management actually hinder communication.

Generally, when a word is used to impress, the report writer assumes that the reader either knows its meaning or will take the trouble to look it up. Don't assume that a word familiar to you is easily recognized by your reader. I recall a few years ago, there was a word "serendipity" which became a fashionable word to impress your reader with. And there was "fulsome" and "pejorative," and more. All are good words, but they're often misused or misapplied. They were shoved into reports to impress, completely disregarding the reader. Your objective is that your reader comprehend your thoughts, and there should be a minimum of impediments to understanding—understanding with first reading, and no deciphering.

Unfortunately, writing to impress is not merely restricted to use of obscure words but also includes unnecessary detail and technical trivia. Perhaps the scientist, chemist, chemical engineer and others become so intrigued with technical fine points that the meaningful (to your audience) elements of a report are buried. And quite often the fault is not so much a lack of removing the chaff from the grain but an attempt to technically impress the reader. Of course there exist reports that are full of technical detail because the nature of the communication is to impart a new chemical process, compound or technique. Even when writing this kind of report, you should eliminate any esoteric technical facts that do not contribute to communication, even though you may be tempted to include them to exhibit your degree of knowledge in the field.

PITFALL 3: HAVING MORE THAN ONE AIM

A report is a missile targeted to hit a point or achieve a mission. It is not a barrage of shotgun pellets that scatter across a target indiscriminately.

Have you ever, while reading a report, wondered where or what it was leading to—and even when you are finished you weren't quite sure? The writer probably had more than one aim, thereby preventing you from knowing where the report was heading.

Having more than one aim is usually the sign of a novice writer, but the pitfall can also trip up an experienced engineer if he does not organize the report toward one objective.

It is too easy to say that your report is being written to communicate, to a specific audience, information about your research, tests, visit, meeting, conference, field trip, progress or any other one of a range of activities that may be the subject. If you look at the first part of the sentence, you will see that "specific audience" and "information" are the key words that have to be modified to arrive at the goal of your report. For instance, you must define the specific audience such as the "members of the research council," "the finance committee" or "the chief process engineer and his staff."

Secondly, you need to characterize the information, such as "analysis of a new catalytic process," "new methods of atomic absorption testing" or "progress on waste treatment programs." You should be able to state the specific purpose of your report in one sentence: e.g., "The use of fibrous material improves scrubber efficiency and life—a report to the product improvement committee."

When you have arrived at such a definition of your purpose and audience, you can then focus both the test results and analysis toward that purpose, tempered with your readers in mind.

The usual error made in writing reports is to follow the chronology of the research in the body of the report with a summary of a set of conclusions and recommendations attached. The proper procedure to follow is to write (while focusing on your report goal) the analysis first (supported by test essentials or any other details), then your introduction or summary—sort of reverse chronology.

But be sure that your goal and audience are clearly known because they become the basis of organizing your report.

PITFALL 4: BEING INCONSISTENT

If you work for an international chemical firm, you may be well aware of problems in communicating with plant managers and engineers of foreign installations or branches. And I'm not referring to language barriers, because for the most part these hurdles are immediately recognized and taken care of. What is more significant is units of measure. This problem is becoming more apparent as the United States slowly decides whether or not to adopt the metric system. Until it is adopted your best bet is to stick to one measurement system throughout the report. Preferably, the system chosen should be that familiar to your audience. If the audience is mixed, you should use both systems with one (always the same one) in parentheses. Obviously, don't mix units of measure because you will confuse or annoy your readers.

Consistency is not limited to measurements but encompasses terms, equations, derivations, numbers, symbols, abbreviations, acronyms, hyphenation, capitalization and punctuation. In other words, consistency in the mechanics of style will avoid work for your reader and smooth his path toward understanding and appreciating the content of the report.

If your company neither has a style guide nor follows the general trends of good editorial practice, perhaps you could suggest instituting a guide. In addition to the U.S. Government Printing Office Style Manual, many scientific and engineering societies have set up guides which could be used.

PITFALL 5: OVERQUALIFYING

Chemical engineers, astronomers, geologists, electrical engineers, and scientists of any other discipline have been educated and trained to be precise. As a result, they strive for precision, accuracy, and detail. That tends to work against the scientist when it comes to writing. Add to that the limited training received in the arts, and you realize why written expression does not come easily.

Most reports, therefore, have too many modifiers—adjectives, clauses, phrases, adverbs and other qualifiers. Consider some examples: the single-stage, isolated double-cooled refractory process breakdown, or the angle of the single-rotor dc hysteresis motor rotor winding. To avoid such difficult-to-comprehend phrases, you could in the first example write "the breakdown of the process in single-stage, isolated double-cooled refractories," and in the second, "the angle of the rotor winding in single-rotor dc hysteresis motors can cause . . . ," and so on. This eliminates the string of modifiers and makes the phrase easier to understand.

Better still, if your report allows you to say at the beginning that the following descriptions are only related to "single-stage, isolated double-cooled refractories" or "single-rotor dc hysteresis motors," you can remove the cumbersome nomenclature entirely.

In short, to avoid obscuring facts and ideas, eliminate excessive modifiers. Try to state your idea or main point first and follow with your qualifying phrases.

PITFALL 6: NOT DEFINING

Dwell, lake, and barn, all are common words. Right? Right and wrong. Yes, they are common to the nonscientist. To the mechanical engineer, dwell is the period a cam follower stays at maximum lift; to a chemical engineer, lake is a dye compound; and to an atomic physicist, a barn is an atomic cross-sectional area (10^{-24} cm^2).

These three words indicate two points: first, common words are used in science with other than their common meanings; and second, terms need to be defined.

In defining terms you use in a report, you must consider what to define and how to define. Of the two, I consider what to define a more difficult task and suggest that you review carefully just which terms you need defined. If you analyze the purpose, the scope, the direction and your audience (reader/user), you will probably get a good handle on such terms.

"How to define" ranges from the simple substitution of a common term for an uncommon one, to an extended or amplified explanation. But whatever the term, or method of definition, you need to slant it both to the reader and to the report purpose.

PITFALL 7: MISINTRODUCING

Introductions, summaries, abstracts and forewords—whatever you use to lead your reader into your report, it should not read like an exposition of a table of contents. If it does, you might as well let your audience read the table of contents.

The introduction, which should be written after the body of the report, should state the subject, purpose, scope, and the plan of the report. In many cases, an introduction will include a summary of the findings or conclusions. If a report is a progress report, the introduction should relate the current report to previous reports. Introductions, then, not only tell the sequence or plan of the report, but tell the what, how and why of the subject as well.

PITFALL 8: DAZZLING WITH DATA

Someone once said that a good painter not only knows what to put in a painting, but more importantly he knows what to leave out. It's much the same with report writing. If you dazzle your reader with tons of data, he may be moved by the weight of the report but may get no more out of it than that.

The usual error occurs in supportive material that many engineers and scientists feel is unnecessary to give a report scientific importance. The truth is that successful scientific writing (which includes reports) is heavily grounded in reality, simplicity, and understanding—not quantity.

The simplest way to evaluate the relevancy of information is to ask yourself after writing a paragraph, "What can I remove from this paragraph without destroying its meaning and its relationship to what precedes and what will follow?" Then, ask another question, "Does my reader require all that data to comprehend, evaluate or make a decision with?" If you find you can do without excess words, excess description and excessive supportive data, you will end up with a tighter, better and more informative report.

These principles should also be used to evaluate graphs, photographs, diagrams and other illustrations. Remember, illustrations should support or aid comprehension rather than being a crutch on which your report leans. The same should be kept in mind when determining just how much you should append to your report. There is no need to copy all your lab notes to show that detailed experimentation was performed to substantiate the results. A statement that the notes exist and are available will suffice.

PITFALL 9: NOT HIGHLIGHTING

Again, I believe the analogy of the painter applies. A good painter also knows what to highlight and what to subdue in a portrait or scene.

If you don't accent the significant elements, findings, illustrations, data, tests, facts, trends, procedures, precedents, or experiments pertinent to the subject and object of your report, you place the burden of doing so on your reader. As a result, he may consider the report a failure, draw his own conclusions, or hit upon the significant elements by chance. In any event, don't leave it up to your reader to search out the major points of your report.

Highlighting is one step past knowing what goes into your report and what to leave out (see Pitfall 8 above). All the key points of your report should define and focus on the purpose of your report. They must be included in your summary or conclusions, but these sections are not the only places to highlight. Attention should be called to key elements needed for the understanding of your material throughout the body of the report. Several methods may be used: you can underline an important statement or conclusion, you can simply point out that a particular illustration is the proof of the results of an experiment, or, as most professional writers do, you can make the key sentence the first or last sentence of a paragraph.

PITFALL 10: NOT REWRITING

Did you ever hear of an actor who hadn't rehearsed his lines before stepping before an audience? An actor wouldn't chance it—his reputation and his next role depend on his performance. The engineer shouldn't chance it either. Don't expect the draft of your report to be ready for final typing and reproduction without rewriting.

Once you have judged what your report will contain and how it will be organized, just charge ahead and write the first draft. Don't worry about choosing the precise word, turning that meaningful phrase, or covering all the facts in one paragraph or section. Once you have written your first draft (and the quicker you accomplish this the more time you will have to perfect the text), you are in a better position to analyze, tailor, and refine the report as a whole. Now you are also able to focus all the elements toward your purpose and your audience.

As you begin the rewriting process simply pick up each page of your draft, scan it, and ask yourself what role the material on that page plays in the fulfillment of the report's objective and understanding. You will find that this will enable you to delete, add, change and rearrange your material very quickly.

After you have completed this process, then rewrite paragraph by paragraph, sentence by sentence, and word by word. Your final step is to repeat the procedure of examining each page's contents. When you are satisfied with its flow and cohesion, then you will have a good report, one you know will be well received and acted upon.

Sheryl Lindsell-Roberts

A Pixel (Picture) Is Worth a Thousand Words

Sheryl Lindsell-Roberts is a consultant in business writing to a number of Fortune 500 companies. In addition to writing Technical Writing for Dummies, *from which the following essay is excerpted, she has also written* Business Writing for Dummies *and* Business Letters for Dummies.

Charts and graphs are super ways to make your point very effectively. You can gather data and prepare a chart to display your findings. Identify opportunities as a result of what visually appears, and update the data to show changes or progress. Many software applications are available to help you prepare graphs in a jiffy. Check the Internet or your local computer to find out more about them.

Keep these tips in mind when you prepare charts and graphs:

- **Write a descriptive title.** Place the title above the chart or graph.
- **Use an appropriate scale.** For example, if your financial range is from $100,000 to $200,000, don't show a scale of $100,000 to $500,000.
- **Create a legend if the chart isn't self-explanatory.** Legends explain the symbols that appear in the chart.
- **Keep the design simple.** Eliminate any information your readers don't need to know.
- **Prepare a separate chart or graph for each point.** If you try to squeeze too much information on one graph, you defeat your purpose of making it simple to read.

If a pixel is truly worth a thousand words, you can eliminate the thousand words with a well-done graphic. Make the graphic self-contained, tie it to the text, and place it as close to the text as possible. Clearly label all the parts so the graphic is self-explanatory and sends a clear message.

PIE CHART

A pie chart is like a pizza with wedge-shaped sections. You may order a pizza with 50% pepperoni, 25% mushrooms, and 25% olives. Each section represents a percentage of the total pie, which is 100%.

Some people think it's important to begin the most important percentage at the 12 o'clock position and continue clockwise. Others believe that (because people read from left to right) the most important information should be to the left of 12 o'clock and continue counterclockwise. It's your choice. In Example 1 [p. 213] you see what a typical pie chart may look like. Example 2 [p. 214] shows a pie chart in three dimensions. (Of course, the 3-D pie has more calories.)

LINE CHART

A line chart shows trends or the change of one or more variables over time periods, as shown in Example 3 [p. 214]. Line charts use points plotted in relation to two axes drawn at right angles. Make the axes descriptive and use clear labels.

A slight variation to the line chart is the *run chart* that shows incidents above and below an established data point. This is evident when you compare Example 3 with Example 4 [p. 215].

BAR CHARTS

A bar chart (which can be vertical or horizontal bars) shows a comparison between categories, as you see in Example 5 [p. 215]. Clearly mark the axes. Variations to simple bar charts are histograms, Pareto charts, and Gantt charts, which you use for specific purposes. I describe and give examples of these charts in the following sections:

Histogram

A histogram shows the relative frequency of occurrence, central tendency, and variability of a data set, as you see in Example 6 [p. 216].

Pareto Chart

A Pareto chart, shown in Example 7 [p. 216], separates vital information from the trivial information. It's based on the Pareto Principle, which says that 20 percent of the problems have 80 percent of the impact.

Gantt Chart

The Gantt chart, shown in Example 8 [p. 217], is a tool used by management to help coordinate resources and activities. It shows timing relationships between the tasks and subtasks of a project.

SCATTER CHART

A scatter chart, shown in Example 9 [p. 217], displays a relationship between two varilables. It may help pinpoint the cause of a problem or show how one variable may relate to another.

FLOWCHART

Example 10 [p. 218] shows symbols used in a flowchart. Example 11 [p. 219] displays the major steps in a process using flowchart symbols.

TABLE THAT THOUGHT

Tables are columns and rows that display specific, related information. Tables carry more information per space than the same amount of text—yet they're often overlooked by technical writers. Find appropriate opportunities to create tables; they have great visual impact. Formal or informal, that is the question? Although there are no hard and fast rules about which tables should be formal or informal, use your judgment based on the formality of your document.

Fonts with personality

Each font has its unique personality, and you should let it shine. Use no more than two fonts, or your document will be too busy. Here are some tips on the use of fonts:

✓ Use a serif typeface (the ones you see here that have little feet) for text on paper documents. It's what we're used to seeing from the time we opened a first-grade primer. A popular serif typeface is Times Roman.

✓ When you generate electronic documents, a sans serif, such as Arial, is easier to read on the screen. Arial is also appropriate for headings on paper or electronic documents.

✓ You probably won't ever use funky fonts in technical writing, but who knows? If you have an appropriate use for such a font, you can choose from a wide selection of them that vary with the software. Play with them and save them for special occasions, such as announcing the company picnic.

ON THE FORMAL SIDE

Separate formal tables from the text with boxed headings, vertical and horizontal rules (lines), and a box, as you see in Example 12 [p. 220]. If you use more than two or three tables in a document, assign a number to each. Place the table heading above the table. If you need to explain any information, place it below the table as a footnote.

When you think that the reader may have difficulty following a table across the rows, consider shading every other line, as you see in Example 12. You do that in Microsoft Word by choosing Format ⇒ Borders and Shading ⇒ Shading.

ON THE INFORMAL SIDE

Informal tables are extensions of the text and don't have headings or table numbers. Merely write a sentence or two that has ties to the table. For example, in Example 13 [p. 220] you see a two-column table about risks that are inherent to a project. . . .

GO FIGURE

The difference between a table and a figure is simple. If a visual element isn't a table, it's a figure. Figures can be sketches (as you see in Example 14 [p. 221]), drawings, photographs, charts, or graphs—in essence, anything other than columns and rows.

If you use more than two or three figures in a document, assign each a number. Include a concise title below or next to the text. Keep figures simple and uncluttered.

When you use a figure, make sure that it paints an accurate and clear picture. Example 15 [p. 221] shows a real-life figure that just boggles the mind. In this case, the thousand words would be better than the picture (to turn a phrase).

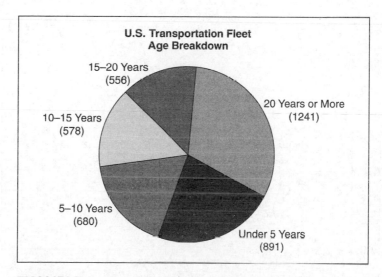

EXAMPLE 1   Pie chart. (Here's pie in your eye.)

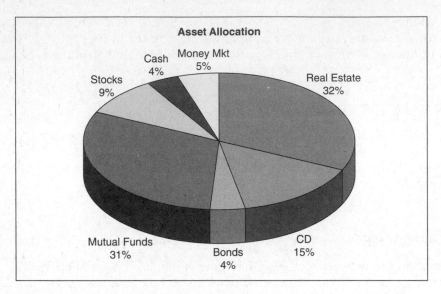

EXAMPLE 2   Three-dimensional pie chart.

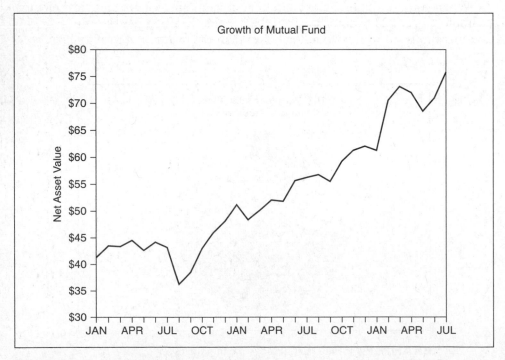

EXAMPLE 3   Line chart. (What's my line?)

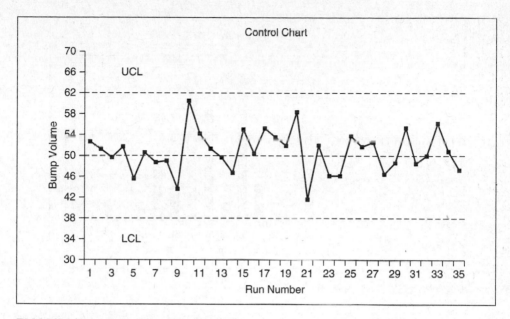

EXAMPLE 4   Run chart. (On the run.)

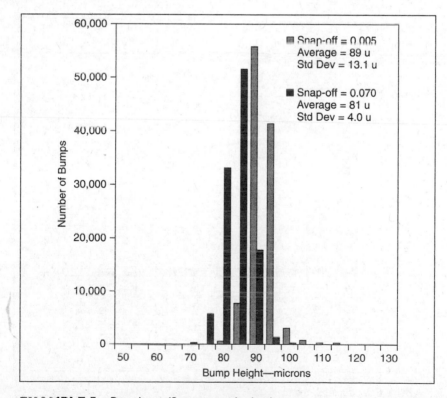

EXAMPLE 5   Bar chart. (Step up to the bar.)

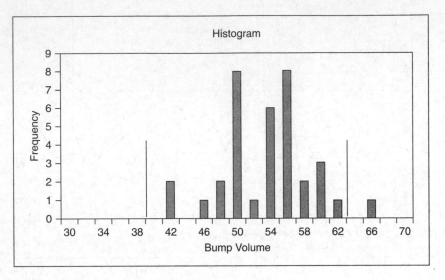

EXAMPLE 6 Histogram.

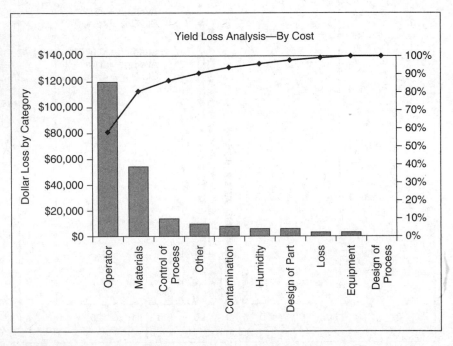

EXAMPLE 7 Pareto chart.

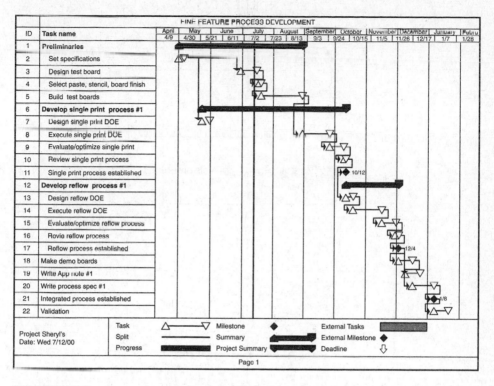

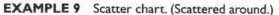

EXAMPLE 8 Gantt chart. (Who's on first?)

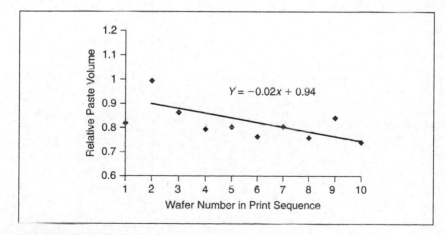

EXAMPLE 9 Scatter chart. (Scattered around.)

Standard Flowchart Symbols

This symbol...	Represents...
	Start/Stop
	Decision Point
	Activity
	Document
	Connector (to another page or part of the diagram)

EXAMPLE 10   Flowchart. (Go with the flow.)

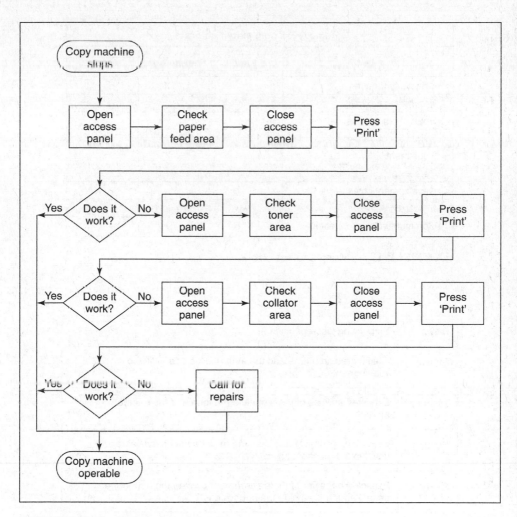

EXAMPLE 11   A flowchart in action.

Table 4-5: Complexity Factors			
Factor	Low	Moderate	High
Originality required		X	
Processing flexibility	X		
Span of Operations	X		
Dynamics of requirements	X		X
Equipment		X	
Personnel	X		
Development costs			X
Processing time		X	
Communication architecture	X		

EXAMPLE 12   Setting a formal table.

Risks	Pinpointing discrepancies
Staffing	Staffing requirements and the staff available to fulfill those requirements.
Technical	Expected abilities of the technical platform and their actual abilities.
Scoping	Level of functionality and the time and resources available to develop the functionality.
External	Expected behavior of the environment outside the boundaries of the project and those inside the boundaries.

EXAMPLE 13   Setting an informal table.

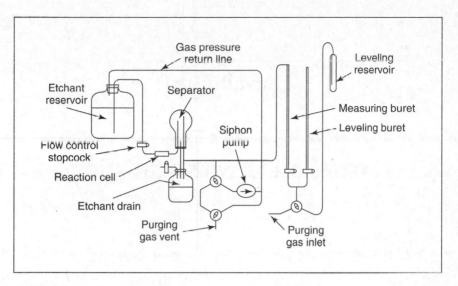

EXAMPLE 14   Sketch. (The greater scheme of things.)

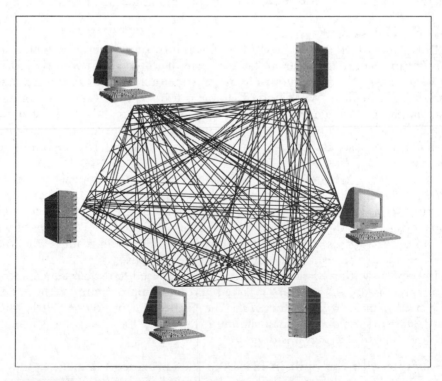

EXAMPLE 15   Mind-boggling figure. (What's the point?)

Darrell Huff

How to Lie with Statistics

Darrell Huff, a freelance writer, expanded this article into a book with the same title (Norton, 1954).

"The average Yaleman, Class of '24," *Time* magazine reported last year after reading something in the New York *Sun*, a newspaper published in those days, "makes $25,111 a year."

Well, good for him!

But, come to think of it, what does this improbably precise and salubrious figure mean? Is it, as it appears to be, evidence that if you send your boy to Yale you won't have to work in your old age and neither will he? Is this average a mean or is it a median? What kind of sample is it based on? You could lump one Texas oilman with two hundred hungry freelance writers and report *their* average income as $25,000-odd a year. The arithmetic is impeccable, the figure is convincingly precise, and the amount of meaning there is in it you could put in your eye.

In just such ways is the secret language of statistics, so appealing in a fact-minded culture, being used to sensationalize, inflate, confuse, and oversimplify. Statistical terms are necessary in reporting the mass data of social and economic trends, business conditions, "opinion" polls, this year's census. But without writers who use the words with honesty and understanding and readers who know what they mean, the result can only be semantic nonsense.

In popular writing on scientific research, the abused statistic is almost crowding out the picture of the white-jacketed hero laboring overtime without time-and-a-half in an ill-lit laboratory. Like the "little dash of powder, little pot of paint," statistics are making many an important fact "look like what she ain't." Here are some of the ways it is done.

The sample with the built-in bias. Our Yale men—or Yalemen, as they say in the Time-Life building—belong to this flourishing group. The exaggerated estimate of their income is not based on all members of the class nor on a random or representative sample of them. At least two interesting categories of 1924-model Yale men have been excluded.

First there are those whose present addresses are unknown to their classmates. Wouldn't you bet that these lost sheep are earning less than the boys from prominent families and the others who can be handily reached from a Wall Street office?

There are those who chucked the questionnaire into the nearest wastebasket. Maybe they didn't answer because they were not making enough money to brag about. Like the fellow who found a note clipped to his first pay check suggesting that he consider the amount of his salary confidential: "Don't worry," he told the boss. "I'm just as ashamed of it as you are."

Omitted from our sample then are just the two groups most likely to depress the average. The $25,111 figure is beginning to account for itself. It may indeed be a true figure for those of the Class of '24 whose addresses are known and who are willing to stand up and tell how much they earn. But even that requires a possibly dangerous assumption that the gentlemen are telling the truth.

To be dependable to any useful degree at all, a sampling study must use a representative sample (which can lead to trouble too) or a truly random one. If *all* the Class of '24 is included, that's all right. If every tenth name on a complete list is used, that is all right too, and so is drawing an adequate number of names out of a hat. The test is this: Does every name in the group have an equal chance to be in the sample?

You'll recall that ignoring this requirement was what produced the *Literary Digest*'s famed fiasco.* When names for polling were taken only from telephone books and subscription lists, people who did not have telephones or *Literary Digest* subscriptions had no chance to be in the sample. They possibly did not mind this underprivilege a bit, but their absence was in the end very hard on the magazine that relied on the figures.

This leads to a moral: You can prove about anything you want to by letting your sample bias itself. As a consumer of statistical data—a reader, for example, of a news magazine—remember that no statistical conclusion can rise above the quality of the sample it is based upon. In the absence of information about the procedures behind it, you are not warranted in giving any credence at all to the result.

The truncated, or gee-whiz, graph. If you want to show some statistical information quickly and clearly, draw a picture of it. Graphic presentation is the thing today. If you don't mind misleading the hasty looker, or if you quite clearly *want* to deceive him, you can save some space by chopping the bottom off many kinds of graph.

---

*Editor's note: The *Literary Digest* predicted that Alfred Landon would defeat Franklin Roosevelt in the 1936 presidential election. Landon carried only two states.

Suppose you are showing the upward trend of national income month by month for a year. The total rise, as in one recent year, is 7 percent. It looks like this:

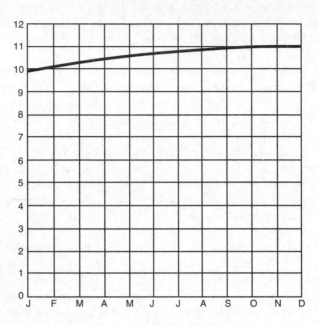

That is clear enough. Anybody can see that the trend is slightly upward. You are showing a 7 percent increase, and that is exactly what it looks like.

But it lacks schmaltz. So you chop off the bottom, this way:

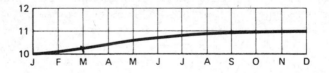

The figures are the same. It is the same graph and nothing has been falsified—except the impression that it gives. Anyone looking at it can just feel prosperity throbbing in the arteries of the country. It is a subtler equivalent of editing "National income rose 7 percent" into ". . . climbed a whopping 7 percent."

It is vastly more effective, however, because of that illusion of objectivity.

The souped-up graph. Sometimes truncating is not enough. The trifling rise in something or other still looks almost as insignficant as it is. You can make that 7 percent look livelier than 100 percent ordinarily does. Simply change the proportion between the ordinate and the abscissa. There's no rule against it, and it does give your graph a prettier shape.

But it exaggerates, to say the least, something awful:

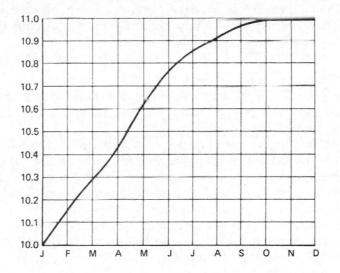

The well-chosen average. I live near a country neighborhood for which I can report an average income of $15,000. I could also report it as $3,500.

If I should want to sell real estate hereabouts to people having a high snobbery content, the first figure would be handy. The second figure, however, is the one to use in an argument against raising taxes, or the local bus fare.

Both are legitimate averages, legally arrived at. Yet it is obvious that at least one of them must be as misleading as an out-and-out lie. The $15,000-figure is a mean, the arithmetic average of the incomes of all the families in the community. The smaller figure is a median; it might be called the income of the average family in the group. It indicates that half the families have less than $3,500 a year and half have more.

Here is where some of the confusion about averages comes from. Many human characteristics have the grace to fall into what is called the "normal" distribution. If you draw a picture of it, you get a curve that is shaped like a bell. Mean and median fall at about the same point, so it doesn't make very much difference which you use.

But some things refuse to follow this neat curve. Income is one of them. Incomes for most large areas will range from under $1,000 a year to upward of $50,000. Almost everybody will be under $10,000, way over on the lefthand side of that curve.

One of the things that made the income figure for the "average Yaleman" meaningless is that we are not told whether it is a mean or a median. It is not that one type of average is invariably better than the other; it depends upon what you are talking about. But neither gives you any real information—and either may be highly misleading—unless you know which of those two kinds of average it is.

In the country neighborhood I mentioned, almost everyone has less than the average—the mean, that is—of $10,500. These people are all small farmers, except for a trio of millionaire week-enders who bring up the mean enormously.

You can be pretty sure that when an income average is given in the form of a mean nearly everybody has less than that.

The insignificant difference or the elusive error. Your two children Peter and Linda (we might as well give them modish names while we're about it) take intelligence tests. Peter's IQ, you learn, is 98 and Linda's is 101. Aha! Linda is your brighter child.

Is she? An intelligence test is, or purports to be, a sampling of intellect. An IQ, like other products of sampling, is a figure with a statistical error, which expresses the precison or reliability of the figure. The size of this probable error can be calculated. For their test the makers of the much-used Revised Stanford-Binet have found it to be about 3 percent. So Peter's indicated IQ of 98 really means only that there is an even chance that it falls between 95 and 101. There is an equal probability that it falls somewhere else—below 95 or above 101. Similarly, Linda's has no better than a fifty-fifty chance of being within the fairly sizeable range of 98 to 104.

You can work out some comparisons from that. One is that there is rather better than one chance in four that Peter, with his lower IQ rating, is really at least three points smarter than Linda. A statistician doesn't like to consider a difference significant unless you can hand him odds a lot longer than that.

Ignoring the error in a sampling study leads to all kinds of silly conclusions. There are magazine editors to whom readership surveys are gospel; with a 40 percent readership reported for one article and a 35 percent for another, they demand more like the first. I've seen even smaller differences given tremendous weight, because statistics are a mystery and numbers are impressive. The same thing goes for market surveys and so-called public opinion polls. The rule is that you cannot make a valid comparison between two such figures unless you know the deviations. And unless the difference between the figures is many times greater than the probable error of each, you have only a guess that the one appearing greater really is.

Otherwise you are like the man choosing a camp site from a report of mean temperature alone. One place in California with a mean annual temperature of 61 is San Nicolas Island on the south coast, where it always stays in the comfortable range between 47 and 87. Another with a mean of 61 is in the inland desert, where the thermometer hops around from 15 to 104. The deviation from the mean marks the difference, and you can freeze or roast if you ignore it.

The one-dimensional picture. Suppose you have just two or three figures to compare—say the average weekly wage of carpenters in the United States and another country. The sums might be $60 and $30. An ordinary bar chart makes the difference graphic.

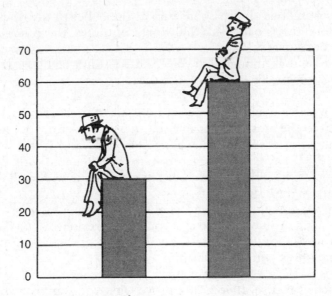

That is an honest picture. It looks good for American carpenters, but perhaps it does not have quite the oomph you are after. Can't you make that difference appear overwhelming and at the same time give it what I am afraid is known as eye-appeal? Of course you can. Following tradition, you represent these sums by pictures of money bags. If the $30 bag is one inch high, you draw the $60 bag two inches high. That's in proportion, isn't it?

The catch is, of course, that the American's money bag, being twice as tall as that of the $30 man, covers an area on your page four times as great. And since your two-dimensional picture represents an object that would in fact have three dimensions, the money bags actually would differ much more than that.

The volumes of any two similar solids vary as the cubes of their heights. If the unfortunate foreigner's bag holds $30 worth of dimes, the American's would hold not $60 but a neat $240.

You didn't say that, though, did you? And you can't be blamed, you're only doing it the way practically everybody else does.

The ever-impressive decimal. For a spurious air of precision that will lend all kinds of weight to the most disreputable statistics, consider the decimal.

Ask a hundred citizens how many hours they slept last night. Come out with a total of, say, 7.813. Your data are far from precise to begin with. Most people will miss their guess by fifteen minutes or more and some will recall five sleepless minutes as half a night of tossing insomnia.

But go ahead, do your arithmetic, announce that people sleep an average of 7.813 hours a night. You will sound as if you knew precisely what you are talking about. If you were foolish enough to say 7.8 (or "almost" 8) hours it would sound like what it was—an approximation.

The semiattached figure. If you can't prove what you want to prove, demonstrate something else and pretend that they are the same thing. In the daze that follows the collision of statistics with the human mind, hardly anybody will notice the difference. The semiattached figure is a durable device guaranteed to stand you in good stead. It always has.

If you can't prove that your nostrum cures colds, publish a sworn laboratory report that the stuff killed 31,108 germs in a test tube in eleven seconds. There may be no connection at all between assorted germs in a test tube and the whatever-it-is that produces colds, but people aren't going to reason that sharply, especially while sniffling.

Maybe that one is too obvious and people are beginning to catch on. Here is a trickier version.

Let us say that in a period when race prejudice is growing it is to your advantage to "prove" otherwise. You will not find it a difficult assignment.

Ask that usual cross section of the population if they think . . . [Blacks] have as good a chance as white people to get jobs. Ask again a few months later. As Princeton's Office of Public Opinion Research has found out, people who are most unsympathetic to . . . [Blacks] are the ones most likely to answer yes to this question.

As prejudice increases in a country, the percentage of affirmative answers you will get to this question will become larger. What looks on the face of it like growing opportunity for . . . [Blacks] actually is mounting prejudice and nothing else. You have achieved something rather remarkable: the worse things get, the better your survey makes them look.

The unwarranted assumption, or *post hoc* rides again. The interrelation of cause and effect, so often obscure anyway, can be most neatly hidden in statistical data.

Somebody once went to a good deal of trouble to find out if cigarette smokers make lower college grades than non-smokers. They did. This naturally pleased many people, and they made much of it.

The unwarranted assumption, of course, was that smoking had produced dull minds. It seemed vaguely reasonable on the face of it, so it was quite widely accepted. But it really proved nothing of the sort, any more than it proved that poor grades drive students to the solace of tobacco. Maybe the relationship worked in one direction, maybe in the other. And maybe all this is only an indication that the sociable sort of fellow who is likely to take his books less than seriously is also likely to sit around and smoke many cigarettes.

Permitting statistical treatment to befog casual relationships is little better than superstition. It is like the conviction among the people of the Hebrides that body lice produce good health. Observation over the centuries had taught them that people in good health had lice and sick people often did not. *Ergo,* lice made a man healthy. Everybody should have them.

Scantier evidence, treated statistically at the expense of common sense, has made many a medical fortune and many a medical article in magazines, including professional ones. More sophisticated observers finally got things straightened out in the Hebrides. As it turned out, almost everybody in those circles had lice most of the time. But when a man took a fever (quite possibly carried to him by those same lice) and his body became hot, the lice left. Here you have cause and effect not only reversed, but intermingled.

There you have a primer in some ways to use statistics to deceive. A well-wrapped statistic is better than Hitler's "big lie": it misleads, yet it can't be pinned onto you.

Is this little list altogether too much like a manual for swindlers? Perhaps I can justify it in the manner of the retired burglar whose published reminiscences amounted to a graduate course in how to pick a lock and muffle a footfall: The crooks already know these tricks. Honest men must learn them in self-defense.

David W. Ewing

Strategies of Persuasion

David W. Ewing was Executive Editor-Planning of the Harvard Business Review *and a member of the faculty of the Harvard Business School.*

When we review reports, letters, and memoranda that get the intended results, we find a fascinating diversity of approaches. Some are gentle in approach, taking readers by the hand and leading them to a certain finding or recommendation. Others are brisk and abrupt. Some are objective in approach, carefully examining both sides of an idea, like a judge writing a difficult decision—at least until the end. Others burst with impatience to explain one side, and only one side, of a proposal or argument. Some flow swimmingly; others erupt like Mount Vesuvius.

How is it possible that communications taking such different approaches can all be effective? It is not sufficient to answer glibly, "It depends on the situation," or "Communications should mirror the personal style of the communicator." How does a written communication depend on the situation? Which style of the communicator should be reflected in a given communication? Examine the writing of most business executives, professionals, and public leaders, and you will find not one but *many* styles of exposition.

RULES EVERY PERSUADER SHOULD KNOW

The explanation lies in a set of relationships among the communicator, the reader, the message, and the time-space environment. These relationships work in predictable ways and are an important part of the knowledge of every good business and professional writer. They come into play in the planning stages of writing, when the writer is considering how he or she will proceed, and in the main body of the presentation, to accomplish what he or she has promised in the opening paragraphs. The relationships affect some of the most important decisions a writer makes—the choice of ideas to use, the comparative emphasis to be given various arguments pro and con, the types of reasons and supporting material used, the establishment of credibility, and other matters.

It is convenient but self-defeating to follow fixed prescriptions for persuasion, such as to put your strongest arguments first or last or to identify with the readers. Such nostrums were fine for the age of patent medicines and snake-oil peddlers, but not for the age of diagnostic medicine. What is more, they are belittling. They assume that writers are witless. Good writers vary their approaches in response to their readings of different situations. Just as a good golfer plays an approach to a green differently depending on the wind, so a good writer uses different strategies depending on the crosscurrents of mood and feeling.

How should you choose your approach to a group of readers? What elements of the approach should be tailored to the situation? These are the topics of this . . . [selection]. Let us assume that the substance of the intended message is clear in your mind. . . .

1. Consider Whether Your Views Will Make Problems for Readers.

J. C. Mathes and Dwight W. Stevenson tell of the student engineer who was asked to evaluate the efficiency of the employer plant's waste-treatment process.[1] He found that, by making a simple change, the company could save more than $200,000 a year. Anticipating an enthusiastic response, he wrote up and delivered his report. Although he waited with great expectations, no accolades came. Why? What he hadn't counted on was that now his supervisors would have to explain to their bosses why they had allowed a waste of $200,000 a year. They were far from elated to read his report.

"If you want to make a man your enemy," Henry C. Link once said, "tell him simply, 'You are wrong.' This method works every time." Under the illusion that their sciences are "hard," physicists, biologists, and others may assume that it is necessary only to worry about setting the facts forth accurately. From posterity's standpoint, perhaps yes—but not from the standpoint of writing for current results. As Kenneth Boulding, head of the American Association for the Advancement of Science, has pointed out, the so-called "hard" sciences are in many ways "soft," and vice versa. "You can knock forever on a deaf man's door," said Zorba the Greek, and the deaf man can be a physicist as well as a marketing manager or public official.

If your views are bad news for readers, you proceed to report them, but with empathy and tact and an effort to put yourself in the readers' shoes. You work as carefully as if you were licking honey off a thorn.

2. Don't Offer New Ideas, Directives, or Recommendations for Change until Your Readers Are Prepared for Them.

"Should I state my surprising findings at the very beginning of my memorandum?" a writer asks. "Should I go slow with my heretical proposal and hold the reader's hand?" asks another.

---

[1] J. C. Mathes and Dwight W. Stevenson, *Designing Technical Reports* (Indianapolis: Bobbs-Merrill, 1976), pp. 18–19.

Generally speaking, the answer to all such questions depends on the extent of your audience's resistance to change, the amount of change you are asking for, the uncertainty in readers' minds as to your understanding of their situation, and what psychologists call the "perceived threat" of your communication, that is, how much it seems (to readers) to upset their values and interests. The more change, uncertainty, and/or threat, the slower you should proceed, the more carefully you should prepare your readers.

For instance, if your boss is enthusiastic about a new promotion scheme that he (or she) has paid a consultant $25,000 to devise, naturally you will want to go slow in shooting it down (at least if you want to stay in his good graces). In fact, any written criticism of the scheme is probably out of order until you have had a chance to talk with him and get a feel for the proper timing of any forthcoming criticism. When you do commit yourself to writing, you should probably review the arguments for the new scheme as fairly as possible, making it crystal clear to him that you understand them. Only then does it become timely to turn to the facts or conditions that, in your opinion, raise serious questions about the plan.

On the other hand, suppose the faulty promotion scheme is of little personal interest to your boss—it is not his (or her) "baby." Now the situation is different. You can launch right into the shortcomings, throwing your heaviest objections first. The fact is that the boss may not even want to know about the lesser objections, much less the supporting arguments once advanced for the plan; the main things he should know are that (a) the plan is in trouble and (b) the major, most compelling reasons why.

Clearly, this strategy is plain, everyday common sense—what you would normally do in communicating orally instead of in writing. Only in writing you must be more explicit and thorough, because a document lacks the expressiveness and visual advantages of a spoken dialogue.

Now consider another type of situation. Suppose it is your unhappy task to write a department manager that the extra appropriations he (or she) was promised have been cancelled. First of all, how would you handle it if you saw him often and could talk with him personally? . . . You would not (we hope) pussyfoot around trying to withhold the bad news from him. Also, once you had indicated the main message, you would probably backtrack a little and make it clear that the step is being taken with reluctance.

"Joe, it looks as if we're not going to be able to give you the extra budget we promised," you might say, getting down to business. That is the message in a nutshell—now for the review of common ground. "We know how much you have counted on getting those people and funds. There's no doubt you could manage them well and put them to good use. And we know that the morale of your people is involved in this, too. But the fact is that the sales we counted on are not coming in. We've got to cut somewhere, and, frankly, we feel it's got to be your department because. . . ."

If you are communicating by letter or memorandum, the strategy is exactly the same (only "Joe" may now be "Mr. Wyncoop"). After your lead, you review the main needs as he and you understand them, perhaps spelling them out more than you would have in a face-to-face meeting but choosing the same ones. Only then do you turn to the new conditions that make it necessary to do an about-face.

3. Your Credibility with Readers Affects Your Strategy.

In general, communication research indicates that the chances of opinion change vary with the communicator's authority with his or her readers. In their succinct summary of the field, *Persuasion,* social scientists Marvin Karlins and Herbert I. Abelson point out that credibility itself is a variable; that is, it can be influenced by the words of the communicator.[2] Above all, as psychologists repeatedly emphasize, credibility lies in the eye of the beholder. . . .[3]

In written communications there are two types of credibility. It may be given or it may be acquired. Between the two lies a world of practical difference.

Given credibility may result from your position in an organization. If, let us say, you are the boss writing directions to a subordinate, your credibility is likely to be high. Given credibility also may result from reputation—a well-known chemist has more credibility in communications about polymers than a good industrial engineer has, but the latter would possess more credibility in communications about time-and-motion studies. It may result from the individuals and groups the writer is associated with—if he or she is a member of the same trade union the reader belongs to, a union held in high esteem by both, he or she has more credibility in a memorandum on grievance procedures than a member of the board of directors would have.

Though you may be high in given credibility, you may yet need to remind some readers of the fact. In the case of an obvious credential, such as a position in an important organization, a letterhead may be enough to do the trick. Another device is to insert a few lines of biographical data at the head of a report or brochure. If you have had experience or associations that carry weight with the reader, perhaps you can interject them early in the message. "During a visit I had last week with Zach Jarvis," you might say, knowing that Dr. Zachary P. Jarvis is a magic name with your reader, or "The Executive Committee of the Aberjona Basin Association asked me to join their meeting on Monday . . ." knowing that group carries a triple-A rating in the mind of the reader.

Of course, you do not want to overplay your hand at such name dropping. A report to a fairly diverse audience by a famous black organization began simply:

> The National Association for the Advancement of Colored People has for many years been dedicated to the task of defending the economic, social and political rights and interests of black Americans. The growing national debate about energy has led us to examine the question to ascertain the implications for black Americans.[4]

---

[2]Marvin Karlins and Herbert I. Abelson. *Persuasion* (New York: Springer, 1970); see pp. 107–132.
[3]See, for example, Ralph L. Rosnow and Edward J. Robinson, eds. *Experiments in Persuasion* (New York: Academic, 1967).
[4]*The Wall Street Journal,* January 12, 1978.

Again, an attorney of the American Civil Liberties Union, in a letter to members of the organization soliciting donations, began:

> My dear friend:
>
> I am the ACLU lawyer who went into court last April to defend freedom of speech in Skokie, Illinois, for a handful of people calling themselves "nazis."
>
> The case has had an enormous impact on my life.
>
> It has also gravely injured the ACLU financially. . . .[5]

Acquired credibility, on the other hand, is earned by thoughts and facts in the written message. I may not know you from Adam. Yet if you send me a letter or report that carefully, helpfully describes something I am interested in, you gain credibility in my estimation.

Some studies suggest that, if you are low in given credibility and seek to acquire it with an audience, a useful technique is to cite ideas or evidence that support the reader's existing views.[6] As Disraeli once said, "My idea of an agreeable person is a person who agrees with me." The very fact that you feel confident and knowledgeable enough to articulate these views is likely to lift you several notches in the reader's estimation.

Still another approach is that old standby of persuaders—identifying yourself, in an early section, with the goals and interests of the audience. Possibly the most famous example of this strategy is the opening of Marc Antony's funeral oration, in Shakespeare's *Julius Caesar:* "I come to bury Caesar, not to praise him. . . ."

Finally, you can acquire credibility by citing authorities who rate highly with your intended audience, or by exhibiting documentary evidence that, because of its source, lends prestige and authority to your proposals or ideas.

"For success in negotiation," says C. Northcote Parkinson and Nigel Rowe, "it is vitally important that people will believe what you say and assume that any promise you make will be kept. But it is no good saying: 'Trust me. Rely on my word.' Only politicians say that."[7]

Even if you have prestigious credentials, you cannot take too much for granted. In an age of television sets, radios, cassettes, and record players in every home, credibility—at least with the public—may come quicker for the singer or comedian than for the judge, business executive, or medical researcher. In fact, because of an association with an organization or profession, you may be stereotyped as a member of "them" or "the establishment." It may behoove you to establish that you are a person with a name, a personality, certain interests, certain experiences—not just a nameless representative.

---

[5]David Goldberger, letter dated March 20, 1978.
[6]Karlins and Abelson, op. cit., pp. 115–119.
[7]C. Northcote Parkinson and Nigel Rowe,"Better Communcation: Business's Best Defense," *The McKinsey Quarterly,* Winter 1978, p. 26.

4. If Your Audience Disagrees with Your Ideas or Is Uncertain about Them, Present Both Sides of the Argument.

Behavioral scientists generally find that, if an audience is friendly to a persuader, or has no contrary views on the topic and will get none in the future, a one-sided presentation of a controversial question is most effective.[8] For instance, if your point is that sales of product X in the St. Louis territory could be doubled and you are writing to enthusiastic salespeople of product X, your best course is to concentrate on facts and examples showing the enormous potential of product X. There is no shortage of evidence showing that people generally prefer reading material that confirms their beliefs, and that they develop resistance to material that repudiates their beliefs. (As we shall see presently, however, this does not mean you cannot change their minds.)

But suppose your audience has not made up its mind, so far as you know? In this case you would do well to deal with *both* sides of the argument (or all sides, if there are more than two). Follow the same approach if the reader disagrees with you at the outset. For one thing, a two-sided presentation suggests to an uncertain or hostile audience that you possess objectivity. For another, it helps the reader remember your view by putting the pros and cons in relationship to one another. Also, it meets the reader's need to be treated as a mature, informed individual. As Karlins and Abelson point out:

> Conspicuously underlying your presentation is the assumption that the audience would be on your side if they only knew the truth. The other points of view should be presented with the attitude "it would be natural for you to have this idea if you don't know all the facts, but when you know all the facts, you will be convinced."[9]

Karlins and Abelson tested the reactions of audiences in postwar Germany to Voice of America broadcasts. They found that the most persuasive programs were those that included admissions of shortcomings in United States living conditions.[10]

Again, observation of businessmen's reactions to scores of *Harvard Business Review* articles advocating controversial measures convinces me that the most influential articles have been those that have acknowledged the shortcomings, weaknesses, and limitations of their arguments. When an author wants to sell a new idea to a sophisticated audience, he or she should be candid about the soft spots in his argument.

5. Win Respect by Making Your Opinion or Recommendation Clear.

Although strategy may call for a two-sided argument, this does not mean you should be timid in setting forth your conclusions or proposals at the end. We assume here that you have definite views and seek to persuade your audience to

---

[8]Experiments supporting this conclusion are reported by Carl I. Hovland, Arthur A. Lumsdaine, and F. Sheffield in *Experiments on Mass Communication* (Princeton: Princeton University Press, 1949). Cited by Karlins and Abelson, op. cit., p. 22.
[9]Karlins and Abelson, op. cit., p. 26.
[10]See *Factors Affecting Credibility in Psychological Warfare Communications* (Washington, D.C.: Human Resources Research Office, George Washington University, 1956).

adopt them. The two-sided approach is a *means* to that end; it does not imply compromising or obfuscating your conclusions. An official at Armour & Company once criticized many reports from subordinates to bosses on the ground that, after presenting much data, they concluded, in effect, "Here is what I found out and maybe we should do this or maybe we should do that." The typical response of a boss to such a memorandum, he noted, was to do nothing. Hence, the time taken both in writing and reading was wasted.[11]

6. Put Your Strongest Points Last if the Audience Is Very Interested in the Argument, First if It Is Not so Interested.

This question is referred to by social scientists as the "primacy-recency" issue in persuasion. The argument presented first is said to have primacy; the argument presented last, recency. Although studies of the question have produced inconsistent findings and no firm rules can be drawn, it appears that if your audience is deeply concerned with your subject you can afford to lead it along from the weakest points to the strongest. The audience's great interest will keep it reading, and putting the weaker points at the start tends to create rising reader expectations about what is coming. When you end with your strongest punch, therefore, you do not let readers down.

If your audience is not so concerned with the topic, on the other hand, it may be best to use the opposite approach. Now you cannot risk leading readers along a winding path. They may drop out before you reach the end. So grab their attention right at the beginning with your strongest argument or idea.

In any case, put the recommendation, facts, or arguments you most want the reader to *remember* first or last. Although experiments by social scientists on the primacy-recency issue are inconclusive, there is a firm pattern on the question of recall. The ideas you state first or last have a better chance of being remembered than the ideas stated in the middle of your appeal or case.

7. Don't Count on Changing Attitudes by Offering Information Alone.

"People are hostile to big business because they don't know enough facts about it," businesspeople are heard to say. Or, "If customers knew the truth about our costs, they would not object to our prices." Companies have poured large sums into advertising and public relations campaigns on this assumption; civic organizations have often based their hopes on it.

"The trouble with the assumption," states Karlins and Abelson, "is that it is almost never valid. There is a substantial body of research findings indicating that cognition—knowing something new—increasing information—is effective as an attitude change agent only under very specialized conditions."[12]

---

[11]John Ball and Cecil B. Williams, *Report Writing* (New York: Ronald, 1955).
[12]Karlins and Abelson, op. cit., p. 33.

Social scientists do concede, however, that presentations of facts alone may strengthen the opinions of people who already agree with the persuader. The information reassures them and helps them defend themselves in discussions with others.

8. "Testimonials" Are Most Likely to Be Persuasive if Drawn from People with Whom Readers Associate.

It is well known that a person's attitudes and opinions are strongly influenced by the groups to which he or she belongs or wants to belong—work units in a company, labor unions, bowling teams, social clubs, church associations, ethnic associations and so on. To muster third-party support for your proposal or idea, therefore, you would do well to cite the behavior, findings, or beliefs of groups to which your readers belong. In so doing, you allay any feelings of isolation readers might have if tempted to follow your ideas. You suggest that they are not alone with you, that there is group support for the points being made.

As every school child learns, the predominant attitudes of a group toward individuals or regarding standards of behavior, performance, or status influence an individual member's perceptions. For instance, a study of boys at a camp demonstrated that their ratings of various individuals' performances at shooting and canoeing were biased by their knowledge of the status of the rated individuals in the camp society. Thus a boy generally regarded as a leader was seen as performing better with the rifle or canoe than was a boy generally regarded as a follower, even though the first boy's performance was not actually superior.[13]

In addition, it seems fair to say that as modern television, radio, records, and cassettes have brought national celebrities into the home and automobile, these people, too, have been stamped with approval or disapproval by millions of groups across the country.

Accordingly, if your readers are young, dissident, or "long hairs," refer to a Richard Dreyfuss or a Joan Baez for supporting statements, not to a Gerald Ford or an Arnold Palmer. If your readers are electrical engineers, quote well-regarded scientific sources as your authority, not star salespeople or public relations people. Take into account also that the more deeply attached your readers are to a group, the greater the influence of the group norms on them. For instance, one experiment by social scientists showed that the opinions of Catholic students who took their religion seriously were less influenced by the answers of nonserious Catholics than were the opinions of Catholic students who placed little value on their church membership.[14]

---

[13]Ibid., p. 50.
[14]See H. Kelley, "Salience of Membership and Resistance to Change of Group-Anchored Attitudes," *Human Relations,* August 1955, pp. 255–289. Cited in Karlins and Abelson, op. cit., p. 58.

9. Be Wary of Using Extreme or "Sensational" Claims and Facts.

Both research in behavioral science and common sense confirm this rule.[15] Do not be misled by the fact that flashy journalists make successful use of extreme and bizarre cases to dramatize a story. The situation in business and professional writing is different from that in journalism.

When you seek the confidence and cooperation of your readers—and typically you do in the kinds of communications we deal with in this . . . [selection]—it is best to write in terms of the real world as you and they perceive it. Observable, believable, realistic statements carry more weight than any other kind. Although you want reader attention, you do not want to shock your audience with outlandish examples or arguments. These may help you to succeed in making the reader sit up—but they will also provoke distrust and suspicion.

Examples are common in the letters sections of newspapers. A writer who identified himself as a former vice-president of a well-known bank opposed a large power company's plan to build a new plant in a rural area near his town. His letter began as follows: "A great many of us . . . are profoundly disturbed by the proposal now being considered to disrupt and destroy the marvelous little valley southwest of [name of town], in order to build bigger and better power plants. This would be a devastating blow to the last unspoiled bit of country left in Connecticut. . . ."[16]

Like a batter who hits the first two pitches foul and quickly gets two strikes against him, this writer managed to distort the first two sentences he wrote. The proposed plant, though a very large one, would not "disrupt and destroy" the valley—only a small section of the valley area would be affected. Moreover, the valley was not "the last unspoiled bit of country" in the state—it was only a small parcel of the state's beautiful countryside. These exaggerations might have drawn cheers from rabid foes of the project, but the writer wasn't interested in appealing to them; he wanted to win uncommitted readers. At the very beginning, however, he antagonized them with hyperbole.

10. Tailor Your Presentation to the Reasons for Readers' Attitudes, if You Know Them.

Your chances of persuading readers are better if you can plan your appeal or argument to meet the main feelings, prejudices, or reasons for their beliefs. For instance, if reader beliefs are the result of their wanting to go along with certain groups they like or associate with, your best bet (as indicated earlier) is to show the acceptability of your point to these groups. If their attitudes reflect personal biases, such as an old grudge against someone in power, it is best to tailor your presentation to that prejudice. And so on.

---

[15]See, for example, *Building Opposition to the Excess Profits Tax* (Princeton: Opinion Research Corporation, August 1952), and R. Weiss, "Conscious Technique for the Variation of Source Credibility," *Psychological Reports,* Vol. 20, 1969, p. 1159. Both cited in Karlins and Abelson, op. cit., pp. 36–37.

[16]*Lakeville Journal,* April 2, 1970, p. 11.

Summarizing the implications of several behavioral studies, Karlins and Abelson present the example of three people who say they are against private ownership of industry. How should their reasons for this position influence one's choice of strategy or persuasion? The authors explain:

One of them feels that way because he has only been exposed to one side of the story and has nothing else on which to base his opinions. The way to change this man's opinion may be to expose him to facts, take him to visit some factories, meet some workers and supervisors. A second person is against private ownership because that is the prevailing norm or social climate in the circles in which he finds himself. His attitudes are caused by his being a part of a group and conforming to its standards. You cannot change this fellow just by showing him facts. The facts must be presented in an atmosphere which suggests a social reward for changing his opinion. Some kind of status appeal might be a start in that direction. A third person may have negative attitudes toward private industry because by making business the scapegoat for all his troubles, he can unload his pent-up feelings of bitterness and disappointment at the world for not giving him a better break. . . . Trying to change this third person with facts may actually do more harm than good. The more evidence shows how wrong he is, the more he looks for reasons to support his beliefs. This kind of person can sometimes be influenced by helping him to understand why he has a particular attitude.[17]

11. Never Mention Other People without Considering Their Possible Effect on the Reader.

Other people may, as we saw earlier, be introduced for the sake of "testimonials." More commonly, however, other people's names are mentioned in the course of explaining a situation, narrating an event, or completing the format of a message. This use of names, too, may affect the power of your message.

A reference to the actions of another person—however simple and unobtrusive it may seem to you the writer—may alter your relationship with readers. If readers consider that person a friend or enemy, their natural reaction is to begin thinking of the possible bearing of your communication on their friendship or antagonism. This reaction can have significant implications for your approach.

To illustrate, a doctoral student who had failed to meet his school's program requirements tried to muster faculty opinion in support of his petition for re-admission by appearing daily at the entrance to the dining hall and handing out leaflets to faculty members. One such leaflet contained these words: "I am very unhappy about the strain my case has created for Professor [name of the program director]. I am distressed if last Friday's handout . . . created the impression that I was harping on his mistakes. I have told him and I tell you that I could understand his actions and decisions. . . ." The leaflet went on at some length to explain the doctoral student's feelings about the problem.

What this writer did not realize was the impact of the professor's name on his communication strategy. Almost everyone who received the leaflet was a colleague of the professor in question. Therefore the leaflet made it necessary for

---

[17]Karlins and Abelson, op. cit., p. 92.

them to think of their relationship with the professor when they made up their minds about the petition. And their relationship with the professor was more important to them than their relationship with the doctoral student.

If the doctoral student considered it essential to mention the professor, he could have elected to: (1) try to win readers over while convincing them that their relations with the professor would not be affected, or (2) show that the professor was so far off base that readers were morally bound to risk their relationship with him. In the latter case, the leaflet should have contained ready-to-use arguments that readers could draw on in explaining to the professor why they sympathized with the doctoral student. Since the leaflet did neither of these things, it was a failure in persuasion.

Don't overlook the possible effect of distribution. Letters often go to third parties, with "cc" typed at the bottom followed by the names of those people. A memorandum often contains the names of several addressees in the "To" line at the top. Covering letters with reports may indicate several groups of readers. All this may affect your strategy. The background information that you could omit if writing only to Jones may be quite necessary if Brown, too, is an important reader; and the rather offhand treatment you give to a certain test or episode if writing to Jones and Brown might not be fitting at all if Larabee also is an intended reader. Many times the wise manager or professional rewrites part of a letter or memo after deciding to send a copy of it to an additional person who was not considered when the first draft was made.

Many people have strong feelings about "blind copies," that is, copies sent to persons other than those indicated after "cc" at the end of a letter or in the "To" line of a memorandum. Some people feel that blind copies never should be sent. Others feel that since a letter or memo is the property of the writer, he or she can distribute it at will. Although the latter view is legally correct, only an obtuse writer will distribute copies thoughtlessly if the content is in any way confidential, personal, or politically sensitive.

SIZING UP YOUR READERS

We have a tendency to abstract written communications from real life, to act as if the customary ground rules of influence and persuasion don't apply to a message that is in writing. We act with a naiveté almost unheard of in our face-to-face relationships. Not seeing readers, we act as if they weren't real people. "If we write the information clearly, accurately, and correctly," we think wishfully to ourselves, "surely that satisfies the requirements of a piece of paper." But Josh Billings's puckish maxim, "As scarce as truth is, the supply has always been in excess of the demand," applies to truth on paper as well as truth in conversation.

Think of your intended readers as the real people they will be when they take your letter or report out of the "in-box." Only then can you decide intelligently what information and ideas to emphasize and in what order to present them.

To help you think of readers as three-dimensional people, ask yourself some questions about their situation and relationships with you. Are they:

- Deeply or only mildly interested in the subject of your communication?
- Familiar or unfamiliar with your views, competence, and feelings about them?
- Knowledgeable or ignorant of your authority in the area discussed, your status, and your associations of possible importance to them?
- Committed or uncommitted to a viewpoint, opinion, or course of action other than the one you favor in your letter, report, or other document?
- Likely or unlikely to find your proposal, idea, finding, or conclusion threatening or requiring considerable change in their thought or behavior?
- Inclined or uninclined to think and feel the way they do about the subject because of identifiable reasons, prejudices, or experiences?
- Associated formally or informally with groups or organizations involved in some way with the idea or proposal you deal with?

With answers to questions like these in mind, you will not see your readers as shadows on the wall. They will sit across from you. You can write as if talking *with* them, not talking to them.

Dan Jones

Determining the Ethics of Style

Dan Jones is Professor of English at the University of Central Florida and the author of several books on technical communication.

Doublespeak is not the product of carelessness or sloppy thinking. Indeed, most doublespeak is the product of clear thinking and is carefully designed and constructed to appear to communicate when in fact it doesn't. It is language designed not to lead but mislead. It is language designed to distort reality and corrupt thought.[1]

—*William Lutz*

Sometimes we want to be unclear. We don't know what we're talking about, and we don't want anyone else to know that. Or we do know what we're talking about, and we don't want anyone else to know what we know. On those occasions, we write unclearly deliberately, and if what we write gets the job done, then we say the writing is "good." But "good" has two meanings. Assassins can be "good" at their jobs but not be "good" people. In the same way, writing can be "good" if it gets the job done, but if the job is ethically questionable, then the writing may be bad just because it is so good.[2]

—*Joseph Williams*

What kind of behavior is "prose behavior"? Prose is usually described in a moral vocabulary—"sincere," "open" or "devious," and "hypocritical"—but is this vocabulary justified? Why, for that matter, has it been so moralistic? Why do so many people feel that bad prose threatens the foundations of civilization? And why, in fact, do we think "bad" the right word to use for it?[3]

—*Richard Lanham*

WHAT IS ETHICS?

Simply defined, "Ethics is the study of right and wrong conduct."[4] More broadly, ethics is "the discipline dealing with what is good and bad and with moral duty and obligation."[5] Ethics also means "a set of moral principles or values" or "a theory or system of moral values."[6] More broadly still, ethics may be defined as a guiding philosophy.

Vincent Ruggiero observes that "the focus of ethics is moral situations—that is, *those situations in which there is a choice of behavior involving human values* (those qualities that are regarded as good and desirable). . . ."[7]

ETHICS AND TECHNICAL PROSE

Just as people must make many ethical decisions throughout their lives, you must make many ethical decisions concerning what you write throughout your career. For example, are you doing your best to document a product honestly and accurately? Are you knowingly omitting any essential information? If you are unclear or imprecise, and if your poor instructions cause injury to someone, are you morally responsible? If you are in a company's marketing department, and you are asked to exaggerate a product's features, are you guilty of lying? If you know you are promising more than you can deliver in a proposal written in response to a request for a proposal (RFP), are you unethical or just keenly competitive? If you fail to point out numerous known bugs in a program in your software manual, are you a good software documentation writer or are you unethical? If you exaggerate your qualifications on your resume or in your cover letter to gain an advantage over the competition, are you unethical? These are just some of many possible scenarios faced by writers of technical prose everywhere.

Why isn't it possible just to make a list of ethical language choices that everyone could agree on and everyone could abide by? Unfortunately, it's not that easy. Suppose that you wrote the clearest instructions you could write, but someone neglected to provide some essential information and a customer is injured following your instructions. Are you unethical in this instance? Suppose because of unreasonable deadlines, you have to cut corners and you just don't have time to document some important features of a software program. Are you a bad person? Suppose you have been told by your boss in marketing that you're expected to hype the product just to keep up with the competition. Are you unethical for trying to keep your job and doing what you are told to do? As these possible scenarios and many others show, it's not always easy to determine which writing decisions are right or wrong, moral or immoral, ethical or unethical.

ETHICS AND THE PROFESSIONS

Of course, ethical concerns are not new to those who must write technical prose. Most professions and professional organizations have published ethical guidelines. The Computer Ethics Institute, for example, published the following guidelines:

The Ten Commandments of Computer Ethics

1. Thou shalt not use a computer to harm other people.
2. Thou shalt not interfere with other people's computer work.

3. Thou shalt not snoop around in other people's computer files.
4. Thou shalt not use a computer to steal.
5. Thou shalt not use a computer to bear false witness.
6. Thou shalt not copy or use proprietary software for which you have not paid.
7. Thou shalt not use other people's computer resources without authorization or proper compensation.
8. Thou shalt not appropriate other people's intellectual output.
9. Thou shalt think about the social consequences of the program you are writing or the system you are designing.
10. Thou shalt always use a computer in ways that insure consideration and respect for your fellow humans.[8]

Search for information on *ethics* using any search engine on the World Wide Web, and you'll see all kinds of databases offering other codes of ethics and all kinds of information on ethics. You'll see medical ethics, business ethics, computer ethics, military ethics, media ethics, journalism ethics, and so on. You'll see links to many professional societies and their published codes of ethics. You'll see course syllabi, papers, online journals, and much more.

It seems as though almost everyone is concerned about ethics in one way or another. Developing ethical guidelines for technical communicators parallels the challenges of doing so for computer professionals and engineers. All three groups have obligations to society, to their employers, to their clients, and to co-professionals and even professional organizations.

In *Computer Ethics,* Tom Forester and Perry Morrison list many ethical questions faced by computer professionals:

- Is copying software really a form of stealing? What sort of intellectual property rights should software developers have?
- Are so-called "victimless" crimes (against, e.g., banks) more acceptable than crimes with human victims? Should computer professionals be sued for lax computer security?
- Is hacking merely a bit of harmless fun or is it a crime equivalent to burglary, forgery and/or theft? Or are hackers to be seen as guardians of our civil liberties?
- Should the creation of viruses be considered deliberate sabotage and be punished accordingly?
- Does information on individuals stored in a computer constitute an intolerable invasion of privacy? How much protection are individuals entitled to?
- Who is responsible for computer malfunctions or errors in computer programs? Should computer companies be made to provide a warranty on software?
- Is "artificial intelligence" a realistic and a proper goal for computer science? Should we trust our lives to allegedly artificially intelligent "expert" systems?
- Should we allow the workplace to be computerized if it de-skills the workforce and/or increases depersonalization, fatigue and boredom?
- Is it OK for computer professionals to make false claims about the capabilities of computers when selling systems or representing computers to the general public? Is it ethical for computer companies to "lock-in" customers to their products?

- Should, indeed, computer professionals be bound by a Code of Conduct and if so, what should it include?[9]

As you would expect, the Society for Technical Communication also has ethical guidelines:

STC Ethical Guidelines for Technical Communicators

Introduction. As technical communicators, we observe the following ethical guidelines in our professional activities. Their purpose is to help us maintain ethical practices.

Legality. We observe the laws and regulations governing our professional activities in the workplace. We meet the terms and obligations of contracts that we undertake. We ensure that all terms of our contractual agreements are consistent with STC Ethical Guidelines.

Honesty. We seek to promote the public good in our activities. To the best of our ability, we provide truthful and accurate communications. We dedicate ourselves to conciseness, clarity, and creativity, striving to address the needs of those who use our products. We alert our clients and employers when we believe material is ambiguous. Before using another person's work, we obtain permission. In cases where individuals are credited, we attribute authorship only to those who have made an original, substantive contribution. We do not perform work outside our job scope during hours compensated by clients or employers, except with their permission; nor do we use their facilities, equipment or supplies without their approval. When we advertise our services, we do so truthfully.

Confidentiality. Respecting the confidentiality of our clients, employers, and professional organizations, we release business-sensitive information only with their consent or when legally required. We acquire releases from clients and employers before including their business-sensitive information in our portfolios or before using such material for a different client or employer or for demo purposes.

Quality. With the goal of producing high-quality work, we negotiate realistic, candid agreement on the schedule, budget, and deliverables with clients and employers in the initial project planning stage. When working on the project, we fulfill our negotiated roles in a timely and responsible manner and meet the stated expectations.

Fairness. We respect cultural variety and other aspects of diversity in our clients, employers, development teams, and audiences. We serve the business interest of our clients and employers, as long as such loyalty does not require us to violate the public good. We avoid conflicts of interest in the fulfillment of our responsibilities and activities. If we are aware of a conflict of interest, we disclose it to those concerned and obtain their approval before proceeding.

Professionalism. We seek candid evaluations of our professional performance from clients and employers. We also provide candid evaluations of communication products and services. We advance the technical communication profession through our integrity, standards, and performance.[10]

Codes of conduct are valuable because they establish ideals and help define the character of a profession. These codes help to establish an atmosphere of professionalism, and they help to encourage members of a profession to act ethically even in the most difficult of circumstances. . . .

NOTES

1. William Lutz, *Doublespeak* (New York: Harper & Row, 1989) 18–19.
2. Joseph Williams, *Style,* 4th ed. (New York: HarperCollins, 1994) 134.
3. Richard Lanham, *Revising Prose,* 3rd ed. (New York: Macmillan, 1992) 96–97.
4. Vincent Ryan Ruggiero, *Thinking Critically about Ethical Issues,* 3rd ed. (Mountain View, CA: Mayfield, 1992) 4.
5. *Merriam-Webster's Tenth Collegiate Dictionary and Thesaurus.* Electronic Edition. CD-ROM, 1995.
6. *Merriam-Webster's Tenth Collegiate Dictionary and Thesaurus.* Electronic Edition. CD-ROM, 1995.
7. Ruggiero, p. 5.
8. Computer Ethics Institute Home Page, http://www.cpsr.org:80/dox/cei.html
9. Tom Forester and Perry Morrison, *Computer Ethics: Cautionary Tales and Ethical Dilemmas in Computing* (Cambridge, MA: MIT P, 1992) 4–5.
10. *STC Membership Directory 1995–96* 42:3A (September 1995) xi.

Part 5

Resumes and Other Written Materials for a Job Search

The written materials that are part of an application for a job face one of the most difficult audiences imaginable: experienced recruiting managers. The selections that follow in this section of *Strategies* offer extensive advice on how to prepare and write resumes and cover letters, as well as on how to follow up on such documents in writing.

Keep in mind that there is no *one* way to write a resume or a cover letter. Slavishly following some model that an applicant mistakenly thinks represents the ideal can defeat the purpose of writing a resume and a cover letter: to get an interview. The shelves of bookstores and libraries across the country are filled with guides offering advice on how to write resumes and cover letters. These guides offer advice, not commandments. Job applicants should consult as many of these guides as they want, read the selections that follow in *Strategies,* but, in the end, let common sense be their guide when they write what are essentially advertisements for themselves.

The best advice on how to write effective resumes and cover letters quite naturally comes from the recruiting managers who read them. Several years ago, my own university's placement bureau sponsored a panel featuring the recruiting managers from the companies that traditionally have hired the greatest number of our graduates. All the managers agreed that they looked at resumes and cover letters to determine as quickly as possible—sometimes merely by scanning a candidate's application materials—what preparation and experience candidates had in the following skills and areas:

- written and oral communication skills
- computer skills
- interpersonal skills, as demonstrated by the ability to work as a member of a team
- self-reliance and initiative, as demonstrated by the ability to work alone
- a sense of what the world of work demands in terms of professionalism and deadlines
- specific skills in at least one business or technical area supplemented by secondary skills in a variety of related areas
- a sense of business and personal ethics
- the ability to manage time, set priorities, and work under stress.

While recruiting managers do not expect job candidates to excel in all these areas or possess all these skills from the start, the list does provide some general guidelines for communicating with recruiting managers by resumes and cover letters—or, for that matter, in person during an interview.

Before you read any further in this section of *Strategies*, you may well want to carry out a useful exercise. Using your word processor, or simply a ruled yellow pad and pen or pencil, compile an extensive inventory of your experiences and the skills those experiences have provided you with. Aim at first to be as inclusive and complete as possible.

List your education and training—omit high school and grade school, however. List all your previous jobs—part- and full-time, volunteer and paid—and don't forget co-op positions, internships, and practica. Again, don't go back any further than the summer after you graduated from high school, and at this stage be as complete as possible. Next think of anything else that you have done in your life, and list it.

Here you might run the gamut of your experiences from actually running in the Boston marathon, to working in a soup kitchen, to editing the college or university newspaper, to belonging to a sorority or fraternity, to working on a political initiative or for a candidate, to work you may have done for your place of worship—though you'll want to tread lightly in both these last areas as a general involvement in politics or religious activities—rather than party or denomination—is what is important.

Don't forget any travel you may have done as well, or any truly unusual experiences you may have had. While he was still in high school, the son of a colleague of mine attended the funeral of Pope John Paul II and an inaugural ball in honor of President Obama. My former department chair, while still a college student, attended the funeral of President Kennedy standing not 200 feet from the President of France and the Emperor of Ethiopia—world leaders have not always had to live in a security cocoon.

Under education and training, flesh things out. If you went to college, you spent two or four (or more years) there. Sure, you had a major or a double major, and maybe also a minor or two. But what other courses did you take? Everyone expects someone applying for an accounting position to have the requisite number of accounting courses and for someone applying for a nursing position to have the requisite number of science courses, but what courses did you take outside the major, and, most importantly, what added credentials or perspectives did those elective courses provide? Check again the list of skills the employers who recruit at my university look for in job applicants.

Also, dig deeper. When you were a student, what topics did you research, speak, and write about; what books did you read; what kinds of debates and discussions did you get into? Was that term paper on the economics of wind power simply an exercise that allowed you to complete a course with a passing grade, or did you gain valuable new perspectives on the interrelationships among energy consumption, energy policy, neighborhood activism, and corporate lobbying? Did that term paper on the New Deal suggest any useful parallels with recent economic downturns? Did that term paper on Bollywood offer you more general insights into the complex relationship between India and the West? Are there items in such term papers, research projects, or class assignments that could now find their way onto your resume or into a cover letter, or be talking points in an interview?

Also, don't forget any specialized skills that your education may have provided you with, such as skills on the computer or skills in foreign languages and culture.

While on campus, what extracurricular activities did you take part in? Were those activities purely for enjoyment, or was there a service or educational component involved? Were you the designated student host for a distinguished visitor? Did you meet with potential job candidates for positions on your campus or in your department, or even ferry them to and from campus? Did you hold any appointed or elective offices? Did a campus publication publish any of your work? Were you interviewed on the campus radio or television station? Did you volunteer as a tutor for children at nearby schools or for your peers? In short, what did you do other than sleep, eat, go to class, and study?

Also, if you worked full- or part-time while also going to school full- or part-time, don't forget to point that fact out. Any student who worked forty hours a week while also going to school full time and managing to maintain a 2.50 GPA may be more impressive to some employers than a scholarship student who simply seems to have hit the books and as a result maintained a 3.75 GPA.

Next, turn to your previous work history. If you are still in school or are a recent graduate, no one expects you to have run a *Fortune* 500 company—or even necessarily to have worked for one. But it is not unreasonable to expect that you have worked. And any job can provide you with skills that you may be able to transfer to another job more closely related to what you really want to do in life. If you had an absolutely horrible summer working at a beach resort in a family restaurant—kids screaming, demanding (of you) and over-indulgent (of those screaming kids) parents, poor tippers, dropped plates, and so on—no one would blame you for not wanting to spend a lifetime in such a job, but in the every cloud-has-a-silver-lining department, that job may have given you an opportunity to demonstrate that you had good people skills, that you could work under pressure, that you could balance competing demands, that you were honest, that you showed up on time, that you showed initiative when you needed to but also followed directions when such actions were called for.

Did you work in a large supermarket as a cashier, notably on Friday nights and all day on Saturdays—typically the busiest, most hectic shifts? Did you balance your cash register every shift? If so, aren't you trustworthy, reliable, good with other people's money? And how much money usually passed through your always-balanced cash register on a typical shift? $5,000? $10,000? More? You really *are* good with other people's money, reliable, and trustworthy if you handled that much money regularly without any shortages.

Did you spend a summer painting houses, mowing loans, babysitting? All these jobs require trustworthiness, reliability, and maybe even some entrepreneurial know-how on your part. No matter what the job and no matter how unrelated that job may seem to the position for which you are currently applying, your previous jobs may have equipped you with a series of skills that translate to and are valuable for any number of other positions: good communication skills, time management skills, people skills toward customers as well as other employees, the ability to follow directions along with the willingness to take initiate when appropriate, loyalty, trustworthiness, number skills, punctuality, reliability, and so on.

Do any special circumstances surrounding your past jobs give you additional credentials or talking points? Again, the demands of working a summer job at a busy family restaurant at a beach resort differ from those working at a two- or three-star restaurant where gentlemen and ladies are "expected to dress." Working at a chain grocery store is not the same as working at and being a member of a food cooperative run by a neighborhood organization. Working at a tennis camp tucked away in exclusive vacation enclave is quite different from running a softball league for an urban branch of the Police Athletic League.

Don't forget nonpaying and volunteer positions as well—you may have gained any number of invaluable skills and experiences in working at them. The same is true of internships, co-ops, practica, even work-study positions at a college or university.

Companies increasingly value employees who are good citizens. That you have been a volunteer for, or work closely with, any number of neighborhood, civic, religious, charitable, or even political organizations can be an asset. But remember that when it comes to religious and political groups, employers want to hire people who will be thoughtful, knowledgeable, civic-minded, and ethical team players, not people who are crusaders for a cause, no matter how worthy you may think that cause may be.

A healthy respect for the environment will get no one in trouble, nor will participation in the electoral process. But employers expect employees to leave the bumper stickers on their bumpers and the placards and even lapel pins and cause-affirming buttons at home. Work with scouting is good, whether you should hit your coworkers up during the annual cookie sales drive may well, however, violate company policy. Employers are, in short, more interested in your being a good citizen in the broadest sense of the term; they are not in general interested in your advocacy for a particular cause, unless that cause is directly related to what that company does, sells, manufactures, or promotes.

Hobbies too can, in some circumstances, work to your advantage. A decent handicap on the golf course may provide opportunities for sealing a sales or other deal. Frequent previous travel may have given you some wider perspectives on issues, or indicate a willingness on your part to travel in the future for an employer. Team sports are a good way of building skills for positions that require team players. Be careful, though, of emphasizing skills that may strike some employers as too risky; no one wants to pay disability and medical bills for employees who love to jump regularly by bungee cord into the canyons of the world, as exciting as such activities may be.

Avoid listing activities that are too generalized ("I like to read."—indicate what kinds of books) or seemingly unrelated to the position for which you are applying. "I like to read medical detective fiction" might connect with a job requiring keen analytical skills, or not. Knitting as a hobby might at first seem fairly irrelevant to a future job or career unless you were applying for a job in fashion or clothing retail. Being a rabid sports fan would seem to be a prerequisite for bartending in a sports bar, not so for being a building inspector, unless talking about sports could be used as an ice breaker when making calls at construction sites.

Finally, did you have any truly "once in a life-time" experiences that can be brought to bear in your written job application materials or in an interview? How many of his peers share my colleague's son's high school experience of having been both to a papal funeral and to a presidential inaugural ball?

Once you have compiled an inventory of your experiences and the skills those experiences have provided you with, start to edit it down, separating what may be potentially useful in pitching yourself to a potential employer. Armed with the data from your inventory, you can begin to flesh out your resume and cover letter, and be better prepared for an interview, where topics discussed may range across a broad spectrum.

But remember that everything that you list on your resume and discuss in a cover letter must be presented in language that will make sense to a potential employer. Recall the distinction made between writer-based and reader-based prose by Linda Flower and John Ackerman in their essay in the first section of *Strategies.* *You* know that Communication 678 is an ethics course. *You* know that Alpha Beta Gamma is a service sorority. *You* know that the Smith-Jones Scholarship is for outstanding academic achievement, but that the Jones-Smith Scholarship is for outstanding athletic achievement. *You* know that ASMU stands for the Associated Students of My University, and even better that the Associated Students of My University is the name of the student government. *You* know that *The Lion's Murk* is the weekly (or is it daily?) student newspaper. But does a potential employer who may have never set foot on your campus know any of these things?

And a final reminder: when it comes to cover letters, resumes, and any employment-related documents, be specific, be clear, don't lie, don't stretch the truth, don't say anything that you cannot in some way or form prove.

The essays that follow offer a number of perspectives on writing to get a job. In a classic piece, the late John Munschauer offers more than advice on writing resumes and cover letters. Based on his many years working at and then eventually directing Cornell University's Career Center, Munschauer offers what amounts to wisdom for job seekers. Using resumes and cover letters from a number of job applicants in a variety of fields, Munschauer shows how some applicants present potential employers with documents that advance their candidacy while others make it more than easy for these same potential employers to reject them. Though Munschauer's job seekers present resumes from the 1980s and 1990s, the advice that he offers is timeless—today the same mistakes need to be avoided, and the same tips can still be used.

Steve Graber, an expert in career management, follows next with additional advice on how to write a cover letter. Graber discusses in full issues of format, content, style, tone, and word choice. He also provides tips on how to avoid common blunders that cover letter writers make, thereby derailing their job search just as it begins. Graber concludes his essay with some advice for job seekers facing what he calls "special situations": responding to "blind" advertisements, sending cold letters, using broadcast letters, writing to an employment agency or an executive search firm, and exploring the possibilities offered by networking letters. By way of coda, Graber reminds us all of the importance of thank you letters after an interview and even after a job rejection.

In Shakespeare's play *The Tempest*, Miranda, the heroine, expressed amazement at "the brave new world" that she encountered halfway through the play. There is a brave new world for job seekers as well, thanks to the Internet. Long gone are the days of manually typing job application materials, photocopying them, and sending them off in the mail.

Today, the Internet is the mode of both composition and of transmittal—and who knows what the future will bring. While the Internet has certainly made composing resumes and cover letters seem easier, that ease has also been accompanied by a host of new problems.

Complementing John Munschauer's earlier advice, both Diana C. Reep and Martin Yate in separate essays comment on the different resume formats available to job seekers. Yate, like Munschauer, writes from the perspective of many years' experience in career management in industry and as a consultant and *New York Times* best-selling author. The essays by Munschauer, Reep, and Yate further reinforce the point that I made earlier in this introduction to the fifth section of *Strategies*: the selections throughout this section offer advice, not commandments. Job applicants should consult as many people, guides, and sources of information as they want, but, in the end, they should let common sense be their guide in writing resumes, cover letters, and other employment-related documents.

There is a whole etiquette to the job search. Unfortunately, employers are in a better position to ignore that etiquette than job applicants, but even in the hardest of economic times and the tightest of job markets, employers who do not treat job applicants well may come to lament their behavior. As the old adage has it, what goes around comes around. Every job applicant knows that she or he will never be better treated by a company than before signing on the dotted line and accepting the job. Shoddy treatment during the application process does not bode well for a period of happy employment later on.

Karl Weber and Rob Kaplan, writing from their complementary perspectives as editors, authors, and consultants in a number of fields, take up the issue of the etiquette of the job search in an essay on follow-up letters. They offer advice on, and provide examples of, networking interview, job interview, job acceptance, job turndown, and networking contact follow-up letters. The golden rule seems appropriate in all cases: do unto others as you would have them do unto you.

In almost all areas of employment and in almost all areas of the country, the job market is tight. Eager applicants need to put their best foot forward. The essays in this fifth and last section of *Strategies* share a common purpose: to help job applicants land first an interview and then a job offer. To repeat and slightly paraphrase a point made by the late John D. deButts when he was Chairman of AT&T in the late 1970s, and quoted at the beginning of the general introduction to *Strategies*: "the ability to express ideas cogently and goals persuasively— in plain English—is the most important skill" in applying for a job.

John L. Munschauer

Writing Resumes and Letters in the Language of Employers

The late John L. Munschauer was Director of the Cornell University Career Center.

[Editor's note: Although Munschauer's job seekers present resumes from the 1980s and 1990s, the advice that he offers is timeless—today the same mistakes need to be avoided, and the same tips can still be used.]

"I am sorry, Father O'Mega, I can't let you in."

"But, St. Peter, I did everything I was supposed to. I changed the Mass from Latin to English. I had the communicants hold their hands the new way when they took communion. Everyone, so far as I knew, genuflected properly, and even Mrs. O'Reilley's Protestant husband stood when I read the gospel. I can't think of a thing I did that was wrong."

"The message, Father O'Mega, what about the message?"

"The message? What message?"

"The message of the Lord, Father. Don't you remember? The Ten Commandments? The Beatitudes? The Golden Rule? It's the *message* that gets people in here, not the ritual. The ritual was supposed to help deliver the message, but you made the ritual the message and the meaning got lost."

Meanwhile, back on earth . . . in Tucumcari, New Mexico, and all over the United States, job hunters are at their typewriters and computers pushing words around to make their resumes look like the ones they have seen in books. Whether to have it professionally printed or not, that is the question. Does it have enough action verbs?

In Peoria, Illinois, and elsewhere, employers are scanning resumes. Some are beautiful to look at; a few are even printed commercially on expensive paper. But the resumes are laid aside. Employers are reading them with one thought in mind: What can the candidates do for us? The message they are looking for isn't there.

WHY USE A RESUME?

The purpose of a resume is to convey a message, a purpose easily forgotten in the ritual of preparing it. At every turn, you will get conflicting advice about how to conduct the ritual:

- You must have a resume to get a job.
- The purpose of a resume is to get an interview.
- Every resume must have a job objective.
- A resume should never, ever be longer than one page.
- On a resume, list experience chronologically.

On the other hand, others advise:

- Don't use a resume if you are looking for an executive position or merely seeking information.
- Resumes typecast you and narrow your options.
- Interview for information first, determine what an employer wants, and then decide whether offering a resume will suit your purposes.
- Two or more pages present no problem if your resume follows a logical, easy-to-read outline.
- List your experience by function, not chronologically.

The more opinions you get, the more confused you become, but you finally work up something. You send it out. You get little or no response. You change your resume from one page to two pages—or from two pages to one. The results are no better. Somebody says to try pink paper; *that* will get attention. You decide you should have used blue. You fiddle and fiddle with your resume, trying to find the magic formula that will get you what you want. You are caught up in the ritual, forgetting that the purpose of a resume is to send a message.

It is hard not to be distracted from the message. You concentrate on developing a format, forgetting the message, instead of concentrating on the message and *then* working on a format that will convey it best. But what is your message? To find the answer, use your imagination to step out of yourself and become an employer. Think about what the employer is trying to accomplish and the talent required to get it done. Now, from your imaginary employer's chair, look back at yourself and ponder the answer. If you can't come up with one, you will have difficulty writing a resume that will say to the employer, "I have something to offer you."

Resumes are not tickets to a job. They are just one of several ways to court employers. And, as in any courtship, sometimes it's just as well not to put everything in print so the other party can't draw the wrong conclusion. Take the case of Cheryl Fender, an alto who learned that the Springfield Opera Company was auditioning for an alto to sing *Carmen*. Cheryl was well-qualified, and her voice teacher was well-known as a coach of only the most gifted singers. On the other hand, her resume, incomplete and with gaps in her history, showed extensive experience as a secretary. Wisely, she did not send the resume, which might have established her as a secretary who wanted to sing rather than as a singer who had supported herself by being a secretary. Instead, she asked herself what was important to the director of an opera company. Voice, of course, so she outlined her training in a letter. But dramatic ability also mattered, so she included pictures of herself on stage in roles that beautifully illustrated her dramatic ability. She got an audition. Cheryl followed a good marketing rule: Don't confuse customers by flaunting things that don't speak to their needs.

GIVING YOUR MESSAGE

While the language of employment for you is "I want" and for employers it is "I need," you can create resumes and letters in your language that will be read by employers in theirs. I don't mean statements such as "I have analyzed my qualifications and feel confident that they fit your needs." If you were one of thousands of employers who read this kind of thing, would you ask what qualifications and what needs? If the answer isn't clear—and it rarely is—there won't be a message.

It isn't all that difficult to create a statement that is effective. Start with the written word, with prose. Even if you are going to be approaching employers in person, go through the exercise of writing letters. Otherwise, like most people, you can get caught up in the resume ritual and neglect to develop the words that can be more effective in telling your story. People sweat over resumes, then dash off letters without much thought. Perfect resumes arriving in the mail won't even be read if the cover letters don't impress and engage employers.

I recall being asked to review a proposed application letter for a job on the staff of a yachting magazine. The letter was beautifully written, but it left the impression of being all "I": "I want to write so very much, and I am sure I can learn if you give me a chance. . . . I got straight A's in English. . . . I love boats. . . . I am a sailor. . . . I was captain of the sailing team in college. . . ."

What do you say to a person who has written a letter like that? He had obviously spent hours composing it. In its appearance and use of language, it met the highest standards. I could not squelch the young man's hopes, so I had him read *Book Publishing,* a pamphlet Daniel Melcher wrote when he was president of R. R. Bowker Company. Although the pamphlet is concerned only with book publishing, I thought its message would be useful for someone interested in magazines as well.

Let me paraphrase a portion of Melcher's pamphlet:

> I like publishing and you might like it too. It is only fair to warn you, however, that publishing attracts a great many more people than the industry can possibly absorb. Sometimes it seems as though half of the English majors in the country besiege publishing offices for jobs each year. While we hope that you will have something to offer us, you might as well face it. Publishers are experts in the art of the gentle brush-off.
>
> The interviewer hopes that you have what he needs, but it turns out that you have never looked into any of the industry's trade journals nor read any books about the industry. You haven't even acquainted yourself with the work of your university press. You tell the

interviewer that you are willing to start anywhere, but it develops that a file clerk's job would not interest you, you do not want to type, you don't think you can sell, and you know nothing about printing.

The fact is, all you have thought about is what you want, but it is his needs that create jobs, and you must address yourself to needs.

Your problem, therefore, is to learn as much as possible about the industry before you go looking for a job. Only in this way will you be able to put yourself in the publisher's place and talk to him about his needs rather than about your wants.

After reading Melcher's advice, the fellow said he got the point, thanked me, and left, returning about three weeks later to show me his revised letter. It began in much the same way as his earlier effort—with "I's"—"I majored in English. . . . I have done considerable sailing. . . ."—but after a few short sentences, he suddenly changed his tack. A new three-sentence paragraph began like this: "With my interests, naturally I want to work for you. But more to the point is not what I want but what you need." He followed this with three words that many women refuse to use and that men almost never think to use: "I can type." Right away, he showed that he knew he must be useful.

So much for the easy part of the letter. Next came the difficult part. Although he had had no experience and had never submitted an article to a magazine or even written for a student newspaper, he still had to come up with something that would interest the editor. He found the solution. The letter continued in this manner:

> . . . In looking into the field of journalism, I visited the editor of our alumni magazine, and I talked to magazine space salesmen and to executives responsible for placing ads in magazines. I also visited a printer who has contracts with magazines. In addition, I have been reading trade journals and several books on the industry. As I looked into publishing, it occurred to me that, of all the things I have done, the one I could most closely relate to the field was, strangely enough, an experience I had as a babysitter.

Immediately, he had the editor's full attention. How could babysitting fit in with publishing? During the summer of his junior year in college, he had taken a job as a sailing instructor, tutor, and companion to the children of a wealthy family that summered on the coast of Maine. The parents often went away for a week or more at a time, leaving a governess in charge, with a cook, chauffeur, maid, and gardener to do the chores and the student to keep the children busy. While the parents were on a cruise, the governess suffered a stroke, sending the cook into a tizzy, the maid into tears, and the chauffeur and gardener to the local bar. Only the student could cope, and he took charge and managed the estate for the rest of the summer.

In his letter of application, he described the crisis and its subsequent problems and told how he had met them. Then he related those experiences to the problems that he had learned editors, advertisers, printers, and others encounter in the publishing industry. Reading his letter, you could picture the student working for a publisher. There would be no slipups with the printers. Advertisers and authors would be handled with tact, yet he would get them to turn in their copy on time. He came through as someone with ingenuity, energy, and reliability; and the letter itself testified to his writing ability.

Did he get the job? Yes and no. He got an offer, but because of the publisher's urgent need, the job had to be filled immediately, and he could not accept it. He was teaching school at the time and felt that in fairness to his pupils he should finish the school year. However, a while later, the letter surfaced again when a group of editors at a meeting chatted during lunch. The subject of good editorial help came up. It followed the usual theme: "They don't make 'em like they used to." The editor of another sailing magazine complained that he had been looking for an assistant, but despite hundreds of applicants he had found no one suitable. At this point, the editor of the yachting magazine described the young man's letter and agreed to share it. The upshot was, again, a job offer. This time the timing was right, and the young man took the job. There is nothing quite like the staying power of a well-written letter. It is remembered.

Later, I complimented the young man, telling him I had never read a better letter. "It was easy," he said. "The first letter was the tough one. I didn't have anything to say other than 'I have a good record. Please give me a chance,' but I knew everyone else was saying the same thing, so I would have to say it better. I struggled with every word, trying to make an ordinary message extraordinary, but even elegant words can't make something out of fluff. I didn't know anything about publishing, so I didn't have anything to say to publishers; nor could I be really convincing without knowing enough about the work to decide whether I wanted that kind of job or not. But publishing sounded exciting, so I thought I would give it a fling."

The Importance of Knowing What the Job Is All About

"When I looked into the field in depth," the young man continued, "I became confident that I had something to offer. Thanks to a few good high school teachers and college professors, I knew where to place a comma and a colon, so I had a technical skill to offer publishers. And I knew sailing. But the big need I saw was one I discovered when I was teaching school and again when I was an assistant manager at a McDonald's—a need for people who can get things done. Such a quality is hard to describe without an analogy. I could have alluded to any number of jobs I had held, but I chose the babysitting job because I thought it would be different and would introduce an element of surprise. Apparently, the analogy worked. I got the job. More important, I wanted it. If I had received a job offer after sending the first letter, before I had really investigated publishing, I would have taken the job with an attitude of 'teach me.' That's a passive role, an observer's role, and observers tend to be critical. The chances are fifty-fifty that I would not have known how or where to contribute and would have quit after a while. Instead of offering my employer solutions to his problems, I would have become one of his problems."

I asked the young man if he had used any other supporting documents, such as a resume, to help him get the job. "I had a resume," he replied, "but I held it back, because my task was to transfer the qualities I had demonstrated as a baby-sitter to the needs of a publisher, and I couldn't seem to do that in a resume. A resume is a good way to outline facts, but I had to use prose to develop the analogy.

"I did think about including a writing sample, but when I studied the magazine I realized that most of the articles were written by contributors rather than staff. Their job was to select and edit articles. If I presented myself as a writer, I wouldn't have received an offer; the magazine didn't hire authors. When a friend of mine saw an advertisement for an editing job, he made a list of the required qualifications, then presented his case point by point, right on target. Then the dope attached a resume that said loud and clear, 'I want to be a writer.' He either should have skipped the resume or prepared a new one."

Are these examples intended to be good arguments for not using resumes? No. They simply emphasize that it is important to determine the best way to get a message across. There are times when there is no substitute for a resume. When employers advertise and list the qualifications they seek, there is no better way to respond than to send a resume outlining qualifications.

LETTERS OF APPLICATION

Sometimes, however, it is hard to figure out how to make the letter of application you send with your resume more effective than those of the hundreds of other people who are responding to the ad. Imagine being on the receiving end of applications at General Motors or Exxon.

To find out about the effectiveness of letters and resumes, I visited corporations and asked employment managers for their comments. "Here," said one employment manager, as he picked up an 18-inch stack of letters and handed it to me. "This is my morning's mail. Read these letters and you'll have your answer."

"I can't," I protested. "I have only 2 hours, and there's a day's reading here."

"Yes, you can," he replied. "Unfortunately, you'll get through the pack in half an hour, because a glance will tell you that most are not worth reading."

It was hard to believe that the letters could be that bad, but he was right. The typical letter was an insult. Among the letters that I did not finish reading was one that was obviously a copy—the machine must have run out of toner thirty copies back. It began:

Dear Sir:

I am writing to the top companies in each industry and yours is certainly that. I want to turn my outstanding qualities of leadership and my can-do abilities to. . . .

Enough of that. Also, the applicant hadn't even bothered to type in the employment manager's name, which he could easily have found in reference books such as the CPC Annual, published by the College Placement Council, and Peterson's Job Opportunities, published by Peterson's Guides.

The next letter was written in pencil on notepaper. There may have been an Einstein behind that one, but I can't imagine anyone taking the time to find it out. Many other letters were smudged and messy. Some applicants tried to attract attention with stunts, such as putting cute cartoons on their letters. One piece of mail contained a walnut and a note that read, "Every business has a tough nut to crack. If you have a tough nut to crack and need someone to do it, crack this nut." Inside the nut, all wadded up, was a resume. Cute tricks and cleverness don't work at the General Mammoth Corporation.

At the same time, the good letters stood out like gold. Five letters, only five letters in that pile of hundreds, were worth reading. They had this in common:

- They looked like business letters. Their paragraphing, their neatness, and their crisp white 8½" × 11" stationery attracted attention like good-looking clothing and good grooming.
- They were succinct.
- There were no misspellings or grammatical errors.

As I read them, I heard a voice—the voice of a fusty old high school English teacher—commanding out of the past:

- If you can't spell a word, look it up in a dictionary.
- Use a . . . [word processor]. Pen and ink are for love letters. . . .
- For format, use a secretarial manual. If you don't have one, borrow one from the library. What do you think libraries are for?

How that English teacher would have loved the following advice given by the late Malcolm Forbes when he was editor-in-chief of *Forbes* magazine:

Edit ruthlessly. Somebody ~~has~~ said that words are ~~a lot~~ like inflated money—the more ~~of them that~~ you use, the less each one ~~of them~~ is worth. ~~Right on~~. Go through your entire letter ~~just~~ as many times as it takes. ~~Search out and~~ Annihilate all unnecessary words and sentences—even ~~entire~~ *paragraphs*.

The following letter is typical of those I saw that day. Give it the Forbes treatment, and see what you can do with it. You may need a scissors as well as a pencil.

Dear Mr. Employer:

I am writing to you because I am going to be looking for employment after I graduate which will be from Michigan where I studied Chemical Engineering and I will be getting a Bachelor of Science degree in June. The field in which I am interested and hope to pursue is process design and that is why I am writing your company to see if you have openings like that. I think I have excellent qualifications and you will find them described in the resume which I have attached to this letter.

The five letters that stood out favorably were characterized by their simplicity. Here is a letter, fictitious of course, but enough like the letter I remember to give you an idea of the ones that created a favorable impression:

February 1, 1991

Mr. Paul Boynton
Manager of Employment
The United States Oil Company
1 Chicago Plaza
Chicago, Illinois 60607

Dear Mr. Boynton:

This June I will receive a Bachelor of Science in Chemical Engineering from the University of Michigan, and I hope to work in process design or instrumentation. I saw your description in *Peterson's Job Opportunities for Engineering, Science, and Computer Graduates* soliciting applicants with my interests. Enclosed is a resume to help you evaluate my qualifications.

While I find all aspects of refining interesting, my special interest in process design and instrumentation developed while working as a laboratory assistant to Professor Juliard Smith, who teaches process design. I wrote my senior thesis on the subject of instrumentation under him, and part of what I wrote will be used in a textbook he is writing and editing.

Would it be possible to have an interview with you in Chicago during the week of March 1? To be even more specific, could it be arranged for 10 A.M. on Tuesday, March 3? I am going to be in Chicago that week, and this time and date would be best for me, but of course I would work out another time more convenient for you. In any event, I will call your office the week before to determine whether an interview is possible.

Sincerely yours,

Charles C. Thompson

Thompson's effective letter, and three of the four others, followed a similar pattern:

1. The first paragraph stated who the writer was and what he wanted.
2. The second paragraph, sometimes the third, and in one case a fourth paragraph, indicated why the writer wrote to the employer and mentioned areas of mutual interest, special talents that might be of interest to employers, or other factors relating to qualifications that could be better described in a letter than in a resume.
3. A final paragraph suggested a course of action.

The fifth letter covered the same points in a different order. I remember it because it complemented the good but not outstanding resume shown in Figure 1 [p. 262]. In that resume, a perceptive employer could see a person he might like, someone who was energetic and personable. Yet it didn't quite hang together,

LANCE ZAROTE

<u>Campus Address</u>   <u>Permanent Address</u>
101 Morril Hall   25 The Byway
University of Puget Sound   Provincetown, Massachusetts 05840
Tacoma, Washington 95840   (617) 555–6026
(206) 555–6206

GOAL:	A SALES CAREER
EDUCATION:	UNIVERSITY OF PUGET SOUND Bachelor of Arts 1991 Philosophy Major

<u>Business-Related Courses</u>

Statistics	Introduction to Computers
Economics	Calculus
Accounting	English

EMPLOYMENT: UNIVERSITY OF PUGET SOUND (Work-Study Program)

Dining hall supervisor	1990–91
Kitchen helper	1987–89

OTHER WORK while in college

Ma and Pa Motel, Tacoma—night clerk	1990
Joe's Bar and Grill—weekend waiter & bartender	1989–1991
Baby-sitting, gardening, house cleaning	1985–1991

WATCHEE OUTEY SUMMER CAMP, Nome, Alaska

Sailing coach and waterfront director	1990
Counselor	1986–1989

ACTIVITIES: CAMPUS
Chair, Campus Chest Drive
Intramural hockey, tennis, and volleyball

LIVING UNIT
House Manager, $25,000 budget
Secretary
Membership Committee

CIVIC
Reader-companion in nursing home
Big Brother-Sister Program, Southside Youth Center

CHURCH
Choir
Youth leader
Sunday school teacher

INTERESTS:

Skiing	Music
Chess	Dancing

FIGURE I   An ordinary resume can become effective when attached to a powerful letter.

because the work history and activities didn't seem to support what the writer wanted to do. But look at the letter that "made" the resume:

Mr. Paul Boynton, Manager of Employment
The United States Oil Company
1 Chicago Plaza
Chicago, Illinois 60607

March 10, 1991

Dear Mr. Boynton:

This June, following my graduation from the University of Puget Sound, I want to pursue a career in sales. Between April 10 and 23, I plan to call on leading companies whose products I would like to sell. The purpose of this letter is to determine whether you would like to have me include you in my itinerary.

Let me tell you why I believe I can sell. It seems to me that I am always selling. As a camp counselor, I persuaded the director to buy a fleet of small sailboats so I could start a sailing program. When our college housing co-op needed painting, I persuaded the members to give up a vacation to do the job. In thinking about how I enjoyed selling these and other projects, I decided to look into a sales career. I persuaded several sales representatives to let me spend a day or more traveling with them to see what it was like.

While with them I realized something more about myself that further convinced me I belong in sales. The best sales representatives were well organized, had high energy levels, and used their time efficiently, qualities I feel I have. As evidence, I have enclosed a resume that outlines my accomplishments in college and during vacations.

I hope to hear from you. United States Oil is in the top group of employers on my list.

Sincerely,

Lance Zarote

Encl: Resume

Hard Work and Attention to Detail Make for a Good Letter

While only the five letters I have mentioned were effective, the rest of the correspondents could have done as well. The point is they didn't. Most people won't. Therein lies your opportunity, because, like Thompson and Zarote, you can write letters that set you apart. You don't have to create a literary masterpiece; just don't knock off a letter hastily with thoughts that wander all over the page. Write it and rewrite it, following Forbes's advice. Unless you are an exceptional typist, you are not good enough to type it yourself. Hire a professional or use a word processor, but be sure the print is letter quality. Also, get an English teacher or someone in the word business to check your spelling, punctuation, and grammar.

Don't Delegate the Job of Letter Writing

More important than style, however, is the thought process used in preparing letters and resumes. Don't shortchange yourself by delegating your thinking to someone else. Be sure it is *your* letter. Somehow, a ghost-written letter always has a phony ring to it. When you write to employers, think about their needs; then think about yourself and what you offer, and relate this to what you would like to do. Putting your thoughts on paper—thoughtfully—will make you sort out your ideas and interrelate them. When you see them on paper they will talk back to you, at times to suggest better ideas, at other times to tell you that you are off the mark. To organize your ideas, create an outline. In other words, prepare a resume even if you decide not to use it. *The value of a resume is frequently more in its preparation than in its use.*

RESUME PREPARATION

When you do give an employer your resume, make it a testimony to your ability to organize your thoughts. Remember, too, it must look sufficiently attractive to get an employer to read it. Unfortunately, most of the resumes I have seen on employers' desks were just as unattractive as the letters; they had sloppy, crowded margins, were poorly organized, and were badly reproduced. At least 30 percent of the resumes had been put aside with hardly a glance because their physical appearance was so awful. The rest got a 20-second scan to see if they were worth studying.

Following are two resumes that pass the appearance test with flying colors. Let's see how they fare during a 20-second scan and beyond.

Nancy Jones—A Good Resume Made Better

Nancy Jones's resume has arrived at the desk of a laboratory director who needs an assistant to help run a quality-control laboratory in a pharmaceutical company (Figure 2). With candidates far outnumbering openings in biology, the advertisement for the job has brought in hundreds of applications, and the director is wearily scanning them one by one to find the few that will be of interest to him. Conditions are not favorable for Nancy. She has to catch his eye with impressive qualifications, or she is not going to get anywhere.

The director picks up Nancy's resume. Immediately, he is impressed, because it looks attractive. He thinks the resume reflects an orderly mind. Most resumes he has looked at just do not put it all together.

He begins to read. The job objective annoys him; it strikes him as being long-winded. Why couldn't she simply say she is interested in applied biology? What is this business about working with people? Is that there because she has doubts about biology?

If resumes are supposed to say only what needs to be said, what about this line?

Born January 6, 1969   5'7"   135 lbs.   Single   Excellent health

Does it say anything about her ability to do the job? The biologist doesn't think so.

NANCY O. JONES

<u>Present Address</u>	<u>After June 1, 1991</u>
105 Belleville Place	1212 Centerline Road
Ames, Iowa 50011	Old Westbury, New York 11568
Phone: 515-555-6674	Phone: 516-555-7664

Born January 6, 1969   5'7"   135 lbs.   Single   Excellent health

<u>Career Objective</u>

Research and development in most areas of applied biology, with an opportunity to work with people as well

<u>Education</u>

Iowa State University, Ames, Iowa
Bachelor of Science, June 1991
Major: Biology   Concentration: Physiology

GPA: 3.3 on a 4.0 scale

<u>Major Subjects</u>	<u>Minor Subjects</u>
Mammalian Physiology	Qualitative Analysis
Vertebrate Anatomy	Quantitative Analysis
Histology	Organic Chemistry
Genetics	Biochemistry

<u>Scholarships and Honors</u>

University Scholarship: $2850/year
Iowa State Science and Research Award

Dean's List two semesters

<u>Activities</u>

Volunteer Probation Officer, 1988–89
Probation Department, Ames, Iowa

Tutor, Chemistry and Math, 1988–91
Central High School, Ames, Iowa

Member, Kappa Zeta social sorority

Women's Intercollegiate Hockey Team

<u>Special Skills</u>

Familiarity with Spanish; PL/C and FORTRAN computer languages; typing

<u>Work Experience</u>

Teaching Assistant and Laboratory Instructor
Freshman Biology   School year, 1990–91

Waitress, Four Seasons Restaurant
Catalina Island   Summers, 1989–90

FIGURE 2   The resume of Nancy O. Jones does not communicate her career-related experience.

His eyes move down the page:

Education	Iowa State University, Ames, Iowa
	Bachelor of Science, June 1991
	Major: Biology Concentration: Physiology
	GPA: 3.3 on a 4.0 scale

Major Subjects	Minor Subjects
Mammalian Physiology	Qualitative Analysis
Vertebrate Anatomy	Quantitative Analysis
Histology	Organic Chemistry
Genetics	Biochemistry

She has used the outline form well, so he is able to take in a great deal of information in one look. Her education impresses him.

Double spacing above and below her grade point average makes it stand out. However, if her average had not been quite as good, and if she had not wanted to feature it, she could have used single spacing to make it less conspicuous, like this:

Education	Iowa State University, Ames, Iowa
	Bachelor of Science, June 1991
	Major: Biology Concentration: Physiology
	GPA: 2.7 on a 4.0 scale

Now that she has told him about her grades and her courses she wants to drive home the point that she was no ordinary student. She flags him down with the headline "Scholarships and Honors," and he sees her financial aid and science awards, which make a favorable impression. Two times on the dean's list may not be important enough to set apart by double spacing, but it makes a modest impression.

Up until now, Nancy has made a favorable impression overall. The director is ready to take in the next batch of information:

Activities	Volunteer Probation Officer, 1988–89
	Probation Department, Ames, Iowa
	Tutor, Chemistry and Math, 1988–91
	Central High School, Ames, Iowa
	Member, Kappa Zeta social sorority
	Women's Intercollegiate Hockey Team

She almost loses him by featuring her work as a probation officer. That is not of primary interest to him, but through good spacing and placement, she draws his eye to the next item, which states that she has tutored chemistry and math. Unfortunately, Nancy now loses him permanently by ranking tutoring along with the sorority and the hockey team. He guesses she has made her major statement about biology, and so he turns to the next resume.

Good as it is, Nancy Jones's resume could be improved by reorganization. Her tutoring chemistry and her two years as a teaching assistant and laboratory instructor in biology reveal a more-than-academic interest in biology. They should be featured. Everything related to biology and any other information of possible use to the employer should be put under a new marginal headline and statement, as follows:

Career Related Experience	Biology Lab Instructor and Teaching Assistant Freshman Biology (1990–91)	
	Chemistry and Mathematics Tutor Central High School, Ames, Iowa (1988–91)	
Skills and Interests	Microscopy Electron Microscopy Histology Spectrum Analysis Small-Animal Surgery	Computer Languages: FORTRAN, PL/1, COBOL Statistics

Now, the director is able to see the things she can do. "Good," he says to himself, "she can use an electron microscope. We need someone with that skill."

By no means should Nancy eliminate mention of the hockey team, but since she is applying for a professional job, the first bait to throw out is credentials; they testify to her ability to do the work. After that, what may sink the hook is how the employer sees her as a person. He may have picked out bits here and there that testify to her diligence, but the picking out depends on chance reading; it would be best not to leave anything to chance. With a slightly different presentation, she might ensure that he receives an impression of her diligence.

There are other areas she could strengthen, things she has underplayed or totally neglected to mention. Sticking the waitress job in down at the bottom of the page is almost an apology for it. She may also have had other jobs, such as baby-sitting, household work, or door-to-door sales, that she belittles in her mind and has not even mentioned. Mention of such things might make a good impression on an employer looking for somebody who is not afraid to work and who is mature for her years.

If we quizzed Nancy, we might find that she could put something like this on her resume:

Scholarships and Financial Support	90% self-supporting through college as follows:
	University Scholarship: $2850/year Iowa State Science and Research Award
	Waitress, Four Seasons Restaurant Catalina Island (Summers, 1989–90)
	Teaching and instructing, baby-sitting, home maintenance, selling

And this, because her activities tell something about her as a person:

Activities	Volunteer Probation Officer (1988–89) Kappa Zeta social sorority Women's Intercollegiate Hockey Team Skiing, sailing, singing, tennis

Double spacing has been cut down so as not to overemphasize the less important items, yet a string of other things not terribly important in themselves has been inserted to support the impression of an active, interesting person. Sometimes you want to leave an impression, at other times you want to emphasize a qualification. For example, Nancy wanted to feature her studies, and the way she brought them out by listing them in a column was good. If she had listed them like this, they would not have stood out:

> Major Subjects: Mammalian Physiology, Vertebrate Anatomy, Histology, Genetics
> Minor Subjects: Quantitative Analysis, Qualitative Analysis, Organic Chemistry, Biochemistry

In Figure 3, you will see the Nancy Jones resume as she might have revised it to emphasize the strong points that would have been of interest to that director who was looking for a resourceful assistant. The added emphasis might have made the difference that would have landed the job for her.

Nancy's revised resume is pure outline, devoid of prose. It works well for her. When she states that she has studied quantitative and qualitative analysis and knows PL/1 and FORTRAN, a scientist reading her resume knows what this means.

Janet Smith—The Proper Use of Headlines

Janet Smith, whose resume is shown in Figure 4 [p. 270], has a different problem in presenting her qualifications. She needs to *describe* what she did in order to tell an employer about her qualifications, so her resume calls for a mixture of key words and prose to get her message across. Yet prose can destroy the effect of an outline. The solution lies in imitating newspaper editors, who use headlines and subheadlines to attract readers. Like a newspaper, a resume should lend itself to skimming so the reader can quickly pick up a good overview of what is important. Then the reader can select specific things of interest and read further. There is an art to using headlines, but Janet Smith hasn't mastered it, at least not in the resume she used to apply for a job with Hermann Langfelder, a hardbitten old hand with thirty years in personnel and labor relations in the machinery business. He picked up her resume and read:

CAREER
OBJECTIVE

A challenging position in personnel administration requiring organizational ability and an understanding of how people function in business and industry.

That was pure baloney, and he choked on it. He thought of the hours he had spent in meetings, listening to a lot of hot air. "Challenging, my foot!" he muttered. Then he read the bit about her organizational ability and her understanding of how people function in business and industry. "I've been at this business for thirty years," he groused to himself, "and I still can't figure out how people function in industry. But she knows all about it."

NANCY O. JONES

Present Address		After June 1, 1991
105 Belleville Place		1212 Centerline Road
Ames, Iowa 50011		Old Westbury, New York 11568
Phone: 515-555-6674		Phone: 516-555-7664

Career Objective   Research and development

Education   Iowa State University, Ames, Iowa
Bachelor of Science, June 1991
Major: Biology   Concentration: Physiology

GPA: 3.3 on a 4.0 scale

Major Subjects	Minor Subjects
Mammalian Physiology	Qualitative Analysis
Vertebrate Anatomy	Quantitative Analysis
Histology	Organic Chemistry
Genetics	Biochemistry

Career-Related Experience   Biology Lab Instructor and Teaching Assistant
Freshman Biology (1990–91)

Chemistry and Mathematics Tutor
Central High School, Ames, Iowa (1988–91)

Skills and Interests

Microscopy	Computer Languages:
Electron Microscopy	FORTRAN, PL/1,
Histology	COBOL
Spectrum Analysis	Statistics
Small-Animal Surgery	

Scholarships and Financial Support   90% self-supporting through college as follows:

University Scholarship: $2850/year
Iowa State Science and Research Award

Waitress, Four Seasons Restaurant
Catalina Island (Summers, 1989–90)

Teaching and instructing, baby-sitting, home
maintenance, selling

Activities   Volunteer Probation Officer (1988–89)
Kappa Zeta social sorority
Women's Intercollegiate Hockey Team
Skiing, sailing, singing, tennis

FIGURE 3   The revised resume of Nancy O. Jones effectively features her career-related experience in a separate section.

JANET V. SMITH
111 Main Street
North Hero, Vermont 05073
802-555-1234

CAREER OBJECTIVE	A challenging position in personnel administration requiring organizational ability and an understanding of how people function in business and industry.
EDUCATION	PURDUE UNIVERSITY Hammond, Indiana Master of Industrial Relations June 1991 SMITH COLLEGE Northampton, Massachusetts Bachelor of Arts, magna cum laude June 1986
WORK EXPERIENCE	UNIVERSAL METHODIST CHURCH 1 Central Square New York, New York 10027 <u>Assistant Personnel Officer.</u> 1988–90 Responsible for interviewing applicants for clerical positions within the organization and for placing those who demonstrated appropriate skills, for accepting and dealing with employees' grievances, and for developing programs on career advancement. CORTEN STEEL COMPANY 10 Lake Street Akron, Ohio 44309 <u>Assistant,</u> Personnel Office. 1986–88 Responsible for all correspondence of Personnel Director and for interviewing some custodial applicants and referring them to appropriate supervisors for further interviewing. BORG-WARNER, INC. Ithaca, New York 14850 <u>Assembly-line worker.</u> Summer 1985 Assembled parts of specialized drive chains in company with thirty other men and women.
COMMUNITY SERVICE	PLANNED PARENTHOOD North Hero, Vermont 05073 <u>Counselor,</u> Summers, 1983–84 Explained various aspects of family planning and provided birth control information to clients of Planned Parenthood. Made referrals to other counselors and physicians where appropriate.
AUXILIARY SKILLS	French: Fluent. Knowledge of office procedures. Experience with mainframe computes and PCs.

FIGURE 4   The resume for Janet V. Smith misleads the reader with irrelevant headings.

Beware of Misleading Headlines

"Well, let's see what she's done," he said to himself, and then his eyes fell on "UNIVERSAL METHODIST CHURCH." That did it! He didn't want to bring any do-gooder into his factory to preach. He rejected her. And the fault was hers, in using the headline.

Janet's job at the church was administrative, not ministerial, and the church didn't care whether she was Jewish, Catholic, or agnostic. Only in its ministerial work does the Methodist Church need Methodists. But people—Langfelder and the rest of us—respond to symbols and make snap judgments on the basis of symbols. Janet had put the symbol of the church—its name—in a heading, when she could have done something better.

When you lay out your resume, think of symbols. Imagine you are a newspaper editor who wants to put a story across. As an editor planning headlines, you must imagine yourself in the position of the reader. Ask yourself, "What words will catch the reader's eye? What words will put the reader off?"

Use words that fit the job in question, and play down those that can lead an employer to think of you in terms that don't relate to the job. Ask yourself, "Does this say something to the employer?" Janet Smith missed Langfelder, and some of her duties would have yielded key words to send appropriate messages.

The following arrangement would have been more effective for her:

WORK EXPERIENCE	ASSISTANT PERSONNEL OFFICER, 1988–90 Universal Methodist Church 1 Central Square New York, New York 10027 <u>Interviewing, placement, grievances, and training</u> of applicants and employees in the clerical and support services of the church organization. Developed programs for the career advancement of employees.
	ASSISTANT, PERSONNEL OFFICE, 1986–88 Corten Steel Company 10 Lake Street Akron, Ohio 44309 <u>Interviewing and referring</u> as an assistant to Personnel Director. Responsible for all correspondence and for interviewing some custodial applicants and referring them to supervisors for further interviews.

Let's suppose that Janet has a chance to send Langfelder the revised resume shown in Figure 5 [p. 272]. This time, she uses headlines that pinpoint the ideas she most wants to get across, so that he makes it past the Universal Methodist Church and gets down to the assembly line. "Hey, now, look at that!" he thinks. "She's worked out there on the floor. That means she's heard all the language and knows the gripes and the tedium. We have a lot of women in this factory, and it might be a good thing to have a down-to-earth, smart woman on my staff." (His sexism may have been showing, but this kind of employer is alive and kicking somewhere out there, and you may have to deal with him.)

JANET V. SMITH
111 Main Street
North Hero, Vermont 05073
802-555-1234

CAREER
INTERESTS   Personnel Administration and Labor Relations

EDUCATION   PURDUE UNIVERSITY   June 1991
                         Hammond, Indiana
                         Master of Industrial Relations

                         SMITH COLLEGE   June 1986
                         Northampton, Massachusetts
                         Bachelor of Arts, magna cum laude

WORK   ASSISTANT PERSONNEL OFFICER. 1988–90
EXPERIENCE   Universal Methodist Church
                         1 Central Square
                         New York, New York 10027
                         <u>Interviewing, placement, grievances, and training</u> of applicants
                         and employees in the clerical and support services of the
                         church organization. Developed programs for the career
                         advancement of employees.

                         ASSISTANT, PERSONNEL OFFICE. 1986–88
                         Corten Steel Company
                         10 Lake Street
                         Akron, Ohio 44309
                         <u>Interviewing and referring</u> as an assistant to Personnel
                         Director. Responsible for all correspondence and for
                         interviewing some custodial applicants and referring them to
                         supervisors for further interviews.

                         ASSEMBLY-LINE WORKER. Summer 1985
                         Borg-Warner, Inc.
                         Ithaca, New York 14850
                         <u>Factory work experience</u> on an assembly line. Worked with a
                         team of thirty other men and women.

COMMUNITY   COUNSELOR. Summers, 1983–84
SERVICE   Planned Parenthood
                         North Hero, Vermont 05073
                         Explained various aspects of family planning and provided
                         birth control information to clients of Planned Parenthood.
                         Made referrals to other counselors and physicians where
                         appropriate.

AUXILIARY   French: Fluent. Knowledge of office procedures.
SKILLS   Experience with mainframe computers and PCs.

FIGURE 5   The revised resume for Janet V. Smith stresses what she did rather than the less important point of where she did it.

What if Janet Smith wanted a job in the computer industry and had ten years' experience with IBM? Employers are impressed by "graduates" of companies like IBM that are known as leaders in their fields. Ten years with them is significant. It might make sense to present her experience this way.

EXPERIENCE   1981–91
                                   IBM Corporation
                                   Binghamton, New York
                                   <u>Assistant Personnel Officer</u>

Were she an engineer after a technical job that could use her IBM experience, highlighting the name of the company would have been a good idea. Imagine employers giving the resume a 20-second scan. What words should you use and how should they be placed to catch the eye and make employers want to read further?

Mark Meyers—The Functional Resume

Janet Smith and Nancy Jones were lucky. Their training and experience translated into satisfactory headlines to highlight their experience, but that doesn't always work. Mark Meyers, whose resume appears in Figure 6 [p. 274], adopted a different technique to help him get a job in community recreation. He got his message across by creating a resume based on functions.

When he began to write his resume, he tried time and time again to get his message across in a conventional form in which he first listed his education, then his experiences in chronological order, and finally his activities, hobbies, and interests. But writing it conventionally raised all sorts of problems. He wanted to highlight his public relations and promotion experience, some of which he had been paid for and some not. Some of it had also been secondary to a primary assignment. Dividing up this experience and placing bits and pieces of it in various parts of the resume to make it conform to a conventional style diluted its impact. Also, his athletic ability and experience would mean a great deal to an employer in his field, but how could he show it effectively? Some of it had been gained as a participant, some through training, and some as a coach. Could he expect an employer to sift through the various sections of the resume to find out all he had done in athletics? (Remember, you can only count on an employer giving a resume a quick scan before deciding whether or not to study it more fully.)

His solution, as seen in Figure 6, was to feature the functions of the job he wanted and then describe things he had done that pertained to each area. Thus, under each function he developed the equivalent of a mini-resume.

Preparing a Resume for a Specific Job

Mark stated his case well, but you can't get blood from a stone. He found he had to look outside his field, because jobs in it were virtually nonexistent due to cutbacks in government funding. In his search, he ran across the following job listing from the publisher of a magazine for parents:

MARK MEYERS

1414 South Harp Road
Dover, Delaware 19901
302-555-4444

CAREER INTEREST
   Community recreation.

RECREATION PROGRAMMING EXPERIENCE
   Planned and implemented programs in stagecraft and drama; assisted with pro-
      gramming in ceramics, photography, and physical fitness for Dover Youth
      Bureau summer program. Summer 1986.
   Lectured and led tours at Atlantic County (Delaware) Park nature trail and visi-
      tors' center. Prepared slides to illustrate lecture; helped in construction of
      nature exhibits. Summer 1985.
   Coordinated men's intramural sports competitions for Hoboken University.
      Had responsibility for equipment and scheduling. 1984–86.

PUBLIC RELATIONS AND PROMOTION EXPERIENCE
   Directed publicity efforts of University Drama Club for several productions. De-
      veloped innovative techniques—such as a costumed cast parade to arouse in-
      terest in an avant-garde staging of "Alice in Wonderland", which gained
      campuswide attention. 1984–85.
   Advertised in various media and became familiar with advertising methods, in-
      cluding writing news releases, taping radio announcements, designing
      graphics for posters and fliers. Drama Club, 1985–87; men's sports,
      1984–87.

LEADERSHIP AND ATHLETIC ABILITIES
   Trained in outdoor leadership and survival skills by Outward Bound.
      Summer 1983.
   Coached hockey and basketball. Dover Youth Bureau, 1986.
   Participate in hockey, swimming, backpacking.

RESEARCH AND EVALUATION ABILITIES
   Prepared college research project on the recreational needs of residents of a
      Hoboken neighborhood. Designed questionnaire to solicit residents' own
      perceptions of their needs; interviewed residents and local officials. Fall se-
      mester 1986.
   Reported on effectiveness of Dover Youth Bureau programming. Summer 1986.

OFFICE SKILLS
   Dealt with unhappy and irate customers at McGary's Department Store, Dover.
      Worked at service desk, tracking down problems and rectifying errors.
      Summer 1982.
   Typing and use of office machinery.

EDUCATION
   Bachelor of Science, June 1987   Major: Recreation
   Hoboken University, Hoboken, New Jersey   Minor: Drama

FIGURE 6   The resume of Mark Meyers illustrates the functional style.

EDITORIAL SECRETARY

BA. in Liberal Arts

Interested in childhood training. Well organized, outstanding language skills. Typing and clerical skills, potential to use electronic text-editing equipment. Reporting to Coordinating Editor, Happy Days magazine. Assist in all editorial functions. Evidence of creativity essential. Entry-level position with career potential.

Can you put yourself in his shoes, analyze the job, and devise a resume that speaks to the stated needs of this employer? The clue to doing it is to go through the job description and step by step take your cue from the employer. Right off, you will hit a bit of a snag because the employer has specified a B.A., while Mark has a B.S. His drama minor might give him appropriate credentials, however. If he shows his education as in the following example it might reflect the liberal background the employer apparently prefers:

EDUCATION   HOBOKEN UNIVERSITY, B.S., 1987
                          Major: Recreation   Minor: Drama

                          Humanities courses:
                          Introduction to Dramatic Literature
                          British Drama to 1700
                          History of Theater
                          Playwriting
                          Introduction to Poetry
                          Shakespeare
                          English History

Next, the job calls for an interest in childhood training, then language skills, and so on. Each specification suggests a headline for a resume. Mark faces another stumbling block when it comes to demonstrating an interest in childhood training, since his experience has been with older youths only. Since a resume makes points by stating facts, he cannot demonstrate an interest in childhood training in his resume because he lacks the appropriate experience. However, he *can* describe his interest in the letter that usually goes hand in glove with a resume. He has a good basis for doing so, because the field of recreation certainly has much to do with the entire range of human development from childhood on. He should be able to point out correlatives in his education and experience with the work being done in childhood training, and he could check a library for information about childhood training to help develop the correlatives. Above all, he should read the magazine and try to tie in as many of his experiences as possible with the purpose of the magazine.

    With his interest in childhood training brought out in a letter to complement his resume, he might then proceed to develop his outline as follows:

EXPERIENCE

HUMAN DEVELOPMENT

<u>Dover Youth Bureau.</u> Planned and implemented programs in drama, photography, athletics, health. Summer 1986.

<u>Research Project.</u> Studied recreational needs of a Hoboken neighborhood. Interviewed residents, developed questionnaire. Project provided an insight into the family life and problems of parents in a neighborhood setting. Fall semester 1986.

<u>Outdoor Leadership Training.</u> Practical experience in human development through a knowledge of nature and survival skills. Summer 1983.

LANGUAGE SKILLS AND CREATIVITY

<u>Writing.</u> Wrote releases, developed advertising, and prepared radio announcements for Drama Club, men's sports programs, and other events. Wrote report on Hoboken research project. 1984–87.

<u>Lecturing.</u> Gave talks and led tours at Atlantic County (Delaware) Park nature trail and visitors' center. Summer 1985.

<u>Audiovisual.</u> Prepared slides for audiovisual presentation for visitors' center. 1985.

<u>Promotional.</u> Created innovative techniques—such as costume parade of cast—to arouse interest in avant-garde staging of "Alice in Wonderland," which gained campuswide attention. 1984–85.

<u>Design.</u> Designed posters, fliers, and other graphics for sporting events, plays, and other campus events. 1984–87.

Constructed nature exhibits at nature center. 1985.

CLERICAL AND ADMINISTRATIVE

<u>Clerical.</u> Typing and use of office machinery. McGary's Department Store. Summer 1982.

<u>Administration.</u> Responsible for equipment, scheduling of programs, and coordinating of competitions. Hoboken University, 1984–86.

    The functional resume allows you to develop a different message for each job or type of job you wish to apply for. Different functions can be highlighted, depending on what the job requires, and your specific experiences rearranged under different headings. It gives you the flexibility you need if your experience has been diverse.

Almost every resume ought to have something of the functional resume about it. With computers making it so easy to change a text, there is no reason why each resume can't be slanted to appeal to the particular employer, even if it's the resume of a generalist like Bruce Gregory Robinson, who hopes to get into a training program.

Bruce Gregory Robertson—A Resume Reflecting an Active Mind and Body

Put yourself in the chair of a merit employer, someone who is interested in candidates not so much for what they know as for what they can learn. Imagine yourself as a banker, a merchant, or a manufacturer. The position you have to fill can be learned easily on the job. What interests you are candidates' traits—their energy, intelligence, leadership qualities—the things that tell you the candidate can grow in your employ and eventually become an executive in the company. You are looking for a resume that reflects an active person with an active mind. Bruce Robertson is such a person, and his resume shown in Figure 7 [p. 278] has been designed accordingly.

Now make yourself a textbook publisher. Again, you are a merit employer and promote from within. Your company hires people with a good liberal education and little or no postgraduate experience. The men and women you hire will travel from college to college either soliciting manuscripts from professors or showing them texts that might fit their courses. Impressive candidates should have a high energy level and be able to show that they have used time efficiently and worked independently. How does Bruce look to you?

Now change the scenario slightly. This time you are a publisher of texts for primary and secondary school. To get your texts adopted, your representatives will have to make presentations to state regents, school superintendents, and other educational groups. Remember that experience and college major don't matter, but do you think it might help Bruce's cause if he did a bit more to highlight his interest in public speaking and his honors as a debater? He has a computer. It would be a cinch for him to change his resume slightly. Can you think how he might do it?

Next, put yourself in the chair of an employer on Main Street. You need someone in customer relations, a person to follow up on complaints and misunderstandings about credit arrangements or bills. You want to hire someone who has had experience of this kind. Still, the work easily could be learned on the job . . . if the right person came along. In response to your classified advertisement, Bruce's resume arrives accompanied by a routine cover letter. He recounts people problems he has resolved and describes his administrative experience in a way that indicates he is a team worker. What's your decision? What if his letter is more inspired?

Michelle Trio—The Curriculum Vitae

A curriculum vitae (literally, "course of life" in Latin), sometimes called a C.V. or vita, is a resume for academic positions and as such does not need a statement of goals or interest. While there is merit in keeping nonacademic resumes brief by focusing on employers' needs, a faculty tends to select colleagues not just to

BRUCE GREGORY ROBERTSON

Home Address   College Address
105 Comstock Drive   5 Erasmus Drive
Pierre, South Dakota 57501   St. Paul, Minnesota 55101
605-555-5445   612-555-4554

CAREER   — The marketing of products or services in industries
INTERESTS   such as banking, publishing, and retailing.

EDUCATIONAL   — Macalester College, St. Paul, Minnesota   A.B.,
BACKGROUND   May 1991
                   Major: English   Minor: Economics
                   Honors: Dean's List, 1990–91

EMPLOYMENT   — Entrepreneurial—Organized a company to paint road
                   markings in parking lots; rented necessary
                   equipment; employed two additional workers; had
                   personal contact with mall managers, store owners,
                   etc., to promote the company's services: summers,
                   1989–90.

                — Administrative and Clerical—Temporary Help, Inc.
                   Typing and other business machine operations,
                   bookkeeping, clerking, complaint adjustments; short-
                   term assignments with auto dealers, banks, real estate
                   operations, schools, and similar employers: summer
                   1988; part-time 1989.

                — Miscellaneous—Camp counselor, stock clerk in
                   grocery store, baby-sitter, newspaper boy. From high
                   school on have earned money for clothes, travel, and
                   purchase and maintenance of an automobile.

ACTIVITIES   — Vice President, Seven-Come-Eleven investment club
                — Varsity basketball
                — Coach and tutor, St. Paul Concordia Boys Club
                — Debate Club
                — Book and Bottle literary club

SKILLS   — Typing
                — PL/C and FORTRAN computer languages
                — German: fluent

HONORS   — Dakota Interstate Scholarship
                — Hubert H. Humphrey First Prize, Minnesota
                   Intercollegiate Debate

INTERESTS   — Public speaking and debate
                — Investments
                — Writing
                — Parachute jumping

FIGURE 7   A resume designed more to reflect an active, energetic personality than specific experience.

teach but for the prestige they will bring to the department, especially in the long run. An eminent faculty attracts eminent associates. Publications, research, memberships, and honors all contribute to telling what a candidate is like; hence long vitae that reflect many achievements are traditional. The same candidate applying for an industrial position wouldn't list a raft of publications, for example, if those publications didn't relate to the job in question.

The C.V. that is shown in Figure 8 [pp. 280–281] lays out in a logical way all the essentials of a good vita. Note the correct way to list publications. In academia, those who list them incorrectly are jeopardizing their chances of being hired.

The Job Objective

"Do I have to have a job objective?" According to my calculations, as of this writing I have been a career counselor for 2,288 weeks, and I have been asked this question at least six times a week, except for the 132 weeks when I was on vacation. When I answer, "No, I don't like the heading JOB OBJECTIVE," the sigh of relief is audible. The job seekers think I have let them off the hook for one of the most important parts of a resume. I haven't. With rare exceptions, a resume *should* open with an objective—it's the way it is stated that can be changed.

I show them the preceding Robertson, Meyers, and Smith resumes and tell them that I prefer the headline CAREER INTEREST, because it leads to a simple and direct way of stating the purpose of the resume. For example, I suggest they try rewriting the Robertson and revised Smith statements of interest as job objectives to see if they don't find it awkward. After a struggle they come up with the same kind of baloney found in the unrevised Jones and Smith resumes.

They listen politely. I may have helped them with a minor problem of phrasing, but I know that I really haven't dealt with their question. Then they tell me what I already know: They don't want to state a goal because they don't know what they want to do. I ask them to imagine themselves as the employers reading their resumes. If theirs is like the revised Nancy Jones resume, which is so obviously slanted toward biology, then employers can figure out what the resume is for without a stated objective. However, I wouldn't fool with a resume that didn't tell me at the outset what it was all about. When I have to start studying a resume to guess what the writer wants, I throw it in the wastebasket.

Next I point to the Zarote and Robertson resumes, which wouldn't make any sense without a statement of purpose. And I can't get up much enthusiasm for a letter as a substitute for an objective. A letter stating a purpose accompanied by a resume without purpose is a wasted letter.

I remember a young woman who, on short notice, got a chance to be interviewed by a recruiter from a large department store. Knowing very little about merchandising, she headed for the nearest department store, where several managers were kind enough to give her information and the loan of their trade journals. In three hours of investigation, her eyes were opened to an industry in which people pursued careers in training, employee relations, promotion, credit, public relations, merchandising, and other occupations. Several of these looked

MICHELLE TRIO

Department of English   406 East Bates Street
Athens College   Athens, NY 14850
Athens, NY 14850   607-555-7654
607-555-4567

EDUCATION

Ph.D., 1984, Cornwall University.

Dissertation: "The Anatomy of Sin: Violations of *Kynde* and *Trawbe* in
                   Cleanness," directed by L. E. Cooper (DAI 40/09, p. 5046-A).
Major Subject: Old and Middle English language and literature.
Minor Subject: Medieval philology.
Courses: Old English; *Beowulf*; seminars on the Junius
                   Manuscript, the Exeter Book, and hagiography;
                   Middle English literature; Chaucer; *Piers Plowman;*
                   Medieval Latin; paleography; Old French; Middle High
                   German; Old Icelandic; Dante.

A.M., 1979, with High Honors, Boston University.

B.A., 1977, *magna cum laude,* Honors in English, State University of New York at Stony
Brook.

PROFESSIONAL EXPERIENCE

1985–present: Assistant Professor, Medieval and Renaissance Literature, Department of
    English, Athens College. Position includes: Engl 325 Chaucer, Engl 323 Triumph of
    English (a course that I instituted on the history of English), Engl 232 Medieval
    Literature, Engl 420 Shakespeare Seminar, Engl 231 Ancient Literature, Engl 107
    Introduction to Literature: Myth, Legend, and Folktale.

1985: Assistant Professor, Department of English, Cornwall University Summer Program.
    One section of Practical Prose and Composition and training of a graduate teaching
    assistant.

1984–85: Lecturer, Department of English, Cornwall University. Two courses in
    Freshman Seminar Program: Shakespeare and Politics, Practical Prose Composition. I
    was Co-director of the latter, with responsibility for planning the syllabus, training and
    evaluating graduate teaching assistants, and leading staff meetings on problems and
    goals of teaching composition.

PUBLICATIONS

"Heroic Kingship and Just War in the Alliterative *Morte Arthure*," to be published in
Acta, 11.

Articles on the Beatitudes, the Handwriting on the Wall, the Parable of the Marriage
Feast, Sarah, and Sodom and Gomorrah in *Dictionary of Biblical Tradition in English
Literature,* ed. David L. Jeffrey, to be published by Oxford University Press and W. B.
Eerdmans.

"On Reading *Bede's Death Song:* Translation, Typology, and Penance in Symeon of
Durham's Text of the *Epistola Cuthbert: de Obitu Bedae.*" *Neuphilologische Mitteilungen,*
84 (1983), 171–81.

FIGURE 8   A Curriculum Vitae.

PROFESSIONAL SERVICE AND ACTIVITIES

1. At Athens College
   1989–90: English Department Library Representative.
   1989–90: Member, Athens College Faculty Enrichment Committee.
   1988–90: English Department Personnel Committee.
   1987–89: English Department Committee on the London Center.

2. Elsewhere
   1985: Organizer and Chair, Latin Section, Northeast Modern Language Association. Topic: "Eschatology and Apocalypticism."
   1980–82: Organizer and Chair, *Quodlibet:* The Cornwall Medieval Forum.
   Memberships in MLA, Medieval Academy of America, International Arthurian Society.

HONORS

Charles A. Dana Fellowship for Excellence in Teaching, Athens College.

Goethe Prize in German Literature, Cornwall University.

George Lincoln Fellowship in Medieval Studies, Cornwall University.

Teaching Assistantship, Medieval Studies program, Cornwall University ("Medieval Literature in Translation").

Teaching Fellowship, English Department, Boston University ("Freshman Rhetoric and Composition").

LANGUAGES

Reading knowledge of Latin, Old French, Spanish, Italian, Middle High German, and Old Icelandic, in addition to the usual French, German, and Old and Middle English.

CREDENTIALS

Dossier may be obtained from the Educational Placement Bureau, Barnes Hall, Cornwall University, Athens, NY 14853.

FIGURE 8   *(Continued)*

interesting, so thanks to word processing, she easily changed a few things on her resume, then listed her objective like this:

CAREER INTERESTS: Training, promotion, and public relations in a retail setting.

Like most of us, her range of aptitudes was wide, so, like a chameleon, she showed the recruiter only those that seemed to match retailing.

One Page or Two?

If a resume can be kept to one page, so much the better. The length depends on the message. In reading resumes in which everything is jammed on one page with none of the white space or headings that can make them attractive and readable, I have wearied of trying to find information and have given up. On the other hand, it has never been the least bit tiring to lift a piece of paper and turn to a second page when scanning an interesting resume. A resume is an outline. It needs a white space. It needs headings that stand out. Don't sacrifice them for some arbitrary notion about a one-page maximum.

Additional Advice About Resumes

No matter how you develop your message, test it before you send it to employers. Get friends to give you a critique of your resume or vita, especially if they are in an occupation in which you hope to find a job. A word of caution, however. Unless you guide them, their critique may relate more to the ritual than to the message. One job hunter had modeled a resume after Janet Smith's. The critic took a red pencil and put all the dates of employment in the left-hand margin. That would have been a good idea if it had indicated long years of experience with a company such as 3M, signifying considerable experience with one of the best-managed companies in the country. But the dates in question referred to short-term summer jobs that were of no consequence to the message and cluttered the margin with information that distracted from the headlines.

One way to get a resume criticized is to hold it up a few feet from the reader and ask for comments on its appearance. Does it look neat? Is the layout pleasing? Does it look easy to read? Is the print good-looking?

Next, give the critics the resume to read. Let them make all the comments they want. You may pick up valuable ideas for improving its style and layout, but be careful you don't get caught up in inconsequentials. What you really want is to have your critics look at the resume as if they didn't know you. You might even show them a resume with an alias, then ask:

- What qualifications does this person have?
- What do you see this person doing with these qualifications?
- What kind of an employer would want to hire this person?
- Does the resume project an image of a certain kind of person? What kind? Aggressive? Thoughtful? Energetic? What?

In other words, ask your critics the most important question about your resume: "What message do you get about me?"

Steven Graber

The Basics of a Cover Letter

Steven Graber is the former managing editor of both the JobBank *and the* Adams Almanac *series.*

Your cover letter, like your resume, is a marketing tool. Too many cover letters are merely an additional piece of paper accompanying a resume, saying "Enclosed please find my resume." Like effective advertisements, effective cover letters attract an employer's attention by highlighting the most attractive features of the product. Begin by learning how to create an effective sales pitch As with resumes, both the format and the content of your cover letter are important.

FORMAT

Before reading a word of your cover letter, a potential employer has already made an assessment of your organizational skills and attention to detail simply by observing its appearance. How your correspondence looks to a reader can mean the difference between serious consideration and dismissal. You can't afford to settle for a less than perfect presentation of your credentials. This . . . [essay] outlines the basic format you should follow when writing a cover letter and shows you how to put the finishing touches on a top-notch product.

The Parts of a Letter

Your cover letter may be printed on the highest-quality paper and typed on a state-of-the-art computer, but if it isn't arranged according to the proper format, you won't come across as a credible candidate. Certain guidelines apply when composing any letter.

Either of two styles may be used for cover letters: business style (sometimes called block style) or personal style. The only difference between them is that in business style, all the elements of the letter—the return address, salutation, body, and complimentary close—begin at the left margin. In personal style, the return address and complimentary close begin at the centerline of the page, and paragraphs are indented.

Return Address

Your return address should appear at the top margin, without your name, either flush left or beginning at the centerline, depending on whether you're using business style or personal style. As a rule, avoid abbreviations in the addresses of your cover letter, although abbreviating the state is acceptable. Include your phone number if you're not using letterhead that contains it or it doesn't appear in the last paragraph of the letter. The idea is to make sure contact information is on both the letter and the resume, in case they get separated in the hiring manager's office (this happens more often than you would expect!).

Date

The date appears two lines below your return address, either flush left or centered, depending on which style you're using. Write out the date; don't abbreviate. *Example:* October 12, 2000.

Inside Address

Four lines beneath the date, give the addressee's full name. On subsequent lines, give the person's title, the company's name, and the company's address. Occasionally, the person's full title or the company's name and address will be very long and can appear awkward on the usual number of lines. In this case, you can use an extra line.

The text of the letter below the date should be centered approximately vertically on the page, so if your letter is short, you can begin the inside address six or even eight lines down. If the letter is long, two lines is acceptable.

Salutation

The salutation should be typed two lines beneath the company's address. It should begin "Dear Mr." or "Dear Ms." followed by the individual's last name and a colon. Even if you've previously spoken with an addressee who has asked to be called by his or her first name, never use a first name in the salutation. In some cases, as when responding to "blind" advertisements, a general salutation may be necessary. In such circumstances, "Dear Sir or Madam" is appropriate, followed by a colon.

Length

Three or four short paragraphs on one page is ideal. A longer letter may not be read.

Enclosure

An enclosure line is used primarily in formal or official correspondence. It's not wrong to include it in a cover letter, but it's unnecessary.

Paper Size

As with your resume, use standard 8½-by 11-inch paper. A smaller size will appear more personal than professional and is easily lost in an employer's files; a larger size will look awkward and may be discarded for not fitting with other documents.

Paper Color and Quality

Use quality paper that is standard 8½ by 11 inches and has weight and texture, in a conservative color like white or ivory. Good resume paper is easy to find at stores that sell stationery or office products and is even available at some drugstores. Use *matching* paper and envelopes for both your resume and cover letter. One hiring manager at a major magazine throws out all resumes that arrive on paper that differs in color from the envelope!

Do not buy paper with images of clouds and rainbows in the background or anything that looks like casual stationery you would send your favorite aunt. Do not spray perfume or cologne on your cover letter. Also, never use the stationery of your current employer.

Typing and Printing

Your best bet is to use a word processing program on a computer with a letter-quality printer. Handwritten letters are not acceptable. You will generally want to use the same typeface and size that you used on your resume. Remember that serif typefaces are generally easier to read.

Don't try the cheap and easy ways, like photocopying the body of your letter and typing in the inside address and salutation. Such letters will not be taken seriously.

Envelope

Mail your cover letter and resume in a standard, business-sized envelope that matches your stationery. Unless your handwriting is *extremely* neat and easy to read, type your envelopes. Address your envelope, by full name and title, specifically to the contact person you identified in your cover letter.

CONTENT

Personalize Each Letter

If you are *not* responding to a job posting that specifies a contact name, try to determine the appropriate person to whom you should address your cover letter. (In general, the more influential the person, the better.) Try to contact the head of the department in which you're interested. This will be easiest in mid-sized and small companies, where the head of the department is likely to have an active role in the initial screening. If you're applying to a larger corporation, your application will probably be screened by the human resources department. If you're instructed to direct your inquiry to this division, try to find out the name of the senior human resources manager. This may cut down on the number of hands through which your resume passes on its way to the final decision-maker. At any rate, be sure to include your contact's name and title on both your letter and the envelope. This way, even if a new person occupies the position, your letter should get through.

Mapping It Out

A cover letter need not be longer than three or four paragraphs. Two of them, the first and last, can be as short as one sentence. The idea of the cover letter is not to repeat what's in the resume. The idea is to give an overview of your capabilities and show why you're a good candidate for the job. The best way to distinguish yourself is to highlight one or two of your accomplishments or abilities. Stressing only one or two increases your chances of being remembered.

Be sure it's clear from your letter why you have an interest in the company—*so many candidates apply for jobs with no apparent knowledge of what the company does!* This conveys the message that they just want any job. Indicating an interest doesn't mean you should tell every employer you have a burning desire to work at that company, because these statements are easy to make and invariably sound insincere. Indicating how your qualifications or experience meet their requirements may be sufficient to show why you're applying.

First paragraph. State the position for which you're applying. If you're responding to an ad or listing, mention the source. *Example:* "I would like to apply for the position of research assistant advertised in the *Sunday Planet*" (or "listed on the Internet").

Second paragraph. Indicate what you could contribute to this company and show how your qualifications will benefit them. If you're responding to an ad or listing, discuss how your skills relate to the job's requirements. Don't talk about what you can't do. Remember, keep it brief! *Example:* "In addition to my strong background in mathematics, I offer significant business experience, having worked in a data processing firm, a bookstore, and a restaurant. I am sure that my courses in statistics and computer programming would prove particularly useful in the position of trainee."

Third paragraph. If possible, show how you not only meet but exceed their requirements—why you're not just an average candidate but a superior one. Mention any noteworthy accomplishments, high-profile projects, instances where you went above and beyond the call of duty, or awards you've received for your work. If you have testimonials, commendations or evaluations that are particularly complimentary, you may want to quote a sentence from one or two of them.

Example: "In a letter to me, Dewayne Berry, president of NICAP Inc., said, 'Your ideas were instrumental to our success with this project.'"

Fourth paragraph. Close by saying you look forward to hearing from them. If you wish, you can also thank them for their consideration. Don't ask for an interview. If they're interested, they'll call. If not, asking won't help. Don't tell them you'll call them—many ads say "No phone calls." If you haven't heard anything in one or two weeks, a call is acceptable.

Complimentary close. The complimentary close should be two lines beneath the body of the letter, aligned with your return address and the date; Keep it simple— "Sincerely" followed by a comma, suffices. Three lines under this, type your full name as it appears on your resume. Sign above your typed name in black ink.

Don't forget to sign the letter! As silly as it sounds, people often forget this seemingly obvious detail. An oversight like this suggests you don't take care with your work. To avoid this implication if you're faxing the letter and resume directly from your computer, you can type your name directly below the complimentary close, without any intervening space. Then follow up with a hard copy of the resume and the signed letter, with your name typed in the traditional place under the signature.

TIPS FOR SUCCESSFUL COVER LETTERS

What Writing Style Is Appropriate?

Adopt a polite, formal style that balances your confidence in yourself with respect for the employer. Keep the style clear, objective, and persuasive rather than narrative. Don't waste space boasting instead of presenting relevant qualifications.

Example: "In addition to a Bachelor of Arts degree in Business Administration, I recently received a Master's, *cum laude,* in International Marketing from Brown University. This educational experience is supported by two years' part-time experience with J&D Products, where my marketing efforts resulted in increased annual product sales of 25 percent."

Tone: Reserved Confidence Is Always in Style

Think of how you'd sell your qualifications in a job interview. You'd probably think harder about what to say and how to say it than in an informal conversation. Above all, you'd want to sound polite, confident, and professional. Adopt a similar tone in your cover letter. It should immediately communicate confidence in your abilities. The trick is to sound enthusiastic without becoming melodramatic. Take, for example, the candidate who expressed his desire to enter the advertising field as "the single most important thing I have ever wanted in my entire twenty-three years of existence." The candidate who was actually offered the position began her letter as follows: "My extensive research into the industry, coupled with my internship and education, have confirmed my interest in pursuing an entry-level position in advertising."

Emphasize Concrete Examples

Your resume details the duties you've performed in your jobs. In contrast, your cover letter should highlight your most significant accomplishments. Instead of stating something like "My career is highlighted by several major achievements," use concrete examples:

"While Sales Manager at Shayko Chicken, I supervised a team that increased revenues by 35 percent in 18 months."

"I published four articles in *The Magical Bullet Newsletter*."

"At MUFON Corporation, I advanced from telephone fundraiser to field manager to canvassing director within two years."

List tangible, relevant skills rather than personal attributes. A sentence like "I am fluent in C++, Pascal, and COBOL" is a good substitute for a vague statement like "I am a goal-oriented, highly skilled computer programmer." Avoid using "etc."—don't expect a potential employer to imagine what else you mean. Either describe it or leave it out.

Use Powerful Language

Your language should be hard-hitting and easy to understand. Your message should be expressed using the fewest words possible. As with your resume, make your letters interesting by using action verbs like "designed," "implemented," and "increased," rather than passive verbs like "was" and "did." Use simple, common language and avoid abbreviations and slang. Change "Responsible for directing" to "Directed" if appropriate. Also steer clear of language that's too technical or jargon-heavy. The first person who reads your cover letter may not possess the same breadth of knowledge as your future boss.

Avoid Catchphrases

In the course of a job search, it's tempting to use catchphrases you've picked up from advertisements or reference materials, phrases that sound as though they *should* go in a resume or cover letter. Many people are tempted to reach for expressions like "self-starter," "excellent interpersonal skills," and "work well independently or as part of a team."

Improve on these descriptions by listing actual projects and goals. For example, rephrase "Determined achiever with proven leadership skills" as follows: "Supervised staff of fifteen and increased the number of projects completed before deadline by 10 percent." Once you begin working, employers will discover your personal attributes for themselves. While you're under consideration, concrete experiences are more valuable than vague phrases or obscure promises.

Mention Personal Preferences?

Candidates often worry if, and how, they should include salary requirements and availability to travel or relocate. Refrain from offering salary information unless the advertisement you are responding to requires it. If you must include salary requirements, give a salary range rather than a number. Another option is to simply indicate that salary concerns are negotiable.

If you're applying to an out-of-state firm, indicate a willingness to relocate; otherwise, a hiring manager may question your purpose in writing and may not take the initiative to inquire.

Proof with Care

Mistakes on resumes and cover letters are not only embarrassing, they will often remove you from consideration (particularly if something obvious, like your name, is misspelled). No matter how much you paid someone else to type, write, or typeset your resume or cover letter, *you* lose if there is a mistake. So proofread it as carefully as possible. Get a friend to help you. Read your draft aloud as your friend checks the proof copy. Then have your friend read aloud while you check. Next, read it letter by letter to check spelling and punctuation.

If you're having it typed or typeset by a resume service or a printer and you don't have time to proof it, pay for it and take it home. Proof it there and bring it back later to get it corrected and printed.

If you wrote your cover letter with a word processing program, use the built-in spell checker to double-check for spelling errors. Keep in mind that a spell checker will not find errors like "to" for "two" or "wok" for "work." Many spell-check programs don't recognize missing or misused punctuation, nor are they set to check the spelling of capitalized words. It's important to still proofread your cover letter for grammatical mistakes and other problems, even after it's been spell-checked.

If you find mistakes, do not fix them with pen, pencil, or white-out! Make the changes on the computer and print out the letter again.

COVER LETTER BLUNDERS TO AVOID

The following discussion focuses on examples that have been adapted from real-life cover letters. Although some of these blunders may seem obvious, they occur far more often than one might think. Needless to say, none of the inquiries that included these mistakes met with positive results.

Unrelated Career Goals

Tailor your cover letter to the position you're applying for. A hiring manager is only interested in what you can do for the company, not what you hope to accomplish for yourself. Convey a genuine interest in the position and a long-term pledge to fulfilling its duties.

Example A (wrong way): "While my true goal is to become a professional dancer, I am exploring the option of taking on proofreading work while continuing to train for the Boston Ballet's next audition."

Example B (right way): "I am very interested in this proofreading position, and I am confident of my ability to make a long-term contribution to your capable staff."

Comparisons and Clichés

Avoid clichés and obvious comparisons. These expressions detract from your letter's purpose: to highlight your most impressive skills and accomplishments.

Examples of what not to do:

"My word processor runs like the wind."

"I am a people person."

"Teamwork is my middle name."

"Your company is known as the crème de la crème of accounting firms."

"I am as smart as a whip."

"Among the responses you receive for this position, I hope my qualifications make me leader of the pack."

Wasted Space

Since cover letters are generally four paragraphs long, every word of every sentence should be directly related to your purpose for writing. In other words, if you are applying for a position as a chemist, include only those skills and experiences most applicable to that field. Any other information weakens your application.

Examples of what not to do:

"As my enclosed resume reveals, I possess the technical experience and educational background to succeed as your newest civil engineer. In addition, I am a certified gymnastics instructor who has won several local competitions."

"I am writing in response to your advertisement for an accounting clerk. Currently, I am finishing an associate degree at Peacock Junior College. My courses have included medieval architecture, film theory, basic home surgery, and nutrition."

Form Letters

Mass mailings, in which you send a form letter to a large number of employers, are not recommended. This approach doesn't allow you to personalize each application. Every cover letter you write should be tailored to the position you're seeking and should demonstrate your commitment to a specific industry and familiarity with each employer. Mass mailings may indicate to a hiring manager that you're not truly interested in joining that organization.

Inappropriate Stationery

White and ivory are the only acceptable paper colors for a cover letter. Also, don't rely on graphics to "improve" your cover letter; let your qualifications speak for themselves. If you're a cat enthusiast, don't use stationery with images of favorite felines. If you're a musician, don't send a letter decorated with a border of musical notes and instruments.

"Amusing" Anecdotes

Imagine yourself in an interview setting. Since you don't know your interviewer, you wouldn't joke with him or her until you determined what demeanor was appropriate. Similarly, when writing, remain polite and professional.

Erroneous Company Information

If you were the employer, would you want to hire a candidate who confuses your company's products and services or misquotes recent activities? To avoid such errors, verify the accuracy of any company information you mention in your cover letter. On the other hand, if you haven't researched the company, don't bluff. Statements like "I know something about your company" or "I am familiar with your products" signal to an employer that you haven't done your homework.

Desperation

In your cover letter, sound determined, not desperate. While an employer appreciates enthusiasm, he or she may be turned off by a desperate plea for employment. However, a fine line often separates the two.
Examples of what not to do:
"I am desperately eager to start, as I have been out of work for six months."
"Please call today! I'll be waiting by the phone."
"I really, really need this job to pay off medical bills."
"I AM VERY BADLY IN NEED OF MONEY!"

Personal Photos

Unless you're seeking employment in modeling, acting, or other performing arts, it's inappropriate to send a photograph.

Confessed Shortcomings

Some job seekers mistakenly call attention to their weaknesses in their cover letters, hoping to ward off an employer's objections. This is a mistake, because the letter emphasizes your flaws rather than your strengths.
Examples of what not to do:
"Although I have no related experience, I remain very interested in the management consultant position."
"I may not be well qualified for this position, but it has always been my dream to work in the publishing field."

Misrepresentation

In any stage of the job-search process, never, *ever,* misrepresent yourself. In many companies, erroneous information contained in a cover letter or resume will be grounds for dismissal if the inaccuracy is discovered. Protect yourself by sticking to the facts. You're selling your skills and accomplishments in your cover letter. If you achieve something, say so, and put it in the best possible light. Don't hold back or be modest—no one else will. At the same time, don't exaggerate to the point of misrepresentation.

Examples of what not to do:

"In June, I graduated with honors from American University. In the course of my studies, I played two varsity sports while concurrently holding five jobs."

"Since beginning my career four years ago, I have won hundreds of competitions and awards and am considered by many the best hairstylist on the east coast."

Demanding Statements

Your cover letter should demonstrate what you can do for an employer, not what he or she can do for you. For example, instead of stating "I am looking for a unique opportunity in which I will be adequately challenged and compensated," say "I am confident I could make a significant contribution to your organization, specifically by expanding your customer base in the northwest and instituting a discount offer for new accounts." Also, since you're requesting an employer's consideration, your letter shouldn't include personal preferences or demands. Statements like "It would be an overwhelmingly smart idea for you to hire me" or "Let's meet next Wednesday at 4:00 P.M., when I will be available to discuss my candidacy further" come across as presumptuous. Job candidates' demands are rarely met with an enthusiastic response.

Missing Resume

Have you ever forgotten to enclose all the materials you refer to in your cover letter? This is a fatal oversight. No employer is going to take the time to remind you of your mistake; he or she has already moved on to the next application.

Personal Information

Do not include your age, health, physical characteristics, marital status, race, religion, political/moral beliefs, or any other personal information. List your personal interests and hobbies only if they're directly relevant to the type of job you're seeking. If you're applying to a company that greatly values teamwork, for instance, citing that you organized a community fundraiser or played on a basketball team may be advantageous. When in doubt, however, leave it out.

Choice of Pronouns

Your cover letter necessarily requires a thorough discussion of your qualifications. Although some applicants might choose the third person ("he or she") as a creative approach to presenting their qualifications, potential employers sometimes find this disconcerting. In general, using the first person ("I") is preferable.

Example A (wrong way): "Bambi Berenbeam is a highly qualified public relations executive with over seven years of relevant experience in the field. She possesses strong verbal and written communication skills, and has an extensive client base."

Example B (right way): "I am a highly qualified public relations executive with over seven years of relevant experience in the field. I possess strong verbal and written communication skills and have an extensive client base."

Tone Trouble

Tone problems are subtle and may be hard to detect. When reading your cover letter, patrol for tone problems by asking yourself, after each sentence, "Does this statement enhance my candidacy? Could a hiring manager interpret it in an unfavorable way?" Have a second reader review your letter. If the letter's wording is questionable, rewrite it. A cover letter should steer a middle course between extremely formal, which can come across as pretentious, and extremely informal, which can come across as presumptuous. Try to sound genuine, not stilted. When in doubt, err on the side of formality.

Gimmicks

Gimmicks like sending a home video or a singing telegram to replace the conventional cover letter may seem attractive. No matter how creative these ideas may sound, the majority of employers will be more impressed with a simple, well-crafted letter. In the worst-case scenario, gimmicks can even work against you, eliminating you from consideration. Examples include sending a poster-sized cover letter by courier service or a baseball hat with a note attached: "I'm throwing my hat into the ring!" Avoid such big risks; most hiring decisions are based on qualifications, not gimmicks.

Typographical Errors

It's easy to make mistakes in your letters, particularly when you're writing many in succession. But it's also easy for a hiring manager to reject any cover letter that contains errors, even those that seem minor. Don't make the mistake that one job-hunting editor made, citing his attention to detail while misspelling his own name! Here are a few common technical mistakes to watch out for when proofreading your letter:

Misspelling the hiring contact's name or title in the address or salutation or on the envelope.

Forgetting to change the name of the organization you're applying to each time it appears in your application, especially in the body of the letter. For example, if you're applying to Boots and Bags, don't express enthusiasm for a position at Shoe City.

Indicating application for one position and mentioning a different position in the body of the letter. For instance, one candidate applying for a telemarketing position included the following statement: "I possess fifteen years experience related to the marketing analyst opening." Another mistake here is that the applicant didn't use "years" as a possessive: ". . . fifteen years' experience. . . ."

Messy Corrections

Your cover letter should contain *all* pertinent information. If, for any reason, you forget to communicate something to your addressee, retype the letter. Including a supplementary note, either typed or handwritten, will be viewed as unprofessional or, worse, lazy. For example, one candidate attached a "post-it" note to his cover letter, stating his willingness to travel and/or relocate. This and all other information must be included in your final draft. Also, avoid using correction fluid or penning in any corrections.

Omitted Signature

However obvious this may sound, don't forget to sign your name neatly in blue or black ink. Far too many letters have a typed name but no signature. Also, don't use a script font or a draw program on your word processor.

COVER LETTERS FOR SPECIAL SITUATIONS

Writing a cover letter can seem like an even more formidable task when you find yourself in what we call "special situations." Perhaps you lack paid job experience, have been out of the workplace to raise children, are concerned about possible discrimination due to age or disability, or are trying to enter a field in which you have no practical experience. The key to improving your cover letter in these special situations is to emphasize your strengths. Focus on your marketable skills (whether they were acquired in the workplace or elsewhere), and highlight impressive achievements, relevant education and training, and/or related interests. And, of course, you should take care to downplay or eliminate any information that may be construed as a weakness.

For example, if you're a "displaced homemaker" (a homemaker entering the job market for the first time), you can structure your cover letter to highlight the special skills you've acquired over the years while downplaying your lack of paid experience. If you're an older job candidate, use your age as a selling point. Emphasize the depth of your experience, your maturity, your sense of responsibility, and your positive outlook. Changing careers? Instead of focusing on your job history, emphasize the marketable skills you've acquired that are considered valuable in the position you're seeking. For example, let's say your career has been real estate and, in your spare time, you like to run marathons. Recently, you heard about an opening in the sales and marketing department at an athletic shoe manufacturer. What you need to do is emphasize the skills you have that the employer is looking for. Not only do you have strong sales experience, you're familiar with the needs of the company's market, and that's a powerful combination!

RESPONSE TO A "BLIND" ADVERTISEMENT

A form of classified advertisements, "Blind" advertisements do not list employer information and generally direct inquiries to a post office box rather than a company's address. Since you're not provided with a company name in a blind ad, your cover letter should sharply define your knowledge of the industry, position (if mentioned) and how your qualifications specifically match up to the stated requirements. In other words, tailor your letter to any information given. For example, consider a blind ad that reads:

> *Large-size law firm in need of paralegal with experience in legal research, writing briefs, and office administration.*

You need to target everything in your response: what you know of the operations of large-size firms; why you want to be and remain a paralegal; how much experience you have in legal research and writing; and exactly what office skills you have. Avoid longwinded passages that don't follow these guidelines. Without knowing your readers, you've caught their attention. They're more likely to invite you for an interview, and suddenly you're one step closer to getting the job.

COLD LETTERS

With a "cold" cover letter, you can directly contact potential employers without a referral or previous correspondence. Job-seekers most commonly use this type of letter to advertise their availability to hiring managers or personnel departments. Presumably, after researching your field, you will have devised a list of the top employers you would like to work for and gathered basic company information for each.

BROADCAST LETTERS

With a broadcast letter, well-qualified candidates can advertise their availability to top-level professionals in a particular field. The candidate attempts to entice the potential employer to consider his or her impressive qualifications for available positions. Although the broadcast letter discusses a candidate's background in detail, a resume is usually included. Since this type of letter is used primarily by seasoned executives, its tone should reflect the candidate's experience, knowledge, and confidence in his or her capabilities.

A candidate using the broadcast letter format might begin, "Are you in need of a management accountant who, in her most recent association, contributed to productivity improvements resulting in an annual savings of $20 million?" This attention-grabbing opening is effective only if the reader understands the significance of such an accomplishment. For this reason, broadcast letters are not recommended for those candidates conducting widespread job searches, where cover letters may end up in the human resources department rather than in the hands of a fellow industry executive.

LETTER TO AN EMPLOYMENT AGENCY

When searching for a job, many candidates rely on the help of employment agencies. These agencies offer services to a wide range of job-seekers, primarily for clerical or support staff positions. Letters addressed to employment agencies should focus on who you are, what type of position you are looking for and in what specific industry, and some of your strongest skills related to that field. For the agency to place you in an appropriate position, mention personal preferences, including geographic and salary requirements.

LETTER TO AN EXECUTIVE SEARCH FIRM

Although executive search firms actively recruit candidates for client companies, don't let this discourage you from writing. A well-crafted cover letter can alert an otherwise unknowing recruiter to your availability. Highlight your most impressive accomplishments and attributes and briefly summarize all relevant experience. If you have certain preferences, like geographical location, travel, and salary, mention them in your cover letter.

NETWORKING LETTERS

For the most part, networking letters refer to a third-party industry contact to garner the reader's attention and induce him or her to assist you in your job search. It is essential to achieve the right tone in your networking letters. Unless you are familiar with a contact, word your correspondence in a businesslike manner. In other words, do not use your addressee's first name or rely on an overly casual writing style. Likewise, if you have been in contact with this person recently, it could be useful to remind him or her, "It was great seeing you at the Chicago Writers' Convention last month" or "It's been several months since we bumped into each other on that flight to London. How are you?"

Many networking letters are written to an addressee whom the candidate has not met but has been referred to by a mutual acquaintance. In this case, immediately state the name of the person who referred you, such as "Jean Rawlins suggested I contact you." It is generally more effective to ask a contact with whom you are unfamiliar for assistance and names of people to contact than it is to ask for a job. Chances are, if your letter is politely persuasive, people will be interested in talking with you.

THANK YOU LETTERS

Your correspondence doesn't end with cover letters. Other types of letters, such as thank you letters, are often appropriate, even obligatory. It's acceptable to handwrite your thank you letter on a generic blank note card (but *never* a post-card). Make sure handwritten notes are neat and legible. If you're in doubt, typing your letter is always a safe bet. If you met with several people, it's fine to send each an individual thank you letter. Call the company if you need to check on the correct spelling of their names. Remember to keep the letters short, proofread them carefully, and send them *promptly*.

Diana C. Reep

Writing Resumes

Diana C. Reep is Professor of English at the University of Akron.

LOOKING FOR A JOB

Beginning a job search means that you actually have taken on the job of finding a job. Maintain a professional approach to all aspects of job hunting. Before applying for a job, follow these guidelines:

- Research the companies that employ people in your field. Find out about the job market and the kinds of skills employers are looking for. Most company Web sites list current job openings with details about the job requirements and instructions for applying. Libraries have business directories and guides. Check the *Wall Street Journal* for information about business in your field and companies you are interested in.
- Assess your own training, education, and experience. Consider how well you match the job requirements being requested.
- Analyze your interests and the skills you enjoy using. These elements will be the most important as you plan your career.
- Study positions advertised online or in the newspapers to determine the training that employers in your field are looking for. If you need more training in a particular skill, plan ways to get it as soon as possible.
- Because so many companies are international, do some research on the global expansion of companies in your field. Consider whether you should learn another language or increase your fluency in a second language.
- Attend career fairs. They allow you to meet several interviewers for potential employers in a short time. Meeting an interviewer in person can boost your possibilities of getting an office interview. Before arriving at the career fair, check the list of companies attending, and select ten that interest you. Research the companies and

the kinds of jobs they offer. Arrive early before the interviewers get tired of talking to people and bring copies of your resume. Get business cards from recruiters you talk to and send a brief thank-you the next day by regular mail.

- Check all possible sources for jobs—newspapers, company Web sites, university placement services, job boards on the Internet, professional association Web sites, friends, professors, and college job fairs.
- Establish a way for prospective employers to reach you. Get an answering machine if you do not have one. Make sure you are the only person to collect the messages. Remove any music or jokes you have on an answering machine or cell phone and record a business-like message for callers.
- Eliminate any Internet postings. Employers now check the Internet to see if job candidates have damaging information online. Profiles in Facebook and MySpace can make a detrimental impression on employers if the profiles reveal illegal or embarrassing activities.

WRITING RESUMES

A serious job seeker today needs at least three styles of resume—a traditional resume with attractive formatting, a scannable resume that employers can add to their databases, and an email resume that can be sent over the Internet. Although the styles of these vary, they include most of the same information, and they all have the same purpose: to attract the attention of an employer and secure an interview for the job applicant. No matter which style you use to apply for a job, always bring a traditional resume to an interview.

Traditional Resumes

A traditional resume is printed on good white bond paper in black ink. The writer uses formatting elements (e.g., boldface, bulleted lists, underlining) that help to create an attractive, easy-to-read page. The usual recommendation for a new college graduate is to keep the traditional resume to one page in length. One report indicates that a two-page resume is equally acceptable and even preferable for those who have outstanding qualifications.[1] . . .

Heading

Put your name, address, and telephone number at the top of your resume. You may include a business telephone number and email address. Appearances are important. If your email address is clever or funny, such as rockon@yahoo.com or

---

[1] Elizabeth Blackburn-Brochman and Kelly Belanger, "One Page or Two?: A National Study of CPA Recruiters' Preferences of Resume Length," *The Journal of Business Communication* 38.1 (January 2001): 29–57.

amazeme@hotmail.com, get a professional email address for your job search. Email addresses that do not look professional may be automatically deleted as spam.

Some people include the address of a personal Web site, but that may not be a good idea. A potential employer might not be impressed by personal photos, diary-style comments, songs, or humorous cartoons. Consider the purpose of your Web site. If the Web site emphasizes professional work, such as graphic design, then including the link might be advantageous in your job search. If the Web site is purely personal, however, omit it from your resume.

Objective

List a specific position that matches your education and experience, because employers want to see a clear, practical objective. Avoid vague descriptions, such as "I am looking for a challenging position where I can use my skills." Availability to travel is important in some companies, so the phrase "willing to travel" can be used under the objective. If you are not willing to travel, say nothing.

Education

List education in reverse chronological order, your most recent degree first. Once you have a college degree, you can omit high school. Be sure to list any special certificates or short-term training done in addition to college work. Include courses or skills that are especially important to the type of position for which you are applying. List your grade-point average if it is significantly high, and indicate the grade-point scale. Some people list their grade-point average in their majors only, since this is likely to be higher than the overall average.

Work Experience

List your past jobs in reverse chronological order. Include the job title, the name of the company, the city, and the state. Describe your responsibilities for each job, particularly those that provided practical experience connected with your career goals. In describing responsibilities, use action words, such as *coordinated*, *directed*, *prepared*, *supervised*, and *developed*. Dates of employment need not include month and day. Terms such as *vacation* or *summer* with the relevant years are sufficient.

Honors and Awards

List scholarships, prizes, and awards received in college. Include any community honors or professional prizes as well. If there is only one honor, list it under "Activities."

Activities

In this section list recent activities, primarily those in college. Be sure to indicate any leadership positions, such as president or chairperson of a group. Hobbies, if included, should indicate both group and individual interests.

References

. . . If you do list references, include the person's business address and telephone number. Be sure to ask permission before listing someone as a reference.

It is best to omit personal information about age, height, weight, marital status, and religion. Employers are not allowed to consider such information in the employment process, and most prefer that it not appear on a resume. . . .

Scannable Resumes

Many large companies use computers to scan and store resume information. When employers want to interview prospective employees for a position, they screen every resume in their electronic files for key qualifications. For employers, the advantages of electronic screening are that it (1) eliminates the difficulty of handling thousands of resumes in a fair manner, (2) quickly identifies candidates who have the primary job qualifications, and (3) processes more applications at less cost.

Electronic screening requires a special resume style. After writing your traditional resume, rewrite it in appropriate electronic style so you have both available. If you are applying to a company that uses electronic screening, you can inquire about a preferred format. If you cannot easily find out what the company prefers, send both a traditional and a scannable resume, and state in your application letter that you are sending both as a convenience to the employer. Following are guidelines for developing a scannable resume.

Name and Address

Your name should be the first line of your resume. Put your address, telephone numbers, and email address in a stacked list.

Key Words

Nouns are more important in scannable resumes than action verbs because computers are set to look for key skills.

Immediately after your opening information, list key words that identify such items as your previous job titles, job-related experience, skills, special knowledge, degrees, certifications, and colleges attended. Be sure to use the terms listed in a job advertisement because these are the terms the scanner is seeking. For example, if the advertisement asks for "public speaking," use that term rather than "oral presentations." Some companies scan only a portion of a resume, so be sure that your key words appear near the top of the page.

Single Columns

Scanners read across every line from left to right. Do not use double columns to list information because it will look like gibberish in the computer files.

Paper and Typeface

Scanners prefer clean and simple resumes. Use only smooth white paper with black ink and 12- or 14-point type. Do not use italics, underlining, boxes, shading, or unusual typeface. Capitals and boldface are acceptable as long as the letters do not touch each other.

Abbreviations

Use abbreviations sparingly. Scanners can miss information if they are programmed to search for a whole word.

Folding and Stapling

Do not staple or fold a scannable resume. The scanner may have trouble finding words that are in the creases or that cover staple holes.

White Space

Organize with lots of white space, so the scanner does not overlook key words. Use wide margins (60–65 characters per line) to avoid having text edges cut off if the recipient's equipment does not read the full line. . . .

Email Resumes

Many employers are now requesting that job seekers send in resumes via email. This method presents certain technical concerns because of the variety of word processing programs and hardware. Do not send your email resume as an attachment. To avoid viruses, many companies set their email systems to reject attachments, and most managers are reluctant to open attachments from strangers. Use the information from your traditional resume to prepare an electronic resume.
Consider these guidelines:

- Do not use bullets, boldface, boxes, underlining, or italics.
- Prepare the resume in ASCII (American Standard Code for Information Interchange), a text that includes no formatting elements but can be easily read by all computers. Save your resume in "text only" or "Rich Text Format" (RTF).
- Use a single-column, left-justified format.
- Use the space bar instead of the tab.
- Use asterisks instead of bullets.
- Use a hard carriage return instead of the word wrap feature in your processing program.

As a test, send your email resume to yourself to check readability and correctness. . . .

Web-Based Resumes

Companies today are using both their own Web sites and Internet job sites to create a pool of applicants for a position. Web sites, such as www.careerbuilder.com and www.monster.com, offer convenient places for job seekers to look for jobs and to post their own resumes for potential employers.

If you decide to post your resume with some of the Internet sites, check the costs carefully. Some charge a fee for posting a resume for a specific length of time. Follow the directions on the Web site. You may be able to use your email version and just paste it in, or you may have to paste in sections under a prescribed format on the site. Eventually, online resume postings will probably become more uniform so that employers can easily compare applicants from different sites.

Update your resume at least every other month and add/change the keywords, so recruiters take another look at your posting.

Matthew Yate

Resume Formats

Matthew Yate is the author of several New York Times' *career bestsellers and a former of director of training or personnel for several national companies.*

We all have different professional backgrounds, and we all have the right and the obligation to package them to our greatest benefit.

Some of us have worked for only one company, and some of us have worked for eleven companies in as many years. Some of us have changed careers once or twice, and some of use have maintained a predictable career path within one profession or industry. For some, diversity broadens our potential, and for others concentration in one area deepens it. While we each require different resume vehicles to put our work history in the most exciting light, the goals are constant.

1. To show off achievements, attributes, and accumulation of expertise to the best advantage.
2. To minimize any possible weaknesses.

Resume experts acknowledge three major styles for presenting your credentials to a potential employer: Chronological, Functional, and Combination (Chrono-Functional). Your particular circumstances will determine the right format for you. You will see resume books with up to fifteen different resume styles. Such volumes are merely filling up space; in the final analysis, each additional style that such books mention is a tiny variation on the above three.

I am going to give you a brief explanation of each style with examples. They are all relevant, depending on your circumstances, and you might even try more than one version in your own job search.

THE CHRONOLOGICAL RESUME [see Figure 1, pp. 308–309]

The chronological is the most common and widely accepted resume format. It's what most of us think of when we think of resumes—a chronological listing of job titles and responsibilities. It starts with the current or most recent employment, then works backward to your first job.

This format is good for demonstrating your growth in a single profession. It is suitable for anyone with practical work experience who hasn't suffered too many job changes or prolonged periods of unemployment. It is not always the best choice if you are just out of school or if you are changing careers, where a chronological format could then draw attention to your weaknesses (i.e., your lack of specific experience in a field) rather than your strengths.

The Work History is the distinguishing characteristic of the chronological resume, because it ties your job responsibilities and achievements to specific employers, job titles, and dates.

There are also optional categories determined by the space available to you and the unique aspects of your professional experience. . . .

THE FUNCTIONAL RESUME [see Figure 2, pp. 310–311]

This format focuses on the professional skills you have developed over the years and bring to a specific target job, rather than on when, where, or how you acquired them. It also de-emphasizes employers and employment dates by their placement on the second page. Job titles and employers can likewise play a minor part with this type of resume. The focus is always on the skill rather than the context or time of its acquisition.

This functional format is suited to a number of different personal circumstances, specifically those of:

- Mature professionals with a storehouse of expertise and jobs
- Entry-level types whose track records do not justify a chronological resume
- Career changers who want to focus on skills rather than experience
- People whose careers have been stagnant or in ebb, who want to give focus to the skills that can get a career underway again, rather than on the history in which it was becalmed in the first place.
- Those returning to the workplace after a long absence
- People closer to retirement than to the onset of their careers

For any resume to be effective, it must be conceived with a specific job in mind, and this is especially true for a functional resume. Because it focuses so strongly on skills and the ability to contribute in a particular direction, rather than on a directly relevant work history, you must have an employment objective clearly in mind.

Though functional resumes are more free-form than chronological ones, there are certain structural features that prevent their becoming what novelist Henry James called "loose, baggy monsters" of the *War and Peace* variety:

- *A Performance Profile or Career Objective/Summary.* Different skills are needed for different jobs, so some kind of functional summary up front is where the functional resume writer puts forward on encapsulated argument of suitability.
- *Relevant Accomplishments/Skills/Knowledge/Professional Behaviors.* Based on your target job, this is where you identify relevant accomplishments, along with the skills and behaviors that made them possible.
- *Dates.* Strictly speaking, a functional resume needn't give dates, but a resume without dates waves a big red flag. So if your employment history lacks stability, a functional resume allows you to de-emphasize dates somewhat by their placement, while an absence of employment dates altogether will do anything but de-emphasize them.
- *Education.* This is always included.

The space available and the unique aspects of your background determine inclusion of other optional categories.

Functional resumes are not as popular as they once were, but in some circumstances, such as those mentioned, they really are the best choice. Below is an example of someone applying for a job as an art gallery or museum curator whose only prior experience was as an art teacher. I want you to read the first page and then ask yourself if you know what such a person does for a living. I'll give you a few more interesting insights after the example.

A couple of interesting observations about the . . . resume [in Figure 2 below]:

- It is more informal in tone than many examples you will see, . . . but as it reflected someone in a profession where personality is a significant part of the job, there is nothing wrong with that. Given these considerations, I decided to give the resume a personal flavor, and the very first words after the contact information immediately draw the reader into a conversation with a passionate and committed professional: "My professional life is focused on art in all it embraces."
- There are professions where a less formal tone is more generally acceptable, usually education, the arts, and the caring professions.
- It is quite clear this person really understands the work of a curator. This resume went out once and resulted in an interview within seventy-two hours, at which a job offer was extended at the end of the first hour.
- Now for the kicker. Everything in this resume is absolutely true. The fact that this person had been the arts department chair of a private elementary through middle school was never an issue, because he so clearly understood the demands of the target job, and that was possible because his TJD* research had allowed the resume to be properly focused and prepared him for exactly the topics that would come up at interview.

---

*Target Job Description

This functional resume was successful because the writer . . . was able to recognize what it was that made a successful curator. He then demonstrated that he had exactly the credentials needed.

THE COMBINATION RESUME [see Figure 3, pp. 312–314]

For the upwardly mobile professional, this is becoming the resume of choice. It has all the flexibility and strength that come from combining both the chronological and functional formats, and it allows you to clearly demonstrate your thorough grasp of the job and its deliverables.

- *A Career Summary or Performance Profile.* The combination resume, more often that not, has either a Career Summary or a Performance Profile, where you spotlight yourself as a professional with a clear sense of self, and a history of relevant contributions. It might include a power-packed description of skills, achievements, and professional behaviors. In the example, the variation is "Executive Summary."
- Alternatively, it may contain a "Job Objective" (not nearly such a powerful headline as an inducement for the reader's attention) that doesn't so much announce what you want in a job, but rather showcases your thorough understanding of the target job and its contribution to the target endeavor. This section comes right after the target job title at the very top of the resume. . . . Some resumes do without the Performance Profile/Career Summary altogether, the argument being that coming right after the target job title it is a given that this paragraph is a performance profile. The choice is yours, but if in doubt, add the headline "Performance Profile"—it gives the reader an immediate positive focus.
- *A Description of Functional Skills.* This is where the combination of styles comes into play. Following the summary, the combination resume starts out like a functional resume and highlights achievements in different categories relevant to the job/career goals.
- *A Chronological History.* Then it switches to the chronological approach and names companies, dates, titles, duties, and responsibilities. This section can also include further evidence of achievements or special contributions.

PARAG GUPTA

104 W. Real Drive • Beaverton, OR 97006 • (503) 123-4286 • parag.gupta@technical.com

SYSTEMS
ENGINEER: Motivated and driven IT Professional offering 9+ years of hands-on experience
              in designing, implementing, and enhancing systems to automate business
              operations. Demonstrated ability to develop high-performance systems, appli-
              cations, databases, and interfaces.

- Part of TL9000 CND audit interviews that helped Technical get TL9000 certified,
  which is significant in Telecom industry. Skilled trainer and proven ability to lead
  many successful projects, like TSS, EMX, and TOL.
- Strategically manage time and expediently resolve problems for optimal productivity, improvement, and profitability; able to direct multiple tasks effectively.
- Strong technical background.
- Highly effective liaison and communication skills proven by effective interaction
  with management, users, team members, and vendors.

Technical Skills

Operating Systems:	Unix, Windows (2000, XP), DOS
Languages:	C, C++, Java, Pascal, Assembly Languages (Z8000, 808x, DSP)
Methodologies:	TL9000, Digital Six Sigma
Software:	MS Office, Adobe Framemaker, Matlab
RDBMS:	DOORS, Oracle 7.x
Protocols:	TCP/IP, SS7 ISUP, A1, ANSI, TL1, SNMP
Tools:	Teamplay, Clearcase, Clearquest, M-Gate Keeper, Exceed, Visio, DocExpress, Compass
Other:	CDMA Telecom Standards – 3GPP2 (Including TIA/ EIA-2001, TIA/EIA-41, TIA/EIA-664) ITU-T, AMPS

Professional
Experience   Technical, Main Network Division, Hillsboro, OR   Jan 1999–Present

                 Principal Staff Engineer • Products Systems Engineering • Nov 2004–Present

- Known as "go-to" person for CDMA call processing and billing functional areas.
- Created customer requirements documents for Technical SoftSwitch (TSS) and SMS
  Gateway products. All deliverables done on/ahead of schedule with high quality.
- Solely accountable for authoring and allocation, customer reviews, supporting
  fellow system engineers, development and test, and customer documentation
  teams.
- Support Product Management in RFPs, customer feature prioritization, impact
  statements, and budgetary estimates.
- Mentored junior engineers and 1 innovation disclosure [patent] submitted in 2007.
- Resolved deployed customer/internal requirements issues and contributed to
  Virtual Zero Defect quality goal.
- TOL process champion and part of CND focus group that contributed to reducing
  CRUD backlog (NPR) by 25% and cycle time (FRT) by 40%.
- Recognized as the TL9000 expert. Triage representative for switching and mes-
  saging products.

                 Senior Staff Engineer • MSS Systems Engineering • May 2002–Oct 2004

- Led a team of 12 engineers for 3 major software releases of TSS product
  included around 80 features/enhancements to create T-Gate SE deliverables.

FIGURE I   A Chronological Resume

- Created requirements for TSS product, 30 features/enhancements contributing to 5 major software releases. Recognized as overall product expert with specific focus on call processing and billing.
- Played integral role in successfully implementing proprietary commercial TSS billing system.
- Supported PdM organization by creating ROMs, technical support for RFPs (Vivo, Sprint, TELUS, TM, Tata, Inquam, Alaska, Reliance, Pakistan, PBTL, Mauritius, Telefonica, Brasicel, and Angola).
- Proactively identified functional areas of improvement for requirements coverage, contributed to resolving several faults, improved customer documentation, and provided reference for future releases as well as other customers.

Senior Software Engineer • EMX Development • Aug 2000–Apr 2002

- Successfully led and coordinated the cross-functional development teams, 30 engineers, to meet the scheduled design, code, and test completion dates ensuring Feature T-Gates are met.
- Feature Technical Lead for Concurrent Voice/Data Services feature, the largest revenue-generating feature for KDDI customer.
- Feature Lead for Paging Channel SMS feature. Created requirements and design; led implementation phase of five engineers' team; supported product, network, and release testing; and created customer reference documentation.
- Performed the role of functional area lead for Trunk Manager and A1 interface functional areas. Provided 2-day Technical Workshops for internal/customer knowledge sharing and functional area transition from Caltel.
- Provided customer site testing and FOA (First Office Application) support for major EMX releases and off-hours CNRC (Customer Networks Resolution Center) support.
- Received "Bravo Award"–May 2001, Sep 2001, Jan 2002

Software Engineer • EMX Development • Jan 1999–Jul 2000

- Developed design and code for SMS feature as a Trunk Manager functional area lead for the largest FA impacted by the feature. Supported product, network, and release testing.
- Contributed to customer release documentation. Supported feature-level SMS testing at various internal labs and customer sites resulting in successful deployment at customer sites.
- Designed and coded phases for wiretap and virtual circuits feature development, initial assessment of internel and customer EMX PRs (problem reports) to route/classify issues and providing problem assessments for many of these PRs.
- Created an implementation process to serve as reference for new hires.
- Provided CNRC support during the Y2K transition.
- Received "Above and Beyond Performance Award"–Jan 2000, Dec 2000 and "Certificate of Outstanding Achievement"–Jun 1999

Education: Master of Science in Computer Engineering • University of Portland, Portland, OR • 1998

Bachelors of Engineering in Electronics • Technology and Science Institute, India • 1996

Significant Trainings Include

- Open Source Software • WiMAX • Agile Management for Software Engineering
- WSG Requirements Process • Product Security

FIGURE 1   *(Continued)*

Charles Chalmers

Manhattan NY 11658 • (212) 232-8269 • fineartist@earthlink.net

Senior Curator Performance Summary

My professional life is focused on art in all it embraces: drawing, painting, sculpture, photography, cinema, video, audio, performance and digital art, and art history and criticism; my personal life is similarly committed. Recently relocated to Manhattan, I intend to make a contribution to the NY arts community that harnesses my knowledge, enthusiasm, and sensibilities.

ART HISTORY

Thorough knowledge of art history from caves of Lascaux through current artists such as Bruce Nauman, Jessica Stockholder, and Luc Tuymans. Film history from Lumiere Brothers to Almodovar. Current with key critical art and film theory. Ongoing workshops and lectures with the likes of Matthew Barney, Louise Bourgeoise, and Andy Goldsworthy.

RESEARCH NEW ARTISTS

Connected to cutting-edge art and artists through involvement with the art communities and galleries of New York and Boston and the faculty, student, and alumni networks of RISD, Columbia, Boston Museum School, New England School of Art & Design, and now Mass Art. Twenty years of Manhattan gallery openings and networking with artists at MOMA, PS1, Guggenheim, Whitney, Metropolitan, Film Forum, and International Center for Photography workshops and lectures.

GATHERING ARTWORK

Through local artists, regional and global artist networks, intercultural artist exchanges, alumni groups, first-rank private collectors, personal and family networks, and Internet calls for submissions.

ART AND THE COMMUNITY

Conception and launch of themed, resourced, and sequenced shows that invigorate campus and community involvement. Reconfigure existing art spaces to create dynamic dialogue with visitors. Education and outreach programs.

INSTALLATION OF ART

Maintain fluidity of gallery space in preparing exhibitions with recognition of size/time considerations for the art, to ensure a sympathetic environment for the presented works. Hang, light, and label shows in sequences that create dialogue between the works.

PR MATERIALS

Energizing invitations, comprehensive press kits, illustrated press releases, and artist binder materials. Sensitive to placing art in historical/cultural context. Photoshop.

Management Experience

Fourteen years art-staff management experience, including curriculum development. Responsible for art instructors, art handlers, maintenance crews, and working with printers, catering, and graphic arts staff.

FIGURE 2 A Functional Resume

Employment
1994–2005 Chair of Visual Arts, The Green Briar School.

Duties: Curriculum development, portfolio preparation, internal and external monthly shows, theater sets, monthly video news show, taught art history and all the studio arts, managed staff of three.

1989–2004 President Art Workshops.
Duties: Private art studio and art history curriculums, staff of four. Private groups to Manhattan museums and gallery tours.

1980–1989 Freelance artist, photographer, and editor.
Highlights include: Taught photography at Trinity School, Manhattan; photographer for the Ramones; editor of *Pioneer,* insurance industry trade magazine; assistant to Claudia Weill documentary filmmaker, director of *Girlfriends.*

Education
MFA. Magna cum laude. Columbia University, 1983
    Awards: ****** ***** Prize for film criticism
    Taught undergraduate Intro to Film, under ****** ***** and ****** ******.

Subscriptions
Art in America, Art News, ArtForum, New York Times, Parkett, Sight & Sound, Film Comment, Modern Painters.

Memberships
MOMA/PS1, Whitney Museum, Guggenheim, Metropolitan Museum of Art, DIA.

Recent Exhibitions
2004. Corcoran Center Gallery, Southampton, NY
2005. Corsair Gallery, 37 West 33rd St., NYC
2006. Fuller Museum, Brockton, MA
2002–2007. Zeitgeist Gallery, Cambridge, MA

FIGURE 2   *(Continued)*

John William Wisher, MBA
2541 Bainbridge Blvd.
West Chicago, IL 60185

jwisher@ameritech.net   630.878.2653/630.377.9117

**Expert leadership in cost effective supply chain, vendor,
and project management within *Fortune* organizations.**

EXECUTIVE PROFILE

A visionary, forward-thinking SUPPLY CHAIN AND LOGISTICS LEADER offering 20+ years of progressive growth and outstanding success streamlining operations across a wide range of industries. Excellent negotiation and relationship management skills with ability to inspire teams to outperform expectations. Proven record of delivering a synchronized supply chain approach through strategic models closely mirroring business plan to dramatically optimize ROI and manage risk.

Supply Chain Strategy:—Successfully led over 500 supply chain management initiatives across a wide spectrum of business, negotiating agreements from $5K to $27M. Implemented technology solutions and streamlined processes to reduce redundancies and staffing hours, improving both efficiency and productivity. Industries include: automotive and industrial manufacturing, consumer goods, government and defense, healthcare, high tech, and retail.

Industry Knowledge:—Extensive knowledge base developed from hands-on industry experience. Began career in dock operations with experience in Hub and Package Operations, multi-site retail operations management, to custom supply chain strategy development over twenty-one-year career with UPS.

Supply Chain Process Costing:—Built several information packets on total cost of ownership (TCO) and facilitated several C-level negotiations to identify and confirm opportunities. Worked to increase awareness among stakeholders on efficiencies and cost-saving measures ROI. Delivered $3.75M total cost savings to client base over three-year period.

Operations Reorganization:—Designed and implemented new sales force alignment and reporting structure; increased daily sales calls by 20%, reduced travel mileage 23%, and head count by nine, total annual cost savings of $920K.

Logistics:—Experienced across all modes of transportation: ocean, air freight, LTL, TL, mail services, and small package. Performs complex analysis to develop strategy based on cost and delivery requirements.

Project Management:—Implemented complete $1.2M redesign of 11 new UPS Customer Centers. Managed vendor and lease negotiations, developed budgets, training, and sales structure. All 11 centers up and operational on time and on budget.

Cost & Process Improvements

- Implemented complete warehouse redesign for a large optical distributor. Optimized warehouse operations through engineering a new warehouse design, integrating and automating technology, and synchronization of goods movement through ocean, air, ground, and mail services. Reduced transportation expense by 15%, increased production levels by 25%, reduced inventory by 15% and staffing by 20%.

- Built custom supply chain for a nationally recognized golf club manufacturer. Improved service levels by 30%, reduced damage by 45%, and integrated technology to support shipping process automation, reducing billing function staffing hours 50%.

Trust-Based Leadership

Vendor/Client Negotiations

Cross-Functional Collaboration

Supply Chain Mapping

Financial Logistics Analysis

Contingency Planning

Risk Management

Competitive Analysis

Haz Mat Compliance

Inventory Planning, Control, & Distribution

Recruiting/Training/Development

Project Management

Organizational Change Management

Distributive Computing

Budget Management

Labor Relations

FIGURE 3   A Combination Resume

John William Wisher, MBA Page 2 of 3

PROFESSIONAL BACKGROUND

United Parcel Service (UPS), Addison, IL 1986 to Present

World's largest package-delivery company and global leader in supply chain services, offering an extensive range of options for synchronizing the movement of goods, information, and funds. Serves more than 200 countries and territories worldwide and operates the largest franchise shipping chain, the UPS Store.

DIRECTOR/AREA MANAGER—SUPPLY CHAIN SALES, 2005–Present

Promoted to lead and develop a cross-functional sales force of 18 in consultative supply chain management services to Chicago area businesses. Directs development of integrated supply chain management solutions across all modes of transportation, closely mirroring client business plans. Mentors team in Demand Responsive Model, a proven methodology to quickly align internal and external resources with changing market demands, situational requirements, and mission critical conditions. Manages $100M P&L.

Accomplishments:

- Implements over 100 multimillion-dollar supply chain integrations per year with 14% annual growth on 8% plan.
- Develops future organizational leaders; four staff members promoted through effective mentoring and development.
- Choreographed a supply chain movement from the Pacific Rim for a global fast-food chain to deliver 300k cartons to 15k locations all on the same day. Utilized modes of ocean, TL, air, and ground services, allowing for a national release synchronized to all locations on the same release date.
- Designed and implemented an automated reverse logistics program for a nationally recognized health food/supplement distributor. Automated returns process to reduce touches and costly staffing hours. Eliminated front-end phone contact using technology and web automation.

MARKETING MANAGER 2004 to 2005

Fast tracked to streamline sales processes, increasing performance. Performed analysis of sales territory, historical data, operations alignment, reporting structure, and sales trends to devise solutions. Managed and coached area managers in business-plan development and execution of sales strategies. Delivered staff development in cost-reduction strategies and compliance requirements. Accountable for $500M P&L.

Accomplishments:

- Drove $500M+ in local market sales. Grew revenues 2004/2005 revenues 12% and 7% respectively.

RETAIL CHANNEL/OPERATIONS MANAGER 2002 to 2004

Charged with turning around this underperforming business unit. Managed development and implementation of new retail strategy across northern Illinois. Rebranded UPS Customer Centers and the UPS Store. Performed vendor negotiations and collaborated with nine regions to support additional implementations.

Accomplishments:

- Developed key revenue-generating initiatives across multiple channels. Attained 65% growth in discretionary sales. Several strategies adopted across the national organization.
- Re-engineered inventory for over 1,000 dropoff locations, reduced lease expenses by 45% and inventory levels by 40% through weekly measurement, inventory level development by SKU, order process automation, and order consolidation.
- Implemented new retail sales associate structure in 1,100 locations; scored highest national service levels by mystery shoppers.
- Selected as Corporate team member on Mail Boxes Etc. acquisition integration.

PROJECT MANAGER 2001 to 2002

Selected to support several underperforming business areas. Managed key segments of district business initiatives and compliance measures for 1,000 dropoff locations. Reported on status to corporate management. Supervised office staff of 16. Negotiated vendor and lease agreements.

Accomplishments:

- Rolled out and managed ongoing Haz Mat compliance program for all locations.
- Generated $6M in sales through cross-functional lead program and increased participation from 20% to 100%.
- Attained union workforce sponsorship of support-growth program through careful negotiations and persuasion.

SENIOR ACCOUNT MANAGER 1999 to 2001

Delivered $2.8M in growth on $1.1M plan, rated 3rd of 53 managers in revenue generation.

ACCOUNT MANAGER 1997 to 1998

Top producer out of 53; $1.3M sales on $500K plan.

FIGURE 3 *(Continued)*

John William Wisher, MBA

SERVICE PROVIDED   1994 to 1996
Top producer out of 53; $1.3M sales on $500K plan.

SUPERVISOR OF PACKAGE OPERATIONS   1994
Managed 65 full-time service providers. Performed post-routine analysis, operating strategy development, compliance, payroll, service failure recovery, and new technology implementation. Met 100% DOT and Haz Mat compliance. Reduced post-delivery staffing time by 50% and missed pickups by 65%.

SUPERVISOR OF HUB OPERATIONS   1988 to 1994
Managed up to 100 union employees and staff processing 75K pieces per day involving 40+ outbound bays. Performed complex staff scheduling and maintained low turnover rates. Designed new management reporting format, reducing administrative time by 20% and improved load quality by 30%.

OPERATIONS DOCK WORKER AND TRAINING LEAD   1986 to 1987

EDUCATION
MBA
National Louis University, Wheaton IL., *4.0 GPA*

BA, Business, Supply Chain Management
Elmhurst College, Elmhurst, IL, *3.84 GPA, Magna cum laude*

Additional Specialized Courses:
- Supply Chain Mapping, 20 Hours
- Financial Logistics Analysis (FLOGAT), 10 Hours
- Hazardous Materials, 20 Hours
- Labor Relations, 30 Hours
- Managers Leadership School, 100 Hours
- Hazardous Materials, 20 Hours
- Managing from the Heart, 30 Hours

FIGURE 3   *(Continued)*

Karl Weber and Rob Kaplan

Follow-Up Letters

Karl Weber is an editor, author, and publishing consultant specializing in books dealing with business, personal finance, and current affairs.

Rob Kaplan has had a long career as a senior editor for several major publishing companies and now heads his own literary services firm.

. . . Follow-up letters provide you with an invaluable opportunity to impress your readers with your skills, your background, your professionalism, and your personality.

In this . . . [essay], we'll show you why writing follow-up letters is so important. We'll help you write effective, professional letters for a variety of situations, including letters to follow-up networking and job interviews, letters for when you've been offered and accepted a position, letters for when you've been offered and turned down a position, letters thanking your interviewer even when you've not received a job offer, and letters to follow up with your networking contacts after you've started a new job.

NETWORKING INTERVIEW FOLLOW-UP LETTERS

It's always appropriate to thank someone, especially someone who doesn't know you well, for taking time out of their schedule to talk to you. And this is true whether they were considering you for a job or not. Although the individual who is actively interviewing potential job candidates obviously has a business interest in talking with you, they're still under no obligation to spend time with you. And people who *aren't* recruiting to fill a position certainly don't have to give you an hour of their valuable time. So thanking these people is courteous, considerate, and appropriate.

More specifically, in the case of networking interviews, sending a follow-up letter [Figure 1, p. 316] serves the purpose of reminding the reader who you are and the fact that you're looking for a job. Remember, the person you met with may

---

Michael Broderick
919 Massachusetts Avenue
Brighton, MA 07122
617-750-9086
E-mail: mikeb@bosnet.com

August 18, 2000

Ms. Corinne Blackman
Nehan, Ross & Blackman
22 Boylston Street
Boston, MA 07125

Dear Ms. Blackman:

I am writing to tell you what a pleasure it was to meet you the other day and to thank you again for taking the time to speak with me.

The information, ideas, and names you were kind enough to share with me will, I'm sure, be extremely helpful, and I appreciate it very much.

I will be in touch with you again to let you know how my job search is progressing. In the meantime, should you hear of any openings for which I might be appropriate, I would very much appreciate hearing from you.

With best wishes,

Michael Broderick

FIGURE 1   Sample Networking Interview Follow-Up Letter.

have a job opening in the near future, and if you've sent a follow-up letter they're more likely to remember you. In addition, because executives in any given industry tend to know each other, the person you follow up with may contact you if he or she hears of a position in another company for which you would be qualified.

Like the other types of letters you've already written, the networking interview follow-up letter can be divided into three elements, or paragraphs—in this case, the opening, your comments on the meeting, and the closing.

FYI

All follow-up letters, regardless of their purpose, should be sent as soon as possible after the meeting—preferably the next day, but certainly within the next few days. It's not only courteous, it's a good way to make sure that you won't forget to do it.

The Opening

The opening should be a brief, straightforward, one- or two-sentence paragraph in which you thank your reader for taking the time to meet with you, such as:

> I'm just writing to say what a pleasure it was to meet you yesterday and to thank you again for spending some time with me.

> I'm writing to say how much I enjoyed our meeting the other day and to thank you for taking the time to help me in my efforts to find a new position.

Comment on the Meeting

The second paragraph of the follow-up letter is the appropriate place to make some comment about the discussion you had. Even if the networking meeting didn't result in your actually gaining a great deal of information, it's still appropriate for you to say something positive about it, for example:

> The information, ideas, and names you were kind enough to share with me will, I'm sure, be extremely helpful, and I appreciate it very much.

> Having the opportunity to discuss the industry with you, as well as hearing your thoughts about its future, was interesting, informative, and enjoyable.

On the other hand, the person you met with may have made some particularly interesting comment, given you an especially good idea, or provided you with several names of people to contact. In this case, it would be appropriate to be more specific about the discussion:

> Your comments about recent developments in the industry were particularly interesting and thought-provoking. I had not considered the impact of gun control legislation on the business and am now beginning to see it in a new light.

> Your suggestion that I contact the National Booksellers Association concerning entry-level positions with their member companies was an especially valuable one, and I will certainly follow up on it.

> In addition to the other valuable suggestions you made, your providing me with the names of so many people to contact will no doubt be enormously helpful, and I sincerely appreciate it.

Finally, if either you or the person you met with promised to do something in the course of the meeting, this is the appropriate place to do what you promised or (tactfully) remind the other person of his or her promise:

> As I promised I would, I'm enclosing the article from the *San Francisco Examiner* about Peter Anderson's new film.

> I very much appreciate your offer to contact Steven Ryan at the Ryan Company on my behalf, and I will follow up with him within the next week or so.

The Closing

The final paragraph of the follow-up letter should include both a promise and a request, for example:

> I'll be in touch again to let you know how my job search progresses. In the meantime, should you hear of any positions in which you think I might be interested, I would very much appreciate hearing from you.
>
> I will let you know how my efforts to find a new position proceed. Should you, in the meantime, learn of any positions for which you think I might be appropriate, I would appreciate your letting me know.

FYI

Remember that the ordering of the elements of the letter is less important than the inclusion of all the elements. Although having a clear opening and closing are essential, the other elements can be moved around and/or combined in a variety of ways.

JOB INTERVIEW FOLLOW-UP LETTERS

It's even more important to send follow-up letters after a job interview than after a networking interview [Figure 2]. One reason is that, since many job candidates do *not* send them, interviewers tend to more clearly remember those who do. It's always important to find a positive way to stand out in the interviewer's mind; sending a well-crafted follow-up letter is a excellent way to do that.

Writing a follow-up letter after a job interview also gives you an opportunity to remind the interviewer of your skills and experience, as well as of their applicability to the position for which you've been interviewed.

As you'll see, there are some similarities between networking and job interview follow-up letters, but one important similarity is timing. Writing *promptly* after a job interview is essential. You have no way of knowing how quickly the interviewer is going to make a hiring decision, so you should always send a follow-up letter within 24 hours of the interview. After all, if the letter is received while the recruiter is still trying to choose a candidate, it could be the thing that tips the scales in your favor.

In certain respects, letters you send after job interviews are like the job-tailored letters you sent to request interviews. Like those letters, the job interview follow-up letter includes three elements divided into four paragraphs: the opening, the two-part pitch ("Why me?" and "Why you?"), and the closing.

The Opening

As with the networking interview follow-up letter, the first paragraph of the job interview follow-up letter is the place to thank the reader for meeting with you, for example:

> I'm writing just to say what a pleasure it was to meet you and to thank you for taking the time to discuss with me the possibility of joining your organization.
>
> I'm taking this opportunity to tell you how much I enjoyed meeting you and how much I appreciate your speaking with me about the opening for an assistant manager in your department.

Cecilia Arnold
5550 Nepperham Avenue
Los Angeles, CA 90233
206-788-8562
E-mail: cece@lanet.com

March 15, 2000

Mr. Brock Peters
Braintree Publishers
1000 Sepulveda Boulevard
Los Angeles, CA 90256

Dear Mr. Peters:

I just wanted to tell you how much I enjoyed meeting you yesterday and to thank you again for spending time with me. It's clear that Braintree's plans for the future will make it an exciting and challenging place to work, and I would very much like to be a part of it.

On the basis of our conversation, I believe that my experience in the industry, my managerial experience, and my experience and interest in acquiring and developing popular reference books would enable me to make a real contribution to your organization as a publishing director. In addition, I sense that you and I share a common philosophy about publishing and that we would accordingly be able to work well together.

I understand that you are not expecting to reach a decision about the position for some time. If, however, I haven't heard from you within the next two weeks, I'll give you a call.

Sincerely yours,

Cecilia Arnold

FIGURE 2　Sample Job Interview Follow-Up Letter.

The Pitch: "Why Me?"

Here is where the real difference between networking and job interview follow-up letters begins. The purpose of the networking letter is basically to thank the interviewer and remind him or her of your interest in finding a new position. By contrast, the purpose of the interview follow-up letter is to make a final argument for your candidacy. In this paragraph you should reiterate the (one or two) best points that you've already made in the interview itself as well as add (one or two) others you may have neglected to mention. A couple of examples:

> On the basis of our conversation, I believe that my experience in the industry, my managerial experience, and my agreement with the goals of your organization would enable

me to make a real contribution in your company as an assistant manager. The fact that I've managed a similar operation in a smaller company should also, I think, make me a good candidate for the position.

As we discussed, the fact that I have managed a similar operation, although in a smaller firm, has provided me with the opportunity to learn and use the same skills that you are looking for in an assistant manager. In addition, the experience I gained in working directly with customers in my previous position would, I think, be very useful in dealing with the sometimes difficult suppliers you mentioned.

One element of my background that we didn't have time to discuss is the year I spent managing the customer database for Little Industries, my previous employer. The experience I gained in managing information technology would be directly applicable to the business reorganization project you mentioned, and I think it could help me be an effective member of the team charged with implementing it.

FYI

Use the follow-up letter as a way to highlight any credential or skill you may have failed to mention in the interview itself. If, like most people, you've ever walked out of an interview and said to yourself, "I wish I'd said such-and-such," a follow-up letter is an excellent way to remedy the situation.

The Pitch: "Why You?"

The third paragraph of the job interview follow-up letter is the appropriate place for you to discuss why you're interested in working for this particular company. Your comments should be based on both whatever you learned about the company during the interview and any information you may have gathered from other sources. If there's been any (positive) "breaking news" about the company, here is a good place to mention it.

From what you told me about your organization, it sounds like a dynamic and exciting place to work. In addition, having heard so many positive things about it from other people in the industry, I believe that it's a company in which I would not only be comfortable but also one in which I would be able to make a substantial contribution.

During our discussion I was particularly impressed with your company's ambitious goals. As we both know, ours is a particularly competitive industry, but I'm sure that with the excellent staff you mentioned you will be able to achieve those goals. On the basis of what you told me, I would very much like to be a part of that effort.

As we discussed, I'm excited about the possibility of working for Mammoth Films. I noted that two of your new releases were among the top ten box-office hits again last weekend—an impressive showing for such a young company. I hope I'll have the opportunity to help contribute to even greater achievements in the future.

The Closing

The last paragraph of the job interview follow-up letter should be short and sweet. You've made your pitch, given it your best shot, and now you just have to wait for the interviewer to make a decision. (Well, more or less.)

Toward the end of the interview, you should have asked approximately how long the interviewer expects it will take to reach a hiring decision. Thus, you'll have at least some idea of her time frame. Bear in mind, though, that many interviewers say, "We want to move quickly on this decision," and then don't. It's not that they're lying, but, rather, that things always take longer than people expect them to.

Although it's unlikely that anything you do will make her come to a decision any sooner, it doesn't hurt to prod her a bit. So the closing of your letter might read:

> Again, I appreciate you taking the time to meet with me and look forward to hearing from you soon. If I haven't heard from you within the next few weeks, I'll give you a call to follow up.

If it's true, you can subtly suggest that you might be in demand from other employers, which could increase the sense of urgency on the recruiter's part:

> Thank you again for meeting with me. As I continue to explore other potential positions, I'll look forward to hearing from you shortly. If we haven't spoken in two weeks' time, I will call you with an update on my status and to find out how your decision-making process is progressing.

FYI

Following up with a phone call to an interviewer a week or so after a meeting is acceptable, but calling him day after day is not. Not only is it unprofessional, but calling frequently is likely to hurt rather than help your cause.

JOB ACCEPTANCE FOLLOW-UP LETTERS

While sending a follow-up letter after you've been offered and accepted a position [Figure 3, p. 322] may seem gratuitous (after all, you got the job!) it's still a good idea to do so. Because writing such a letter is both courteous and professional, it's likely to impress and please your new boss. It will help to confirm in his or her mind that they've made a good decision in hiring you, and it'll help you start your new job on a positive note.

The job acceptance follow-up letter is very different from the other types of follow-up letters we've discussed. Since you've already closed the sale, it's neither necessary nor appropriate to include any kind of sales pitch. Your letter should, however, be enthusiastic, warm, and to-the-point.

Joshua Kriegel
224 Sansom Street
Phoenix, AZ 04405
602-890-8165
E-mail: joshk@aol.com

February 17, 2000

Ms. Marjorie Simpson
Phoenix Power & Light
2000 Arizona Avenue
Phoenix, AZ 04412

Dear Marjorie:

I'm just writing to tell you how pleased I am that we were able to come to an agreement about my joining your staff at Phoenix Power & Light as a senior planner.

I am looking forward to working with you and helping to find efficient and cost-effective ways of meeting the challenges of the increasing need for electricity in our growing community.

I will be leaving my current position a week from now, and then taking the short vacation I mentioned prior to my starting the job on March 1st.

Sincerely yours,

Joshua Kriegel

FIGURE 3 Sample Job Acceptance Follow-Up Letter.

JOB TURNDOWN FOLLOW-UP LETTERS

It's entirely possible that you'll receive job offers for positions that you're not interested in accepting. It may be that they're not paying as much money as you'd like, or that you've simultaneously received an offer from another company that you'd prefer working for, or for any number of other reasons.

Whatever the reason may be, in such a situation it's likely that you'll turn down the offer over the phone (since companies extending job offers generally need a fairly prompt response). It is still, however, advisable to write a follow-up letter [Figure 4] for one very good reason.

Most industries tend to be small worlds. That is, as people move from one company to another within any given industry (and they do) they get to know a lot of other people in the industry. Moreover, they tend to run into those people again and again over the years. So the chances are that you may at some time in the future find yourself being interviewed again by, or working with, a person

Sandra McGregor
620 Centennial Avenue
San Francisco, CA 90366
818-755-0236
E-mail: sandymc@sfnet.com

June 1, 2000

Mr. Albert Decker
White Industries, Inc.
4050 Michigan Avenue
Detroit, MI 86420

Dear Mr. Decker:

I'm writing to thank you again for spending time with me to discuss your need for a market research assistant.

Although, as I told you on the phone yesterday, I am pleased and proud that you are interested in having me join your team, I have been offered and have accepted a position with another firm that I think would be a more suitable match for me at this point in my career.

I sincerely hope, however, that we may be able to work together at some time in the future. In the meantime, if I can be of any assistance to you, I hope you won't hesitate to let me know.

Yours truly,

Sandra McGregor

FIGURE 4   Sample Job Turndown Follow-Up Letter.

whose offer you rejected. When that happens, it won't hurt if they remember that you turned them down in a graceful and professional manner.

JOB REJECTION FOLLOW-UP LETTERS

While it may seem odd to write a letter thanking someone for *not* hiring you, it's a good idea to send follow-up letters even when you *haven't* received a job offer [Figure 5, p. 324]. Hard though it may be to do, writing such letters may well bear fruit at some later date.

For example, although you may have no way of knowing it, you may have been your interviewer's second choice, and just a tad behind his or her first. (You may even have been the first choice of some people involved in the hiring decision, who were overruled by the boss.) If they have another opening in the near future, you'll probably be the first person they'll call anyway—especially if

Howard Seaview
777 Pittsburg Avenue
Chicago, IL 66666
302-888-0050
E-mail: howards@aol.com

January 17, 2000

Ms. Barbara Harris
Dillon Bank
4406 Finance Way
Evanston, IL 99755

Dear Barbara:

I am writing to thank you again for meeting with me a few weeks ago and for
considering me for the position of assistant treasurer with the Dillon Bank.

Although I am of course sorry that you chose another applicant for the position,
I enjoyed meeting you very much, and sincerely hope that we may be able to
work together at some time in the future.

In the meantime, if I can be any assistance to you, I hope you won't hesitate to
let me know.

Sincerely yours,

Howard Seaview

FIGURE 5   Sample Job Rejection Follow-Up Letter.

you send a gracious, professional letter thanking them for considering you for
the position.

In addition, as we've already mentioned, you never know when you might
run into the same interviewer again, and it could well be to your advantage if
they remember that you accepted their decision with maturity and class.

A rejection follow-up letter is probably the hardest kind of letter to write.
But it you can bring yourself to do it, it may have very positive results at some
time in the future. Like the job acceptance follow-up letter, this one should be
short, to the point, professional, and infused with as much warmth as you can
manage under the circumstances.

FOLLOW-UP LETTERS TO NETWORKING CONTACTS

It's likely that by the time you've found a new position, you will have spoken
with a good number of people, both people you already knew and those you
met as a result of your networking. It's not only courteous to contact them

---

FYI

Being successful in business sometimes really is about who you know, so it's in your best interests to make an effort to stay in touch with highly placed individuals in the industry whom you've met during your job-search networking efforts. Make it your business to call your networking contacts periodically "just to catch up"; invite them for breakfast, lunch, or a cup of coffee once or twice a year; and send a quick note, a relevant clipping, or a bit of news from time to time.

---

again, especially if they either directly or indirectly led to your finding a job, it also makes good business sense [Figure 6]. Your personal network is a lifetime career tool because keeping those connections strong and positive will pay dividends for years to come.

Dorothy Arnold
36 Pleasant Avenue
Tacoma, WA 90877
704-654-0022
E-mail: dottya@ATT.com

May 14, 2000

Mr. Howard Bean
World Communications, Inc.
666 Fifth Street
Tacoma, WA 90874

Dear Mr. Bean:

You will, I hope, remember your being kind enough to meet with me some months ago when I was in the process of seeking a position in the communications industry.

As I promised to let you know how my job search progressed, I'm writing now to tell you that I have just received and accepted an offer to become an assistant engineer with KBAL-TV here in Tacoma.

Your suggestions for who to contact were extremely helpful, and I just wanted to tell you again how much I appreciate all your help. I hope and look forward to meeting you again, and if there's ever any way I can be of help to you, please don't hesitate to ask.

Sincerely yours,

Dorothy Arnold

FIGURE 6   Networking Contact Follow-Up Letter.

JUST THE FACTS

- Networking interview follow-up letters are not only courteous but also help remind your contacts of who you are and that you're looking for a job.
- Sending a follow-up letter after a job interview may make the difference between an offer and a rejection.
- Writing a follow-up letter to someone from whom you've just accepted a job offer will help you get off to a good start on your new job.
- Follow-up letters after you've turned down a job, or been rejected, show style and professionalism and may pay long-term career dividends.
- Once you've started a new job, send follow-up letters to all your networking contacts; you never know when they may be in a position to help again in the future.

Acknowledgments

Part 1

USING PAFEO PLANNING. By John Keenan. Reprinted from *Feel Free to Write* by John Keenan. Copyright © 1982 by John Wiley & Sons, Inc. This material is used by permission of John Wiley & Sons, Inc.

THE WRITING PROCESS. By Michael E. Adelstein. Reprinted from *Contemporary Business Writing* (New York: Random House, 1971). Copyright © 1971 by Michael E. Adelstein. Reprinted by kind permission of Michael E. Adelstein.

EVALUATING AND TESTING AS YOU REVISE. By Linda Flower and John Ackerman. Reprinted from FLOWER, *Writers at Work*, 1E. Copyright © 1994 Heinle/Arts & Sciences, a part of Cengage Learning, Inc. Reprinted by permission. www.cengage.com/permissions.

THE PROJECT WORKSHEET FOR EFFICIENT WRITING MANAGEMENT. By John S. Harris. Reprinted from *Publications Management: Essays for Professional Communications*. Edited by O. Jane Allen and Lynn H. Deming (Amityville, New York: Baywood Publishing Company, Inc., 1994). Copyright © 1994 by Baywood Publishing Company, Inc. Reprinted by kind permission of John S. Harris and of the publisher, Baywood Publishing Company, Inc.

THE COMPOSING PROCESS OF AN ENGINEER. By Jack Selzer. Reprinted by kind permission of the National Council of Teachers of English (NCTE) from *College Composition and Communication* 34.2 (May, 1983), pp. 178–187. Copyright © 1983 NCTE.

Part 2

GOBBLEDYGOOK. By Stuart Chase. Reprinted from *Power of Word*. Copyright © 1954, 1953 and renewed 1982, 1981 by Stuart Chase, reprinted by permission of Houghton Mifflin Harcourt Publishing Company.

"WHAT DO YOU MEAN YOU DON'T LIKE MY STYLE?" By John S. Fielden. Reprinted by permission from the *Harvard Business Review* (May–June, 1982). Copyright © 1982 by the Harvard Business School Publishing Corporation; all rights reserved.

CLEAR WRITING MEANS CLEAR THINKING MEANS. . . . By Marvin H. Swift. Reprinted by permission from the *Harvard Business Review* (January–February 1973). Copyright © 1973 by the Harvard Business School Publishing Corporation; all rights reserved.

A GUIDE TO NONSEXIST LANGUAGE. By the University of Wisconsin-Extension Equal Opportunities Program Office and Department of Agricultural Journalism. Reprinted with the kind permission of the Board of Regents of the University of Wisconsin System and the University of Wisconsin-Extension.

INTERNATIONAL COMMUNICATION AND LANGUAGE. By Gwyneth Olofsson. Reprinted with permission from *When in Rome or Rio or Riyadh . . . Cultural Q & As for Successful Business Behavior Around the World* by Gwyneth Olofsson, Intercultural Press, A Nicholas Brealey Company, 2004. Copyright © 2004 by Gwyneth Olofsson.

Part 5

WRITING RESUMES AND LETTERS IN THE LANGUAGE OF EMPLOYERS. By John L. Munschauer. Copyright © 1991 by Peterson's Guides, Inc. Reprinted from *Jobs for English Majors and Other Smart People* by John L. Munschauer. Used by permission of Walter Pitkin for the estate of the late John L. Munschauer.

THE BASICS OF A COVER LETTER. By Steven Graber. Copyright © 2000 by Adams Media. Reprinted from *The Everything® Cover Letter Book* by Stephen Graber. Used by permission of Adams Media, an F+W Media, Inc. Co. All rights reserved.

WRITING RESUMES. By Diana C. Reep. From *Technical Writing, Principles, Strategies, and Readings* by Diana C. Reep. 7th edition. Copyright © 2009 by Pearson Longman. Reprinted by permission of Pearson Education, Inc.

RESUME FORMATS. By Matthew Yate. From *Knock 'Em Dead Resumes, 8th edition.* Copyright © 2008, 2006, 2004, 2003, 2002, 2001, 1995, 1993 by Martin John Yate. Used by permission of Adams Media, an F+W Media, Inc. Co. All rights reserved.

FOLLOW-UP LETTERS. By Karl Weber and Rob Kaplan. From *The Insider's Guide to Writing the Perfect Resume* by Peterson's. Copyright © 2001. Reprinted with permission of Peterson's, a Nelnet Company.

Index